W9-BNT-943

WOE TO THE
REBELLIOUS CHILDREN

Avery managed to pull himself up so that he
was sitting on his knees. Lundgren raised his pistol. As he looked down on the bound man who
had considered him to be his "very best friend,"
Lundgren's right hand tightened on the .45.

"I told Dennis Avery what would happen if he
continued to sin, continued to deny the truth, continued to reject my teachings, but he continued to
choose darkness rather than light and he has no
one to blame but himself for leading himself and
his family into this pit of damnation."

He slowly squeezed the trigger.

PROPHET OF DEATH

THE MORMON BLOOD-ATONEMENT KILLINGS

PETE EARLEY

AVON BOOKS ◆ NEW YORK

AVON BOOKS
A division of
The Hearst Corporation
1350 Avenue of the Americas
New York, New York 10019

Published in hardcover by William Morrow and Company, Inc.; for information address Permissions Department, William Morrow and Company, Inc., 1350 Avenue of the Americas, New York, New York 10019.

The William Morrow and Company edition contains the following Library of Congress Cataloging in Publication Data:

Earley, Pete.
    Prophet of death : the Mormon blood-atonement killings / by Pete Earley
        p.   cm.
    1. Murder—Ohio—Kirtland—case studies.   2. Cults—Ohio—Kirtland—Case studies.   3. Mormons—Ohio—Kirtland—Case studies.
4.Lundgren, Jeffery.   5. Avery, Dennis   6. Avery, Cheryl.   I. Title.
HV6533.O5E37   1991   91-25557
364.1′523′09.771334—dc20   CIP

First Avon Books Printing: January 1993

AVON TRADEMARK REG. U.S. PAT. OFF. AND IN OTHER COUNTRIES, MARCA REGISTRADA, HECHO EN U.S.A.

Printed in the U.S.A.

RA   10   9   8   7   6   5   4   3   2   1

In Memory of Alice Lee Earley
and Belle Patterson

Contents

The easiest thing of all is to deceive one's self; for what a man wishes he generally believes to be true.

—DEMOSTHENES, OLYNTHIACA

Prologue

J UST before dawn on a cool April day in 1989, a lone man climbed a hill a few miles outside Kirtland, Ohio, a village of six thousand, located directly east of Cleveland. As the morning sunshine began to filter through the branches of the apple and maple trees that towered over him, the man dropped to one knee and began to pray.

"What is thy will?" Jeffrey Don Lundgren asked out loud. "Give me a sign. Tell me what to do."

Lundgren stared upward into the morning light. He didn't move, didn't speak. For several minutes he waited, and then he nodded his head.

"I understand," he said, addressing a vision that only he could see. "Thy will be done."

It was misty on the night of April 17. There was no moon. The only light outside the farmhouse that Lundgren rented came from the neglected barn out back. It was a New England-style barn, painted red. It smelled inside of hay, rabbits, chickens, oil dripping from an abandoned car. An extension cord snaked across the floor leading into a little room at the rear of the barn. The cord had been tacked up the wall of the room and stretched out into the center of the ceiling. A single, naked bulb dangled down, illuminating a hole in the room's dirt floor. The hole had been carefully dug and was precisely six and a half feet wide and seven feet seven inches long. It was four feet deep. Underground water had seeped into it, turning the bottom into two-inch-deep mud. The water gave the brown clay walls of the pit a sheen that glistened in the overhead light.

Just before 7:30 P.M., two men could be heard talking as they walked from the Lundgren farmhouse toward the barn.

1

One of them cried out as soon as they stepped through a door into the barn.

"Ouch! What are you doing? This isn't necessary. Goddamn it!"

The fifty-thousand-volt electric charge emitted by the hand-held stun gun was supposed to immobilize a man for several seconds, possibly even knock him unconscious. But when it was jabbed into Dennis Avery's side by the man walking beside him, it neither immobilized Avery nor knocked him down. It only stung and made him mad.

"Goddamn it!" Avery yelled when the gun was jabbed once again to his neck. "This isn't necessary!"

Four men had been hiding in the barn and when it became apparent that the stun gun wasn't working, they jumped out and grabbed Avery, forcing him down onto the floor. Avery didn't fight. He was in poor physical shape, with a watermelon belly. Even his friends regarded the forty-nine-year-old Avery as weak. His attackers, mostly men in their late twenties, were all in excellent physical condition. Within seconds, Avery's mouth, feet, and hands had been bound with gray two-inch-wide duct tape. His eyes, however, had not been covered. Jeffrey Lundgren had given specific instructions about Avery's eyes. "I want him to see who is administering justice," Lundgren had explained to his followers. "I want to look him eye to eye when I break his heart."

As he was carried from the front of the barn back into the lighted room, Avery's eyes flashed with anger. It was as if he were trying to communicate: "As soon as I'm loose, you are going to pay for doing this to me!" But the two men carrying him weren't afraid. They gently slid Avery down into the pit in the floor. He fell clumsily onto his side in the mud. Without speaking, the two men dashed toward the door.

The lone light bulb served as a spotlight over the pit, casting shadows into the room's corners. As Avery's eyes adjusted to the brightness, Jeffrey Lundgren stepped forward out of the darkness. He held a .45-caliber, stainless-steel, semiautomatic pistol in his right hand.

Avery managed to pull himself up so that he was sitting on his knees now. Lundgren raised his pistol. He would later recall with complete clarity void of all emotions what his thoughts were at that moment as he looked down on the bound man who had considered him to be his "very best friend." Lundgren was thinking about verses from the Old Testament book of Isaiah, chapter 30.

Woe to the rebellious children, saith the Lord, that take counsel, but not of me. . . . You are a rebellious people, you lying children, you children who will not hear the law of the Lord.*

Lundgren's right hand tightened on the .45. "I had told Dennis Avery what would happen if he continued to sin, continued to deny the truth, continued to reject my teachings, but he continued to choose darkness rather than light and he had no one to blame but himself for leading himself and his family into this pit of damnation."

He slowly squeezed the trigger.

The first hollow-pointed slug smacked Avery's torso and knocked him sideways; the second round hit so quickly that it almost went in the same hole even though his body was recoiling. Avery's taped face hit the muddy bottom of the pit with a loud *smack*.

Iniquity shall be to you as a branch ready to fall, and you shall break it—you shall not spare the wicked.

It was another verse from Isaiah.

"All right, everybody, come look at this, come see what death is," Jeffrey called to the others. The five men who had subdued Avery came into the room and gathered around the hole. Lundgren had warned them earlier that God would someday demand each of them to "slay the wicked." They would be forced to kill dozens, possibly more.

---

*All biblical passages are from The Holy Scriptures, inspired version as translated by Joseph Smith, Jr.

Lundgren examined the face of each man. He was still holding his .45 pistol. The men seemed terrified, yet mesmerized by the body in the pit. He knew that most of them had doubted him, doubted that he would actually go through with it.

"Okay, bring in the next one," he said. He had tasted death and was eager to continue.

Lundgren's plan was simple. Dennis Avery's wife, Cheryl, forty-two, would be the next to be put into the pit and executed. While Dennis was being murdered, Cheryl and her three daughters were sitting in the Lundgren farmhouse less than fifty yards away, visiting with the wives of the men in the barn. She would be lured from the farmhouse by one of Lundgren's accomplices, who would tell her that Dennis needed help in the barn sorting through some personal belongings stored there. Once inside the barn, she would be overpowered by Lundgren's followers and bound with duct tape. Her husband had no idea that he had been sentenced to death by Lundgren, nor would Cheryl. After Lundgren executed her, the Averys' daughters—Trina, fifteen, Rebecca, thirteen, and Karen, six— would be brought into the barn and put into the pit one at a time, the oldest first. Not only would their hands, feet, and mouths be bound, but their eyes would be covered with duct tape. The scriptures, Lundgren had explained, only required that the man of the family be allowed to see his executioner.

As Jeffrey waited for his followers to bring Cheryl into the barn, he glanced down into the pit. Blood was soaking into the back of Avery's plaid wool shirt. There was no sign of life. Killing him had been easy. The pistol in Jeffrey's hand felt good. Jeffrey decided that he had been smart to choose the .45 semiautomatic. He had considered using a shotgun, but had rejected the idea because of the noise. Someone driving past the farm might have heard the blast and been curious. The cracking sound of a handgun was more crisp. He had considered using a .357 Magnum or a .9 millimeter, but was afraid that neither was powerful enough. Lundgren had read stories about police officers who had shot criminals three or more times with rounds from a .357 and still not killed them. There was no reason to prolong the Averys' pain. Of course, the .45 had certain disadvantages. Little Karen Avery only weighed thirty-six pounds and shooting her with the big handgun seemed a bit extreme. Only a few nights earlier, Lundgren had gone to the Averys' house for dinner and had bounced Karen on his knee. While she giggled at the excitement of being tossed up and down, he had wondered if he should use a smaller caliber pistol to kill her. But Lundgren had eventually settled on the .45 on the assumption that it would be better to use too much rather than too little firepower.

Lundgren could hear voices from outside the barn now. Cheryl Avery was being brought into the trap. Another scripture came to him: Revelation, chapter 6, the opening of the seven mystical seals that signal the second coming of Jesus Christ, Judgment Day, the beginning of the Millennium, the end of the world. He thought about verses 2 through 8, passages that describe the Four Horsemen of the Apocalypse.

> And when he had opened the second seal I heard the second beast say, Come and see . . .

Cheryl was in the barn now. Lundgren could hear the sound of duct tape being ripped from its spool. It was only seconds before she would be brought to him. He stepped back into the shadows with his .45 semiautomatic.

> . . . and there went out another horse that was red; and power was given to him that sat thereon to take peace from the earth, that they should kill one another . . .

Part One

———

Con Man

If there arise among you a prophet,
or a dreamer of dreams . . .

—DEUTERONOMY 13:1

Chapter 1

ALICE Elizabeth Keehler was eighteen when she met Jeffrey Don Lundgren. She was a senior in high school. He was a freshman at Central Missouri State University in Warrensburg, Missouri, about forty miles southeast of Independence. Alice had caught a ride to the campus with the youth minister from her church in Odessa, a farming town north of the school. Usually her parents, Ralph and Donna, didn't let Alice go out of town without a chaperon, but they figured she was safe with the pastor, and Alice was intent on using the college library. She was writing her senior English term paper about the origins of the Book of Mormon and the public library in Odessa had only a few books on the Mormon religion and its founder, Joseph Smith, Jr. Alice was a member of the Reorganized Church of Jesus Christ of Latter Day Saints, a branch of Mormonism, and she wanted to make certain that her paper was thoroughly documented. Most of the "Gentiles" in her English class would scoff at her beliefs. She considered Joseph Smith, Jr., a prophet, was convinced that God had spoken directly to him, and believed, as all good Mormons did, that the Book of Mormon was as important as, if not more important than, the Old and New Testaments in the Bible. That was why Alice had to use the college library. If her paper swayed just one of her classmates, then all the ridicule would be worth it. Alice loved her God and she was confident that He loved her.

On this particular Friday night in the spring of 1969, Alice finished at the library earlier than expected so she walked across campus to a former two-story house that had been converted by the RLDS Church into a student union. Alice immediately spotted an older girl from Odessa who offered

9

to introduce her to the other students. The only boy Alice would later remember was Jeffrey. "He was dressed in a neatly pressed white short-sleeve shirt with tiny thin blue-and-yellow pinstripes," she gushed to her best friend later back in Odessa. "His shirt matched his blue corduroy slacks. He was also wearing brown penny loafers and *no* socks! Can you believe it. He wasn't wearing any socks!"

Although they had talked for only a few minutes, Alice was smitten. "Jeffrey was like no other man I had ever met," she said. Neither of them made any effort to keep in touch after that chance meeting. Alice returned home, graduated, and spent a week at a church-run summer camp. But she didn't forget Jeffrey. One of the other girls there had just finished her freshman year at CMSU and she had gone out on a date with Jeffrey. Alice quizzed her about him. "He tried to get me drunk and take advantage of me," the girl confided. Alice was horrified. She couldn't believe that the friendly boy she had met would be so pushy.

During evening vespers at the camp, Alice decided to ask God whom she would eventually marry. Alice had been taught that a woman's role was to serve her husband and raise a family. What would her husband be like? she asked, as she prayed silently with the other campers perched on a split-log bench around a bonfire. After several minutes of silence, one of the adult counselors stood up and began to prophesy. One by one, the counselor called out each camper's name. He was being moved "by the spirit" to give them a message from God. This was a common practice in the RLDS Church and Alice believed that whatever the counselor said was from the Lord.

"Unto my sister Alice," the man proclaimed, "thus saith the spirit. I have seen your tears and I have heard your prayers and I will never leave you comfortless. I will direct your path and I will hold your life in the palm of my hand for there I have engraven you."

While others might have thought the prophecy obscure, Alice understood. She felt God was telling her not to worry about her future husband. "God was going to direct me to him!"

On the final day of camp, the group held a Sunday morning testimonial service. Because it was raining, they met in the dining hall and one of the RLDS's most revered patriarchs spoke. "We were told that the fellowship we had enjoyed that week had been acceptable in God's sight and that it was pleasing unto Him," Alice said. "The patriarch said that our generation was the one that would see the establishment of God's kingdom here on earth and that many of us would be instruments in His hands in the bringing forth of His kingdom in these latter days."

And then the speaker had looked directly at Alice, picking her out of the group for no apparent reason. He called her by name and said that God had given him a message for her.

"And unto you, my daughter Alice," he said, "thus saith the Lord. You shall have the answer to your prayers. You shall marry a companion whom I have prepared to bring forth my kingdom and he shall be great in the eyes of these people and shall do much good unto the children of men, for I have prepared him to bring forth a marvelous work and wonder."

Alice hadn't told anyone about her prayers. Yet the patriarch had known exactly what she had asked God. She began to cry. "God had chosen me," she said, "lowly me, to help bring about His kingdom on earth."

A few weeks after summer camp ended, Alice was asleep in her bedroom at night when she felt something pressing down on her. She was being crushed by what she would later describe as "an evil presence." Alice couldn't raise her arms, lift her legs, or roll off the bed. She was paralyzed, and as she lay there terrified, the weight of the evil presence began to increase until she felt as if she were about to be crushed by Satan himself. In a panic, Alice began to pray and when she called out Christ's name, the evil spirit was jerked off her as if a hand had reached down and grabbed Satan by the neck and pulled him away.

No one doubted Alice when she described her experience the next Sunday at the RLDS church in Odessa. Many in the congregation had shared similar supernatural experiences during testimonials at church. If anything, Alice's story was a comforting confirmation that Jesus Christ protected those who called for His help. After the church service, Alice was congratulated by members for giving such an inspirational and moving testimonial. She was clearly someone special and destined to do great things in the church.

When Alice enrolled at Central Missouri State University that fall as a freshman, one of the first boys she bumped into was Jeffrey. He was playing cards with his best friend, Keith Johnson, at the RLDS student union. Alice knew Keith from various church events and when he saw her, Keith waved her over and began introducing her to everyone.

"We've already met," Alice beamed when Jeffrey was introduced.

Years later, after Jeffrey had formed his cult in Kirtland, he would often reminisce about the first time he met Alice. "From the instant that I first saw her," he would say, "I *knew* she was my wife." It was as if he had always known her, as if they had been together before, he would say, as if they had always been together since the beginning of time. It was an enchanting story. It was also a lie.

When Alice looked up at Jeffrey on that fall day in 1969, she realized that he didn't remember anything about their first meeting a few months earlier.

"We met last spring," she said. "You weren't wearing any socks."

Jeffrey glanced down. He wasn't wearing any now either. They laughed. Keith invited Alice to play cards. He and Jeffrey let her win every hand. Afterward, they asked Alice if she wanted to go with them to a nearby ice cream parlor.

En route, Keith said: "Jeffrey wants to ask you out but he's too shy."

Jeffrey turned bright red. Alice laughed. Keith explained that he was having a picnic at his parents' farm that weekend. He already had a date, but Jeffrey didn't.

"Would you like to go?" Jeffrey finally asked.

"How many other couples are going?" she replied, recalling what she had heard during the summer about Jeffrey's bold conduct on dates.

"Eight or nine," Keith volunteered.

"Okay," Alice replied. "I'll go if there's a group."

As it turned out, all of the other couples except for Keith and his date dropped out. But Alice went anyway and she had a wonderful time with Jeffrey. At dusk, Keith and Jeffrey built a fire in a dry creek bed and spread out blankets to sit on. After a few moments, Keith and his date went for a walk. Jeffrey moved closer to Alice. Nervous, she began talking fast. What tumbled out was a jumbled version of her life story. When she finished, Alice pelted Jeffrey with questions about his past. He was more guarded, but Alice was so persistent that he ended up telling her much more than he intended. He liked her.

As the fire crackled, Alice and Jeffrey discovered that they had come from much different backgrounds. Alice's family was poor. Jeffrey's was well off. Alice had low self-esteem. Jeffrey was arrogant. Yet psychologists would later testify that they had one common bond. They were desperately searching for someone who would love them.

Born in Independence on January 21, 1951, Alice was the oldest of four children. Her parents had both moved to Independence because of the RLDS Church's belief that it is where Jesus Christ will return and build Zion, a perfect city of peace and beauty. Ralph Keehler had met Donna at an RLDS church service shortly after World War II. They married in 1947 and he went to work as a welder. She stayed at home and raised four children.

For the first thirteen years of her life, what Alice wanted she generally got. New dresses, shoes, spending money—it wasn't that Ralph earned a huge salary. He didn't. But both parents put their children's desires first. If there wasn't enough money, Ralph and Donna would scrimp to get it. "Alice was very, very, very spoiled as a youngster," Donna recalled later. "All my kids were. I wanted them that way really. You see, I wanted them to have all the things that I never had, so if they wanted something, we generally did whatever we could to get it for them." Donna had been the youngest of eight children. Ralph was number eight in a line of nine.

One day in 1964, Ralph felt a pain in his right leg. By nighttime, he had lost all feeling in it. The next day, doctors diagnosed him as having multiple sclerosis. It was difficult for him to walk. He was put on disability. Donna, who had never finished high school, was forced to go to work. She was hired as a cook at an all-night café and worked from seven P.M. until seven A.M., leaving Alice to run the home. "It was very difficult for Alice to understand," her mother said. "When she wanted a new dress, I'd tell her, 'I'm sorry, honey, but we can't do that anymore. We can't afford it.' And that made her angry. I think she felt cheated."

Alice's role as a surrogate parent often put her at odds with her sisters, Susan and Terri, ages eleven and seven, and brother, Charles, age two. She was the nag who demanded that her sisters pick up their clothes, make their beds, do their homework. Susan and Terri were best friends and rough-and-tough tomboys. Alice was, in the words of her younger siblings, picky and prissy. Her escape from the family was the church. "I think the thing that I loved most about church was that they truly welcomed me there," she later told a psychologist. "I was loved and accepted and I didn't always feel loved and accepted at home. I felt alone and insecure."

Alice had officially become a "latter day saint" at age five in Independence when she was baptized by Carlos Kroesen who, in the close-knit world of the Mormon church, happened to be Jeffrey Lundgren's uncle. But it was as a teenager that Alice really became engulfed in religion. She rarely missed a service, participated in every youth activity, and developed a chilling certainty to her beliefs. While others might doubt Joseph Smith, Jr.'s unconventional claims and teachings, Alice didn't.

"Alice always wanted to be the center of attention," her sister Susan Keehler Yates said later. "She loved being in the spotlight, and at church, she was on center stage." Alice was particularly revered after she told the congregation about her experiences at summer camp and her bedroom bout with the devil. But at home, her sisters and brother viewed Alice's claims with skepticism. "Alice lives in her own little fantasy world and always has," brother Charles Keehler said later. "When we were growing up, she had her own room and she would go in there and fantasize about this and that." Alice was always looking for some knight in shining armor to come carry her away, he said. Alice's sister Susan agreed. "I'm not certain Alice knows sometimes the difference between the truth and lies. Alice has always been able to convince herself that whatever she wants to believe is the truth and nothing else matters. She was that way about religion and that way about her life."

Jeffrey had grown up in the RLDS Church just like Alice, but no one had ever prophesied over him and he had always questioned claims about visions and prophecy. "I would sit there on Sundays and people would be in tears talking about the Lord's presence and His love and all these strange events that they claimed had happened to them," Jeffrey recalled, "and I would think that something was wrong with me because I felt absolutely nothing and nothing had happened to me like what they were describing. I was stone cold to all this emotional drivel."

Jeffrey went to church because it got him out of the house.

The older of two sons born to Donald and Lois Lundgren, Jeffrey came from a well-pedigreed RLDS family. Lois's parents, Alva and Maude Gadberry, had helped found two RLDS congregations in Independence. Alva was a pastor at both. Maude ran the Sunday-school programs. On the Lundgren side, it was Donald's mother, Mabel, who was the religious stalwart. She had converted from the Lutheran faith as a young mother and had seen to it that her children rarely missed a service. Mabel later taught Sunday school for thirty years at the Slover Park RLDS congregation in Independence, one of the more prestigious in town. Everyone there called her "Grandma Lundy." Don and Lois had met at church. They married in 1948. Don rose to the rank of elder, a high-ranking post in an RLDS congregation. On most Sundays, he and Lois could be found sitting and holding hands in the sanctuary.

While Don and Lois were well known at Slover Park, they were not always well liked. Don was considered too opinionated by some, while Lois was viewed as being flashy. "In every church you have your show people who see if they can dress better than anyone else," a church member later explained. "You know the type—if someone shows up in a fur coat one week, they have to have one the next week. That was Lois Lundgren. Appearances were everything to her."

Don had spent his early years in rural South Dakota, where he had learned to hunt and fish, and, according to his younger sister, Mary Bennett, had earned a reputation for being a "terror" and "bully." By the time he had grown into adulthood, Don was no longer a hellion, but he was still seen as "a tough guy," his brother-in-law George Gadberry said later. Don was a man's man who spoke his mind, stood his ground, and was prepared to back up what he believed. There were two things, he often told other church members, about which he was fanatical. Don had served in the navy and was an unabashed flag-waving patriot. He also detested slackers. No one had ever given him anything, he was fond of saying. He had earned his own way, had never welshed on a debt, and couldn't abide those who did.

Unlike the Keehlers, Don and Lois were well off financially. Don had started as a construction worker but had been put in charge of a work crew that installed microwave towers for the telephone company. He was a handsome man, well built, self-assured, the leathery sort that cigarette companies liked to feature in advertisements. By the early 1960s, Don was earning $100 per day when the average salary in the nation was $100 per week. When George Gadberry got into financial trouble operating a formal-wear rental shop in Independence, it was Donald who put up the $5,000 in cash to keep the store open. Eventually, he bought out his brother-in-law, put Jeffrey to work there after school and on weekends, and soon had it operating in the black. No one was surprised when Don sold it for a tidy profit.

Jeffrey would later joke that the reason his father had to earn a good income was because of his mother's unabashed spending. Lois liked to collect things, and her home was filled with so many knick-knacks that it often reminded visitors of a museum. During the first years of their marriage, Lois bought old furniture in secondhand shops and refinished it with painstaking care. Later, when she could afford it, Lois searched area antique stores and brought home their finest pieces. Each room of the house looked as if it had been arranged to be photographed for display in a magazine. As children, Jeffrey and his brother, Corry, who was nearly six years younger, were permitted to sit on the living room sofa only when guests visited. At all other times, they sat on a rug dropped in front of the television.

As a young woman, Lois had chestnut hair, ivory skin, and a figure that other girls envied. Even when she was a grand-mother, she bleached her hair blond, dressed immaculately, and had a youthful sparkle.

Jeffrey would later insist, however, that his mother was cold toward him. "My parents were madly in love with each other, so much so that I don't think they had any love left over for me and my brother. I always had to fight for affection and my parents' love was always conditional," he charged. "It was always used as a reward and taken away as punishment when I was inadequate. I loved playing sports, but there was also a lot of pressure. I was always onstage. When the game ended, my parents would want to know how well had I done? How many hits did I get? Had I embarrassed the family? They were completely success orientated and worried constantly about how the Lundgrens looked in the community."

When Jeffrey played his first basketball game in sixth grade, he scored seven of the team's eleven points. After the game, his mother harangued him because of the "plopping" noise that his feet had made when he ran up and down the wooden floor. "She was so embarrassed that she made me practice running on my toes in the kitchen while she watched so I'd learn how to run quietly."

Jeffrey had only one close friend when he was young. Sarah Stotts lived just down the street from the Lundgrens. They first met as toddlers in the church nursery at Slover Park. By the time they were in high school, they had become close friends. "We would talk on the phone a couple hours each day after school about what was happening," Sarah remembered. "It wasn't a boyfriend-girlfriend relationship. He just happened to be a boy and I happened to be a girl. But for me, talking to Jeffrey was just like talking to one of my girlfriends. He seemed to really understand me and he listened."

Both felt awkward around others. "Jeff wasn't popular and neither was I. We were very quiet, but we both wanted to be part of the group at church so we'd encourage each other. I'd say, 'Okay, I'll play volleyball if you'll play it,' and he'd say, 'I'll try this if you will try this.'"

Sarah didn't have a happy homelife and she didn't think he did either. "Jeff never felt that he was good enough for his father. He didn't think he could please him."

Jeffrey would later reiterate that same feeling of inadequacy to a psychologist. "No matter what I did, I never felt I was man enough for him. I always wanted an 'I love you' but what

I got was male-on-male competition. We would play burnout. I'd throw a hardball as hard as I could for him to catch and he'd throw it back to me. I used to endure the pain when I was seven or eight just because I wanted to be with him. I can still remember one of the best moments in my life was when I was a freshman in high school and I had become strong enough to hurt him when I threw the ball back."

At William Chrisman High School in Independence, Jeffrey excelled as shortstop on the baseball team. He lifted weights every day, and by his senior year, he could throw a pitch close to one hundred miles per hour. But other students considered him a geek. "Here was this guy who wanted to be liked and was shy and afraid to participate, yet when he opened his mouth, he was a know-it-all," recalled a classmate. "You felt sorry for him until you started talking to him and then you realized that he was arrogant. No one really liked him."

Jeffrey didn't have a date to the senior prom so he asked Sarah to go with him. When she suggested that he invite someone he was interested in romantically, Jeffrey appeared hurt. "I don't like anyone but you," he told her.

Jeffrey's graduation picture in the 1968 high school yearbook stuck out. Other boys in the class were shown wearing long hair, a few brandished peace symbols, most were smiling, clearly eager to get on with their lives. And then there was Jeffrey, his hair cut in a 1950s buzz, dressed in a crisp white shirt, narrow tie, and jacket, completely out of step with his classmates. But it was the expression on his face that caught the eye. His uncle George Gadberry would later remember how one day when he was cleaning out a desk drawer, he had come across several school pictures of Jeffrey that had been taken as the boy moved up through the various grades. "Jeff was never smiling. He never seemed very happy as a boy." The photographs chronicled a boy who seemed to be angry and bitter inside.

During their picnic at Keith Johnson's farm, Jeffrey told Alice how he had played shortstop in high school and briefly mentioned his parents. But the only comment that she would later recall as odd was something Jeffrey said jokingly, or at least it sounded as if he were kidding. "My mother is not going to like your name," he told Alice. "She'll think it is much too plain." Alice didn't respond. She was having too good a time. Despite what she had heard about him, Jeffrey was a perfect gentleman. He didn't even try to kiss her. After Keith and his date returned, the four of them drove back to campus and Jeffrey escorted Alice to the front stoop of the women's dormitory. He politely asked if he could kiss her good night. Alice nodded.

A few minutes later, Alice was upstairs in her room when she heard the telephone ring in the hall outside her door. There was only one telephone on the entire floor and Alice's room was the closest to it. She hurried out to answer it, figuring she would page whoever it was for. It was Jeffrey. He wanted to thank her for spending the afternoon with him and he wanted to know what time she was getting up in the morning.

"Why?" she asked, giggling.

"Because I want to be waiting outside to carry your books," he replied.

"Oh, Jeffrey, you don't have to do that," she said.

"I plan to walk you to every one of your classes tomorrow," he said firmly.

They chatted for a few minutes and then Alice went to bed. The next morning when Alice stepped outside the dormitory, Jeffrey was waiting.

At the time, she thought it was simply wonderful.

Chapter 2

THE Mormon religion that Jeffrey and Alice learned as children was peculiarly American and unlike any other sect. Its founder, Joseph Smith, Jr., claimed he had a vision in 1820 at the age of fifteen while living with his parents on a farm near Palmyra, New York, about thirty miles east of Rochester. At the time, western New York was on the verge of what later became known as the Second Great Awakening—a religious revival marked by impassioned conversions and sensational Elmer Gantry-style tent meetings. So many Methodist circuit riders, itinerant Baptist preachers, and self-proclaimed evangelists swarmed into western New York State that it was soon nicknamed the "burned over" district because of the hellfire and brimstone preached there. Amid this fervor, young Joseph was trying to decide, as he wrote later, "Who of all these parties are right? Or, are they all wrong together?"

Smith's questions were answered one day while he was praying alone in the woods. A "pillar of light" fell down around him, he later said, and God and Jesus Christ appeared. It was Christ who told him that the existing churches "were all wrong" and "their creeds were an abomination in his sight." Christ ordered Smith not to join any denomination but to continue to pray for guidance.

Three years later, while Smith was saying his nightly prayers in his bedroom, an angel named Moroni appeared. The angel said that fourteen hundred years earlier, when he was still a mortal man, he had hidden a book made of golden plates in a stone box about three miles from the Smith farm. The plates contained the history of a band of ancient Hebrews who had traveled from Jerusalem to the New World before the birth of Christ. These Hebrews had settled in the Americas and were the forefathers of the Indians. Their history was nothing less than a volume of holy scriptures that God now wanted brought forth so that "the fullness of the everlasting Gospel" could be known.

Smith found the plates exactly where the angel had told him to look, but Moroni wouldn't let him take them from their hiding place. During the next three years, Moroni steadfastly refused to surrender the plates, but on September 22, 1827, the angel relented. Along with the plates, Smith was given two magical stones called the Urim and Thummim that were needed to translate the ancient writings into English.

Smith wanted to translate the plates immediately, but he was broke, and by this time he had a family to support. He contacted a wealthy farmer, Martin Harris, and asked him for help. Harris was intrigued by Smith's story about Moroni, but when the farmer mentioned it to his wife, she suspected a scam and demanded proof that the plates were genuine. Harris asked Smith to show him the plates. Smith politely refused. Moroni had instructed him not to show them to anyone, he explained, but he gave Harris a sheet of paper that contained strange markings which Smith said he had copied directly from the golden plates. Harris gave Smith fifty dollars and rushed the paper to Charles Anthon, a Columbia College classics scholar familiar with ancient writing. Anthon studied the markings and pronounced them fake. A dejected Harris returned home, where Smith was waiting with a ready explanation. Engraving the golden plates had been such a tedious process that the ancient Hebrew prophet and historian who had compiled the records had developed his own form of shorthand to save time and space. Smith identified the author as Mormon, who happened to be Moroni's father. He said that Mormon had transcribed the golden plates in "Reformed Egyptian," a dialect that only Smith could read.

Harris agreed to help bankroll Smith's venture and also offered to aid in translating the plates. Exactly how this was done is unclear. One historical account says that Smith placed the Urim and Thummim into his hat, buried his face in the hat, and then, covered with a blanket, dictated to a scribe what he saw. Other stories say that Smith wore the Urim and Thummim like eyeglasses, held the plates in his lap and read them aloud to Harris from behind a screen. Regardless, by 1830 the translation was finished. Smith called it the Book of Mormon, and on March 26 a local Palmyra printer, Egbert Grandin, published five thousand copies of it. The $3,000 printing bill was paid by Harris, who had become such an ardent supporter of Smith that he mortgaged his farm to raise the necessary cash. While Smith's "Gold Bible" caused an immediate stir, it didn't sell well and Harris lost his farm.

From the moment it was published, the Book of Mormon came under attack. Scholars pointed out that it described animals and plants in the New World that didn't exist in North and Central America until after Spanish and English explorers arrived. Prophets, who lived decades before Jesus Christ was born, were quoted talking about Christ's death on the cross as if it had already happened. The fact that Smith couldn't produce the golden plates didn't help his credibility. The angel Moroni had reappeared, Smith said, and had taken them back.

Smith's local reputation also raised suspicions. Four years earlier, he had been convicted in Chenango County, New York, of accepting money from a farmer in return for finding buried treasure with a "peepstone," a native crystal much like those used by fortune-tellers. The court had declared Smith "disorderly and an imposter."

Not everyone, however, was skeptical. Written much like the Bible, the Book of Mormon was filled with inspirational stories about religious heroes. It contained detailed descriptions of military battles and a slew of commandments that seemed to clarify statements by Jesus and others in the Bible. Most of all, it promised those who believed in it a chance to reign over the earth with Jesus Christ.

Smith taught that Christ was on the verge of returning to earth where he would judge every man, woman, and child. Christ would then rule the earth with a selected few for a period of one thousand years known as the Millennium. Those who joined Smith's church during these "last days" on earth were "the saints of the latter days," he said, and they would be the ones whom Christ would choose to rule with Him over everyone else.

On April 6, 1830, Smith and six other men officially incorporated a new religion which they called the Church of Christ. At the time, Smith was only twenty-four years old. He boldly declared that his new church was the "only true church" in the world. A short time later, Smith renamed his church to emphasize his teachings about the "latter days." He called it the *Church of Jesus Christ of Latter-Day Saints*. Anyone who didn't accept the Book of Mormon was a Gentile and was automatically doomed.

Besides offering his followers a new testament, Smith also taught that God played an active role in the lives of his "saints." Smith's God hadn't changed much from the one described in the Old Testament. He still sent prophets to direct his people through revelations and His spirit. Smith claimed that God had chosen him to be His church's first "prophet, seer, and revelator."

Despite such grandiose claims, Smith's church got off to a sluggish start in New York. Few joined. But shortly after

the Book of Mormon was published, one of Smith's converts
delivered a copy to Sidney Rigdon, one of the most influential
preachers of the time. Rigdon would eventually fall from
favor in Mormon circles and be relegated to a footnote
in the church's archives, but he was far more charismatic
than Smith. The bushy-haired, bearded, barrel-chested Rigdon
could keep a congregation entranced for hours with his oratory.
Even hardened men had been known to burst into tears at his
services. Rigdon had already been a minister in two other
denominations when he began reading Smith's new testament.
Overnight, Rigdon was converted. Like Smith, Rigdon believed
that the Millennium was imminent. He also believed that only
a prophet who had been selected by God could have brought
forth the Book of Mormon.

Rigdon lived in Kirtland, Ohio, and during his first thirty
days as a Mormon convert, he baptized one hundred twenty-
seven people into the new religion. Back in New York, Smith
had attracted a following of less than half that number. In
December 1830, Rigdon rode his horse to New York to
meet the self-proclaimed prophet and tell him of the budding
Mormon movement in Kirtland. Smith was so thrilled by
Rigdon's success that he invited him to spend the night in
his home. The next morning, Smith said that God had spoken
to him during the night. Just as John the Baptist had prepared
the way for Christ, God wanted Rigdon to prepare the way for
Smith. He announced that he and his family were moving to
Kirtland and he commanded all faithful Mormons to follow
him there.

At the time, Kirtland boasted a population of 1,020,
mostly former New Englanders. It had a rooming house,
two churches, and a mill. The richest citizen was Newel K.
Whitney, owner of the general store and one of Rigdon's
recent Mormon converts. Smith immediately moved into the
Whitneys' home and lived there until his followers built his
family their own house. Once Smith was settled, he said
that God had commanded him to rewrite the Holy Bible.
Over time, it had been filled with errors because of sloppy
translators and wicked church leaders, he explained. God
had told him to publish an "inspired" version for the saints
to use.

During the coming months, Rigdon and Smith recruited more and more converts, eventually developing a following of five hundred in the Kirtland area. Smith also began having almost daily revelations. Some dealt with minor events. When Smith and Rigdon tipped over in a canoe and almost drowned in a river, God revealed that He no longer wanted His prophet and Rigdon to travel on water, unless it was on a man-made canal. Other revelations contained sweeping theological announcements. One of the most important dealt with Zion. Smith said that God wanted the Mormons to "gather" together and establish Zion, a perfect community of love and trust where they would wait for Christ's return. Even though Kirtland had become the church's stronghold, the prophet said that God had designated Independence, Missouri, as the site of His "new Jerusalem." That was where Christ would eventually return.

On August 3, 1831, Smith, Rigdon, and other Mormon leaders held a dedication service in Independence at the "center spot" where Zion was to be built. Most of the land in Independence, however, was owned by Gentiles who didn't want anything to do with Smith or his religion. When Mormons began moving to Missouri, the Gentiles there turned hostile. One night, a mob tarred and feathered the Mormon bishop and forced other saints to flee at gunpoint. Faced with growing hatred in Missouri, Smith decided that the saints could remain in Kirtland a short while longer. He announced that God wanted His saints to build a temple in Kirtland as a demonstration of their love and faith.

Construction of the "House of the Lord" began June 5, 1833, and it was Rigdon who became the driving force behind it. Church historians would later write that Rigdon had "wet the walls with his tears" by coming to the construction site daily and offering emotional prayers there. Although the fledgling church had little money, the Mormons managed to construct what then was the tallest temple in Ohio. As a show of devotion, women donated their finest china to the church. It was crushed and mixed with the exterior plaster so that the walls would sparkle when hit by sunlight. At the dedication in 1836, Rigdon gave a two-hour sermon. Smith spoke too, blessing the building. Some of the saints at the service later claimed that an angel had appeared standing next to Smith when he spoke. One week later, Smith announced that while he was praying in the temple, Christ appeared, followed by Moses and Elijah.

Although the Mormons were prospering in Kirtland, they still were having trouble in Independence. On February 24, 1834, a mob attacked Mormon settlers. When word reached Kirtland, Smith made an angry declaration. God, he said, had promised to one day send a prophet to lead the saints against their enemies and redeem Zion.

"I will raise up unto my people a man, who shall lead them like as Moses led the children of Israel. . . ." Smith quoted God as saying.

There are conflicting stories about what happened next in Kirtland. The official church version says that the cost of constructing the temple put the Mormons heavily in debt. The completion of the temple also frightened Gentiles who feared the Mormons were becoming too strong. Anti-Mormons called for a boycott of the saints' stores and Gentile bankers stopped making loans to Mormon families. Smith responded by opening his own bank for Mormons, called the Kirtland Safety Society Bank. The saints were told that God expected them to exchange gold and silver for paper notes printed by the bank. Unfortunately, the Mormon bank went belly up during a national bank panic in 1837 and Smith and Rigdon were forced to leave Kirtland when angry Gentiles threatened legal action.

A less flattering account is told in the records at the Lake County deeds office and in old county-court documents. According to these records, Smith began buying large tracts of land, apparently in the hope that a railroad would run a line over his property and make him rich. When Smith ran out of places to borrow money, he opened the Mormon bank and used its deposits as if they were his own. To ease any qualms that Mormons might have about exchanging gold and silver for bank notes, Smith put several strongboxes filled with silver coins on display in the bank lobby. It wasn't until later, court records reveal, that Mormon depositors learned the strongboxes had been filled with sand and only the top layer had been made up of shiny fifty-cent pieces. When the bank went bust, Smith and Rigdon fled town at night to avoid furious creditors.

Whatever version is true, Smith moved his church first to a Missouri settlement that he called Far West, located just north of Independence, and then later to Hancock County, Illinois, where he established his own town, which he named Nauvoo. Once Smith and Rigdon left Ohio, Rigdon's standing began to slip. When Rigdon's daughter accused Smith of locking her in a room and demanding that she have sex with him because God had ordered it, Rigdon's relationship with Smith was ruptured even more.

Seven years after the two men fled Kirtland, Joseph Smith, Jr., and his brother, Hyrum, were murdered by a mob in Carthage, Illinois. Their deaths left the Mormon Church without a leader. Rigdon argued that he should be in charge, but he no longer had enough clout to declare himself the new prophet. He was excommunicated and returned to his native Pennsylvania, where he died penniless.

The saint who stepped into Smith's shoes was Brigham Young, a charismatic and determined man who led the biggest bloc of Mormons on a difficult trek westward to Salt Lake City, Utah. Not everyone followed Young, however. A small faction of saints stayed behind in Independence, where they chose Smith's eldest son, Joseph Smith III, to head their church. Because he was only eleven at the time, his mother, Emma, took control.

Over time, the Mormons in Utah grew into a worldwide church of seven million members with tremendous wealth, power, and prestige. The saints who stayed behind in Independence renamed themselves the *Reorganized* Church of Jesus Christ of Latter Day Saints [RLDS]. Unlike their better-known Utah counterparts, the RLDS never attracted more than 250,000 members and its members were so poor that until recently they couldn't afford to build a temple of their own in Independence.

Besides wealth and membership, the two Mormon sects differed in their religious teachings. One point of contention was Smith's 1834 declaration that God would someday raise up a leader like Moses who would redeem Zion. Many Utah saints felt that Brigham Young had fulfilled that prophecy. Young, they argued, had successfully led the saints "out of bondage" in Missouri into the "new promised land" of Utah where he had "redeemed Zion." But such talk was heresy to the saints in Missouri. They considered Young a false prophet. Zion was supposed to be built in Independence—not Salt Lake City—they argued.

For many in the RLDS, the 1834 promise had never been fulfilled. They were still waiting for God to send them a prophet. Alice was among those RLDS members eagerly awaiting this new Moses, and in the fall of 1969, she was more confident than ever that Smith's 1834 revelation was about to come true. After all, one of the church's patriarchs had told her and the others during summer camp that their generation would establish Zion and that could mean only one thing. God was planning to raise up a prophet in her life time. The patriarch had also revealed that Alice's husband was going to help prepare the way for Christ's return. She had carefully memorized the patriarch's words:

"You shall marry a companion whom I have prepared to bring forth my kingdom and he shall be great in the eyes of these people and shall do much good unto the children of men, for I have prepared him to bring forth a marvelous work and wonder."

After her first date with Jeffrey, Alice began to wonder: Could he be the man whom God had chosen to be her husband? Was Jeffrey the one who would help bring forth God's kingdom?

The very thought made her tingle.

Chapter 3

A long-stemmed rose arrived every day during the first week. Jeffrey was waiting outside the women's dormitory each morning to carry Alice's books. He was there after every class. If Alice needed to go to the library, the school cafeteria, the gymnasium, Jeffrey would escort her. Everything that he did revolved around Alice. Even after Alice had gone into the dormitory at night, he telephoned.

"What are you going to wear tomorrow?" he'd ask.

"I don't know yet," Alice would reply. "Haven't decided."

"I think you should wear that blue outfit," he'd volunteer. "You look beautiful in it."

"Okay," she'd say.

They'd talk for a while and then he'd tell her, "Say, you'd better get to sleep. Go right to bed now."

Alice would hang up the telephone, get her blue outfit ready to wear, and go to bed. The next morning, he would be waiting outside and would compliment her.

There was only one time that he upset her. He had suggested that she wear a white blouse and black skirt the next morning, but she forgot and chose something else. He didn't speak to her when they walked together to her first class.

"What's wrong?" she asked later.

"I'm just disappointed," he said. "I asked you to wear the blouse and skirt. I thought you agreed."

Once Alice was sitting in her freshman chemistry class when she felt as if someone were staring at her. She glanced over at the door and spotted Jeffrey watching her through a tiny window. Ten minutes later, she looked over again and he was still there, just staring at her.

Alice loved the attention.

"He's fascinating. He's handsome. He's athletic," she confided to a schoolmate. "He is everything that I have ever thought the perfect man should be and he is crazy about me."

One week after their first date, Jeffrey and Alice went on a hayride sponsored by the RLDS-run student union. During the ride, Alice looked at Jeffrey and he began to say something, but stopped.

"What'ya gonna do," she asked teasingly, "ask me to marry ya?"

He continued to stare at her.

"Yes," he replied solemnly. "I want you to be my wife."

Alice smirked and then she realized that he was serious.

"If you promise to fall in love with me, I will," she replied solemnly.

"I already am in love with you, Alice," he said.

In 1969, women could get married at age eighteen without parental consent in Missouri but men had to be twenty-one. Jeffrey was nineteen and he knew his parents would not approve. They wanted him to finish college. He was worried that Don and Lois were not going to like Alice. She was poor and had no status within the church.

"We'll have to figure out some way to get my parents' permission," he told her.

Alice would later tell psychologists that as soon as she and Jeff agreed that they were going to get married, he began to pressure her for sex. Despite her religious training, she didn't resist. Did it really matter? After all, they planned to get married. "It was as if I had opened the floodgates," Alice later confided to a friend. "All Jeff ever wanted to do was have sex, sex, sex. It was so contrary to my upbringing that I felt very ashamed. I felt dirty. But to him it was a sign that I loved him. 'If you love me, you'll do this,' he said. And I wanted him to love me."

When the Thanksgiving school break arrived, Jeffrey asked Alice to come to Independence to meet his family. Alice was terrified. Jeffrey's descriptions of Don and Lois didn't put her at ease.

"Don't be surprised if my father makes faces at you during the meal," Jeffrey said as they pulled into the driveway at his parents' home on Thanksgiving Day.

"What?" Alice replied.

"He's been practicing making faces at you so he can do it during the meal."

She thought he was joking.

"Alice, they don't think you are good enough for me," he said coldly. "They think you want to marry me because of their money."

Alice was about to cry. All during the meal, she stared at her plate. She was afraid to look at Don because she thought he might make a face at her. She was afraid to compliment Lois on her decorating skills because she might think all Alice cared about was possessions. Don and Lois were both gracious during the meal. They were friendly to her. But she was too scared to speak. Afterward, she and Jeffrey went to see the movie *Romeo and Juliet*. Alice spent most of the time in the ladies' room throwing up.

Jeffrey got called into the Dean of Students' office when college resumed. He had spent so much time escorting Alice around campus that he had missed most of his own classes. If he didn't stop cutting class, he would be put on academic suspension.

"You'd better tell Jeffrey to study for the final," a friend told Alice. "You know he's never even been to class."

Alice was shocked. She'd never asked him about his grades. When she confronted him the next day, Jeffrey lied.

"I'm going to class," he said. "It's just that no one sees me." He told Alice that after he walked her to her classes, he would dash across campus and slip into a seat in the back of his class. He'd leave a few minutes early so he could meet Alice. "The reason no one sees me is because I slip in and out so quietly.

"Besides," Jeffrey added, "I'm majoring in Alice. It doesn't matter if I go to class."

Jeffrey's grades weren't the only ones that had dropped. Alice's began slipping. There just wasn't enough time during the day for her to study. Jeffrey loved to play table tennis and he wanted Alice to watch him. He'd taught her how to play too, and together they had won the school's doubles championship, although Alice joked that her major contribution was jumping out of Jeff's way when he charged for the Ping-Pong ball.

She'd never met anyone as competitive as Jeffrey, nor anyone who hated to lose as much as he did.

The semester passed quickly and it was soon time for the Christmas holidays. Jeffrey failed every one of his classes. He was told that he couldn't come back for the spring semester. Alice panicked. She knew that Jeffrey was going to lose his draft deferment. Even if he didn't get called up right away, he would still have to move back to Independence and live with his parents.

Alice telephoned her mother. "We've got to get married," she said. "We can't wait."

"If you truly love each other, then you'll still love each other in a few years after you finish college," Donna insisted.

Alice wasn't so certain. What she didn't and couldn't tell her mother was that sex had become such a big part of her relationship with Jeffrey that she was afraid he might break off their relationship if they spent time apart. "Sometimes I think the only reason Jeff wants to be with me is because of sex," she told a friend. "I don't know what he'd do if I ever told him no." Alice returned to Odessa at Christmas afraid that she might lose Jeffrey for good.

In Independence, Jeffrey telephoned Sarah Stotts over the holidays. She was home from Graceland College, a small school in Lamoni, Iowa, sponsored by the RLDS Church. When Jeffrey dropped by Sarah's house to visit, he was surprised. "I had decided to change my image when I went away to Graceland," Sarah said. "No one there knew that I was shy and scared to death so I jumped right in and decided to overcome my fears and it worked." Sarah had turned into an outgoing, self-confident woman.

After telling Jeffrey about Graceland, Sarah asked him what was happening in his life. Jeffrey was quiet and then he told her that he wanted to ask her an important question.

"I need to know if there is any chance at all of us getting together, you know, romantically," he asked.

"What?" Sarah replied.

"Is there a chance that we might end up getting together someday?" he said. "You know, getting married."

"I don't think so," said Sarah.

"Well, how about if you kiss me one time?" Jeffrey continued.

Sarah agreed, but when Jeffrey leaned over to kiss her, she burst out laughing.

"I guess it wouldn't work," he said. "The reason I had to know was because if I can't have you, I guess I will marry someone else who is as close to you as possible."

Sarah stopped laughing. She hadn't realized that he felt as strongly as he did about her. More than two decades later, Sarah would still remember what Jeffrey said that night.

"Jeff told me that Alice was pressuring him to get pregnant because she had a bad homelife and she wanted to get out of the house, you know, to get married. I told Jeff that he really needed to be careful or he was going to get into something that he didn't need to get into and he said it didn't matter."

"What do you mean, it won't matter?" she asked.

"If I can't have you, I'll marry Alice. But if you and Alice and I were all three in a boat that was sinking and I could only save one of you, I would save you first and if I had a chance, I'd go back and save Alice because I do love Alice, but if it came down to choosing between you and Alice, I'd save you first."

"Jeff," Sarah said, "if you really feel that way, you shouldn't be even talking about getting married. You shouldn't be rushing into this."

Sarah would later recall that conversation with confusion and sorrow. "I remember thinking that I had gone away to college and had changed. I had overcome my insecurity. But I don't think Jeff had ever gotten to the point where he really believed in himself. I think he was looking for someone to love him and tell him that he was worth loving."

Jeffrey invited Alice to his house on Christmas Day, but she felt self-conscious when she got there. She had brought gifts for the Lundgrens, but no one had bought her anything. When she and Jeffrey had a chance to talk in private, she asked if he had told his mom and dad that they wanted to get married. He avoided answering her.

A few weeks after the spring semester started at CMSU, Jeffrey and Alice drove to Odessa to talk to her parents. They had thought of a way to force Don and Lois to give their consent. This is how Donna Keehler remembers what happened. "We were sitting around the kitchen table when Alice and Jeffrey asked us if we would tell Jeff's parents that Alice was pregnant. I immediately asked her if she was and Alice said no, but they wanted us to lie to Don and Lois so they would have to agree to the marriage."

"I'm not going to lie for you," Donna told Jeffrey and Alice. "That's no way to start a marriage."

A month later, Jeffrey and Alice returned to talk to Donna and Ralph. This time, Alice said, no one was going to have to lie. Jeffrey called his parents from the Keehlers' kitchen and broke the news. Don and Lois were furious. Jeffrey asked Donna and Ralph if they'd go with him and Alice to face his parents.

Don led everyone into the family room where he had lined up six chairs. He and Lois had never met Ralph and Donna before.

"I have something to say," he announced, and for the next several minutes, he blistered Jeffrey. "My dad said I had embarrassed the entire family. That I had ruined the Lundgren name. That he and mom were so embarrassed by what I had done that they couldn't show their faces at the Slover Park congregation. Then he turned and looked at me and said, 'It is a great sorrow to me that my first grandchild has to be born a bastard.' "

During the next few minutes, Lois and Donna argued. Lois claimed Alice had trapped Jeffrey. "Lois called Alice a whore," Donna recalled. Alice began to cry. Donna fired back. This was no way for the Lundgrens to treat their future daughter-in-law. Don jumped into the fray. Jeffrey didn't have to marry Alice just because she was pregnant. Jeffrey stomped out of the room. He packed a few things and left with Alice and her parents.

The next day was Sunday and everyone cooled off. On Monday morning, Jeffrey, Alice, and Donna drove to the Independence courthouse to get a wedding license. Don and Lois had agreed to give their consent as long as Jeffrey and Alice promised not to have a big church wedding.

Lois was waiting at the courthouse but she told Jeffrey that she wanted to talk to him privately before they went inside. She led him to her car where his grandparents, Alva and

Maude Gadberry, were waiting. For several minutes, Lois and the Gadberrys explained to Jeffrey all of the reasons why he didn't need to marry Alice. Jeffrey would later tell Alice that his mother had upped the ante. "She offered to pay me off if I would denounce you and walk away."

On May 5, 1970, Jeffrey and Alice were married at her RLDS church in Odessa. Jeffrey didn't tell his parents the time, date, or location because he was afraid they might disrupt the ceremony. Just to make certain that none of the Lundgrens showed up, Jeffrey had two of Alice's relatives stand guard at the front door. The church pews on the left side of the sanctuary, traditionally reserved for the friends and relatives of the bride, were packed with guests. The pews on the groom's side were completely empty except for one person. Jeffrey's college pal, Keith Johnson, came to wish him well.

Jeffrey didn't have enough money to rent a tuxedo. Donna and Ralph paid for it and slipped him another six hundred dollars from their savings to pay for a honeymoon. Jeffrey borrowed the Keehlers' car and drove his new bride to Arlington, Texas, where they checked into a hotel near the Six Flags Over Texas amusement park. He had been there before with his parents and he figured Alice would enjoy the rides. He had booked a room in the same hotel that he had stayed in with his mom and dad. The morning after their wedding, Jeffrey and Alice arrived at the park early. Jeffrey wanted to spend as much time as possible on the rides. But when they got to the park, Alice's stomach was upset. It was morning sickness. Jeffrey took Alice back to their hotel, but he soon became jittery. He had already paid for two all-day passes. There wasn't much point in their both being stuck in the hotel. He kissed her on the forehead and left for the park. He would be back when it closed.

As soon as he shut the door to the room, Alice began to cry. She couldn't believe that Jeffrey had left her alone on their honeymoon. What had happened to the obsessed college boy who had sent her a long-stemmed rose each day for a week?

Chapter 4

MARRIAGE had seemed so simple when Jeffrey and Alice first fell in love. But that was before Jeffrey flunked out of school and before Don and Lois stopped paying for his room and board. When the newlyweds returned from their honeymoon in May 1970, they had no car, no money, no jobs, and no place to live. Donna Keehler came to the rescue. Jeffrey and Alice could live with her and Ralph rent-free in Odessa until they could afford a place of their own.

Jeffrey knew he was going to be drafted. It was a terrible time to be inducted into the army. By January 1970, some forty thousand Americans had already been killed in Vietnam. Ten thousand of them had died during 1969 alone. And even though Henry Kissinger had secretly begun negotiating an end to the war, some of the most intense fighting still lay ahead. Jeffrey decided to enlist in the navy under a delayed-entry program that didn't require him to report until late 1970.

Donna had always said that no household was big enough for two families, and between May and November, her axiom proved painfully accurate. What bothered Donna was Jeffrey's selfishness. He was fairly good at pitching in with household chores, but he refused to share. Whenever Jeffrey earned a few dollars doing odd jobs, he'd immediately spend it on himself without offering to chip in for groceries, gasoline, or other costs at the Keehler house. Some nights, Jeffrey would bring home a large pizza, but rather than sharing it, he would scurry into his bedroom with Alice and shut the door so that they could eat in private. Jeffrey's between-meal snacking also irked the Keehlers. Three or four times a week, he would buy a liter of Pepsi and frozen chocolate-chip cookie dough. After taking a few sips of the Pepsi, he would cut off the top of the plastic bottle and fill the container with ice, making it into a giant cup. He would drink the entire liter as he ate the raw dough.

There were other problems too. Jeffrey would borrow Donna's car at night so he could take Alice on rides. Donna understood how the young couple might want to get away. But when Donna got up early the next morning to leave for work, she would always find her gas gauge registering empty. Jeffrey never thought to fill the tank. He didn't seem to care about anyone but himself.

When Jeffrey left on November 8 for navy training at San Diego, California, only Alice was sorry to see him go. Their baby was due any day and she wanted Jeffrey at the hospital with her. Three weeks after he left, Alice gave birth to Damon Paul Lundgren. She called Jeffrey and told him they had a son. The arrival of a baby at the Keehler household caused new friction between Alice and her two sisters. "Alice always claimed that she was too tired to get up at night, so Sue and I got out of bed and took care of Damon, got him a bottle or whatever," Terri remembered later. "My mom was working nights so she wasn't home and didn't know we were doing all the work at night. We were gone to school by the time she got home. We all found out later that Alice was telling our mother that she had been the one who was up all night. She'd say she was exhausted, and our mother would end up taking care of Damon all day long. That was typical of Alice. She liked to get other people to do her work."

Jeffrey wasn't permitted to come home over the Christmas holidays. When he finally got back to Odessa on February 13, 1971, he told Alice that he had two big surprises for her. Alice had bought Jeffrey a mushy Valentine card and she immediately suspected that he had bought her something special to celebrate their first Valentine's Day as a married couple.

"Okay!" she said, excitedly. "Tell me, tell me!"

"I've been studying the scriptures," he announced. "Go ahead, say a verse; I bet I can tell you where it's located."

Alice didn't know what to say.

"C'mon, Alice," he pushed. "Test me. Just name one."

All Alice could think of was a well-known verse from the Book of Mormon. Jeffrey beamed when he named its location.

"I wanted to impress her," Jeffrey remembered years later. "The scriptures were very precious to Alice and I wanted to show her how much I had learned. At that time, she knew the scriptures much better than I did and she was always harping about them, so I had decided to study them for her."

Still expecting a Valentine present, Alice urged Jeffrey to tell her his second surprise.

"My father has agreed to bless Damon. It's all arranged."

While in San Diego, Jeffrey had written to Don and Lois and asked his father if he would perform a blessing, a major event in the Mormon Church. Jeffrey hadn't bothered to consult Alice or her parents. Instead, he and his parents had chosen a time, date, and place for the ceremony.

"Is there anything else?" she asked. Jeffrey didn't know what she meant. Without uttering another word, she handed Jeffrey the Valentine card. He opened it and blushed.

"Alice," he stammered. "I was so busy, I didn't have a chance to buy you one."

The next weekend, Jeffrey and Alice took Damon to Independence to meet his grandparents. Don scooped up Damon in his arms. Lois wasn't as friendly. Neither of them acknowledged Alice. The afternoon went well as far as Jeffrey was concerned, and Don and Lois asked them to stay for dinner. By the time it was over, Jeffrey was telling his father all about the navy while Lois rocked Damon.

"I was a non-person," Alice complained on the ride back to Odessa. "I was invisible, like I wasn't even there. I never want to go back to their house again."

Damon's blessing was scheduled for the following Sunday at the Slover Park congregation. The Keehlers drove to Independence with Jeffrey, Alice, and Damon. It was a beautiful ceremony. Damon was carried to the front of the sanctuary during the regular church service. Don held him and said a blessing. He had spent hours preparing it and after he finished, some in the congregation were wiping tears from their eyes.

Don and Lois invited friends to their house after church. Ralph and Donna were noticeably absent. Alice reluctantly tagged along. When she arrived, her mother-in-law was waiting. Lois threw her arms around Alice and gave her a hug. All of the anger and hatred she had felt toward Alice had "melted away" during Don's blessing of Damon, she explained. Alice was no longer a ghost, she was family. Lois began introducing Alice to her friends as her new "daughter." Jeffrey had to return to San Diego a few days later. Alice and Damon moved to California with him.

Jeffrey was assigned to work as an electrical repairman on the USS *Sperry*, a supply delivery and repair ship that serviced submarines. But it wasn't scheduled to leave San Diego harbor for several months so he was temporarily assigned to work as a lifeguard at a base swimming pool. Nearly every day, Alice and Damon would go to the pool with him. He and Alice would play badminton, sunbathe, and gossip about how the wives of other sailors flirted with men at the pool. "We both felt out of place in San Diego," Jeffrey later said. "It was just too wild for us. We weren't ready for the California life-style." A fellow crew member invited them to a party one night, but when they got there, everyone was smoking marijuana. Jeffrey was afraid the police would arrive at any second so he and Alice quickly excused themselves and hurried home.

Alice would later describe that summer as one of the happiest periods in her marriage. Yet there were problems. Jeffrey earned less than $200 per month and the monthly rent for their off-base apartment was $105. They could have lived in military housing for less, but Jeffrey didn't like having his co-workers as neighbors. Even if they had spent their money frugally, they would have had a tough time. But neither tried to budget or save. Jeffrey continued to snack on Pepsi and cookie dough. Alice hated to cook, preferring to eat out. They both called their parents at various times and asked for cash. Nearly every month, they ran out of food. When that happened, Jeffrey would go over to the ship and raid its galley. He'd smuggle some bread and sandwich fixings out to Alice, who waited in the car.

Besides money, sex was becoming a problem. "Alice wasn't warm sexually after we got married," Jeffrey later complained. "She felt guilty because she had gotten pregnant before we were married. She started getting these migraine headaches. I was very frustrated and I told her that she simply wasn't satisfying me." Alice later blamed Jeffrey for their sexual problems. "Jeffrey was fixated on sex. Sex, sex, sex. That was all he thought about, all he wanted to do. He'd do it several times a day if I let him, and when we did it, he just wanted to satisfy himself. He didn't care about me and my feelings."

In the spring of 1972, Jeffrey was transferred to the USS *Shelton*, a battle-tested Korean War destroyer with a crew of 275 men and two twin five-inch guns. On May 30, Jeffrey was told that the ship was going to Vietnam. He wrote his parents and asked if Alice and Damon could live in Independence with them while he was gone. They agreed. On June 13, Jeffrey kissed Alice and Damon good-bye. Twenty-seven days later, the USS *Shelton* arrived off the coast of Vietnam.

On board the ship, Jeffrey spent all of his free time reading the Book of Mormon. Like the Bible, it was divided into books, rather than chapters, and he studied all fifteen. He still wanted to know the scriptures better than Alice. One verse that Jeffrey read while studying bothered him. Verse 65 in the Second Book of Nephi said: "For the Spirit is the same, yesterday, today, and forever." Jeffrey was confident that he knew what it meant. God hadn't changed since the time of Moses. God was God. But if that was true and God hadn't changed, then why didn't He still do all of the wonderful things that He had done in biblical days? Specifically, why hadn't He intervened in Jeffrey's life? Alice had told him about her experiences at the summer camp and how an evil presence had tried to crush her in her bedroom. Jeffrey had never experienced any supernatural event. He had prayed for some sort of sign, but there was none.

While Jeffrey wrestled with the spiritual, back in Independence, Alice was learning about the secular. Lois was keeping her promise of accepting Alice as a member of the Lundgren family. Like Professor Henry Higgins, she was supervising a transformation. She taught Alice how to style her hair. She got Alice to stop biting her fingernails, and when she did, Lois rewarded her with a manicure. They went shopping together and Lois taught Alice how to select outfits that complimented her figure, how to mix and match blouses and skirts so they didn't clash. Lois taught Alice about antiques and showed her how to refinish furniture. She instructed her on etiquette, simple things really, such as how to correctly set a table and host a party. In the kitchen, Lois showed Alice how to cook meals that were more exotic than the meat and potatoes that she had grown up eating.

While Lois kept busy with Alice, Don focused on Damon. They became buddies. Each morning, the twenty-two-month-old would fuss unless he got to eat his rice crispy cereal with his "paw-paw." Jeffrey had told Alice that his father was a cold and harsh taskmaster. But she saw none of that in the way Don treated his grandson. If anything, he spoiled him.

On the clear and sunny Sunday morning of October 15, 1972, Jeffrey's scripture studies were interrupted by a loud boom. The USS *Shelton* was under attack. Naval Intelligence had assured the destroyer's captain that the island of Hon Co, called Tiger Island by U.S. troops, was free of enemy artillery, but the reports had been wrong. The first round fired by enemy artillery dropped short. The second overshot the ship. Obviously, the North Vietnamese were sighting in their weapon for the kill. But when the third round was fired, it dropped short too. And then the firing ended. The ship's captain described the brief attack in the ship's log as an "extremely close call."

Four days later the destroyer was in the Gulf of Tonkin when enemy artillery again began shooting. This time, the battle was much more fierce. For thirty minutes, enemy guns exchanged fire with the USS *Shelton* and a nearby cruiser, the USS *Providence*. The two U.S. ships fired more than 120 rounds at the enemy. The North Vietnamese fired just as many back. Yet neither U.S. ship was hit. While the destroyer's crew joked about the enemy's poor marksmanship, Jeffrey began developing a different theory.

In mid-December, the destroyer again came under attack. The captain of the USS *Shelton* would later report that more than 190 shots were fired at his ship. None hit. Two days later, the destroyer was engaged in the biggest battle of its history. More than *seven hundred* shots were fired at the USS *Shelton* by a battery of shore guns. As Lundgren and other crew members manned their battle stations, rounds peppered the water causing geyserlike eruptions. Despite the repeated firing, not a single round hit the destroyer. "Many splashes within fifty yards were observed," the captain wrote in the ship's log, "with one missing the port bow by only twenty feet." It was, the captain noted, a "miracle" that the USS *Shelton* escaped the onslaught of enemy rounds.

That was exactly how Jeffrey felt. "The enemy had us. They fired shells over us. They fired shells short. They had us locked on with radar. There was no way they could miss. But they fired and fired and fired and they couldn't hit us. There was no reason for them to miss except for one reason. God made it impossible for them to hit the ship."

As the USS *Shelton* sailed out of the Gulf of Tonkin on December 22 and made its way home, the crew celebrated its good luck. Jeffrey watched with a knowing grin. None of his shipmates realized that the only reason they were alive was because of him, he explained later. He had been the only saint aboard the ship. A scripture popped into his mind. "For the Spirit is the same, yesterday, today, and forever."

"God had showed me a sign," Jeffrey said. "He had protected the ship because he didn't want me to die in Vietnam."

For the first time in his life, Jeffrey looked upon religion as something useful. He also remembered what Alice had told him about the patriarch's prediction. Alice's husband was going to do great things for the church. All the way home, Jeffrey studied his scriptures.

Chapter 5

WHEN the USS *Shelton* returned to San Diego on January 13, 1973, Jeffrey and the other crew members were awarded a slew of military decorations. Jeffrey received three from the navy: the National Defense Service Medal, Vietnam Service Medal with one Bronze Star, and the Combat Action Ribbon. The South Vietnamese government issued him its Republic of Vietnam Campaign Medal and he received a special letter of commendation for the outstanding job that he had done keeping electronic equipment aboard the ship in good working order. His evaluations by his superiors showed Jeffrey was an above-average sailor, skilled at his job and eager to please.

"I had an excellent time aboard that ship and if it weren't for Alice, I would have made the navy my career," Jeffrey complained later. "I liked the life-style, but the first thing that Alice said when I stepped off the ship and met her was 'Promise me that you'll never leave me again.' Those were her exact first words. She was so insecure."

Alice hadn't had time to find an apartment in San Diego before Jeffrey returned from Vietnam. They needed a place to stay while they looked. A friend mentioned that Louise Stone lived in San Diego with her husband, Muril, whom everyone called Sonny. He was a chief petty officer assigned to the United States Marine Corps Recruit Depot just up the bay from the naval station where Jeffrey was stationed. Louise had grown up attending the Slover Park congregation. Her father, Damon Binger, had been the pastor. Because Louise was two years older than Jeffrey, she had been friends with a different crowd at church, but she recognized his voice when he called her.

"I was wondering if we could stay with you for a while?" Jeffrey asked. Even though Louise hadn't seen him in nine years, she agreed. It was common for saints to open up their homes to other church members in need. Sonny didn't care either. "Sailors help out sailors," he remarked.

During the week that Jeffrey, Alice, and Damon spent with Louise and Sonny, the two women became lifelong friends. "There was a chemistry between us," Louise said later. "I think I know her better than any other person on earth."

Sonny and Jeffrey got along too, but they were not close. There was something about Jeffrey that Sonny didn't like, although he couldn't pinpoint what it was that made him uneasy. After the Lundgrens found an apartment, they still got together nearly every weekend with the Stones. Once or twice a week, Alice and Louise would chat on the telephone, sometimes for hours.

Two months after the USS *Shelton* returned to port, the navy decommissioned it and the destroyer was sold to the Taiwan government. Jeffrey was put in charge of planning the farewell party for the crew. He asked Alice to help and she got to show off everything that she had learned from Lois. Jeffrey and Alice didn't drink alcohol, but there was plenty of liquor at the party and several crew members got drunk. At one point, an officer stopped at the table where Jeffrey and Alice were sitting with several couples. Throwing one arm around Alice's shoulders, the officer broadcast in a slightly slurred, booming voice: "Little lady, I want you to know that your husband was the *only* man who was faithful to his wife during our cruise." Alice's face blushed as she whispered a quick "Thank you." The other women sitting at the table were not as bashful. "What?" one shrieked. The officer repeated himself: "That's what I said. Good old Jeffrey was the only man who kept his pants zipped." Tempers flared as wives demanded explanations and husbands denied their accusations. Jeffrey and Alice slipped out of the room.

"Weren't you even tempted?" asked Alice.

"You are the only woman in the world that I will ever want," he replied.

Alice couldn't wait to tell Louise. Most of the time, Jeffrey was always criticizing Alice, calling her stupid, but sometimes he could say just what she wanted to hear.

"Sonny and I both thought that Jeffrey was tremendously rude to Alice," Louise said later. "Jeff would make decisions without consulting her or even telling her about them. He had complete control in all decision making, and he just expected Alice to accept that."

One night Louise got a telephone call from Alice after Jeffrey had gone to sleep. Alice had crept out of the bedroom to call her. She told Louise that Jeffrey had gotten angry because she had asked him how much money was in their checking account.

"I am not allowed to even touch the checkbook or to even know how much is in it," explained Alice. She was worried because Jeffrey hadn't been paying all the bills.

"Well, why don't you just ask him about it?" Louise asked.

"I can't," said Alice. "He'll explode."

"That's ridiculous," Louise replied.

That weekend when the two couples got together, Jeffrey was cold toward Louise. She learned later that he was irritated because he had heard about her conversation with Alice. "He thought I had too much influence over Alice."

Louise knew that many conservative RLDS members believed that God had created a strict hierarchy in every marriage. Much of this attitude was based on the New Testament writings of Paul in his first letter to Timothy, chapter 2, verses 11 through 15:

Let the women learn in silence with all subjection. For I suffer not a woman to teach, nor to usurp authority over the man, but to be in silence. For Adam was first formed, then Eve. And Adam was not deceived, but the woman being deceived was in the transgression. Notwithstanding they shall be saved in childbearing if they continue in faith and charity and holiness with sobriety.

What surprised Louise was how readily Alice accepted Jeffrey's dominance. "Jeffrey says it's a man's job to love and obey and to serve his God," Alice explained to Louise one afternoon. "God is the man's master. That means the man must submit his will to God. The woman's job is to love and obey and serve her husband. He is her master."

Such talk exasperated Louise. "I felt Jeffrey was in the process of making Alice into exactly what he wanted her to be. He wanted to control every part of her life and she gave him that control in return for his love. She tried to be exactly what he wanted—the perfect little housewife. She cleaned, she cooked, she canned, she changed diapers, washed clothes, and took care of Jeffrey, and she did it without complaining because she had total faith that he would take care of her and he would love her."

Jeffrey's next assignment was aboard the USS *Schofield*, a guided-missile frigate, which had a well-deserved reputation for being a lemon. He abhorred the ship and was unhappy. Alice had tired of navy life too and she hated the idea of Jeffrey's going away on another eight-month cruise. During 1973, Alice began complaining about migraine headaches that were so painful she was hospitalized for treatment. When Jeffrey learned that his ship was scheduled to leave on an extended cruise that fall, Alice became depressed. She was so distraught that Jeffrey suggested that she see a psychiatrist. If Alice could get a doctor to say that her mental anguish was caused by Jeffrey's going away on cruises, maybe the navy would grant him an early discharge. Alice underwent a psychiatric exam and blamed her problems on Jeffrey's career, but the navy didn't buy it. "My commanding officer told me, 'Lundgren, if we had wanted you to have a wife, we'd have packed one in your seabag.' There was no way the navy was going to let me go early."

Sonny Stone was a "lifer," and when he heard how Jeffrey had tried to use Alice's migraines as an excuse to get a discharge, he got angry. Other rifts began developing between the Lundgrens and Stones. Louise had decided that Jeffrey was fixated with sex. She and Sonny had bought a house with a swimming pool, and on warm nights, they would often skinny-dip together. "It became a joke. People would say, 'Hey, wonder if Sonny and Louise are in the pool tonight,' " Louise said. One morning, Alice and Jeffrey dropped in unannounced and spotted some of Sonny's clothing tossed beside the pool. Obviously, he and Louise had gone for a romantic swim the night before.

"We all joked about it at first," Louise recalled, "but Jeffrey just wouldn't let go of it. Every time we got together after that, he would bug us about having sex in the pool. 'Hey, did you use the pool last night?' he'd say. Or 'Hey, when are you and Sonny going to let us use your pool?' He put a lot of pressure on Alice to ask us to invite them to baby-sit our kids when we went out so that he and Alice could have sex in our pool. He just went on and on and on about it until it wasn't funny at all."

By the time that October arrived, the couples weren't meeting regularly although Alice and Louise remained close friends.

On November 23, Jeffrey's ship left San Diego for Pearl Harbor, the first stop on an eight-month trip that would take it to the Indian Ocean. Alice and Damon returned to Missouri, only this time they moved in with Alice's parents. She had just learned that she was pregnant again. Jeffrey promised to write every day. Alice said that she would too. She also told Louise that she would call her whenever she could afford it.

As he had done when he went to Vietnam, Jeffrey carried his copy of the Book of Mormon with him on the ship. Kevin Currie worked for Jeffrey in the electronics repair shop and was assigned to a bunk next to his. But Kevin didn't have much in common with his supervisor. Jeffrey was somber, humorless, a by-the-regulation boss. Although Kevin was only one year younger, the thin New York native didn't take life seriously. He had a tattoo on his leg that said "Just Passing Through," and that expressed his philosophy. Whenever his ship dropped anchor, Kevin was one of the first to race to the waterfront whorehouses and bars. Religion meant nothing to him. He had been raised in the Episcopalian Church, but had stopped going as a youngster.

Kevin didn't like Jeffrey at first. "Jeffrey always gave people the impression that he was looking down on them, that he was somehow better," Kevin said. But after they had spent a few months at sea, Kevin's opinion changed and he became intrigued. Jeffrey was always studying his scriptures. He didn't cuss, shunned coffee, wouldn't smoke, and he wrote letters to his wife every day, sometimes two or three times each day. Yet Jeffrey didn't browbeat anyone about the Bible or try to evangelize. If anything, he seemed to like keeping whatever he was reading a secret. It was as if he had made some important discovery that he wasn't that eager to share.

It turned out that Jeffrey was just as interested in Kevin. "Jeffrey was curious about my carefree attitude," Kevin said. "I did whatever I wanted and I think, to a certain degree, Jeffrey was envious."

Still neither made any effort to get to know the other until the USS *Schofield* stopped to refuel at the Anzuk Naval Base in Singapore. The crew received eight days of liberty and, by chance, Kevin and Jeffrey found themselves crammed into the same taxicab one morning with four other sailors going into the city. Jeffrey asked if any of the men wanted to go sightseeing with him. They laughed. They were headed to a whorehouse. But Jeffrey made the cultural sites on the island that he was going to see sound so interesting that the men finally agreed to join him. They hired pedal-carts, two-seat carriages powered by a man on a bicycle, to take them on their tour. Kevin and Jeffrey sat together. By nightfall, all of the men except Jeffrey had had enough culture. They stopped at a nightclub. Jeffrey waited outside while the others paid to see two women engage in lesbian sex acts. After the show, all the men but Kevin came outside. When he eventually appeared, he was carrying a cucumber.

"Why do you have that?" Jeffrey asked.

Kevin smirked.

"It's ah, uh, souvenir," he announced, as the other sailors guffawed.

Jeffrey later learned that the two women had used the cucumber to have sexual intercourse with each other. Kevin had paid one of the women after the show to have sex with him and then had stolen the cucumber. When they got back to the ship that night, Jeffrey wrote a long letter to Alice describing that day's events. He mentioned Kevin and talked about how the women had used the cucumber on each other. Jeffrey went into such detail that Alice incorrectly suspected that he too had seen the act.

The frigate left Singapore on March 13, 1974, and eventually returned to San Diego on June 5. Alice was waiting with Damon. They had flown to California a few weeks earlier and found an apartment. She was nine months pregnant. A few days later, Kevin asked Jeffrey at work one day about the Book of Mormon. Jeffrey invited Kevin to come to his apartment for dinner. Alice was appalled. All she could think of was the cucumber story. But Jeffrey insisted. When Kevin arrived, Alice began to relax. He was nicely dressed, polite, rail thin, and spoke with a quiet voice. He was nothing like she had imagined. As Kevin walked into the Lundgren apartment that night, he suddenly felt a "warmth" and he decided to tell Jeffrey and Alice about his past. As a child, he had been shuffled between relatives. "I attended fourteen different schools before I graduated." At age five, he had also been sexually molested. He had joined the navy to start a new life, but had begun using drugs. Nothing in life seemed to matter, he explained. Jeffrey began telling Kevin about Mormonism. He explained that the Book of Mormon was the history of a group of ancient Hebrews who had crossed the Atlantic Ocean before Christ was born and had settled in the New World where they split into two groups, called the Lamanites and Nephites. The Lamanites were

wicked and they eventually waged war and destroyed the good
Nephites during a great battle at the Hill Cumorah. Mormon
was a prophet and historian and he recorded the history of the
two tribes on golden plates. His son, Moroni, finished the last
portion of the record and hid the plates on the Hill Cumorah
before he was killed. Centuries later Moroni returned to earth as
an angel and directed Joseph Smith, Jr., to where the plates were
hidden. The saints were different from other religions, Jeffrey
said, because they believed that God intervened in their lives
and still sent them prophets. God had also given the saints a
purpose in their lives. They were to build Zion and prepare for
the second coming of Christ.

Kevin was impressed. He began stopping by the Lundgrens'
apartment every night. Some weekends, he would sleep on the
couch after he and Jeffrey ended their marathon late-night
debates about various scriptures.

One night Jeffrey told Kevin about an event that had
happened aboard the USS *Schofield* when the frigate was
in the Indian Ocean. Jeffrey had gone up onto the deck to
lift weights and exercise. He was all by himself. "The sea
was like glass and a brilliant full moon made it possible for
me to see in the darkness," he said. "It was clear except for
one peculiar cloud. Rather than being white, this cloud was
inky black, darker even than the rest of the sky.

"As I began working out, I noticed this cloud seemed to
be following the ship," Jeffrey explained. "We were moving
along, probably at twenty knots, cruising speed, and the cloud
seemed to be trailing us, following behind us as we moved
across the water.

"I decided to investigate. So I walked over to the rail that ran
along the deck. As I looked at the cloud, it suddenly zoomed
down. It took the shape of a human hand and it came directly
toward me and attacked me. It began pushing me back against
the guide wire and railing. I grabbed onto it because the cloud
was literally pushing me off the deck, but I couldn't hold on
very long because the cloud kept pushing and it was stronger
than me. It was pushing against my chest and I suddenly
realized that I was going to be pushed overboard, that I was
going to be pushed into the ocean and drowned by this cloud.
So I cried out, 'My God, save me! Deliver me!' and as soon as

those words left my lips, I was released and within seconds the cloud had disappeared, completely vanished, and I was safe."

Why had the cloud attacked him? Kevin asked. What did it mean?

"I believe the cloud was Satan and the forces of evil, and he was trying to kill me to keep me from doing something that God has chosen me to do."

What? Kevin asked.

"I don't know," Jeffrey replied. "But there is no other interpretation. There has to be a reason why God is saving me and why Satan wants me dead."

On June 24, Alice gave birth to another boy, whom she and Jeffrey named Jason. When she came home from the hospital, she jokingly said that the family had really gained two "new" children. Kevin was spending so much time with them that he was their other "son."

Jeffrey asked a group of elders at a local RLDS congregation to conduct "cottage meetings" for Kevin. During the sessions, the elders explained the official history of the church and its doctrines. Since Jeffrey wasn't a member of the RLDS priesthood, he couldn't officially conduct a "cottage meeting" although he knew his scriptures better than the elders who spoke to Kevin. In October, Kevin was baptized into the RLDS. On November 4, 1974, Jeffrey was discharged. He had decided to return to Missouri. Jeffrey wasn't the sort of man who hugged another man, but when he and Kevin shook hands and said good-bye, he thought that he saw tears in Kevin's eyes.

Although the elders had officially prepared Kevin for membership, Jeffrey knew that he was really responsible for bringing him into the church. Jeffrey felt good about that. He had never thought of himself as being terribly persuasive, but he was learning.

Chapter 6

ONCE Jeffrey was discharged, he and his family returned to Missouri and moved in with Ralph and Donna. Jeffrey didn't know what he wanted to do, so he decided to enroll in classes at Central Missouri State University. The GI Bill would pay his tuition and give him a bit more for living expenses. James Postlethwait, the assistant dean for admissions and records, agreed to give Jeffrey another chance at college despite his terrible academic record. As soon as Jeffrey was accepted, he went to the RLDS student union. His old pal Keith Johnson was playing Ping-Pong in the recreation room. It was as if time had stopped while Jeffrey had been gone. Keith explained that he had graduated, married, divorced, and returned to school to earn an advanced degree. While the two men were talking, a younger student interrupted.

"We need some help, Keith," he said, nodding toward the next room. "It's the liberals."

"C'mon, Jeff," Keith said. "You'll enjoy this."

A crowd of students were arguing about scriptures. Without waiting to be asked, Jeffrey jumped into the fray. Keith was surprised. The Jeffrey he'd known hadn't been much of a Bible student. "I've been doing quite a bit of studying," Jeffrey beamed afterward.

Jeffrey and Alice found an apartment not far from the campus, and when the first semester ended in late spring of 1975, Jeffrey had earned straight As—much to the delight of Assistant Dean Postlethwait. One of Jeffrey's professors, Hal Sappington, offered him a lab-technician job. It paid only $120 per month, but he took it. "I really liked working in the lab. I liked the interaction with students and I enjoyed the way the professors treated me. I decided that I wanted to be part of that world." That summer, Jeffrey told Alice that he planned to become a college professor. Dr. Jeffrey Lundgren. He liked how it sounded.

Besides doing well academically, Jeffrey quickly became a spokesman for "fundamentalists" at the RLDS student union. They were conservative RLDS students who were unhappy with changes taking place in the church. The students who favored the changes were the "liberals." The daily arguments that took place between the two factions mirrored a bitter debate that was going on within the RLDS church. During the late 1950s, the church had started to modernize under the leadership of the church's new "prophet," W. Wallace Smith, a grandson of Joseph Smith, Jr. By 1975, most RLDS churches were split between members who favored the old ways and those pushing for change.

Jeffrey loved arguing about religion. He spent all of his free moments at the student union. The most heated arguments were about the role of women in the church. The liberals favored letting them become priests. Jeffrey and the other conservatives claimed that only men could be ordained. During one bitter argument, tempers flared, and someone said the student union wasn't big enough for the liberals and Jeffrey Lundgren. Jeffrey reacted by inviting all of the conservatives at the union to walk out and come to his apartment.

Assistant Dean Postlethwait, who was an RLDS Church member and helped run the student union, eventually soothed the hurt feelings. But not before Jeffrey held a few meetings of his own at his apartment. Dennis Patrick and Tonya McLaughlin were two fundamentalists who attended.

Dennis and Jeffrey had first become allies during debates at the student union. Jeffrey had a photographic memory and was excellent at spouting scripture. No one could match him when it came to reciting verses. But Jeffrey had a high-pitched, almost whiny voice, and he was a bully. Dennis, on the other hand, had a booming, well-trained voice, and a salesman's knack for swaying people.

Slim, athletic, and personable, Dennis was the son of a career air force officer who had moved his family from base to base when Dennis was growing up. Whenever anyone asked Dennis where he was from, he would say Oregon because that was where he had gone to high school, but his real home had always been the church. The RLDS had been the common thread that had given Dennis continuity and stability. "My father was a district RLDS president and a high priest in the church," Dennis told Jeffrey shortly after they first met. "I used to go with my dad on his calls and I fully intend to carry on as I have been raised and taught. The church to me is not just a way of life, it is my life."

Tonya McLaughlin's parents had not been as active as Dennis's family. But like many other saints, when Tonya was growing up all of her friends had been church members. As a teenager, Tonya had lived only a few blocks from Don and Lois Lundgren, but she hadn't known Jeffrey, although she knew his brother, Corry. Shy and chunky, Tonya had beautiful bright red hair and ivory skin. She had met Dennis at a summer party at the student union. He had fallen in love immediately. Tonya hadn't. But she liked his company. Three weeks after they met, Dennis proposed and Tonya agreed. She figured she'd learn to love him. They had just gotten engaged when they met Jeffrey and Alice.

After Jeffrey led his fundamentalist revolt, he and Dennis began spending more and more time together studying the scriptures. Tonya and Alice also became friends. Alice was older, married, the mother of two boys, now ages five and one, and eager to give Tonya advice. One night Dennis asked Jeffrey if he would like to take a break from studying scriptures to play tennis. Jeffrey agreed and Dennis thrashed him on the court. Jeffrey was furious and swore that he'd practice round the clock if necessary, until he finally could beat Dennis.

Dennis, who was just as competitive, gladly accepted the challenge. They began meeting at the tennis court every day. The games quickly became an obsession. Try as he might, Jeffrey couldn't defeat Dennis. And then, after more than one hundred matches, Jeffrey finally won.

Afterward, Dennis noticed that Jeffrey made it a point to bring up his victory whenever he was talking to other students. "Jeffrey would tell everyone about how he had worked and worked and worked and had finally defeated me," Dennis later recalled. "But what he never mentioned was that after we played that set, we played again and I won. In fact, I don't think he beat me after that one time. But he made it sound like he had absolutely defeated me and that I was so crushed that I was never able to beat him again. I remember thinking, 'This is really odd.' But it was important to Jeff to be seen as a champion. He wanted people to believe that he could do anything he wanted once he put his mind to it. He really wanted to be somebody important."

In the fall of 1975, Jeffrey set his mind to something else besides tennis. Dennis was in line to become a priesthood member and Keith Johnson already had been ordained. Jeffrey could recite scripture better than either of them. It was time, he decided, for him to join the priesthood and get on with God's work.

In the RLDS, priesthood members ran local congregations. Unlike most denominations, the RLDS didn't have salaried, professionally trained ministers. Sunday services were conducted by men from each congregation who had been "called" by God to serve as priests. These men, who worked during the week at non-church jobs, divvied up the chores each Sunday. They either took turns preaching or chose one of their own to serve as the regular pastor.

The first step to joining the priesthood was to "receive the call." At least two priests had to feel "moved by the spirit" to recommend a saint as a priesthood candidate. Once two priests recommended a candidate, the district or "stake" office conducted a discreet background check to make certain the candidate was worthy. After that was completed, the candidate was asked if he wanted to become a priest, and if he agreed, his name was put before all of the priests in his local congregation for a vote. When he was approved, he served an apprenticeship under other priests and was finally ordained.

On paper, the process looked tough. In reality, it wasn't. In most congregations any man who came to church regularly and expressed an interest could become a priest. Jeffrey began dropping hints at the local RLDS congregation that he attended and he soon found two priesthood members willing to submit his name. By late 1975, Jeffrey felt certain that he was on his way.

Chapter 7

J EFFREY'S life seemed grand. His college professor, Hal Sappington, had decided to take a sabbatical at the start of 1976 and the university had asked Jeffrey to help fill in by teaching a basic electricity course to freshmen even though he was still an undergraduate. The Farmers Home Administration had loaned $22,500 to Jeffrey and Alice so that they could buy a new three-bedroom, ranch-style house in Knob Knoster, a town of 2,040 people about ten miles east of Warrensburg. The months rolled by quickly and, on the surface, happily.

So Louise Stone was surprised when she received a telephone call from a tearful Alice.

"I need to see you," Alice anxiously explained. "I got to get away from here."

"Well, come on out," Louise said, reassuringly. "Stay as long as you need to."

Louise no longer lived in San Diego. She and Sonny had moved to Norfolk, Virginia, home of the Atlantic naval fleet. Sonny had just left on a nine-month cruise, leaving Louise home with their three children.

Alice brought Damon and Jason with her to Norfolk. After the two women got all of the children settled into bed, they went down to the living room to talk and Alice burst into tears.

"It's Jeffrey," she sobbed. "He's lying to me. Hiding things from me. My life is a total wreck."

Jeffrey had unhooked the bell on the telephone, Alice said. He had gotten a post-office box and had stopped having mail delivered to the house. At first Alice couldn't figure out what he was trying to hide. But then a bill collector had come by the house while Jeffrey was in school. "We are thousands and thousands of dollars in debt," she said. "He hasn't paid anything. I had to get away from it all. It's so embarrassing."

All that week, Louise and Alice talked about Jeffrey. Sometimes they would stay up until dawn. Each night, Alice seemed to grow more irritated at him. "Alice was just miserable," Louise said later.

And then Jeffrey arrived.

He had driven to Norfolk in a brand-new Chevrolet Monte Carlo that he had just bought. When Alice saw him pull into the driveway, she rushed outside and clapped her hands in excitement as Jeffrey proudly showed off their new car, opening the doors, trunk, and hood as if he were a salesman hustling a buyer.

"I couldn't believe what I saw happen," said Louise. "Alice was completely thrilled over this brand-new car."

While Jeffrey was outside loading Alice's luggage, Louise pulled Alice aside in the house.

"What about all the things that he hid from you? What about the bills? How'd he afford a new car?" she asked.

Alice brushed off her questions with a shrug.

"He's here," she gushed. "That's all that matters."

"I remember watching them drive away," Louise recalled later, "and thinking that the bottom line was that Alice had terrible self esteem. The fact that someone loved her enough to buy her a car and come and get her simply overshadowed everything else."

Jeffrey had financed the car through a credit union that was largely owned by RLDS church members. His father was on the board, which is why he got the loan despite his terrible credit rating. Within a few months, Jeffrey's name appeared on the list of delinquent borrowers. Don, who knew nothing about the car loan, was so embarrassed that he resigned from the board.

In later years, Jeffrey blamed Alice for their financial woes. "Alice became just like my mother. Getting possessions, accumulating things, became extremely important to her. My mistake was in not putting my foot down and just telling her no. But I had trouble doing that because Alice and I were having a difficult time in our personal relationship and she wanted physical manifestations from me that showed that I loved her."

Alice's continuing guilt over being pregnant before they were married had turned her into a frigid spouse, Jeffrey claimed. "Alice would say that if we made love once every three months that was a compromise on her part. And I would tell her, 'Alice, what you don't realize is that the eighty-nine days that we didn't make love was a compromise on my part.' "

Not surprisingly, Alice would tell psychologists later that Jeffrey was to blame for their financial and sexual problems. "The first five years of our marriage, I never had an orgasm. I didn't even know what one was until I read about them in a magazine. All he cared about was getting off. He didn't care about my feelings."

There were problems outside the bedroom as well, Jeffrey said. "Alice was angry because she wasn't getting all the attention that she wanted. I wasn't spending enough time with her, she'd say. She'd complain about how much I was studying and working. Those were more important than she was. I'd tell her, 'Well, I have to support you and the family,' but she wouldn't accept that. The truth was that she wanted to be the focal point of the world and so she started demanding things.

"She'd say, 'Oh, if we just could afford to move into our own house, I'd be happy.' So I went down and got a loan from the Farmers Home Administration and we bought a house and she would be happy for a while and then she would say, 'Oh, Jeffrey, if you would just buy me . . . ' It never ended. She wanted me to prove that I loved her, over and over and over again.

"And then she started feeling the need to compete with my mother," he continued. "My mother had told Alice that we would never have as much as they did and this superiority complex of my parents, which was entirely my mother's doing, really got to Alice. When my mother got a one-point-one-karat diamond ring for her wedding anniversary, Alice fussed until I bought her a one-point-two karat diamond ring. It had to be bigger than my mother's."

Exactly who was to blame for the couple's runaway expenses is impossible to tell. But relatives and friends later suggested that Jeffrey and Alice were both irresponsible with money.

Much of their cash went for frivolous expenses—eating meals in restaurants, Jeffrey's constant snacking. Both loved to go to movies, as many as three or four per weekend. By January 1977, Jeffrey and Alice had accumulated $22,000 in unpaid bills and that didn't include their $22,500 house mortgage.

One morning, they were served with an eviction notice. Alice telephoned her mother. Unless they came up with $300, they were going to be kicked out of their house. Donna wrote them a check and Alice and Jeffrey drove over to get it. Alice said they were going to take the check directly to the Farmers Home Administration office, but on the way home, Jeffrey and Alice stopped to get something to eat. They cashed the check and used some of it to pay for the meal. The money never made it to the FmHA. The mortgage went unpaid.

Without explanation, Jeffrey quit school even though he was only a few credits short of graduation. Hal Sappington, who had returned to campus, was dumbfounded. "It was like Jeffrey vanished. He was here one day and gone the next." Assistant Dean Postlethwait was just as shocked. "Something was wrong, but no one knew what."

Jeffrey would later tell his followers that he had been forced to quit because of Alice. "She told me that her father could get me a good-paying job in the ironworkers union. We needed the income so I quit school and went to the union hall," he explained. "But I only got one job before there was a strike and I was out of work."

Alice would later tell investigators that Jeffrey had been forced out. "Jeffrey got caught stealing money. He had collected some sort of student fee in the electrical lab and instead of turning the money in, he spent it."

The records office at CMSU does not keep disciplinary files from 1977. Those records were shredded years ago. But a school official recalled that Jeffrey had been involved in some sort of disciplinary dispute. "He didn't just leave," this official recalled. "There was a reason."

Although he was now out of work, broke, and still deeply in debt, Jeffrey remained optimistic about becoming a priesthood member. It was the one area of his life where he was still successful. In the Knob Knoster RLDS congregation, he was earning a reputation as a spokesman for the fundamentalists, just as he had done at the student union. One evening after dinner, however, the priest who had recommended Jeffrey stopped by to tell him that the district RLDS office had decided against recommending Jeffrey for ordination. The president of the RLDS stake didn't know Jeffrey that well, the priest explained, so he had telephoned Keith Johnson, who had grown up in the area, and asked him about Jeffrey. "Keith told him that I wasn't mature enough spiritually to be ordained," Jeffrey recalled. He didn't take the news well. "I felt betrayed, totally betrayed."

Jeffrey was so angry that he decided to drop out of the RLDS. Joseph Smith, Jr., hadn't needed a church to teach him about God and neither did Jeffrey. "They're going to regret doing this to me," he told Alice.

A few days before he was supposed to be evicted, Jeffrey telephoned his parents and they, in turn, talked to Jeffrey's grandfather, Alva Gadberry. He knew a contractor who needed someone to help do some electrical wiring at the Andrew Drumm Institute, commonly called Drumm Farm, in Independence. Some strings were pulled and Jeffrey was hired at five dollars per hour. It wasn't enough to keep the government from foreclosing on his house, but it was enough to buy groceries. Jeffrey worked hard and made a good impression on the institute's director. He offered Jeffrey a full-time job as the farm manager and Jeffrey agreed. The job included use of a rent-free cottage. Jeffrey and Alice moved to the farm. A short time later their house in Knob Knoster was sold on the courthouse steps.

Jeffrey's job at Drumm Farm was to repair equipment and oversee the livestock. Founded in 1930 by cattleman Andrew Drumm as a home for "orphan and indigent" boys, the institute was designed to be a working farm. Between fifty and sixty boys, ages six through seventeen, milked cows, tended livestock, and raised crops on some 360 acres. Jeffrey liked the work, and when he learned that the institute needed a couple to work as houseparents and oversee ten boys, he telephoned Dennis and Tonya. They had just finished college, were married, and were looking for work.

Dennis and Tonya took the houseparents job and moved to Drumm Farm, where they quickly resumed their friendship with Jeffrey and Alice. Most nights, the Patricks would drop

by the Lundgrens' cottage. Alice and Tonya would chat while
Jeffrey and Dennis studied their scriptures or played chess.
Occasionally, Dennis and Jeffrey would go hunting at night.
"The place was overrun with skunks and Jeff was afraid that
one of them might bite one of the boys," Dennis recalled.
The two men would ride across the farm at night on a tractor
searching for the animals, who would stop and stare when hit
by the beams from the headlights. Dennis wore glasses and was
a lousy shot. Jeffrey had perfect vision and rarely missed. "I
think I can see almost as good as an eagle," he told Dennis.

The Patricks were not the only friends who spent time with
the Lundgrens at Drumm Farm. Sonny and Louise Stone
stopped by once while passing through town. Alice was
thrilled, but Jeffrey was aloof. He spent most of the night
ignoring them. Near the end of the visit, however, someone
asked Jeffrey about the farm manager's job and he began
telling the Stones about his plans to artificially breed cattle.
For the next hour, Jeffrey described in unnecessary detail how
cattle reproduced and were artificially inseminated. "It was
the most bizarre conversation I have ever heard," Louise later
remembered, "because it became clear during it that Jeffrey
was absolutely and totally fascinated with the sex life of cows.
It was weird."

Less than a year after he had started work at Drumm Farm,
Jeffrey abruptly resigned. When the Patricks asked why, Jeffrey
told them that he had quit because he was worried about his
children. Andrew Drumm had stated in his will that the farm
was only supposed to be used to help good boys who didn't
have a home. But Jeffrey claimed that the school was starting
to admit juvenile delinquents and he told the Patricks that he
didn't want Damon, who was now nearly eight, and Jason,
age four, to be influenced by them.

Once again, Alice would later tell authorities a much different story. "Jeffrey got caught stealing hay from the farm.
He was selling it and keeping the cash."

Jeffrey and Alice were broke and didn't have anywhere to
go. What's more, Alice was pregnant again. She turned to
her relatives for help. Her father had a sister who worked at
Drumm Farm as a cook and she agreed to loan them enough
cash to rent an apartment. Within a week, Jeffrey announced

that he had found a job at Trans World Airlines. He was part of a "preflight inspection crew" that checked airplanes when they were on the ground at night to make certain they were safe to fly. Jeffrey would leave for work just before 7:00 P.M., but he never came home at the same time. He told Alice that his hours varied because he could never be certain how much work any individual aircraft might take. If the airplane was in good shape, he'd come home early. Otherwise, he'd have to work late. It made sense to Alice, but she began to get suspicious after a few weeks when she noticed that things were disappearing from the house. A pair of candlesticks vanished. Jeffrey had also sold a rifle that he owned. Alice suspected that Jeffrey was either selling or pawning their valuables to get cash for groceries. She decided to ask him when TWA was going to give him a paycheck.

"I won't get a check until the end of the month," he replied.

Alice thought it was odd that TWA would make a new employee wait a full month before paying him, but she believed Jeffrey. When six weeks went by and there was still no sign of a paycheck, she once again confronted him. This time, Jeffrey told her that someone in the accounting department had made a mistake and had given his check to the wrong person. It was going to take several days to fix the error. Alice was angry, but not at Jeffrey. She blamed TWA.

"Well how do they expect you to feed your family?" she asked.

Jeffrey promised to press TWA for the money.

The next morning, Alice used her neighbor's telephone to call Donna. She explained that TWA still hadn't paid Jeffrey and she asked Donna to loan her $300. Donna sent Alice a check. When another week passed and Jeffrey still hadn't gotten paid, Alice decided to take matters into her own hands. After Jeffrey left for work, she jimmied the drawer to his desk. She was looking for some sort of employment papers from TWA that would tell her when Jeffrey was supposed to be paid. She suspected that he was hiding his paychecks from her. What Alice found instead was a stack of hard-core pornographic magazines and an angry letter from their landlord telling them that they were going to be evicted because their rent was overdue.

The next day when Jeffrey left the apartment to run an errand, Alice raced next door to use her neighbor's telephone. She called TWA's personnel office and demanded to know why her husband hadn't been paid for nearly two months.

"I'm sorry, lady," the TWA clerk replied, "but we have no record of a Jeffrey Lundgren working at TWA."

"That's impossible," Alice said. "He goes to work at the airport every night."

During the long pause that followed, Alice realized that Jeffrey had lied to her. She called Donna. "He's doing it again—lying to me," she sobbed. That night, she confronted Jeffrey.

"What have you been doing at night?" she demanded.

"Working at TWA," he said.

"You're a liar!" she screamed. Alice told him that she had called TWA's personnel office.

Jeffrey began to cry. "I've been out looking for jobs," he said.

"At midnight?" Alice demanded.

He changed his story. "I knew you'd worry if I told you I couldn't find work," he said. He had been depressed. Most nights he went to a movie. Sometimes he sat in a nearby diner and ate a piece of pie. Alice didn't know whether or not to believe him.

The police arrived a few days later. In front of Alice and their two sons, Jeffrey was handcuffed and taken outside to a waiting squad car. "He had written a check for some gun that he wanted to buy and the check had bounced, but by then he had sold the gun for three hundred dollars and spent the money."

Alice was pregnant again. She had no money. No way to post bond. No telephone and no car. Jeffrey had wrecked the Monte Carlo a few weeks earlier. She put her two boys to bed and walked into the living room. She turned out all of the lights, sat down on the floor, and began to sob.

"I remember sitting in the corner crying and I kept saying to myself, 'What am I going to do? What am I going to do?,' and then Jeffrey came home and he picked me up and held me and he told me everything was going to be all right. I don't know how he got released and I never found out how he had gotten home. All I knew was that he had come home. I said, 'Jeffrey, what's happening to us?,' and he said, 'Don't worry, Alice, it is going to be okay. I will work it out.' And I believed him. I believed he would take care of me."

Jeffrey decided to ask his parents for money. "They can afford to help us," he said. Don and Lois had helped them out before, but this time, they refused. Don lectured Jeffrey. "I'm getting old. Who's going to take care of me if I spend all my savings on you?" he asked. Lois marched into the kitchen and returned with half a loaf of bread and a jar of peanut butter, which she handed to Alice. It was time, Don and Lois said, for Jeffrey to support his own family.

Alice decided to telephone Donna. "Mom, I don't have any money," she said. "The kids don't have any food to eat."

Donna was irritated. She and Ralph were just barely making it themselves. She was in her sixties but retirement was out of the question because of Ralph's medical bills. Still, Donna couldn't turn her back on Alice. She told Alice that she and Jeffrey could move in with them.

By this time, the Keehlers had moved from Odessa to Macks Creek, a town of fewer than one hundred residents in the rolling hills of southwestern Missouri. They lived in a modest prefabricated modular home on a gravel road. Jeffrey and Alice arrived late on Friday, June 15, 1979. The next morning, Donna handed Jeffrey the local want ads. Incredibly, he found a job that seemed promising. A new ninety-bed hospital had just opened in Ozark Beach, a resort community about thirty miles east. It needed a biomedical technician, a fancy title for someone who repaired medical equipment. With his navy experience in electronics, Jeffrey felt he was qualified. On Monday morning, Jeffrey borrowed Donna's car and drove up state highway 54, to Ozark Beach. Bernie Wilson, the head of the hospital's maintenance department, spent less than thirty minutes talking with him before offering Jeffrey the job. Jeffrey rushed back to Macks Creek to tell Alice, but when he got there, she had news of her own. She was in labor. Jeffrey hustled Alice back to the Lake of the Ozarks Hospital where he had just been hired. Alice gave birth to a daughter, Kristen. Jeffrey was in the delivery room, and when he stepped outside, Bernie Wilson was waiting to congratulate him and hand him a stack of employment forms to sign. Eager to impress his new boss, Jeffrey volunteered to begin work that same day. Later in the afternoon, he stopped in Alice's room to see how she felt. Jeffrey had always wanted a daughter and he began to cry as he rocked "Krissy" in his arms. Alice began to cry too. "Everything's going to be okay, Jeffrey," she said. Surely, the worst was over.

Chapter 8

BERNIE Wilson considered himself a good judge of character. He'd spent twenty-three years in the navy, rising to the rank of chief petty officer, and during that time he'd come across all kinds. He could tell Jeffrey was smart when he first interviewed him and he seemed enthusiastic. The hospital job paid six dollars per hour. It wasn't a big salary in 1979, but it was enough for a family to live comfortably on in rural Missouri if they stayed within a budget. One thing Wilson liked was that Jeffrey told him straight out that he was in bad financial shape and would be staying with his in-laws until he could save enough to pay rent.

Jeffrey did a good job at first. The hospital had just opened and there were plenty of maintenance chores. Jeffrey even volunteered to help Wilson with his paperwork. Because the hospital was new, the administrator wanted every department head to write out all the policies and regulations that they followed in their areas. Jeffrey ended up drafting most of Wilson's papers. "He did a darn fine job at writing," Wilson said later.

There was only one hitch during Jeffrey's first month. One morning when Wilson walked through a section of the hospital that still hadn't been opened, he found a room full of household furniture. Jeffrey said it was his. He needed a place to store some personal things that he'd moved down from Independence and he didn't think anyone would mind.

"You got to ask permission before you do something like that," Wilson said. Jeffrey turned red and apologized. He still didn't have enough money to rent a house and there was no room for his furniture at his in-laws.

"Look, I got a two-car garage," Wilson replied. "Why don't you store it there."

"Great!" said Jeffrey. But a week later, the furniture was still in the hospital. This time the problem was transportation. Jeffrey had been using his mother-in-law's car but now she needed it. Wilson again offered to help. He had just bought a new 1979 pickup truck, so he said Jeffrey could buy his older 1972 Chevrolet truck for $1,200. Jeffrey could pay him whenever he got the cash. It was a good deal. Wilson's "old" truck was dazzling. Its blue and white paint gleamed under thick coats of heavily applied wax, the eight-cylinder engine was tuned perfectly, the truck's cargo area looked unused. Jeffrey drove it home that night and moved his furniture into Wilson's garage that weekend.

Three months later, Wilson began to get irritated. Jeffrey's stuff was still in the garage. Wilson told him to come get it. When Jeffrey pulled up, Wilson was shocked. The 1972 truck that he had babied was a wreck. Its paint was scratched, the body was covered with mud, and the pinging noise coming from the engine reminded Wilson of the sound that after-dinner speakers at the hospital made when they tapped their spoons against their water glasses to get everyone's attention.

Jeffrey didn't seem to care that Wilson was upset. He'd found a place to rent, he announced. Wilson felt odd. Jeffrey hadn't paid him a cent for the truck. He clearly wasn't taking care of it. He had stored furniture in Wilson's garage all summer without ever bothering to say thank you. And yet when Wilson had started to complain, Jeffrey had a way of making *him* feel guilty.

Jeffrey moved the furniture into a house owned by Jacob Wilcox on eighty acres east of Macks Creek in a heavily wooded area. Wilcox and his family had restored much of the 1940s farmhouse by themselves. It had two bedrooms and a bath on the top floor, another bedroom and bath on the main level and an unfinished basement. The only reason Wilcox had decided to rent the place was because he and his family were going to be leaving town for about a year. He didn't want to sell it, but he couldn't afford to leave it sitting empty. A friend had told Donna that Wilcox might be willing to rent his home cheap to a family if they took good care of it. Donna had passed the message on to Jeffrey who had immediately telephoned Wilcox. The novice landlord had put Jeffrey off at first. "I wanted to check Jeff out," Wilcox later said. "This wasn't a rental property. It was my home. I planned to come back and live here." Wilcox called a friend who knew the Keehler family.

"Don't do it," the man warned. "That guy has been nothing but trouble."

Despite such advice, Wilcox decided to let Jeffrey move in. "The guy seemed so sincere," Wilcox recalled, "and to tell you the truth, I felt sorry for him." The rent was $100 per month, a figure well below the house's rental value. There was only one stipulation. Wilcox had moved all of his personal belongings into the garage and had put a padlock on the door. He told Jeffrey to stay out of there. Jeffrey agreed and wrote Wilcox a check for the first month's rent. That same day, Wilcox left Macks Creek. A few weeks later, Wilcox got a letter from his bank telling him that Jeffrey's check had bounced. Wilcox called Jeffrey, who quickly apologized and mailed him another check. It bounced too. Wilcox made another call and this time Jeffrey promised to mail him a check that was good. When it cleared, Wilcox figured the first two had been harmless errors. He would soon discover that he was wrong.

From the start, Alice didn't like the farm. It was too isolated. Every day when Jeffrey left for work, she was stuck alone with a new baby and two boys with no neighbors. The only adult she ever got to speak with was Jeffrey and their relationship was once again in trouble. Jeffrey claimed that Alice was a nag. She was always complaining and demanding attention, he said. Alice claimed that Jeffrey was cold and harsh. He didn't care about anyone's feelings but his own, she complained. Both agreed that sex was a problem.

Said Jeffrey: "Being happy sexually with Alice wasn't possible. She couldn't give me what I wanted. I would not be out of line to say that if we had sexual intercourse six times a year that was a great year. I used to say that you could tell how many times Alice and I had made love by counting our kids—it was supposed to be a joke, but it wasn't funny anymore."

Said Alice: "Jeffrey was impossible to satisfy when it came to sex. If Jeffrey didn't have seven or eight orgasms a day, he felt deprived."

One night, Jeffrey confronted Alice.

"Let's stop playing games," he said. "Let's deal with the issue. This is a marital relationship and I have certain sexual expectations and I expect you to meet those expectations."

Jeffrey later insisted that Alice got angry and refused to have sex with him. "She simply refused to meet my needs," he said, "and made it clear that she wasn't going to." Her refusal, he claimed, made him so frustrated that he began flirting at work with other women.

Alice later told a much different story about why she and Jeffrey were having sexual problems.

"Just before Thanksgiving, Jeffrey took me out to the farm we had rented. He left the kids at my mom's and he told me we were going out there to be alone and to make love. I went along with him because I wanted to make him happy but I wasn't prepared for what happened."

After they went into the farmhouse, Jeffrey told Alice to go upstairs and take a bath. While she was still in the tub, Jeffrey walked in naked. He told her to open the drain and let the water out, but he ordered her to stay in the tub. He then stepped into the tub so that he was facing her feet. According to Alice, Jeffrey bent down over her and defecated onto her breasts.

"I discovered that Jeffrey was fascinated with his own feces," Alice later told investigators and her psychologist. "He told me that he had been using it since he was thirteen. He would smear it on himself and masturbate with it."

After Jeffrey rubbed feces on Alice's breasts, they had intercourse and then bathed together, she said. "It wasn't that I was cold and uncaring," Alice explained. "I just didn't want to do all the things that he wanted me to do. I knew that my role as his wife was to satisfy him and I wanted to do that and make him happy, but after we moved to the farm, he not only wanted to smear his feces on me, he got so he liked holding me down and putting it on my face. . . . It was just too much . . . so I began telling him no and that is what made him angry and that is what caused all of the fights."

Jeffrey refused during interviews to discuss his sexual practices with Alice. He considered their sexual life to be private. All he would say was that he had never done anything with Alice that "she didn't want to do too." Later, when he was specifically asked if he had smeared his feces on Alice, Jeffrey became upset. "That's an outright lie!" he said. "That is not part of my life-style." He accused Alice of making up stories about their sex life in order to win sympathy for herself. He had never abused her or engaged in any unusual sexual acts with her, he said.

Shortly after Thanksgiving, Jeffrey began coming home late from work at night. He told Alice that he was taking a night class at the hospital so that he could become an emergency medical technician. Alice didn't seem to mind until one Wednesday in December. Alice didn't have a washing machine or clothes dryer at the rental house, so once a week, usually on Wednesday nights, Jeffrey drove her into Macks Creek to a Laundromat. He'd drop her off and go to his night class at the hospital and then return to take her home. On this particular night, Alice finished the laundry and waited for Jeffrey but he didn't show up on time. She waited another hour and then called the hospital.

"Is the class still in session?" she asked.

The nurse, whom Alice knew, was confused. There were no night classes being taught at the hospital, she replied.

Alice tried to hide her embarrassment. "Oh, I must have been mistaken," she said. Alice didn't know what to do so she waited another hour and then finally called Donna. They drove to the rental house together. Jeffrey wasn't there. Donna took everyone home with her.

The next day, Alice borrowed her mother's car and she and Kristen drove to the farm. Jeffrey answered the door.

"What's going on?" Alice demanded. "Why didn't you pick me up at the . . ."

Before she could finish, Jeffrey slammed the door. She beat on it with one hand for several minutes until Kristen began to cry and then she drove back to her parents' house. "I didn't know what was going on," she later said. "I knew he was mad at me because of our sex life, but he wouldn't tell me what was the matter."

Alice and the kids spent Thursday at the Keehlers'. On Friday morning, Jeffrey called. He wanted to take Alice and the kids to McDonald's for hamburgers that night after work, he said. He wanted to talk to Alice about their marriage and whether she was willing to become a "good, subservient wife." Alice dressed the boys in their best outfits and put ribbons in Kristen's hair. All of them waited in the living room. Five o'clock. Six o'clock. Around nine o'clock, Alice put the children to bed and she and her sister Terri went out to find Jeffrey. His truck was parked at the hospital, but he was gone. The following morning, Alice again drove to the farm in her mother's car looking for Jeffrey but he hadn't been there. It looked as if he had spent the night somewhere else. She sat down in the kitchen and wrote him a long letter. In it, she apologized for being, in her own words, "such a bad wife." She was sorry that she had made his life so miserable, that she couldn't satisfy him sexually or be obedient as the scriptures demanded. She begged him for forgiveness and finished the letter by asking him not to hate—or leave—her. "I felt that I had caused this entire mess," she recalled. "Not only had I displeased Jeffrey, but I'd also disobeyed God because I had not been subservient to my husband."

On Monday morning, Jeffrey pulled into the Keehlers' driveway. He hadn't talked to Alice for three days. He'd simply disappeared. He told Alice that he needed to speak with her in private. They went for a walk.

"Where have you been?" she asked.

Jeffrey said he had spent the weekend in Springfield, about fifty miles south of Macks Creek, at a motel with a woman who also worked at the hospital. He said the woman wanted to marry him.

"You're having an affair?" Alice later remembered asking.

"No," Jeffrey said, "I was going to, but I didn't." Jeffrey explained that he and the woman had ended up staying in separate rooms. She had wanted to make love with him, but he had been physically incapable of having sex because "I'm still in love with you, Alice, and I couldn't break our marriage vows."

Alice was stunned. "I knew he was angry with me, but I didn't know he was seeing another woman. He told me that he had gone with her because he was so unhappy with me and because I wouldn't do what he wanted. He said she told him that he was masculine and macho and everything that a woman wanted in a man, and she had offered herself to him and that he felt good about that, because that is how a woman was supposed to act, but that he didn't love her. He loved me."

Years later, Jeffrey repeated much the same story in an interview. "I got involved with this woman at work because I was sexually frustrated. It wasn't love. She had her problems, I had mine. It was nothing but animal heat. But I felt so guilty that I just couldn't do anything and then I confessed everything to Alice."

Jeffrey told Alice that he wasn't going to answer any questions about the Springfield trip. He just wanted her to know what she had driven him to do. "He blamed me totally and considered himself a hero because he had turned down this woman," Alice said.

Incredibly, Alice thanked Jeffrey for not committing adultery and for not leaving her and the children. Jeffrey then drove all of them back to the rental house. When it was time for bed that night, Jeffrey told her that he wanted to make love. He pointed toward the bathroom.

"I'll draw your bath," Jeffrey told her.

Alice said later that she understood what he wanted. She followed him into the bathroom and disrobed without complaint.

The next day after Jeffrey went to work, Alice telephoned her parents and told them where Jeffrey had spent the weekend. Ralph Keehler was angry. Was Alice really so naïve that she believed Jeffrey had spent a weekend in a motel with another woman and never touched her sexually?

"Drop that son of a bitch," he told his daughter. "Divorce him."

Donna was more conciliatory. "You decided to marry him, not me, and I'm not going to make the decision on whether you should break up your marriage," she said. "That's up to you." Then she asked her daughter if she still loved Jeffrey.

"Yes," said Alice. Besides, she added, "Who else would take me? I have a baby, two boys, and I'm twenty-eight years old."

All that week, Alice and Jeffrey avoided talking about his tryst. But on Friday afternoon while Jeffrey was at work, his girlfriend called and boldly asked Alice to give Jeffrey a message.

"Tell him I can't go away with him this weekend," she said.

Alice slammed down the receiver. When Jeffrey got home, she screamed at him. Jeffrey got angry.

"I can't believe you believe her!" he snapped. "She is making all this stuff up because I wouldn't have sex with her. It's all a lie! She's trying to get even with me."

Alice was caught off guard.

"Do you think she would call you if she wasn't angry and jealous?" he continued.

Jeffrey's explanation seemed to make sense, at least to Alice. "I believed him. I honestly believed that they hadn't gone to bed together." On Monday, Alice decided it was time for her to turn the tables. As soon as Jeffrey left for work, she telephoned the hospital and asked to speak to the woman.

"Why are you bothering my husband?" she yelled. "Why are you making this stuff up? Is it because Jeffrey ditched you? Because he didn't want to have sex with you?"

"Is that what he told you?" the woman replied, mockingly. With a steady voice, she then recited the names of the motels and the times and dates that she and Jeffrey had been together. And then she added something else.

"She told me that Jeffrey had taught her how to have oral sex," Alice recalled, "and the way she described it and the words that she used—she was using Jeff's vocabulary—I knew she was telling me the truth because they were the words that he had used to teach me about oral sex. She wasn't lying. I knew that he had been the one telling lies."

Alice hung up and grabbed a telephone book. She called each of the motels and asked the clerks if a "Jeffrey Lundgren" had been a guest on the dates that had been quoted to her.

"Every one of them told me that he had checked in. He even had used his real name. He didn't even try to hide it. Everything she had told me was true."

Alice dialed the long-distance number of her friend Louise Stone and told her about Jeffrey's affair. "I drove him to it," she said between sobs. "I am not as sexually active as he wants me to be. If I'd only done what he had wanted and accepted it, then Jeffrey wouldn't have looked elsewhere."

At this point, Alice didn't mention Jeffrey's fascination with feces. She was too embarrassed. She simply told Louise that Jeffrey wasn't happy with her attitude toward sex.

"Alice told me that she had decided that to make Jeffrey happy she was going to become a very sexual partner," Louise Stone said later. "She said she didn't know whether she could do it or not, but she said that she was going to convince Jeffrey that whatever he wanted was okay even if she couldn't enjoy it. I felt that she was trying her best to become what Jeff wanted her to become sexually."

When Jeffrey got home, Alice told him that she thought it was best if they never mentioned his affair again. "She said that she forgave me and for two weeks, she reclaimed me and I reclaimed her, and we had a good sexual relationship," Jeffrey said. "She did what wives are supposed to do and submitted her will to her Lord—me."

But the second honeymoon didn't last long. One night in February, Jeffrey told Alice to put the children to bed early and come to bed. There was something new that he wanted to teach her, he said.

"Jeffrey came up with two glasses and a bottle of cherry vodka and I was shocked because we didn't drink, but he told me that he wanted me to drink some Coke and cherry vodka and we began drinking."

While they sat on the bed, Jeffrey asked Alice what it was like to be a woman during sex. He was curious about how it felt. What was it like for a woman to have an orgasm? How did it feel to have a penis thrust inside her?

"I was getting pretty drunk and he told me that he wanted to do something different. He told me that he wanted me to give him a bath and wash his hair, which I did, and then he had me comb it and set it in rollers. He had me clean and file his fingernails and toenails and then polish them. Then he asked me for one of my nightgowns and he put it on. He asked me to shave his legs and I did and he put on a pair of my panty hose and I was pretty drunk by this time and he decided to model for me so I put makeup, women's makeup, on his face and took out the hair rollers.

"All this time, he was telling me to drink this vodka and Coke and I was really getting drunk. I was sloppy drunk and then he pulled this package out from under the bed and he said that he wanted to show it to me and he opened it up and took out a dildo and a leather harness and I thought, 'My God, what is he going to do to me?' But he told me that the harness was for *me* to wear. He wanted me to put on the dildo and he wanted me to have sex with him! He wanted me to have anal intercourse with him and it was supposed to be a rape. I said, 'No.' I said, 'Jeffrey, this is too weird. I may be drunk, but I'm not going to do that.' He said, 'Oh yes you are,' and we started arguing and that is when I decided just to get out of the bedroom so I went into the hallway and he came after me and he said, 'You are going to do what I tell you to do,' and I said, 'Oh no I'm not,' and he said, 'Well then, I'll get someone who will.' I was drunk and furious and I yelled at him. I said, 'Oh, you going to get your hospital whore?,' and he said, 'Yeah, she'll do it for me.' I yelled, 'You son of a bitch,' and I went for his throat. I dug my fingernails into his neck. I wanted to hurt him, hurt him so bad, hurt him like he had hurt me. I was so angry. I mean, I had tried and tried and tried to get him to tell me that he was sorry about having an affair, but he always refused. He always said, 'I'm not going to grovel in the dirt for you, Alice. It's your fault that it happened.' I was so furious about everything—the lies, the affair, everything— so I grabbed him around the throat and tried to hurt him and he grabbed me and pulled me off and when he did, he threw me against the wall and my back hit the door, the doorknob, right in the middle of the back and I remember just going limp with the pain and sliding down the wall. I remember the pain was excruciating. I crawled into the bathroom and I locked the door and I passed out. He was trying to take the hinges off and was yelling at me to unlock the door, but I wouldn't and I passed out."

Jeffrey later recalled the confrontation in the hallway differently. He did not mention anything about a sexual encounter or dildo. "One night I went downstairs to get something to eat and when I came back upstairs, she was waiting for me at the door of our bedroom with a baseball bat. She was enraged about the affair, almost catatonic, and she went on an angry tirade. She swung at me with the baseball bat and missed. I caught her with my arms and picked her up. I didn't have any feelings of anger. She claims that I threw her against the doorknob, but that isn't true. She didn't hit anything when I tossed her back. A few days later, she slipped while she was walking down the stairs and fell and hit her back. That's how she got hurt."

No one except Alice and Jeffrey actually knows what happened, but the result is documented in medical records at the Lake of the Ozarks Hospital. Regardless of the cause, Alice's spleen was ruptured and began leaking blood. The injury went unnoticed for two weeks until Alice collapsed and lost consciousness one morning while visiting Jeffrey at the hospital. He carried her into the emergency room, where doctors discovered massive internal bleeding and operated to remove her spleen. Twice during surgery, Alice almost died.

Jeffrey's parents came down from Independence to the farm to take care of the children while Alice was in the hospital. By the end of March, Alice was released, but her medical problems were far from over. She developed a series of painful complications and remained bedfast. One night when she was lying in bed half asleep and under heavy medication for pain, Jeffrey had sexual intercourse with her. She was so groggy that she thought it was a dream at first. A few weeks later, she discovered that she was pregnant again. Alice, who was still taking large doses of painkillers, was terrified. She was afraid that the drugs that she was taking might harm her baby.

Jeffrey, meanwhile, was facing his own worries. He had written bad checks to several area merchants. Some of the checks had been written on accounts that had been closed months earlier; other checks were from accounts that contained no money. A merchant tipped off Donna. A local businessman was so angry that he was going to ask the county attorney to prosecute Jeffrey. "I went over and paid the checks," Donna recalled later. "I collected quite a few of them. We do quite a bit of business with people and we live here. Credit was extended to Jeffrey and Alice because of us and I felt morally responsible to not leave them hanging." Once merchants heard that Donna was paying Jeffrey's bad checks, they began calling her at home. The calls came every night. None of the checks that Jeffrey was writing was for more than thirty dollars. Most were for gasoline or milk or other groceries. But as quickly as Donna paid them, he wrote more. Within a month, she had depleted what little savings she and Ralph had. She decided to confront her son-in-law.

"Jeff, you got to stop doing this," she said. "This is the third time that I've gone around and gotten these checks for you and we can't afford to do it anymore."

He didn't respond.

"If you got many more floating around, you better make them good because the prosecutor comes down real hard on bad checks around here."

Jeffrey nodded, but didn't follow her advice. He wrote another bad check to his landlord. The Lundgrens had lived at the Wilcox farmhouse for nearly one year, yet had paid only two months' rent. Wilcox started eviction procedures. Once again, Jeffrey and Alice and their children were forced to move in with Ralph and Donna.

Wilcox had felt bad when he decided to evict the Lundgrens, but when he visited the farmhouse after they were gone, whatever sympathy he had for the family vanished. The first thing that he noticed was that Jeffrey had broken into the garage where Wilcox had stored his personal belongings. Jeffrey had taken several items and had been using them inside the house. As soon as Wilcox stepped through the back door of his house, Wilcox's heart sank. "The place was a wreck. It looked like a tornado had sucked up everything and thrown it around." He suddenly smelled a pungent odor coming from the basement. Wilcox walked downstairs and nearly gagged. For some reason, Jeffrey had used a saw to cut through the pipe that drained the toilet. "There was toilet paper, feces, urine, everything— dropped directly down onto the basement floor just like in an outhouse," Wilcox recalled. "There was a pile of human waste at least one foot deep and six feet in diameter." Covering his mouth, Wilcox hurried back up to the kitchen. How could someone live with such filth in the basement? he wondered. And why would Jeffrey have done such a thing? Why would someone want a pile of feces in the basement?

Wilcox went through the entire house looking for damage. There was plenty. Holes had been knocked in the walls, carpets were stained and filthy. When he reached the master bedroom upstairs, Wilcox found something else that he thought was curious. Inside one of the closets were stacks of pornographic magazines that Wilcox later described as sadomasochism and bondage publications. Something tossed in the corner of the closet also caught his eye. Wilcox reached down and picked it up, but as soon as he realized what it was, he dropped it.

"It was a plastic dildo that was still caked with feces," Wilcox said. "I mean it was caked with it. They hadn't washed it. They'd just tossed it in there."

As he left the house, Wilcox couldn't help but wonder at the contradiction Jeffrey posed. "He was radical in his religious beliefs. He was intensely conservative and in one room of the house he had left about every book you could think of about the RLDS religion. He had rows and rows of them." Yet upstairs Wilcox had found the opposite sort of literature. It was almost as if there were two different Jeffrey Lundgrens, both extremes. One holy, one evil. "He just wasn't operating from the same perspective that most people operate from. I have never met a person who wanted to be liked more than Jeffrey. He wanted to be liked, he wanted to be admired, yet he didn't want to do anything to earn you liking him. At the same time, I also never knew anyone who thought so much of himself. It wasn't arrogance; it was intense self-importance. He simply looked upon himself as someone who was unique, you know, special, and he felt people needed to treat him special."

On August 6, Jeffrey came home from work and announced that he had quit his job at the hospital. He had not said anything that morning about quitting. He didn't have another job lined up. Alice was dumbfounded. She was six months pregnant, they hadn't found another house to rent, Jeffrey still owed local merchants for bad checks.

"Why did you do it?" she asked. "What's wrong?"

"I can make more money in Independence," Jeffrey replied. "Besides, they don't appreciate me at the hospital."

Jeffrey would not say anything more.

Years later, Bernie Wilson would recall why Jeffrey had resigned. That morning, a hospital employee had walked into an office and caught Jeffrey and his girlfriend embracing. "Jeffrey denied that he was having an affair, but he had been caught fondling this woman's breasts and there was little doubt in my mind what they were up to," Wilson said. "I didn't give him much choice but to quit."

Jeffrey left for Independence the morning after he resigned. He moved into an apartment with his brother, Corry, and told Alice that he would send money whenever he could. During the four-month period that Jeffrey was gone, he mailed her a total of five dollars, Alice later said. In December, Alice went into labor and was taken to Lake of the Ozarks Hospital. Jeffrey drove down from Independence but was clearly uncomfortable at the hospital. Alice still didn't know the truth about why he had resigned. Jeffrey spent the night sleeping in the car in the parking lot rather than in the lobby. The next morning, Alice gave birth to a boy.

"I was so terrified that the drugs I'd taken after my spleen was removed had harmed my baby, but the doctor said, 'Alice, he's got all of his fingers and toes.' And I was so happy that I started crying. You see, I had wondered why God had spared my life when my spleen ruptured. I should have died. My life was so miserable but He spared me so that I could give birth. I looked over at Jeffrey because I wanted to tell him and share it with him and I reached for his hand and he knocked it away. He was crying and I said, 'What's wrong? The baby's okay! He's okay!,' and Jeffrey glared at me and he said, 'HE!,' and I said, 'Yes, honey, it's a boy,' and Jeffrey said, 'Alice, I wanted a girl! Can't you do anything right?,' and he turned around and he walked out. He left me there with my son and just walked out."

Alice named the boy Caleb, after Caleb the son of Jephunneh, mentioned in the Old Testament book of Numbers. "I named him by myself. I chose the name Caleb because Caleb in the Bible hadn't been scared off by adversity and run away from things. He had also told the truth when everyone else lied."

The day after Caleb was born, Alice mentioned to the doctor that she wanted to have a tubal ligation. She didn't want any more children.

"I don't think we can do that," the doctor replied.

Alice asked why. She was certain that her insurance would cover the cost.

"What insurance?" the doctor asked.

"I thought that our insurance had covered all of my medical bills," Alice later explained, "because Jeffrey had been covered by the hospital's employee policy and he had told me that we were still covered by it even though he had quit. What I found out was that Jeffrey had taken me and the kids off the policy months earlier and had been pocketing the extra cash that he saved. We owed the hospital thousands and thousands of dollars from my spleen surgery and they weren't going to do anything else for us until they were paid."

When Donna came to visit her daughter and new grandson later that day, she found Alice in tears.

"Mama," Alice blurted out. "I married Jeffrey for better or worse, but it just keeps getting worse and worse and worse."

Chapter 9

EVEN though Jeffrey was spending his weekdays in Independence searching for work, he would come to the Keehlers' on weekends, and late at night, he and Alice would explore what Jeffrey liked to describe as their "secret world."

"My mother had a sunken bathtub in the bathroom that we used and that is where most of this stuff with feces and urine took place," Alice later said.

During one visit, Alice mentioned that her parents were going to be gone during the upcoming weekend. She and Jeffrey, along with their children, would have the Keehler house to themselves. Jeffrey arrived home earlier than usual the next Friday and was impatient with the kids. As soon as Alice got them to bed, he hurried her into the bedroom. "Jeffrey told me to strip and I did, and then he told me to lie down on the bed. He had bought some rope and he had already cut it into four pieces that he used to tie me onto the bed. He told me that he wanted to see what it was like, you know, bondage. I went along with it because it didn't seem like such a big thing."

They had sex, and when it was over, Alice asked Jeffrey to untie her. He refused. "I began to panic and I said, 'Jeffrey, untie me,' and he said, 'Then it wouldn't be any fun.' " Alice would later claim that during the night, Jeffrey had sexual intercourse with her numerous times. The entire time, she was tied in various positions on the bed. In the morning, she told him that she needed to use the bathroom. He untied her legs but tied her hands together after freeing them from the bed. He led her into the bathroom and then he climbed into the sunken bathtub. "He ordered me to urinate on him and I did," she said. "Then we went back into the bedroom and he tied me back up." Alice later told a friend that Jeffrey had kept her tied to the bed all day Saturday and most of Sunday. He only released her a few hours before her parents came home. "He told the kids that I was sick and couldn't be disturbed so they stayed out of the room."

Although she later said that she did not enjoy the experience, she candidly acknowledged that she had not complained to Jeffrey at the time. "I wanted to please him. I wanted to make him happy. I kept thinking, 'Well, at least we are spending time together. At least he is not with some other woman.' "

Jeffrey found work at a hospital in Kansas City and he moved Alice and the kids up to live with him. But he only kept the job for a few weeks before quitting without explanation. He and Alice were broke as usual. When their landlord knocked on the door in late February 1981 demanding rent, Alice begged for more time. With tears running down her cheeks, she showed him her baby and her three other children and explained how Jeffrey was doing odd jobs to earn enough to feed them. He felt sorry for her and agreed to wait. Jeffrey, meanwhile, began writing bad checks.

One afternoon Alice received a telephone call. It was Jeffrey. He had been arrested by police for passing bad checks. Alice telephoned Donna for help. Jeffrey needed $300 in cash for bail.

"Honey, we just don't got it," Donna replied. Ralph suggested that they leave Jeffrey in jail, but Donna disagreed. She offered to put up their house as collateral.

Alice paused. "No, Mama, I can't let you do it. I'm afraid Jeffrey won't pay it back."

Donna sent her son, Charles, in her car to Independence to pick up Alice. She also telephoned Ralph's sister—the same woman who had worked at Drumm Farm as a cook and had helped them before when they needed cash. The aunt gave Alice a $300 check.

"Don't make it out to Jeffrey," Alice warned. "If I take it to our bank to cash it, they'll simply confiscate the money to pay for other bad checks."

The woman made the check out to Ralph. Alice and Charles drove to Macks Creek to get Ralph's signature and cash it. En route, Alice began to pray. "I reached the bottom, the absolute bottom. I had been married to this man for eleven years and we had nothing to show for it, absolutely nothing. I had always dreamed about having a house with a white picket fence and a nice family. But now I was thrilled just to have enough money to buy milk for the children. What had gone wrong? I remember Charles had fallen asleep in the front seat while I was driving and it was raining and I just started talking to God. 'What am I supposed to do?' I said. 'I'm married to this man for life. He lies to me. He can't keep a job. He cheats on me. Why, God, are You doing this to me?' "

As she drove toward Macks Creek, Alice remembered the summer of 1969 when the patriarch had said that she would marry a companion who would do great things for the church. "I began to think that maybe God had a purpose for doing this, but I just didn't see it."

A few days after Jeffrey was bailed out of jail, he got a job at one of Independence's oldest hospitals, St. Mary's, a 365-bed institution operated by the Roman Catholic Church. He worked as a biomedical technician and was paid $32,000 per year, the most money he had ever earned. Under pressure from Donna, Jeffrey used most of his first paychecks to clear up the bad checks that he had written in Macks Creek. In return, the charges against him were suspended and later expunged from his record.

For the first time in their lives as a couple, Jeffrey and Alice had enough cash to pay the rent, buy groceries, and still have a few dollars left over. Jeffrey began buying rifles. "I want to have a better gun collection than my father," he told Alice. She began buying antiques. "I want to have a better collection than your mother's," she told Jeffrey.

In the fall of 1981, Alice found a beautiful two-story stone house to rent located directly across from the Independence Medical Center on East Twenty-third Street. The rent was $400 per month.

Now that they had the money, Jeffrey and Alice began entertaining. Alice telephoned Dennis and Tonya Patrick, whom they hadn't seen since all of them worked at Drumm Farm. Dennis was now a manager at Bendix Corporation and Tonya had given birth to a daughter, Molly. They had just bought a new house in Independence and were attending the Slover Park congregation. Dennis had risen to the rank of elder in the church, which meant that several nights each week he called on other saints. The Patricks and Lundgrens had a good time when they got together. But Tonya told Dennis later that she felt Jeffrey and Alice had changed. Jeffrey's sexual jokes had made her feel uncomfortable.

"Oh, that's just Jeff," Dennis replied. "He's always been that way, saying things."

"No, Dennis," Tonya said. "This time it was different." In the past, she explained, Jeffrey had always tried to be funny. But this time she felt his innuendos were serious. "I think if I would have shown an interest, he would have jumped at the chance."

One day in autumn of 1982, Alice was outside the rental house raking leaves when an elder from the Slover Park congregation pulled his car to the curb and stepped out to speak with her. He told Alice that an adult Sunday school class at the church was going to begin a new series about the Book of Mormon on Sunday and he invited her to attend. When Alice mentioned the invitation later that night to Jeffrey, he became irritated.

"Why'd you even talk to him?" he asked. "You're my wife. Men shouldn't be walking up and talking to you in the front yard like that."

Jeffrey told Alice to forget about going to church, but Sunday morning, he awoke early. "I sat upright in bed for no reason," he recalled, "and I woke Alice up and told her to get the kids ready for church. She was shocked and so was I, but for some reason I had decided to go—no—it was more than that, I felt *compelled* to go."

The Book of Mormon class was being taught by Raymond C. Treat, a tall, lean man in his early forties, who had dedicated his life to proving that the Book of Mormon was an accurate historical account of early life in the New World. Treat had grown up in Wisconsin, where his parents owned a profitable cranberry marsh. They were not Mormons and neither was he, but in 1959, an employee at the marsh gave Treat a copy of the Book of Mormon and he was mesmerized. He converted to the RLDS and in 1961 married Mary Lee, whom he had met at church. She was fascinated by anthropology and together they decided to pinpoint where the ancient Nephites and Lamanites mentioned in the book had actually lived. Their studies took them to Mexico, and after months of work and study, they decided that the early Hebrews had settled in Mesoamerica, an area extending from central Mexico to Honduras and Nicaragua in which diverse pre-Columbian civilizations once flourished. Treat eventually inherited his family's lucrative cranberry marsh, but he felt moved by God in 1975 to sell it. He used the proceeds to establish the Zarahemla Research Foundation, a nonprofit operation dedicated to investigating the archaeological aspects of the Book of Mormon. The Treats chose the name Zarahemla because that was what the Nephites and Lamanites called their homeland. The foundation operated out of a nondescript brick building in downtown Independence and had two employees— Ray and Mary Lee. They lived on a shoestring budget, made trips to archaeological sites in Mesoamerica, and published their findings in their own newsletter called *The Zarahemla Record*.

Jeffrey and Alice had found Treat's slide presentation about Maya ruins fascinating but it was a comment that Treat made about how the Book of Mormon had been written that made Jeffrey snap to attention. "Everything in this book," Treat said, lifting up his well-worn copy, "every word is there for a reason. God had some reason for including it."

"It was like Ray Treat had put a key into my heart and turned it on full speed," Lundgren recalled. "I began to ask myself, 'Why is this story here? Why is this word used here? Why did God use this particular phrase? What is He really trying to tell us?' I began to look at the scriptures in an entirely different way. Each one was a clue left by God. Memorizing a scripture wasn't enough. You needed to examine each individual word and discover its meaning. When you did that you could actually see God's thought process. From that point on, no one could keep me away from church. I had to know more."

Jeffrey decided to make another try at joining the priesthood. Only this time around, he decided to lay the necessary groundwork so he wouldn't be rejected. "I volunteered to play the piano on Wednesday nights before the evening service. Every Sunday, I made certain that my family was in Sunday School and church. Churches are always looking for someone to volunteer and I was that person. I did all the jobs nobody wanted." Jeffrey also clued in Alice and together they used Dennis and Tonya to make contacts at Slover Park.

"Jeff and Alice were anxious to get prestige," Tonya later recalled. "They didn't have it, they wanted it. . . . They were constantly pushing us to introduce them to important people and then they would either latch onto them or try to."

Jeffrey's plan worked. Two elders told him privately that they were going to recommend that he be "called" into the priesthood. "I was actually amazed at how easy it was really," said Jeffrey. "I discovered that it really doesn't take much effort to take charge in a church and what really was shocking was how easily people were led. Most people didn't even read the scriptures. They had no idea what was in them." Alice agreed. Jeffrey could have hidden a *Reader's Digest* in his Book of Mormon and read from it and most people at Slover Park wouldn't have known the difference, she said.

While things were going well at church, Jeffrey was in trouble again at work. He had been given access to a company car because he was frequently required to drive between the main hospital and a satellite hospital in an adjoining community. One weekend in December 1982, Jeffrey was seen driving the company car when he clearly wasn't at work. Jeffrey's boss, Henry Thomas, asked him if he had been using the car for personal trips. Jeffrey said that he hadn't, but a few days later Thomas found out otherwise. "I called Jeffrey into my office again and I told him straight to his face that he had lied to me," Thomas later said. "He got all red and huffy. I wrote a disciplinary report about the incident and I told him that the next time he took that car and used it on his personal business and then lied about it, I was going to fire him. I came down hard and I figured that threatening him with termination would make him straighten out." It didn't.

Two days later, Thomas caught Jeffrey using the car to run personal errands. He fired him. It was three weeks before Christmas and Jeffrey was out of work. Alice called Dennis and Tonya. What was she going to do? she asked. She and Jeffrey didn't have any money to buy their children presents. Dennis and Tonya offered to help. Tonya took Alice shopping and spent $400 which was charged to the Patricks' credit cards.

"I didn't mind helping at first," Dennis remembered, "but Jeffrey started stopping by all the time and he'd be broke and he'd need gas money and he'd just sort of sit there until I gave him ten or twenty dollars. It was like he just expected it."

Three months after Jeffrey was fired from St. Mary's Hospital, his former boss received a telephone call from the personnel director of a company in Independence that sold equipment to hospitals.

"I'm thinking about hiring Jeffrey Lundgren," he explained.

"Oh, my God!" Thomas recalled saying. "I sure as hell wouldn't do that if I were you."

The director asked why, but Thomas was prohibited by hospital privacy regulations from telling him.

"Well," the director said, "I've interviewed him and I think he could help us and I'd like to help him. He's got a wife and kids and he is really active in his church."

"Let me give you some advice if you do," Thomas replied. "Hide the company credit cards, don't let him have a company car, and watch his expense accounts or it will come back to haunt you."

Despite the warning, the director hired Jeffrey as a salesman in April 1983 and issued him a company credit card and automobile. Both were to be used only for business purposes. Within a few weeks, Jeffrey was asked to resign because of questions over the charge card and car expenses. It was the last paying job that Jeffrey ever held.

Chapter 10

WITHIN the RLDS Church, Dr. James H. Robbins was held in reverent esteem. A gentle, soft-spoken man in his early forties, Jim Robbins had converted to Mormonism in 1965 and had moved to Independence a short time later to help build Zion. By 1978, he had developed a lucrative medical practice and was regarded as one of the city's most successful podiatrists. But just as he reached the peak of his profession, Jim began to feel guilty. "I felt that God was advising me to give it up," he later told his fellow saints. "Money and status should not be the most important goals in life." For six months, Jim prayed, and then one evening he was visited by two church elders. Jim asked them to anoint his head with oil and pray for him by a "laying on of hands"—touching him on the head with their hands. While they were praying, one of the men said that he felt led by the spirit to tell Jim that God was "opening a door" for him and that he should not be afraid to go through it. After they finished praying, one of the men turned to Jim. "Are you thinking about selling your practice?" the elder asked.

"I was taken back by that question," Jim recalled, "and I said, 'Why yes.' And he said, 'I thought so, that came to me while I was praying for you.'"

Jim considered that incident a divine revelation. He felt God was instructing him to sell his medical practice. So he did just that. He stopped performing lucrative foot surgery, opened an office in his house, and began providing medical care to the elderly and poor, frequently without charge.

In the spring of 1982, at about the same time that Jeffrey was starting to work at his short-lived job as a biomedical equipment salesman, Jim was about to join two other devout Mormon families in what the church calls a "living in common endeavor." It was a concept that dated back in the Mormon Church to Sidney Rigdon's early teachings at Kirtland. Rigdon believed that the first Christians mentioned in the New Testament had lived communally and he encouraged his followers to do the same. One group established a commune outside Kirtland in 1830, but within a year they began quarreling over possessions. "What belonged to one brother, belonged to any of the brethren; therefore we would take each other's clothes and property and use it without leave," a member wrote in his diary. When Joseph Smith, Jr., moved to Kirtland, he disbanded the commune. Over time, numerous other devout Mormons had organized similar communes but few lasted.

"I was interested in a 'sharing all things in common' living arrangement," Jim later explained, "because I felt that God wants every man, woman, and child to live for one another, not simply to accumulate as much as they can for themselves." In October 1982, Jim and his wife, Laura, and their children were about to move into a commune when Jim suddenly became ill. Doctors found that he had stomach cancer. He was forced to back out of the commune but the other two families went ahead and combined their assets. Jim, meanwhile, was readied for surgery. As he prayed one night, Jim felt a "calmness" come over him.

"The peace of God settled upon me to a degree that I had never experienced before in my life. If you try to use logic, it will not make sense, but it was real and I found myself carrying on a two-way conversation with the Lord. I didn't hear voices or anything like that. What happened was that whenever I thought of a question in my mind, the answer would suddenly come to me. What he told me was that He was prepared to heal me when I first got cancer but that the unbelief of the saints was so monumental that if I had stood up and announced in church that the Lord had cured me of cancer, no one would have believed me. So what He said was that He had decided to go ahead and let me be stricken with cancer. That way, everyone would know that I had it. He then told me that I could go ahead and have surgery, but not anything else. 'I will take care of you,' He said. God didn't tell me how long I would live and He didn't tell me that He was curing me. He simply said that He would take care of me."

Jim underwent surgery and had a large section of his stomach removed, but his doctors were not able to remove all of the cancer before it spread into his lymphatic system. His surgeon told Jim that he would have to undergo immediate chemotherapy. Jim refused and, despite the doctor's protests, returned home without undergoing any additional treatment.

Two months after his surgery, Jim and Laura Robbins were randomly paired with Jeffrey and Alice at a weekend church retreat for married couples. The two couples were supposed to spend most of the weekend together as part of the program. Jeffrey recognized Jim. By that time, Jim had already shared his "personal testimony" about his cancer operation with several congregations and his moving story was becoming well known in Independence. Some saints suspected Jim would soon die from cancer, but others believed that God was using Jim and his faith to inspire other saints. Regardless, Jim Robbins was a genuine celebrity and Jeffrey and Alice were eager to get to know him and Laura.

At first, Jim didn't like Jeffrey. He thought he was arrogant and pushy. But he was impressed by Jeffrey's ability to recall scriptures. After the weekend retreat, the two couples began socializing. They would get together in each other's homes for what Jeffrey and Jim called "scripture shootouts." Jim would cite a scripture and Jeffrey would counter with a scripture that seemed to either say the same thing or contradict it. Then the two men would continue citing verses until one of them ran dry.

"Jeffrey didn't enjoy light conversation, but he was captivated by the Book of Mormon and digging for hidden or deeper meanings in the scriptures," Jim said. "I was in the priesthood and he wasn't yet ordained but it soon became apparent that he was far more brilliant than I when it came to knowing verses."

In February 1983, two months after meeting the Lundgrens, Jim and Laura told Jeffrey and Alice that they wanted to help support them. "We knew Jeffrey was out of work and they were hard up so we decided to give them two hundred dollars a week," Jim said. In a moment that he would later have difficulty explaining, Jim also announced that if the Lundgrens were interested, he and Laura would like to combine their two families into an "all things in common relationship." Jeffrey and Alice quickly agreed.

"As soon as I brought up the subject, I knew in my heart that I was making a mistake," Jim recalled years later. "In looking back on it, my only explanation is that I think I felt guilty. You see, we had originally planned to join with these two other couples before I was diagnosed as having cancer. They had gone ahead and had disbanded after about a year. I think asking the Lundgrens to form an 'all things in common relationship' was sort of like marrying on the rebound after a divorce."

The day after he first mentioned communal living to Jeffrey and Alice, Jim returned to their house and added a caveat. He and Laura would participate only if they didn't have to go into debt.

What Jim and Laura didn't know was that Jeffrey and Alice were being supported by other church members as well. Along with the $200 that the Robbinses were giving them each week, the Lundgrens were receiving periodic donations from two other families, and the church was paying their rent and utilities from a special fund set aside for poor Mormons. Jeffrey and Alice were also calling on Donna and Ralph when they needed cash and were still borrowing small sums from Dennis and Tonya.

Sonny and Louise Stone, the Lundgrens' friends from their navy days, moved to Independence at about this time and

Louise was shocked when she saw how Alice and Jeffrey were living. "I met Alice one afternoon and we went shopping. She told me that Jeffrey was unable to find a job and that she didn't know how they were going to feed the kids that night. She literally didn't have any food in the house. All the time that we were gone, she was fussing about how they were broke. When we got back to her house, we walked up the steps and their front porch was covered with groceries. I mean, bags and bags of food."

"Help me carry these inside," Alice told Louise.

"Alice, where did all this come from? Who left it here?" Louise asked.

"Oh, I don't know. Jeffrey told me that he was going to pray about getting us enough to eat and he prayed last night about it."

"What?" Louise asked incredulously.

Alice became irritated. "Louise," she lectured, "I don't question God and neither should you."

"I told Alice that it wasn't right for her and Jeffrey to live off other people," Louise remembered. "I asked her why Jeffrey didn't go get a job like everyone else. She told me that Jeff had things to do for God and therefore he wasn't required to work like everyone else. Other people were supposed to take care of him. That was their job. His was to serve God."

Once the Lundgrens became friends with the Robbinses, they no longer had as much time for Dennis and Tonya or Sonny and Louise. Jeffrey, in particular, didn't want to bother studying scriptures with Dennis. "He can't keep up with me," Jeffrey complained to Alice. "He's just not as sharp as Jim."

There was one passage of scriptures in particular that Jeffrey and Jim were trying to decipher. It was recorded in the Doctrine and Covenants, a Mormon book that contained all of Joseph Smith, Jr.'s revelations from God, as well as those given by God to Smith's successors. This particular revelation was identified as "Section 76." [The book listed revelations in numerical order but used the word "section" rather than "number" to identify them.] According to it, Joseph Smith, Jr., and Sidney Rigdon had been meditating on February 16,

1832, when they were shown a revelation and a vision. What the two men saw was eternity and it was quite different from the simple heaven and hell concept that most other religions described. There were actually three different levels in heaven, Smith later explained. These included the Celestial [highest], the Terrestrial [middle], and Telestial [lowest]. Only the most devout saints could make it to the Celestial where God himself dwelt. Section 76 described in detail what kind of person would be assigned to each level. In the final sentences of the passage, the revelation also said that God had permitted Smith and Rigdon to see other "great and marvelous . . . works." But He told them that they couldn't reveal what they had seen.

> "For they are only to be seen and understood by the power of the Holy Spirit, which God bestows on those who love him and purify themselves before him; to whom he grants this privilege of seeing and knowing for themselves."

Jeffrey and Jim wanted to know what "great and marvelous" mysteries the two men had seen but had been forbidden to describe. So they came up with a plan. If God had appeared to Smith and Rigdon in Kirtland, Ohio, then Jeffrey and Jim would drive to Kirtland and ask God to show them what He had shown Smith and Rigdon.

They made plans to leave with their wives in March. Jeffrey had never seen the Kirtland temple but he had read about its history. He knew that after Joseph Smith, Jr., and Rigdon had fled Kirtland because of the Mormon bank failure, the temple had been abandoned and had fallen into disrepair. At one point, a Gentile farmer had used it as a sheep shed. After Smith was murdered in 1844, the Mormons in Utah and those in Independence both claimed ownership of the church. But in February 1880, a county judge ruled that it belonged to the RLDS. Since then, the RLDS had restored the temple and opened it for tours.

The Robbinses and Lundgrens drove to Kirtland in an old station wagon that the Lundgrens had been given. They stayed in the home of a local church official who knew the Robbinses.

Jeffrey and Jim had gotten permission to pray inside the temple after it was closed to tourists. About an hour before it was time for them to go inside, Jeffrey became fidgety.

"What's bothering you, Jeffrey?" Alice asked, but he didn't reply. Jim and Laura Robbins noticed that Jeffrey was acting strangely.

The two men had been told that they would have thirty minutes to pray in the temple before they would have to leave. They quickly hurried inside and sat on one of the wooden pews in the front. All of a sudden, Jim realized that he didn't have any idea what to do next.

"I guess we should pray," he finally said. Jeffrey nodded, so Jim knelt down and asked God if He would show them the hidden mysteries described in Section 76.

Nothing happened.

Jim returned to his seat, feeling rather foolish. "It was obvious to me that we were in no condition spiritually to have such a marvelous experience as Smith and Rigdon had had."

Jeffrey stood up and began to pray out loud, but rather than asking God to show him a vision, Jeffrey asked God to heal Jim of his stomach cancer. As Jim listened, Jeffrey became so emotional that he could hardly speak. He began to weep.

"I was touched by what he said, that he would ask God to cure me, and I was touched by his show of emotion because I had never seen that before in Jeffrey," Jim later recalled, "but I told Jeffrey as we were leaving the church that I didn't expect God to heal me. God had promised before my operation to take care of me and I trusted Him to do that. He never said that He'd cure me of cancer."

When Jeffrey later told his followers about his prayer and experience with Jim Robbins at the Kirtland temple in March 1983, he would claim that Jim collapsed as soon as he stepped outside the building. Jim would remember what happened a bit differently. According to Jim and Laura, the two couples rode to a nearby restaurant for dinner and while they were eating, Jim began to shake and became faint. He had recently had a bad viral infection and he thought that he was suffering a relapse. By the time Laura had paid the restaurant bill, Jim was shaking uncontrollably with chills. Jeffrey helped him crawl into the back of the station wagon and they left immediately for Independence.

"I think we should get him to a hospital," Alice said after they had ridden on the highway for about an hour. Jim's entire body was shaking. Laura didn't know what to do, but Jeffrey was calm.

"He is going to be fine," he said. "He didn't get sick in a day and he's not going to be cured in a day."

Alice glanced over at Laura. Neither one of them knew what Jeffrey was talking about. They stopped for the night at a motel in Richmond, Indiana. The next morning, Jim still felt ill. When they reached Independence, Jeffrey helped Laura put Jim in bed. The next morning, Jim said he felt fine when Jeffrey came to see him. Jim was certain he had been suffering from a virus. Jeffrey wasn't.

"Jim, I want you to know what happened," Jeffrey said. "The reason that I was so nervous before we went into the temple was because God had spoken to me. He said that I had a choice. I could see the vision—the same one that Joseph Smith and Sidney Rigdon had seen—or I could choose to have you healed of your cancer." Jeffrey paused. "The reason why I was so upset was because I actually had to think about it before I told God to heal you. I felt terrible. That's when I realized that I had come to the temple for the wrong reasons. I had come because I was selfish. That's why I prayed in the temple for God to cure you."

Jim didn't know what to say.

"You see," Jeffrey continued, "that's why you were sick after we left the temple. God was healing you. He was healing you of cancer because I had made the right choice. I've come over here today to tell you that you are completely healed. The cancer is gone."

After a few moments, Jim spoke. He had chosen his words carefully. "Jeffrey, I appreciate what you are saying, but I don't have that same testimony. All I know is that God promised to take care of me. I don't know that I'm healed."

"Well, I'm telling you that you are healed," Jeffrey replied. "You are healed because I chose that rather than to see the vision."

On Sunday when the Robbinses went to church, a woman hurried up to them. "Isn't it wonderful!" she exclaimed. Jim looked confused. "I'm talking about how Jeffrey Lundgren prayed for God to heal you and He did! Jeffrey told us all about it this morning. It's a miracle."

Jim Robbins wasn't so sure.

Chapter 11

THE friendship between the Robbinses and Lundgrens became strained after their trip to Kirtland for reasons besides Jeffrey's claims that his prayers had healed Jim. Jeffrey and Alice had found a piece of land in Independence that they felt would be ideal for a "communal" duplex. They could live on one side and the Robbinses could live on the other. Jeffrey estimated that it would cost about $60,000 to buy the land and build a duplex. That sounded reasonable to Jeff and Alice, but Jim and Laura balked. Jeffrey was still unemployed and, Jim suspected, wasn't really looking for a job. If the Robbinses sold their home, they still would have to borrow at least $10,000 to cover all the construction costs. "I'm wondering if the hand of God isn't protecting us," Jim told Laura one afternoon. "Maybe He doesn't want us to move in with Jeffrey and Alice." Later that day, Jim reminded Jeffrey of the caveat in their deal. "I'm not going to do this if we have to go into debt," he said. Jeffrey scrapped the duplex plans.

It was income-tax time, and when Laura began going over her records, she discovered that she and Jim had given the Lundgrens more than $2,000. She also realized that they weren't going to be able to continue supporting the Lundgrens and keep up their financial pledge to the church.

"We can't keep doing both," she told Jim. "One of us has to tell Jeff and Alice, and soon."

That night when the Lundgrens came over to visit, Laura kept waiting for Jim to tell them, but the closest he came was asking Jeffrey if he'd had any luck finding work. He hadn't. The next Sunday, Laura cornered Alice at church.

"Is Jeff really looking for a job?" she asked.

"Why?" Alice replied, coldly.

"Because we just don't have the money to keep supporting you," Laura blurted out.

Badly embarrassed, Alice hurried to find Jeffrey. Laura thought she had better warn Jim, who had stayed home that morning. She got there too late. Jeffrey had beat her home. He had pounded on the Robbinses' door and had come right to the point when Jim answered.

"Your wife told my wife that you don't want to continue your relationship with us," Jeffrey huffed.

"What are you talking about, Jeffrey?" Jim asked.

"Your wife informed my wife that you can't help us any longer financially."

"That's right, Jeff," Jim said solemnly. "We just can't afford it. It's too much of a burden right now."

"What kind of an excuse is that?" Jeffrey demanded. "I expect you to keep your commitments to me."

Jim got mad. "Jeff, you are the most ungrateful person I've ever known. How can you stand there and carry on like this because now I'm telling you we can't afford it anymore? You act like we owe you this money."

Jeffrey spun around and walked away.

The next Sunday at church, the Lundgrens and Robbinses avoided each other.

In early October 1983, Jeffrey was ordained at Slover Park into the RLDS priesthood. He had been out of work for more than one year, but the elders in the church didn't hold that against him. Jeffrey asked his father to perform the ordination ceremony. Dennis Patrick, whom he had befriended again, assisted. Now that Jeffrey was in the priesthood, he could preach on Sundays. Years later, regular members would still recall his first sermon. He didn't speak from a prepared text. Instead, he read a series of scriptures. Every one of the verses was about God's wrath and how he would destroy the wicked.

Jim and Laura were in the congregation. Neither had ever heard such a scathing denunciation, but Jim wasn't surprised. "During our scriptural studies, Jeffrey always focused on scriptures that would enable him to mentally put people he didn't like into the lake of fire and brimstone. He would say, 'See this scripture? Why, God could be talking about so-and-so. He could be calling that person a Son of Perdition [evil].' And I'd say, 'Why, Jeff, you don't know what you are talking about. That person is not a Son of Perdition. It's like you are finding pleasure in condemning people. The Lord wants to save lives, not destroy them by casting them into the pit.' But he always argued with me. 'So-and-so fits all the criteria of that scripture,' he'd say. 'They should be destroyed.' "

So many members complained about Jeffrey's discourse that the church sent an elder to talk to Jeffrey. "Our God is a God of love, not damnation," he told Jeffrey.

"I reminded the pastor that all I had done was read scriptures," Jeffrey later recalled, "and I asked him if he was telling me that a member of the priesthood shouldn't be allowed to read scripture in church."

The pastor didn't argue. Jeffrey was not asked to preach again.

A few days later, on Halloween night, Damon Lundgren tripped while running across a parking lot after a youth group meeting at the church. By the time an adult reached the thirteen-year-old, he was holding his rib cage in obvious pain. They hurried him home.

"I think you should get Damon to the hospital," the church's youth group sponsor told Jeffrey.

"We don't have any insurance," Jeffrey replied. "He'll be okay." He yelled at Damon to get out of the car, but the sponsor interrupted.

"The church will pay for it. This kid is in pain."

"Well, I can't take him because I'm here alone with the other kids," Jeffrey replied. The sponsor offered to stay with them so that Jeffrey could take Damon across the street to the emergency room at the Independence Medical Center.

"I don't like leaving my children with strangers," Jeffrey replied.

Exasperated, the sponsor decided to admit Damon into the emergency room by himself. Jeffrey went along to sign the necessary hospital paperwork and then hurried back home and telephoned Alice, who was visiting Tonya. Alice asked Dennis if he would come to the hospital and pray for Damon. He anointed Damon's head with oil and asked God to comfort him. A short while later, doctors told Alice that Damon had broken a rib, which, in turn, had punctured his liver. They were going to operate to stop the internal bleeding. Dennis went across the street to fetch Jeffrey. Jeff had telephoned Don and Lois and once they arrived, he and Don went to the hospital, leaving Lois with the children. As soon as Damon saw his grandpa, he smiled. Damon had always been Don's favorite. When Damon was little, Don used to squeeze his leg and count. Damon would see how long he could take the pain before he yelled. They called it the "pain game."

"I think I made a ten on the pain scale, Grandpa," Damon said.

"I think you did too, honey," Don replied. Jeffrey noticed that there were tears in his father's eyes. He was surprised and jealous.

The surgery went well, and after it was completed, Jeffrey went home and Don and Lois left. Alice slept on a cot next to her son in the hospital. She had Jeffrey bring her clean clothes in the morning. She showered and ate there too. "I don't want to leave him," Alice told Jeffrey. "I know what it's like to be alone in a hospital after surgery." Alice's comment was a reference to when her spleen was removed following her confrontation with Jeffrey. He hadn't been there when she woke up after the operation.

Five days after Damon's surgery, Jeffrey told Alice that he wanted her to come home, if not to see him, then to spend some time with the other three children. She agreed, but when she walked across the street, she found that Jeffrey had already put the children to bed. He had grilled two steaks over charcoal and set the table for a romantic candlelight dinner. When they finished their vanilla ice cream dessert, Alice stood up to leave.

"I think I'll dash over to check on Damon," she said.

Jeffrey exploded. He grabbed her arm and pushed her against the dining-room wall.

"By God, woman, you belong in this house and this is where you are going to stay!" he yelled. "Now get in the bedroom."

Now it was Alice's turn to get angry.

"What's wrong, Jeff?" she asked mockingly. "Are you feeling neglected because you had to go five whole days without any sex?"

He threw her onto the floor. "He tore open my blouse and he raped me. He raped me on the floor and when he got done, he got up and took my bathrobe and threw it at me. I went into the bathroom and I sat on the floor and cried and cried and then I got into the tub and after about a half hour, he came in with a red rose that he had put into a vase and he put it next to me and he sat down next to the tub and he stroked my face and he told me that he loved me and he was glad that we were married. It was like we were two normal persons, like nothing had happened."

(When asked later about Alice's account, Jeffrey said that it was impossible for a husband to rape his wife since her purpose in life was to please him sexually.)

The next day, Alice telephoned Louise Stone. "Jeffrey raped me," she said. Alice decided to tell Louise everything, including how Jeffrey liked to smear his feces on her. "What am I going to do?" she asked.

Louise suggested a divorce and offered to help her find a lawyer. "I'll stand by you no matter what you want to do," she offered. Alice promised to think about it.

When Jeffrey got home later that day, he told Alice that he had to tell her something important. He began by reminding her of the summer in 1969 when the patriarch made his prophecy about Alice and her husband.

"Alice, on the night that Damon was taken to the hospital, I had a vision," he announced. Years later, he would repeat during an interview what he told Alice that night in October 1983. As he spoke, he became emotional and began to cry. It was, he explained, the most heartrending experience in his life.

"I had gone out onto the front porch of our house because I could see the emergency room from there and I was trying to see what was happening with Damon across the street. I began to pray but I didn't know what words to use. Suddenly words started coming into my mind and I began to pray for the son, but it wasn't Damon that these words were about, it was the son of God, Jesus Christ, and just as I started to say them, the hospital dissolved away and I was no longer in Independence. I was at Calvary and I was facing the cross. I was standing to the right of it. This was not like a movie. I was actually there. I was physically, totally, completely there, and I looked up at Christ and He was in total agony and I realized that there were plenty of people who could pray for my son, but no one had prayed for the *son*—Jesus Christ. All of the disciples had been upset about losing Him, but no one had prayed for Him. And I heard Him call out with a loud voice. He was calling for Elias and it was horrible. I could hear Him struggle and see His breath. He would struggle to raise Himself up to get a gasp of air and then His entire body would sag, and I wanted to take Him down and He looked at me and I could tell that He wanted me to take Him down, but I couldn't take Him down because I needed Him to die just as every other creature needed Him to die. We all helped crucify Him because we needed Him to die for our sins so I didn't help Him. I rejected Him. I had to say 'Crucify Him' just like everyone else because I needed that atonement. It was like I had put a nail in His hand. I looked at Him and I knew and He knew that I was rejecting Him. You see, I understand rejection. I understand what it is like to be rejected and He knew too. So I just walked up to the base of the cross and I began to weep and, I don't know how to explain this, but all of a sudden, all I can say is, I was looking out of Christ's eyes. I saw everything and I was aware that I was in His head and in His consciousness and I could see all things, all eternity, from the beginning of time to the present into the future. It was like a giant panorama, and then I felt His pure and total love and I understood that there was no anger in Him at all. Then I saw my own life and I realized that love was a foreign object to me, that I didn't understand love, especially love like Christ's. And then it was over. The scene dissolved back and I found myself staring at the hospital. I began to weep and the next thing that I knew, Dennis Patrick was walking up the steps to see if I was okay. He thought I was crying about Damon, but I was crying because I had been with Christ and felt His love and then been brought back to reality."

Alice told Jeffrey that she thought his vision was the most beautiful religious experience that she had ever heard anyone describe. "But what does it mean?" she asked.

"I'm not sure yet," he replied, "but God is preparing me for something. He is directing both of our lives."

Later that day, Louise telephoned Alice to learn whether or not she was going to divorce Jeffrey.

"I can't leave Jeffrey," Alice told her. "He told me about a vision that he had. He told me that he has work to do for God. He told me that if I left him, he wouldn't be able to do what God wanted."

"What are you talking about, Alice?" Louise asked.

"Louise, haven't you been listening to me? God told Jeff that He is preparing him for an important mission in the church. I can't leave him now. It's impossible."

Chapter 12

THE pastor at Slover Park asked Dennis Patrick to teach an adult Sunday school class in the fall of 1983. Dennis asked Jeffrey to help. They were supposed to teach a course about Zion. Twenty adults attended the first session and Dennis was pleased. But the next Sunday he told Jeffrey that there was a problem. Dennis had been asked to coordinate a new training program for young church leaders. "I'm not going to have time to teach the class anymore," he told Jeffrey. "Would you mind taking over?"

Jeffrey was delighted. He saw God's hand at work. The next Sunday, he strolled into the classroom. "We are going to change this class into a study of the Book of Mormon," he announced. "I am going to be the teacher, you will be the students. I will teach, you will learn. If there is time for questions at the end, I will answer them. Otherwise, don't interrupt. I'm not here to debate." With that, Jeffrey opened his books and began his lecture.

His classes were immediately controversial. Nearly everything Jeffrey taught was based on fundamentalist RLDS doctrine, but those conservative beliefs were no longer in vogue. The fight between the liberals and the fundamentalists, which Jeffrey had first gotten involved in back in 1975 at the student union at CMSU was still going on, but the liberals were clearly winning. The reforms started in the late 1950s by RLDS president-prophet W. Wallace Smith had made it possible for his son and successor, Wallace B. Smith, to steer the RLDS even closer toward mainstream Protestantism. The idea that the RLDS was God's "only true church" was being deemphasized. Some liberals had even suggested that the Book of Mormon was a fictional "morality play," not holy scripture. Such talk infuriated fundamentalists, and in 1978, when Wallace B. Smith took charge, a group of conservative church members in Vancouver, Washington, voted to secede. They announced that their congregation was going to become a "restoration" RLDS church, which meant that its members were going to "restore" their church to the RLDS's original traditions. The new president-prophet responded by "silencing" the elders at Vancouver and by going to court to seize their church, a recreational building, and the congregation's $3,000 bank account. By the time Jeffrey began teaching the adult class at Slover Park, Wallace B. Smith had gone to court five times in Texas and Missouri to prevent fundamentalists from breaking away. Despite such efforts, the RLDS Church was clearly headed toward a split and most members expected the final break to occur when the church held its worldwide conference in April 1984 in Independence. That was when Wallace B. Smith was going to recommend that the church permit women to become priests.

Jeffrey's class soon became a refuge for fundamentalists, particularly those opposed to ordaining women. As far as Jeffrey was concerned, Wallace B. Smith was misguided and history was repeating itself. God had picked Joseph Smith, Jr., to restore the "only true church" on earth because the other

denominations had been corrupted over time by men. Now
Smith's church was heading down that same path. Such talk
did not endear Jeffrey to the elders at Slover Park. But even
though his views were in the minority, his class still drew about
twenty loyal members so he was allowed to continue teaching.
Georgia Milliren was an avid Jeffrey supporter. Like Jeffrey,
Milliren had been raised in the Slover Park congregation, but
she was six years older than he and didn't really know Jeffrey
until she began attending his class. "Jeffrey was a dynamic
teacher, a real challenger," she recalled. "He and Alice used
to tell us that they wanted to stretch our thinking, and he
really did."

Jeffrey peppered his lectures with dire predictions of God's
coming wrath and destruction. He was so convincing that
Milliren began tucking extra clothing into her children's back-
packs just in case Christ returned to earth while they were
in school. The fact that Jeffrey was unemployed bothered
Milliren. "But," she said, "you had to admire the fact that
he spent so much time studying. No one knew scriptures like
Jeffrey did. He knew them and he could interpret them and
even if you didn't agree with him, you couldn't disprove him
because everything he said, he backed up with scriptures."

Another fervent backer of Jeffrey's was Cheryl Avery. She
and her husband, Dennis, were appalled with the liberalization
of the church and privately suspected that Wallace B. Smith
was being led astray by Satan. Cheryl thought Jeffrey was an
extraordinary teacher, so much so that others in the class began
to joke that Jeffrey had become Cheryl's "personal guru."

In April, the delegates at the RLDS worldwide conference
did exactly what the fundamentalists feared and supported a
"revelation" by Smith that allowed women to be ordained.
Cheryl was devastated and Jeffrey became even more bellig-
erent in his class toward Wallace B. Smith and the church hierarchy. That June, Jeffrey taught a lesson that simply pushed the
Slover Park elders too far.

"God and Christ are the same entity," Jeffrey announced.
"They are not separate and distinct personages as you have
been taught by the church. If they were, then we have a very
selfish God because that means He sent someone else to do
His dirty work on earth and to die on the cross. It means that

He let His own son die, rather than giving up His own life and saving His son's."

As several class members listened in horror, Jeffrey read scriptures from the Book of Mormon and Joseph Smith, Jr.'s inspired version of the Bible that suggested that God and Jesus Christ were the exact same being.

"God wasn't selfish," Jeffrey continued. "He didn't send His son to die on a cross. He came down Himself. He was on the cross. He was so loving that He created mankind knowing in advance that mankind would reject Him and later crucify Him."

Jeffrey's comments not only contradicted RLDS doctrine, they also raised questions about Joseph Smith, Jr.'s first vision. The saints had been taught that God and Jesus Christ had appeared as two separate individuals in front of Smith.

A woman in the class jumped to her feet. "Are you saying Joseph Smith was a liar? That he made up the story of his vision?" she asked.

Jeffrey tried to explain that he had discovered at least four different accounts in church archives of Smith's first vision and each was substantially different from the others. But the woman refused to listen.

"You're not preaching God's word," she yelled. "You're preaching the devil's."

Georgia Milliren would later recall the trouble that Jeffrey's lesson sparked. "I remember when he said that God and Jesus were one—it simply blew me away. . . . It was very troubling to me and others in the class." The elders in the church told Jeffrey that he was through teaching. His class was discontinued.

As he had done when in college, Jeffrey reacted by inviting Georgia, Dennis and Tonya Patrick, Dennis and Cheryl Avery, and about six other couples to his house on Sunday afternoons for scripture classes of his own. He was not going to let anyone tell him what to preach. About fifteen people showed up. Like the Averys, most were unhappy with the RLDS.

Shortly after Jeffrey's class was disbanded at the church, he had another vision. "I was in a room and there was a table in it that was filled with great riches and I was told to make a choice. I could take the riches and live a normal life or I could choose to go down a path and worship God. I told the Lord that I wanted to walk down that path and serve him. I rejected the world's riches.

"The wealth suddenly disappeared and I found myself walking on a path. Dennis Patrick was there and two other personages [angels]. The path led me beside a tiny stream and there was a highway nearby and a rowdy bar where sinners were drinking and there was evil all around, but the path was light and if you stepped off it, people could grab you, but you were safe as long as you remained on it.

"While we were walking, we came to a place where there was heavy fog and I was told to reach into the fog, and I did, and I was given a set of gold plates. These were not the golden plates that Joseph had been given and had already transcribed. These were other plates that God had not yet revealed to mankind.

"God told me that He wanted the plates translated so I began searching for someone who could transcribe the plates and I went to the world church headquarters in Independence because I was going to give the plates to Wallace B. Smith to translate, but when I went into the building, God asked me why I had brought the plates there and when I told him, He told me that Smith couldn't translate them. He told me that the church had been given the greatest truth that mankind had received but it had done the least with it and because of this, it had lost the truth.

"I continued my search but there was no one who could translate the plates. There was no one to give them to so I returned to the path and when I got there Dennis Patrick tried to wrestle the plates from me and we struggled and finally I got them loose from him."

Neither Alice nor Jeffrey spoke for several minutes after he finished describing his vision, and then Alice asked him: "What do you think this means?"

"I'm not certain," he replied, "but I think that it means that God wants me to bring forth some new revelation. I think it means that Wallace B. Smith is a fallen prophet and is leading the church to destruction. I think it means that Dennis Patrick will try to stop me from accomplishing my task because he will be more worried about winning the glory of the world than about winning the glory of God."

"Jeffrey, are you telling me the truth?" Alice asked, immediately realizing that her question had insulted him. Before he could answer, she said: "Oh, I know it's true. I'm sorry I doubted. I know it's true because it's exactly what I was told when I was growing up. Remember, I was told by the patriarch that I was going to marry a man whom God was going to 'prepare to bring forth a marvelous work and wonder.'"

The next day, Jeffrey told the Patricks about his vision, but he skipped over the part about how Dennis would try to wrestle the gold plates from him.

Jeffrey seemed sincere, they later recalled. "In our tradition, visions are not uncommon and the vision that Jeffrey described was not something that either Dennis or I would have questioned or thought odd," Tonya explained. "If you had gone to any Wednesday night prayer service that week, you probably would have seen someone stand up and talk about how God had inspired them to say something or shown them a vision. It just wasn't that unusual."

While the Patricks did not see Jeffrey's account as anything spectacular, he considered it momentous. "When I had that vision, I became convinced that I would walk on an actual path someday like the one that I had seen and would actually be given or shown some sort of mysterious records. I was going to be instrumental in bringing them forth. I did not see myself as a prophet at that point, but after I had that vision, I began studying what kind of man I needed to become to be acceptable to God so that I could do what He wanted. My entire attention was focused on the prophets and how I could be like one of them."

One afternoon in July, Jeffrey was mowing the grass and thinking about God. "I began asking God questions in my mind. I was trying to figure all of this out and I asked, 'What would you have me do?,' and God put a thought in my mind. 'The answer is already written,' He said."

Jeffrey shut off the lawn mower and ran inside where he grabbed his copy of the Doctrine and Covenants and began flipping pages. He stopped at Section 38.

"I got it!" he suddenly hollered. "I know what I am supposed to do!"

Jeffrey showed Alice paragraph 7b of Section 38, one of Joseph Smith, Jr.'s earliest revelations from God. In it God orders Smith to leave New York and go to Kirtland to be with Sidney Rigdon.

> For this cause I gave unto you the commandment, that you should *go to the Ohio* and there, I will give unto you my law and there *you shall be endowed with power from on high*, and from thence, whosoever I will, shall go forth among all nations, and it shall be told them what they shall do.

"We are moving to Ohio," Jeffrey proclaimed. "We must go to the Kirtland temple because that is where the scriptures are telling me to go if I want to be endowed with the power."

He shut the book, walked outside, and finished mowing the lawn, leaving Alice in the house dazzled. Later that night, Alice asked Jeffrey how he planned to finance the move. "God will show us," he told her.

A few days later, Alice noticed an advertisement in a church newsletter. The RLDS was seeking volunteers to work as tour guides at the Kirtland temple. Applicants had to be financially self-sufficient because they would not receive a regular salary, but the church would provide a house and pay for the utilities.

"God is showing us the path," Jeffrey explained. He answered the ad that same day. When asked about his finances, Jeffrey lied. He said that his parents had decided to give him his inheritance and that it was enough for his family to live on for one year without his earning a salary.

A short time later, the church offered him the job. That same day, Jeffrey received a job offer from an Independence company. He would later tell his followers that the company had offered to pay him $65,000 per year. "It was just like in my vision," he said. "I was being given a choice. I could have the riches of the world or I could choose to go down the path that God was showing me. I chose God."

Alice was just as certain as Jeffrey that God was leading them to Kirtland. "I told Jeffrey, 'Don't take that company job because if you do, it will be the only reward you will have in life.' The Lord wanted us in Kirtland."

Jeffrey decided they needed $1,500 to move. He began selling his gun collection and ordered Alice to sell her antiques. He borrowed $600 from various church members and asked his parents for a donation as well. "I wrote my parents a fifteen-page letter describing why I was going to Kirtland, citing all the scriptural references." Don and Jeffrey's grandfather, Alva Gadberry, responded by coming to Jeffrey's house. "Grandfather Gadberry told me that God was not calling me to Kirtland, Satan was. He warned me against going and told me that I would be following the devil if I did."

When Jeffrey broke the news to the group who met at his house each Sunday afternoon for class, Cheryl Avery and Georgia Milliren immediately suggested that they have a going-away picnic at a nearby park for Jeffrey and Alice. About ten couples came to say good-bye. They gave $120 to Jeffrey and Alice as a going-away present. Georgia wanted the group to get up early the next morning and surprise the Lundgrens by waiting at the outskirts of town and waving to them when they drove past. But she decided that the class might not spot them on the busy highway so she dropped the idea. Dennis Avery told Jeffrey that he admired his dedication. "This is so exciting," Cheryl said. "You've got to tell us what you find there." Alice was crying by the time the picnic ended. Dennis and Tonya followed them back to their house for a final good-bye.

Jeffrey told Dennis that he was still $50 short of the $1,500 that he needed to raise. As they were talking, someone knocked on the door. "We had an old washer and dryer sitting on the porch and this couple had seen them and our garage-sale sign and had come up to buy them," Jeffrey recalled. "They gave us fifty dollars."

Once again, Jeffrey saw God at work.

The next morning, Jeffrey, Alice, and their children climbed into their old station wagon. All of their possessions were in a U-Haul trailer that they were going to tow. Jeffrey would later recall how he felt that morning. "Everyone considered me a failure. My father, my mother, even Alice, because I had not accumulated a bunch of possessions or stayed at one job. But it suddenly dawned on me why. God had been trying to get my attention. He didn't want me to succeed at all those other jobs. He wanted me to fail so that I would eventually come to Him and do what He wanted me to do. In fact, I believe that He caused me to fail.

"I had been created for one purpose and it wasn't working in a hospital. I loved the scriptures and everyone told me that I knew them better that anyone. Why? Because it was all part of His plan."

As they left Independence, Jeffrey knew that he was not going to fail this time. He would prove to Don, to Lois, to his grandparents, and to Alice and everyone else who had ever doubted him that he was not a loser. He was special and important.

"The Lord had chosen me—me—for a great mission. He hadn't chosen them. He hadn't given my father this vision. He hadn't given it to Wallace B. Smith. He had chosen me. I truly believed that and I saw this as a new adventure, a new start. We were going down God's path and I wasn't going to let Him down.

"I was going to do whatever God commanded."

Part Two

Prophet

Thou shalt not hearken unto the words
of that prophet, or that or that dreamer
of dreams . . .
—*DEUTERONOMY 13:3*

Chapter 13

THE first white settler in Kirtland arrived in May 1811 from Berkshire County, Massachusetts, aboard an ox-drawn covered wagon. Legend has it that he built his log cabin along the Indian trail that he had followed through the dense woods and rocky inclines of northern Ohio. Those who came later also built their cabins next to this Indian trail and over time, a town emerged. It was not a carefully platted community with neat square blocks. Rather, it grew haphazard much like wild flowers sprouting next to a meandering stream. Wherever the ground was level enough for a house, one was built. Today, most homes and shops face this same trail that once Erie Indians walked. It is officially designated on maps as State Highway 306. But the five-mile section that runs through Kirtland is called Chillicothe Road by the locals. It's the town's de facto main street. Beginning in the north, the narrow two-way blacktop guides motorists past a dilapidated red brick combination city hall and police department, a smattering of shops, Kirtland's public schools, a well-tended football field, and a failed Dog & Suds restaurant now painted dark brown with boarded up windows. Farther south it passes the entrance of Chapin Forest, a large park and nature reserve, before it finally intersects with State Highway 6 near the end of the city limits. The Kirtland cemetery is located adjacent to this one-stoplight interchange; so is a feed store and Lupica's Country Corner which promises customers genuine Amish-made cheese and handpacked fruit baskets.

There is no McDonald's in Kirtland, no local movie theater, no bowling alley, no Wal-Mart with discount prices. But the town does have churches—ten of them at last count, including six that broke off from either the Baptist or Mormon denominations. About halfway through town, a sign proclaims JESUS SAVES. It was not erected by any religious group. It was made by a Kirtland man who stuck it in his front yard much as a realtor puts up a For Sale sign. On the outskirts of Kirtland, the city council has erected welcome signs that describe Kirtland as a community of "faith and beauty."

On August 19, 1984, Jeffrey Lundgren and his family turned onto State Highway 306, the last leg of their move from Independence to Kirtland. They had been traveling on Interstate 90, a restless major east-west thoroughfare that runs parallel to the southern shoreline of Lake Erie and connects Cleveland with the myriad of bedroom communities to its east. Had Jeffrey turned left when he exited the bustling interstate, he would have driven into Mentor, a sister-city to Kirtland, and a much larger and more prosperous mecca of strip zoning. Mentor is everything that Kirtland has avoided: neon-lighted fast-food eateries, budget hotels, and sprawling shopping malls. But Jeffrey had turned right and bypassed Mentor. The Lundgrens' car had swooped down a steep hill and crossed the bridge that spans the eastern branch of the Chagrin River where Sidney Rigdon first baptized Mormon converts. As their station wagon sputtered up the incline on the southern bank, Jeffrey gazed through the windshield at a sight that brought tears to his eyes and caused Alice to whisper a quick "Praise God!"

The "House of the Lord" towered before them, its white walls glistening in the afternoon sun as light reflected off the slivers of broken china mixed in the exterior stucco. Joseph Smith, Jr., had chosen this location on the northern tip and highest hill in Kirtland because he wanted the Gentiles in Mentor, which even in the early 1830s was considered a much more worldly place than Kirtland, to see the kerosene lamps burning inside the temple at night. Like a lighthouse beacon, the church would pierce the darkness and silently witness to the world that God's "only true church" was standing watch and eagerly awaiting Jesus Christ's imminent return.

A one-story clapboard building identified as the VISITORS' CENTER was located a few hundred feet from the temple's front doors. Directly across Chillicothe Road from the temple was the red-brick Kirtland RLDS Church and next to that building was a large house where Sidney Rigdon had once lived.

Eleanor Lord was the first to welcome the Lundgrens when Jeffrey stepped into the visitors' center, causing a bell dangling from the door to jingle. She and her husband, Bill, were in charge of the temple staff, although there really wasn't much of one to oversee. Besides the Lords, there was another retired couple who gave tours, and during summer months, three or four college students were paid by the church to help out.

An attractive, gracious woman in her mid-sixties, Eleanor explained with a bit of embarrassment that Bill was running an errand and she didn't know where he had left the keys for the church-provided house where the Lundgrens would live. It was a two-story house, circa 1950, built right next to the visitors' center. Like all of the other temple property, it was painted white. Jeffrey didn't want to wait for Bill, so he jimmied open a window and Damon crawled through and unlocked the doors. Alice almost began to cry when she stepped inside. "We discovered the church was a slumlord," Jeffrey later recalled.

"Alice, you got to give me a couple of weeks," said Jeffrey optimistically. "We'll get it into shape. I promise."

By the time they had unloaded the trailer, Bill showed up and quickly invited them to a backyard cookout that he and Eleanor were hosting the next day in appreciation of the four college students who had spent their summer as temple tour guides. Jeffrey accepted the invitation and then asked: "When can I start work?"

The question surprised Bill, who had figured that the Lundgrens would need at least a week to get settled. But Jeffrey didn't want to waste time. "I'd like to learn how to give tours as quickly as I can." At Bill's urging, he agreed to wait for at least a day.

The next morning while Alice unpacked, Jeffrey took his children for a ride. Less than an hour later, he returned home and burst inside.

"I want you to go with me now!" he exclaimed. "You've got to see what I've found!"

They left Damon in charge of the others and drove to Chapin Forest. "Look at that!" Jeffrey said excitedly after he parked the car. "Over there!"

Alice saw a pond shrouded by trees and a footpath.

"That's it!" Jeffrey said. "The path in my dream. The path that I walk down to get the plates. C'mon."

He hustled her to it and then suddenly stopped. "Do you feel something?" he asked. Without waiting for a reply, Jeffrey told Alice that most of the rock used in the foundation of the Kirtland temple had been cut here in Chapin Forest.

"This feels like hallowed ground," said Jeffrey.

"I was thinking the exact same thing," Alice replied.

"Remember how I said the path was by a little stream, and a highway, and how there was a bar nearby? Look, look, look!"

The path in the park was next to a brook that ran parallel to Chillicothe Road. Through the trees, Jeffrey could see a building, which he told Alice was a local bar and restaurant called PJ's Pub.

"Joseph left something for me here," he said. "I'm sure of it."

"Oh, Jeff, this is so exciting," Alice replied. "Do you really sense that?"

The comment irritated him. Why did she always doubt him? They walked down the path for several minutes, but they didn't find anything so they returned home for lunch.

Later that day, Jeffrey, Alice, and their children went to the cookout across the street at the Sidney Rigdon house where Bill and Eleanor Lord lived.

"I remember watching them as they came up the driveway," Eleanor later said. "I remember thinking how happy I was that they had come. It was so unusual for someone so young to be able to work as tour guides. I felt they would bring a youthful vitality to the temple."

Neither Jeffrey nor Alice mentioned their experience in Chapin Forest, nor did they volunteer much information about themselves. Instead, they quietly ate their hamburgers and potato salad and let Bill and Eleanor do the talking. They were a devout and kindhearted couple. Bill had worked for U.S. Steel and later as a maintenance supervisor at a college in Long Island, New York, before retiring in 1981. At age sixty-five, he was a small, thin-framed man with close-cropped hair, metal glasses, a quick laugh, and ready smile. His grandfather had been a fervent Methodist minister, but his parents hadn't seen much use in religion and neither had Bill as a teenager. But when he was in his twenties, a friend gave him a copy of the Book of Mormon and he converted.

Eleanor had grown up in the RLDS and it was one of two great passions in her life. Her other love had been the stage. When she was twenty-two, Eleanor was living in New York and trying to decide whether she should be a music teacher or audition for roles on Broadway. During a prayer meeting, an elder told her that God had a message for her. God wanted Eleanor to use her talents in His service. Eleanor interpreted that to mean that she should forsake the stage and teach music. "From that point on, I offered my talent to the Lord and within six months all of that burning desire to be onstage was gone," she recalled. "I felt a wonderful peace with God." She and Bill had met shortly after that and married in 1953. The church had been the focal point of their lives, and after Bill retired they decided to become temple tour guides to, as Bill put it, "give something back to the Lord." The Lords had studied their church's history and were familiar with the stories about Joseph Smith, Jr.'s treasure hunting and alleged attempts to seduce Sidney Rigdon's daughter. But such talk didn't shake their belief in the validity of the Book of Mormon. "There is just too much in it to be the creation of a boy's imagination," Eleanor explained. Besides, she asked, who were they to question why God had chosen Joseph Smith, Jr., as His prophet? Hadn't God blessed King David even after he committed adultery with Bathsheba and arranged for her husband, Uriah, to be killed?

As the two couples became better acquainted that night, Bill asked Jeffrey how he could afford to work as an unpaid tour guide at such a young age. Jeffrey said that his grandparents were giving him $800 per month as part of his inheritance, and then he quickly changed the subject by asking Bill questions about the temple, visitors' center, and tour-guide job. About 25,000 persons toured the temple each year, Bill said. No one was ever permitted to go inside unless a guide was with them. There was always a chance that some anti-Mormon visitor might deface the temple. Before each tour, visitors were shown a fifteen-minute slide show in the visitors' center that explained the highlights of Joseph Smith, Jr.'s life and how the temple was built. After that, a tour guide led the visitors into the temple.

The tours always began in the temple vestibule, a narrow room in the front of the building. It was there that guides would explain that the temple contained three floors. The bottom floor, called the lower court, was used as a sanctuary; the second floor, which was nearly identical to the lower court, had been built as a school for priests; the attic story with its dormer windows made up the third floor. It was divided into a series of rooms which could be used either as offices or for classes. There was also a steeple and belfry complete with a weather vane whose tip was one hundred twenty feet above ground. One of the first features of the temple that the guides would mention was how the three floors were connected. There were two winding staircases on each side of the vestibule and there were exactly thirty-three steps between each floor—"One step for each year of Christ's life," said Bill.

The temple was a jumble of architectural styles: Greek Revival, Georgian, Colonial, Federalist, and Gothic. The most curious designs inside were the intricate decorative carvings on the columns, doors, and moldings. Guides often speculated about what these hand-carved designs represented.

The tours always ended exactly where they had started—in the church's entryway, where visitors, if they felt so inclined, could make a cash donation to the temple.

When Jeffrey wasn't giving a tour, he would sit inside the visitors' center where souvenirs and religious books and pamphlets were for sale. The most expensive item was the Holy Scriptures, Joseph Smith Jr.'s rewritten version of the Bible, which sold for twenty-six dollars.

After the Lundgrens had gone home that night, Bill told Eleanor that he felt Jeffrey should be given some sort of responsibility besides being a tour guide because he was younger and eager to prove himself. "I think I'll put him in charge of the financial records," Bill said. The temple generated at least $20,000 per year in souvenir sales and offerings.

"Yes," Eleanor agreed. "That would be a good job for him."

The next morning, Bill gave Jeffrey a copy of the standardized speech that tour guides used, issued him a set of keys to the temple, and told him that besides his regular duties, he would be in charge of collecting the offerings left at the temple and keeping track of sales at the visitors' center.

A few nights later, when Bill and Eleanor went for a walk after dinner, they noticed that someone was inside the temple even though it was closed. Bill was about to telephone the police, when he thought of Jeffrey. He decided to investigate and found Jeffrey inside the temple.

"I didn't mean to worry you," Jeffrey said. "It's just that I want to investigate every nook and cranny in this place." Bill didn't complain. When he and Eleanor resumed their walk, Bill remarked that he had never seen anyone so enthusiastic when it came to learning about the House of the Lord. Eleanor agreed. "They are an answer to our prayers," she said.

Chapter 14

FOUR days after the Lundgrens arrived in Kirtland, Cheryl Avery knocked on their front door. She and Dennis and their three daughters had come to visit. Jeffrey was not happy to see them, but Alice invited them in. The Averys were planning on staying the weekend. Cheryl was distressed. She and Dennis had gone to a Wednesday night prayer meeting at Slover Park and hadn't felt comfortable. She still couldn't get over the fact that the church had decided to ordain women. She and Dennis had talked about leaving the RLDS. But where could they go? No other denomination believed in the Book of Mormon except for the Utah Mormons and they were considered worse heretics than other Protestants.

Jeffrey took the Averys on a tour of the temple. Although he was only beginning to investigate the building, he said he'd already made two important discoveries. "God, Himself, was the architect of this temple," he explained solemnly. "It is the only temple in the world that we know was designed by Him." According to historical records, Joseph Smith, Jr., Sidney Rigdon, and church member Frederick G. Williams saw a vision of the temple while they were praying in the summer of 1833. The temple was constructed, under Smith's direction, based on that vision. The fact that God had shown Smith how to construct the temple was extremely significant, Jeffrey said. "By studying it, we can see how God thinks." It was the same logic that Jeffrey had applied to his studies of the Book of Mormon. Why had God decided to use a specific word in a parable? Why had God designed a temple with two separate front doors? "The entire building is a clue."

Jeffrey's second discovery was a carving in the temple. He had found it on a pulpit used by a priest. "This is the symbol of man," Jeffrey said. "Every book about symbols says that this design means man. I have searched and searched and there is no symbol on any of the pulpits for woman. None." To Jeffrey, the message was clear: "God never intended for women to be ordained as priests; otherwise he would have put the symbol for woman on a pulpit."

Dennis and Cheryl were astounded. It was just like the Old Testament story in Daniel, Cheryl said, where King Belshazzar blasphemed God by using the Hebrews' sacred vessels from their temple as wine goblets at a feast. The fingers of a man's hand had suddenly appeared and the hand had written a strange warning to the king on the palace wall. Only the prophet Daniel could interpret the strange writings. In Cheryl's mind the fact that God had once communicated with men by writing a message on King Belshazzar's wall was prima facie evidence that He might have included a few messages on the walls and pulpits of the Kirtland temple.

The Averys' reaction was so enthusiastic that Jeffrey decided to tell them about his dream and the path that he had found in Chapin Forest, but first he swore them to secrecy. When he finished, Dennis asked Jeffrey what the dream meant. "I'm not certain," Jeffrey said, "but clearly the RLDS is without a prophet and God is going to bring forth a new one to preach the truth."

Dennis and Cheryl asked Jeffrey to show them the path in Chapin Forest, so Jeffrey and Alice drove them to the park.

But when they got there, Dennis began complaining about how cold it was outside and Cheryl slipped on a wet stone and fell, hurting her hip. Jeffrey grew impatient and the enthusiasm that the two couples had felt at the temple waned. They returned to the Lundgrens' for dinner. After everyone had gone to bed that night, Jeffrey told Alice that he didn't think Dennis's chill and Cheryl's fall were accidents. "God was keeping them from walking down the path," he said. "The Lord doesn't want them to know the truth."

The rest of that weekend, as far as Jeffrey was concerned, was unbearable. "All the Averys did was complain about life," said Jeffrey. "They were not people we would have sought out as friends."

The relationship between the Lundgrens and the Averys had always struck people who knew them as odd. Behind their backs, Jeffrey and Alice constantly belittled the Averys. And yet the Averys often described the Lundgrens as their best friends.

To most, Dennis and Cheryl seemed strange. Dennis was mousy. Cheryl was uncomfortable around strangers. Neither dressed fashionably or was good at small talk. Cheryl had grown up in Centralia, Washington, a town of about 10,000 south of Tacoma. She had never really known her own father, Hiram Clisby. He had been in the merchant marine during the 1940s when he met and married Donna, Cheryl's mother. At the time, Donna was working in Yakima, a town in central Washington, and living with her aunt. She had gone to college for one year, but was forced to drop out because she couldn't afford tuition. Donna met Hiram at an RLDS church meeting. They met, married, and then just as quickly, Hiram left for sea, leaving his bride behind at her aunt's house pregnant with their first child. Lance Clisby was born in 1945. Two years later, when Cheryl was born, Donna was still living with her aunt waiting for Hiram to finish another one of his Pacific voyages. In January 1948, Donna filed for divorce and moved with her two children to Centralia to live with her parents. Cheryl was seven months old. Two years later, Donna married Howard Bailey, a carpenter and general handyman. They moved into a house just across the railroad tracks from where her parents lived, only a block away from the RLDS church. Donna gave birth to another son, Donald, in 1951. By that time, Cheryl was four. "We never had much money," Donna recalled. "We were almost on welfare sometimes, particularly in the winter when my husband was off work. But Cheryl never seemed to mind."

As a youngster, Cheryl's closest friends were her two brothers. "Cheryl was very loyal to Lance, in particular," her mother said. "They'd walk to school together even when both of them were in high school. She helped out Donald too, even though he was younger. She was almost like a mother to both of the boys."

Cheryl didn't participate in many high school activities after school. She didn't date, didn't give a hoot about being popular, and really had only one close friend: Barbara Carter. "Cheryl wasn't ever a goofy person—even as a teenager," Carter recalled. "She didn't go crazy over the Beatles and didn't care a bit about boys, like most of us. She was uncomplicated, stubborn, modest, and serious." When Carter had a slumber party for her sixteenth birthday, she invited Cheryl. It was the first sleep-over that Cheryl had ever attended. No one had ever invited her before.

Carter knew that Cheryl was deeply religious although she rarely mentioned it. She didn't drink alcohol, didn't smoke, never used profanity, and considered makeup, trips to the beauty parlor, and fancy clothes to be worldly vanities. "I remember when all the girls began wearing nylon stockings and flats in high school," Carter recalled. Cheryl continued to wear white bobby socks and saddle oxfords. "She simply wore what she wanted to wear, without being influenced by others' opinions," said Carter.

When Cheryl graduated in 1965, a teacher called her by the last name of Clisby, not Bailey. Carter was surprised. "Although I was her closest friend, she had never told me that Mr. Bailey was not her father. Even after this revelation, Cheryl supplied no details and was very angry that her real name had been divulged. She was a very, very private person."

After high school, Cheryl enrolled at a community college in Centralia, but didn't like it. She was even more out of sync in college than she had been in high school. It was the dawning of the Age of Aquarius, the antiwar movement was just getting started, feminists were burning their bras. By contrast, Cheryl's favorite movie star was John Wayne. Her favorite song was Tennessee Ernie Ford's "Sixteen Tons." She had never been out on a date. Cheryl stayed in school one semester and then transferred to Graceland, the RLDS's conservative college.

Located about four miles from the Iowa-Missouri state line in tiny Lamoni, Graceland had an enrollment of eight hundred, nearly all white students from middle-class homes. Cheryl arrived for the spring term in 1966 and was assigned to a room in "Kimball Manor," a fancy name for the third floor of the women's dormitory. At Graceland, each floor had its own name to give the dormitory a more homelike atmosphere. Ann Sherman, a shy freshman from Independence, lived down the hall, and the two women became friends. During spring break, Ann invited Cheryl home with her. Cheryl had never been to Independence. She loved it, and Ann's parents, Robert and Velma, adored Cheryl. Ann was an only child. "We liked to joke that we were the sister that neither of us ever had, but both wanted," Sherman later remembered. "We both felt the same way about most things."

The Shermans were not wealthy. Robert made his living by refinishing furniture. Velma was a secretary. But they were devout RLDS members, and when the spring semester ended and they learned that Cheryl might not be able to return to Graceland in the fall because of money problems, Robert and Velma decided to help. They invited Cheryl to spend the summer with them and Robert found her a job as a clerk at a Montgomery Ward store. Cheryl faithfully saved her earnings, but when it was time to enroll at Graceland, she still was short of cash. The Shermans wanted to help her, but they couldn't afford to pay for both girls to attend Graceland. Ann unselfishly suggested that she and Cheryl transfer to Central Missouri State University in Warrensburg, the same school that Jeffrey and Alice would later attend. Cheryl agreed and the Shermans had enough to pay for both women's tuition. Ann and Cheryl roomed together. "The school cafeteria didn't serve Sunday supper and neither of us had much money so we would buy a can of spaghetti and heat it up and for dessert we would have baby food—a little jar of pudding or peach cobbler," Ann Sherman remembered.

Although Cheryl would sometimes tag along with Ann and her boyfriend to a football game, Cheryl didn't go out on dates. She wasn't unattractive, but she was plain and she did little to enhance her appearance. She had a round face and black wavy hair that had first started showing streaks of gray in college. She wore it cut short and most mornings simply brushed it. "I let it do what it wants to do," she often joked, "because it will do that anyway." She was five feet three inches tall, weighed one hundred and thirteen pounds, and had a nice figure, but even when she was in her early twenties, Cheryl had a matron's air to her. Finding a husband wasn't as important as earning a college degree in elementary education. "Cheryl was a very determined person," said Ann. "If she wanted something done, she went out and did it and if you got in her way, tough luck."

During Labor Day weekend in September 1969, Ann and Cheryl attended a weekend church retreat for singles held at a campground in Excelsior Springs north of Independence. The men and women were paired off on Saturday night so that they could get to know each other. Cheryl was matched with Dennis Avery. Despite Ann's probing later that night, Cheryl didn't say much about Dennis. But that weekend, he called. They went to church together. She was twenty-two. It was her first date and it was his first date too. He was twenty-nine. Eight months later they were married. The wedding was held on May 29, 1970. They picked that date because Cheryl's birthday was May 27 and Dennis's birthday was May 28. They figured it would be easy for them to remember their May 29 wedding anniversary.

Donna Bailey came to Independence for her daughter's wedding. "I was let down when I first saw Dennis. I had been introduced to Ann Sherman's boyfriend and I remember thinking, 'Why couldn't Cheryl get someone like him instead of someone like Dennis?,' but I changed my mind after I got to know him and realized what a kind person he was."

Dennis didn't make a good first impression. A neighbor of the Averys would later tell a reporter for the Cleveland *Plain Dealer* that Dennis was "the typical nerd, with his pocket protector and everything." He was a small-framed man, standing only five feet seven inches, weighing less than one hundred twenty-five pounds. Yet in photographs, he seemed to be overweight and to have a double chin. He slumped, wore thick glasses with self-darkening lenses, had a receding hairline, and seemed, according to several who knew him, to be rather slow-witted except when it came to quoting scriptures. Dennis pored over his Bible and the Book of Mormon. There wasn't a time in Dennis's life when the RLDS wasn't important to him.

The oldest of four children, Dennis grew up in Baldwin Park, a suburb of Los Angeles, where his father worked at a company that manufactured electrical medical equipment. His mother stayed at home until her children were grown. Then she became a librarian. She had been raised in the RLDS. His father was a convert. Their family life revolved around the church and Dennis never questioned his faith.

Like Cheryl, Dennis was always serious. As a child, he was chosen to appear on *The Art Linkletter Show*. Along with four other children, he was interviewed by Art during a segment called "Kids Say the Darndest Things." Dennis gave short, somber replies that didn't spark many laughs. Art quickly moved on.

At Baldwin Park High School, Dennis was later remembered as one of those students who passed through unnoticed. "He was not someone who stuck in your mind," said a classmate who graduated with Dennis in 1958. After graduation, Dennis worked as a clerk at a bank and then landed a job in the mail room at Edwards Air Force Base. "He never did go off, like some youth in the area, with those who were protesting back in the sixties," Lois Hartnet, an elder at the Covina RLDS congregation, later told reporters. "He was a dependable churchgoer who lived a good, puritanical life-style." Dennis lived with his parents for eleven years after high school. When he finally decided in 1969 to move out, he decided to "gather" to Independence. He rented a room from a family and a short time later met Cheryl.

Dennis couldn't afford a honeymoon. He didn't own a car. Money was a problem. It always would be. Dennis worked nights at the Centerre Bank in Kansas City, where he ran a machine that sorted canceled checks. He would eventually work there for seventeen years, and during that time, he would never be promoted to a better job nor earn more than $24,000 per year. "He was a pleasant fellow," said a fellow employee, "but he had absolutely no ambition. I think he was scared to try new things. I always thought he was rather simpleminded, but one day he began talking about religion and he really knew his scriptures."

Each year, Barbara Carter received a Christmas card from Cheryl. "She would talk about how poor they were. She wasn't complaining, it was just a fact. No matter how hard they tried, they always were broke."

Cheryl taught school after she got married. But she quit when their daughter, Trina Denise, was born on March 7, 1974. They had another daughter, Rebecca Lynn, on January 23, 1976. Shortly after that Dennis suffered from prostate and urinary problems and didn't think that he could father any more children. But on August 3, 1982, Karen Diane was born. Dennis and Cheryl called her their "miracle" baby.

No one was certain why Dennis and Cheryl decided to attend the Slover Park congregation because they clearly didn't fit in. Cheryl either made her family's clothing or bought it secondhand at a Salvation Army store. "I think one of the reasons why the Averys latched onto Jeffrey and Alice was because they were nicer to them than most people in the church," recalled Georgia Milliren. "The Averys were not particularly easy to like. They were wimpy, mousy people and a lot of members just simply avoided them."

When Cheryl first mentioned Jeffrey Lundgren in a letter to her mother, Donna was pleasantly surprised. She knew his mother. Lois had lived in Centralia with her parents, Alva and Maude Gadberry, for a short time. She and Donna had been in the same Sunday school class as children. It was one of those ironic twists of fate, Donna told Cheryl, that frequently happened in the close world of the RLDS saints.

Even though Jeffrey and Alice complained about the Averys, they did nothing to sever the friendship. When Cheryl had to go into the hospital for an appendectomy, it was Alice who volunteered to prepare a meal for Dennis and his girls. Later, she got Tonya Patrick to go with her to tidy up the Averys' house before

Cheryl came home. The place was filthy and cluttered with junk. There were holes in the walls, the toilet was leaking water, the yard needed to be weeded and mowed. A storm had damaged the roof and the roofers had simply tossed the old shingles down on the grass when they made the repairs. Dennis hadn't bothered to pick them up. Nor did he volunteer to help the women clean. Instead, he sat in his easy chair as they worked around him. When it was lunchtime, he told his daughters to make him a sandwich and bring it to him. Tonya was exhausted and irritated when she got home later that night. She told her husband that Dennis Avery was the laziest man that she'd ever met.

At Slover Park, there were lots of other stories about the Averys. One church member recalled how he had stopped by the Averys' house on a particularly cold winter night and found their living room icy cold. "Dennis was sitting in his chair complaining about how cold it was, so I looked around and noticed that someone had closed the air vents in the room. There was no way for warm air to blow inside. I said, 'Well, Dennis, here's your problem—someone closed your vents. Just open them up.' What amazed me was that he knew the vents were closed! He said, 'Oh, I just haven't had time to get around to opening them.' That family spent the entire winter freezing in the living room because he was too lazy to open the vents!"

Another church member recalled how she had gotten a panicky telephone call from Cheryl one night. "What do you use to get orange juice off the floor?" she asked. The church member suggested a well-known cleaner. "Oh, that's wonderful," Cheryl replied. She explained that one of the girls had spilled the juice four days earlier. "Cheryl had been fretting the entire time about what to use to get it up. She couldn't make up her mind," the woman recalled. "I often wondered how either of them ever made it in this world."

Ann Sherman would recall Cheryl and Dennis much less critically. "Cheryl was definitely the strong one in the family, and sometimes she would complain about Dennis because he didn't help out much around the house. But he wasn't lazy. He went to work faithfully. The thing about Dennis was that he had an easygoing nature about him. He didn't get real concerned about most things and he didn't always follow through on things once he got started." Years later, Ann would also recall that Dennis seemed to withdraw even further after he befriended Jeffrey and Alice. "He sort of adopted an attitude that the Lord will provide. He felt the Lord was directing his life, almost to the point that he didn't have to do anything in terms of planning. It was like he was depending on God to figure out a way to make things happen. That was kind of his philosophy. God was in charge."

Donna Bailey also saw a change in her daughter once she and Dennis became friends with the Lundgrens. Cheryl and Dennis became "fanatical," she said. "Cheryl had always studied her scriptures, but she was reading them over and over and over again." When the RLDS held its controversial worldwide conference in April 1984, Cheryl asked Donna if she would come to Independence to baby-sit for her granddaughters. She and Dennis wanted to attend the debate at the conference about ordaining women into the priesthood. Neither Cheryl nor Dennis told Donna the entire reason why they wanted her there. Both of them felt that a vote in favor of letting women become priests would be a clear signal that Satan had successfully steered the RLDS away from God's truth. Dennis even speculated that God might respond by bringing the earth to an end. If that happened, Dennis and Cheryl wanted Donna to be with their daughters.

Donna agreed to make the trip, but before she left for Independence, she received a letter from her daughter that troubled her. "Cheryl told me that she and Dennis had decided that their girls couldn't watch television anymore and she said that they were against playing cards too." Donna and her husband both liked to watch television and play cards. Donna decided to telephone Cheryl.

"Won't you make an exception for Dad's sake?" Donna asked.

"No," said Cheryl. No television. No card playing. Donna agreed to baby-sit anyway. "Cheryl and Dennis were heartbroken when the church decided to ordain women," she recalled. "Cheryl told me that there was only one man at Slover Park who was brave enough to tell the truth and oppose women being ordained. That was Jeffrey, and she said that he had told her that he had gotten death threats because of what he preached."

Unlike the Lundgrens, Dennis and Cheryl enjoyed their weekend visit in Kirtland during August 1984. They returned to Independence electrified about what Jeffrey had showed them in the Kirtland temple. Cheryl was so excited that she wrote her mother a long letter. Because Jeffrey had sworn her to secrecy, she didn't mention Jeffrey's dream, the path in Chapin Forest, or how God was going to choose a new prophet to replace Wallace B. Smith. But she did mention that she had, at last, found someone who could give her the "answers" that she had been seeking. There was something about Jeffrey Lundgren, she wrote, that was special.

Chapter 15

JEFFREY'S discovery of a symbol for man, but not for woman, convinced him that he was on the right track. But the temple was filled with other carvings and no one knew what they meant. During his first two weeks on the job, Jeffrey went through all the historical records in the temple archives. He'd even got Eleanor Lord to check art books at the local libraries. But the meaning of most designs remained a mystery. In October, Jeffrey learned that Raymond Treat was lecturing for several nights at an RLDS church in Pittsburgh. As always, Ray was talking about similarities that he had found between the Nephites and Lamanites in the Book of Mormon and the Maya culture in Mesoamerica. Jeffrey figured that Ray might be able to identify some of the symbols in the temple because he was a trained archaeologist. So Jeffrey and Alice drove to Pennsylvania to listen to Ray's speech. It wasn't too different from the one that Jeffrey had first heard at the Slover Park congregation in 1982, but as Jeffrey watched the color slides of Maya ruins, he noticed that a few of them contained symbols that looked to him like those in the Kirtland temple. After

Ray completed his speech, Jeffrey introduced himself and explained how it was Ray who had first gotten him excited about reading the Book of Mormon. Jeffrey then mentioned that several of the designs in the Kirtland temple seemed similar to those in Ray's slides. Ray was intrigued.

Although there was some printed material available before 1830 about archaeological discoveries in Mesoamerica, Ray was confident that Joseph Smith, Jr., and other early Mormons in Kirtland would not have known about the Maya. If Maya symbols were in the temple, then Ray would be able to add another bit of proof to his theory that the Mormon religion and the Maya were somehow linked. He told Jeffrey that he would gladly drive to Kirtland the next morning to look at the symbols. Another man joined Ray and Jeffrey as they talked. Tom Miller had accompanied Ray from Independence to Pittsburgh. Tom was an elder in the church and was interested in seeing the temple too.

When the two men arrived in Kirtland the next day, Jeffrey hustled them into the temple and Ray carefully examined all of the symbols. He agreed that some seemed similar to those found in Mesoamerica, but he couldn't be certain until he had done more research. Tom was impressed by Jeffrey. "He clearly had a special understanding about the temple," he later recalled. "Jeffrey was seeing things there that others had missed." Both men found Jeffrey's discovery of the symbol for man interesting, especially Tom. He had been a delegate at the 1984 world conference and had personally felt that women shouldn't be ordained. Yet, when it came time for a vote, he had raised his hand in favor of permitting women to be priests simply because all those around him had raised their hands. Now he was certain that his decision had been a mistake.

After the tour, Jeffrey invited Ray and Tom to his house to meet Alice and talk more about the temple. Within an hour, Jeffrey and Tom were, as Alice later put it, "clicking like crazy." Tom was well versed in the scriptures and there was an authority to his voice when he spoke, partly because of his background. At age thirty-eight, Tom had worked as a police officer and as a game warden. But he had eventually quit both jobs, he explained, because of "politics." Tom prided himself on being a man who didn't "kiss up" to anyone. If he thought that his boss was doing something stupid, he told him so.

Tom and Ray had met at a church service in Independence and become friends. Ray had invited Tom to come with him to Pittsburgh because Tom was between jobs. His wife, Patti, worked at a medical lab in Independence.

Jeffrey decided to take Ray and Tom to Chapin Forest so they could see where the stones used in the foundation of the temple had been cut. He told them that he felt that the quarry area was hallowed ground, but he didn't tell either of them about his dream or the significance of the footpath. As they walked down the path, Tom spotted several holes that had been drilled into stones in the creek bed that ran adjacent to the path. Tom's college degree was in agronomy and he told Ray and Jeffrey that in the 1800s, stonemasons frequently cut stones in a quarry by drilling a line of holes in them. The holes would be four or five inches apart. The masons would then fill the holes with water and when it froze, the water would expand and cause the stone to crack along the line of holes. "These holes were probably made by the men who built the temple," he said.

Jeffrey, Tom, and Ray climbed down a small embankment to get a closer look at the holes in the creek bed. It was about a five-foot drop to the stream from the path. After the men examined the holes, they turned around and started to climb back up the embankment, but Tom suddenly stopped. "Hey! Look at this!" he hollered. Part of the embankment was made of stone—the same gray stone found in the creek bed and the temple foundation—and someone had drilled nearly a dozen holes into it. These holes, however, were different from the ones in the creek bed. They were nearly twice as large and they had been drilled at angles and in a circular pattern. Each hole looked as if it eventually met the others somewhere deep inside the rock.

"Why would someone drill there?" Jeffrey asked.

Tom put his mouth against one of the holes and blew into it. There was no resistance. "There's got to be a chamber in there," he announced. Tom Miller would later recall during an interview the excitement that he felt that afternoon in October 1984. "We broke off a branch and stuck it in one of the holes and we never hit the end," he said. "Man-oh-man, we were really having fun. The more we talked, the more convinced we all became that we had really found something. We speculated that these were air holes that led to some secret chamber. The next thing we knew, we were convincing ourselves that Joseph Smith, Jr., had hidden something in this chamber—gold plates probably. We were on a roll." Tom decided to ask God if there was a hidden chamber behind the stone. He left Jeffrey and Ray and walked down the path to pray alone. "I can't tell you now whether I wanted to see something so bad that I imagined it or whether I truly had a vision that day," Tom said later. "But I came back to Jeff and Ray and I said, 'My understanding is that there is a chamber hidden here and there are gold plates hidden in it.'"

Ray and Tom needed to get back to Pittsburgh for Ray's lecture that night, but they promised to return to Kirtland the next day. After they had gone, Jeffrey told Alice about Tom's statements in the park. It fit perfectly with his dream. They began speculating about what might be hidden there. The Book of Mormon contained plenty of stories about brass and gold plates that had never been found. There was another mystical artifact mentioned in the book that had vanished centuries ago. It was a magnificent gold-and-jeweled sword known as the Sword of Laban, and it played a role in one of the most important and controversial stories in the Book of Mormon. According to the Mormon scriptures, God told a Hebrew prophet named Lehi that He wanted him to leave Jerusalem and go to the New World. But Lehi didn't want to make the journey without several brass plates that contained the genealogy of his family. The plates were being held by a man named Laban, so Lehi sent his son, Nephi, to fetch them. Laban, however, refused to give up the plates and no matter what Lehi offered him, he wouldn't budge. One night Nephi decided to make a final attempt at getting the plates. He went to talk to Laban and found him drunk. Nephi also spotted Laban's magnificent gold sword.

According to the Mormon scriptures, God told Nephi to kill Laban, but Nephi hesitated because he knew that murder was wrong.

And it came to pass that the Spirit said unto me again, "Slay him, for the Lord hath delivered him into thy hands. *Behold the Lord slayeth the wicked to bring forth his righteous purposes.*"

Nephi grabbed Laban by his hair and cut off his head with the golden sword. He then took the brass plates and the sword with him. Although the sword appeared in other passages in the Book of Mormon, it wasn't clear what finally happened to it, and over time it developed into a symbol of mystical power. In December 1836, for example, the sword was mentioned in a prophecy that Joseph Smith, Sr., the father of the Mormon prophet, said in the Kirtland temple on behalf of his grandson, Joseph Smith III. [It was Joseph Smith III who eventually became the leader of the RLDS Church.] The senior Smith prophesied that his grandson would someday "have power to wield the Sword of Laban." From that point on, the sword became synonymous with the leadership of the church. As with the mythical Excalibur that young Arthur pulled from the stone, proving that he was the rightful heir to the English throne, Jeffrey believed God would permit only His chosen prophet to wield the Sword of Laban. Obviously, if someone found the sword, he would automatically be declared the church's true prophet. At least that is what Jeffrey thought.

"Do you think it could really be hidden in the park?" Alice asked.

Jeffrey was sure of it. He showed Alice a map of New York and drew a line from the spot where Joseph Smith, Jr., said he found the golden plates to the Kirtland temple. The line went directly through Chapin Forest. "It's entirely possible that the angel Moroni hid the Sword of Laban and other golden plates in a secret chamber in Chapin Forest while he was alive and on his way to New York to hide the other golden plates," Jeffrey said.

"Do you think you can find it?" Alice asked.

Jeffrey wasn't sure, but he intended to try.

The next morning, Alice told Jeffrey that she had something important to share with him.

"I had a dream last night," she gushed. "You were standing

in the temple and a tall thin man was on your right and a shorter, more muscular man was on your left. I was sitting in the temple in the back row and when I looked up, there was this beam of pure white light coming down on the three of you and it was so white and so intense that all I could see was the outline of you three and then a pure white personage appeared and talked to you and exchanged something with the three of you. I couldn't quite make out who it was until I saw his hands."

"Who was he?" Jeffrey asked.

"His hands had nail prints in them," Alice said, her eyes filling with tears. "It was Jesus, Jeffrey! Jesus appeared to you!"

She was certain, she added, that the two men in her dream with Jeffrey were Ray Treat and Tom Miller.

"Oh, Jeffrey," she continued. "This is just like the patriarch said it would be. God wants you to bring forth a great message. He wants you to prepare the way for Christ's return."

That night, Ray and Tom again drove to Kirtland from Pittsburgh. Alice didn't mention her dream and Jeffrey didn't mention his theory about the Sword of Laban. If it was there, he was going to find it by himself.

The three men ended up talking about the symbols in the temple just as they had the day before, and then Jeffrey suggested that the three of them spend the night at the temple praying. If they did, perhaps God would show them a sign. Ray and Tom agreed to stay over. Jeffrey was excited. He had successfully set the stage for Alice's dream to come true.

"All of them expected something to happen that night," said Alice. The three men prayed and meditated until three in the morning, but despite their efforts, nothing happened.

"So much for your dream," Jeffrey told Alice the next morning.

Ray and Tom returned to Pittsburgh and Ray taught his last class that night. The next afternoon, he and Tom left for Independence. They stopped in Kirtland around dinnertime to say good-bye to Jeffrey and Alice. Jeffrey invited them in and both men were shocked when they saw what the family was having for dinner. All the Lundgrens had to eat was a basket of biscuits. It looked as if there was only enough for one biscuit per person.

"We had asked Jeff earlier how he survived and he had told us that he depended on the Lord to feed his family," said Tom. "It was pretty clear that they were broke and the kids were hungry."

Even though Tom was unemployed and strapped for cash, he gave one hundred dollars to Jeffrey. Ray added another hundred. Jeffrey thanked both of them and they left. A few miles outside of Kirtland, Tom began to feel uneasy. He and Ray had told Jeffrey that they would be stopping by their house around dinnertime, and for a brief moment, he wondered if Jeffrey hadn't staged the dinner-table scene. There was something about how he and Ray had gotten there at exactly the same moment that Jeffrey and Alice were sitting down at the table. It all seemed too perfect. But then Tom pushed his suspicions out of his mind. It was his old police training, he decided.

Saints were supposed to trust each other.

Chapter 16

ALICE would claim later that she never knew that Ray and Tom had given Jeffrey money. She never knew where any of Jeffrey's money came from, she said. She never asked. The $1,500 that she and Jeffrey had raised to finance their move to Kirtland was quickly spent. The church didn't pay Jeffrey. He didn't have any obvious financial support. Yet whenever Alice and Jeffrey went to the grocery store or to buy clothing, he would pull a five, ten, or twenty dollar bill from his pocket. "I just assumed that the Lord was providing," she later claimed.

Had she asked, Jeffrey was ready with a heart-tugging story. "We ran out of money almost immediately," he later recalled.

"There wasn't any food in the house and everyone was hungry. It was just about dinnertime when two elderly ladies knocked on the door and I explained to them that the temple was closed. But they had driven a long distance, so I decided to break the rules and let them in. They were inside the temple for only about fifteen minutes, but when they came out, they were crying and one of them took my hand to shake it and when I took her hand, I felt paper. 'This is for you,' she said. 'God made me aware that you need this.' I didn't look at it until she had gone. It was a one-hundred-dollar bill and that is what we lived on that week. The rules said we were supposed to turn in all the money that we received. But she had told me that God wanted *me* to have it and that's how I operated. If people said it was for me, I kept it. God had directed me here. He wanted me to do His business, so I expected Him to take care of me and my family."

In October, a group of priesthood members from upstate New York held a weekend retreat at the temple. Most arrived Friday afternoon but it began to snow and some were delayed. Bill Lord gave the men a tour of the temple. Jeffrey stood inside the temple at the door waiting for stragglers. When he heard the sound of footsteps, he opened the door. As soon as he saw who was coming, he began to smile. Kevin Currie, his buddy from the navy, walked up the steps. They hadn't seen each other in ten years. Jeffrey quickly explained that he was a tour guide and pointed next door to the white house where he lived.

"Be sure to stop by later," he said. "There are some things that I've got to share with you."

Jeffrey hurried to tell Alice about Kevin. When he came over to their house, Alice gave him a big hug. Kevin told them that something significant had happened that night. Back in 1974 when Jeffrey first introduced him to the Book of Mormon, Kevin had seen a vision. "Just for an instant in my mind's eye, I saw a door and it had a brilliant white light coming from behind it," he said. Kevin didn't know what it meant so he hadn't paid much attention to it. "But tonight as I was walking up to the temple, I saw that very same door and it opened and there was a bright light shooting out from behind it," Kevin said. He paused and then continued:

"Jeffrey, the door that I saw in my mind ten years ago was the door to the Kirtland temple. It was the door that you opened tonight."

Kevin didn't think their reunion was a coincidence. There had to be a reason why he had had his vision. "Why are you here?" he asked.

Jeffrey said that he had come to Ohio "to be endowed with the power—just like it says in the scriptures." He then told Kevin that he had recently made an astounding discovery. After swearing Kevin to secrecy, Jeffrey opened his copy of the Doctrine and Covenants and read out loud the first eight paragraphs of Section 83, a revelation that Joseph Smith, Jr., said God gave him on September 22 and 23 of 1832. The first three paragraphs were about Independence, but it was the fourth paragraph that Jeffrey wanted Kevin to hear:

> Verily, this is the word of the Lord, that the city New Jerusalem shall be built by the gathering of the Saints, beginning at this place, even the place of the temple, which temple shall be reared in this generation.

"Kevin," Jeffrey said excitedly. "I'm going to prove to you that for all these years everyone has been waiting at the wrong place for Christ to return."

Kevin was intrigued.

"I'm going to prove to you," Jeffrey continued, "that the real site of Zion is Kirtland—not Independence."

During the next hour, Jeffrey read Kevin more than a dozen scriptures from the Bible and the Book of Mormon that were messages from God delivered by prophets. In each case, the prophet began by saying "This is the word of the Lord" or "Thus saith the Lord."

"A prophet has got to make it clear right up-front that he is delivering a message from God," Jeffrey explained. He then told Kevin to read the first three paragraphs of Section 83. Those paragraphs didn't have any such declaration. "The reason is because God never said those three paragraphs. Those were words written by men," Jeffrey said, his voice becoming a whisper now, as if he were afraid someone might overhear.

"Those words were added after Joseph fled Kirtland to justify the saints moving to Independence."

Jeffrey told Kevin to read the fourth paragraph of the revelation. It began with the sentence: "Verily, this is the word of the Lord."

"This is where God's message really starts," Jeffrey explained, "and it says 'the city New Jerusalem shall be built' at the same spot as the temple—right here in Kirtland."

That night in the Lundgrens' kitchen, Kevin once again felt that God was speaking to him through Jeffrey. What Jeffrey was saying seemed to make sense. Other revelations in the Doctrine and Covenants began with a "Thus saith the Lord" preface. Why didn't Section 83?

"It became clear to me that Jeffrey was correct. The only commandment that God had ever given was that He wanted His people to go to the Ohio to be endowed with the power."

Kevin was hooked. Every weekend during the next two months, Kevin rode the bus to Cleveland on Friday nights. Jeffrey picked him up and they studied the scriptures together until Sunday afternoon when Kevin caught another bus back to his hometown of Buffalo, New York. During their visits, Kevin confided in Jeffrey and Alice. He had gotten married after he left the navy, he said, but it didn't last and he ended up divorced and depressed. He'd stopped going to church, started drinking heavily, and had gotten involved in a homosexual relationship. Nothing in life seemed important. Eventually, Kevin had returned to Buffalo where his mother lived and gone to work at the Veterans Administration hospital. He had started attending church again, but he still was miserable—until he started studying again with Jeffrey.

"For the first time in years," Kevin told them, "I feel a purpose to my life."

This is how Jeffrey later recalled his feelings toward his navy pal. "Kevin was a leech really and a leech needs to be attached to a host. I became that host. You see, religion seemed to touch Kevin from time to time, and give him stability and a purpose in his life. He also wanted to be part of a family. He'd never had his own. In a way, Kevin wasn't that much different from all the others who eventually joined my group. They all were drawn to me because there was something lacking in their own personalities and lives. They wanted me to provide it for them. They were weak. I was strong. I was their host."

In January 1985, Kevin requested a transfer to a VA hospital outside Cleveland, and when it was approved, he moved in with Jeffrey and Alice. He slept on a bed that Jeffrey put in the room where Damon and Jason slept. In the beginning, Kevin gave Jeffrey money each week to help pay for groceries. But Jeffrey and Alice took Kevin aside in early March and suggested that he give them all of his paycheck each month. "They told me that in order for Jeffrey to maintain respect in his children's eyes as the breadwinner of the family, I needed to turn over my entire paycheck to them," Kevin said. "And that is basically what I did." Kevin earned about $1,600 per month. On paydays, Kevin would find Jeffrey waiting on the porch for him when he got home. Jeffrey said that he didn't want to get the money inside because the children might see it.

Kevin was happy to turn over his pay. "I was having a good time. Jeffrey and Alice were fun to be around and Jeffrey was revealing new things all the time in the scriptures. I was glad I lived with them."

Besides, Jeffrey was making more-and-more-dramatic discoveries and Kevin was eager to hear about them. One night, Jeffrey shook Kevin awake and motioned to him to follow. They walked into the kitchen where Alice was waiting. Jeffrey quickly explained that he had been praying in the temple when he saw a ghost.

"I saw a personage, totally white, moving up the stairs," he explained, "and I knew who it was—I immediately recognized him."

Jeffrey paused to catch his breath.

"I asked God, 'What do I need to do to repent before I meet this person? What would you have me do?,' and after a period of time, I felt that God was telling me that it was okay for me to go before this personage, to meet him, so I followed him up the stairs."

Alice and Kevin were clearly mesmerized.

"I could feel the power of his glory as I walked up the stairs. It was like when you get near to an electric power generator, you can feel the power. I went up to the third level and there he was and—"

Jeffrey stopped. He suddenly began crying. "When I came into his presence, I suddenly saw myself as I truly am. For the first time in my life, I saw myself as a dirty rag, the filthiest thing on the face of the earth. I didn't have a right to be in the same room with this figure. I was so unclean. I couldn't move. I couldn't touch him. I couldn't engage him in conversation because I was so unworthy. I had to shrink away because I was so filthy."

"Who was it?" Alice asked, excitedly.

"It was Joseph," he said. "I saw Joseph Smith, Junior, in the temple."

The next Sunday, Jeffrey stood up during the worship service at the RLDS Kirtland congregation and recalled what had happened, only rather than telling everyone that he had seen Joseph, he simply said that he had seen an "angel." He also added a moral.

"If I had been clean, who knows what I could have asked or what this angel could have shared with me. But I lost out because I am a sinner and unclean."

Afterward, some members of the church said it was the most dramatic personal witness that they had ever heard. As far as Kevin was concerned, it was completely believable.

"Among the more traditional RLDS church members, spiritual experiences were something sought after because having a spiritual experience is a sign that God is communicating with you. I figured that if God was going to talk to anyone, it would probably be Jeffrey because he was the most pious person I knew."

Chapter 17

TOM Miller kept in touch with Jeffrey after he returned to Independence, and by the spring of 1985, the two men chatted weekly on the telephone about their scriptural studies. A robust, powerfully built man with short blond hair, chiseled features, and a hearty laugh, Tom was having trouble with the liberal changes taking place in the RLDS. "Things have to be logical for me to accept them, and when they aren't, it's tough for me to believe in them," he told Jeffrey during one call. Lots of changes in the church, he added, weren't logical in his view. "I find nowhere in the scriptures where it says women should be priests."

Tom had always had problems with the church, dating back to when he had served a stint as pastor of a small RLDS congregation in Iowa. While he enjoyed preaching on Sundays, he felt uncomfortable when it came to recommending young men for the priesthood. What bothered Tom was the church's policy about having each candidate recommended by two priests who both felt that they had received a "call" from God. Pastors were supposed to recommend young men, but no matter how hard Tom prayed, he never felt that God was telling him to "call" anyone. So Tom didn't, and the men in his Iowa church who wanted to become priests began to complain. "I got to thinking, 'Hey, is it me or are all these other guys who are claiming to have revelations from God about who to call just a bunch of liars?' " Tom decided to ask the pastor who had submitted his name as a priesthood candidate. What sort of revelation had he received about Tom? "I asked him: 'Why did you recommend me for the priesthood? What did God tell you about me?' And this man sort of hemmed and hawed, and he finally admitted that he really hadn't had any special experience. He just felt that it was the right thing to do, so he did it. I began to wonder if the whole process was all a farce."

Tom might have left the RLDS had it not been for the voice that he heard a short while later. He was asleep in the bedroom of his house when it woke him up. "I mean to tell you it *was* a voice! I thought it was my imagination at first, but then I heard it again and then it repeated itself one more time. The voice said: 'Arise, cleanse thyself and clothe thyself for I am coming.' My first thought was that I should take a shower and put on my suit because the Lord is coming tonight, but then I thought, 'Come on, is putting on a suit going to make me less of a sinner?' "

Tom got out of bed and walked outside onto the wooden deck behind his house. "It was the most beautiful night that I'd ever seen. The moon was full and the shadows cast by the oak and hickory trees were just fantastic. I was standing there, reveling in the beauty, just praising the Lord, when I looked over to the east and there were two bright stars and between them I saw a figure. It was Christ on the cross. I rubbed my eyes. I slapped myself on the head. I told myself that I was seeing something that wasn't there. But I looked and it was. It was there and it was not something that I was imagining. Believe me, I put it through every test that I could think of and everything I did convinced me that what I was seeing was real. Christ was hanging there."

When Tom moved to Independence, he and his wife, Patti, joined the Enoch Hill RLDS congregation, an ultraconservative group where prophecy was viewed as a vital part of every Sunday service. After several Sundays, Tom was asked to anoint a woman with oil and join other elders by putting his hands on her head and prophesying. Everyone waited for Tom to begin. "I didn't know nothing from nothing, but I got caught up in the emotion of it and I started prophesying and pretty soon I was spouting out all sorts of things about this woman and what she was going to do with her life. It was purely emotional and none of it ever came true. I was really going wild." Afterward, Tom felt guilty. "I knew that this woman believed everything I had said and I knew it was nonsense so I went to see her and I told her that I had been making stuff up, but she refused to believe me. She still thought what I had told her was from God. It seemed that there was no place in the church for intelligence. You either had to be caught up in the emotionalism of religion or you weren't seen as a true believer. Intelligence was viewed as a block to being religious."

Tom talked about his experiences with Jeffrey, who quickly agreed that most RLDS members were caught up in the emotionalism of religion, rather than intelligent study. Tom decided to read every verse in the Bible and the Book of Mormon that described contact between God and the Hebrew people. When he finished, he called Jeffrey. "Emotions are more a response to Satanic influence than the things of God," Tom announced, "because emotions cloud your vision and your understanding of the truth."

Jeffrey agreed, so Tom continued. "The truth is purely intellectual. In order to understand God, we must find out how He thinks and then attempt to become one with Him, make our thoughts into His thoughts, and share His intelligence and His truth. And that is an intellectual process, not an emotional one."

Tom and Jeffrey were both excited by what Tom was saying. They talked for nearly an hour on the telephone. The next Sunday, Jeffrey claimed credit in the adult RLDS Sunday school class in Kirtland for an important discovery. He announced that he had studied every scripture that described God's contact with the Hebrews and had found that "intelligence, not emotion" was the key to understanding God. Jeffrey repeated Tom's conclusions almost verbatim. There was only one slight change. Jeffrey made it sound as if everything he said was *his* idea, not Tom's.

No one in Kirtland said much about Jeffrey's "discovery," but in Independence, Tom's denouncement of emotional outbursts had irked most members of Enoch Hill. One night, however, a couple from the church stopped at Tom's house. "They told me that I had all the indications of being ready to receive a special truth. I listened and what they said was so astounding, I didn't know whether to continue listening or run through the door without bothering to open it."

The couple told Tom that there was a secret way to decipher God's truth by using intelligence, rather than emotion. It was called chiasmus. During the next two hours, the couple explained the process to Tom. Most Old Testament books, such as Psalms, Proverbs, Lamentations, Micah, Obadiah, Habakkuk, Nahum, and Zephaniah, were long Hebrew poems, they said. Prophetic books, such as Isaiah, Job, Joel, Amos, Hosea, and Jeremiah, also contain lengthy segments of poetry. Unlike English poetry, Hebrew poetry doesn't have rhyme or meter. Instead, Hebrew poems were written in a style called "parallelism." Put simply, Hebrew poets always repeated themselves. A poet would write a line and then repeat the same thought in the next line only in a slightly different way. This was called "rhyme of thought rather than sound." In Psalm 19, verse 1, the Hebrew poet wrote:

> *The heavens declare the glory of God;*
> *and the firmament showeth his handiwork.*

Both lines say the same thing but in different ways. Over time biblical scholars found a variety of "parallel" poems. Some poets alternated lines that were synonymous. In Psalm 27, verse 1, the poet wrote:

> *The Lord is my light and my salvation:*
> *Whom shall I fear?*
> *The Lord is the stronghold of my life;*
> *Of whom shall I be afraid?*

Scholars were finding so many different types of parallel writing that they developed a way to diagram them. They marked the first line of a poem with the letter A and whenever they came to another verse that was synonymous, they marked it with an A too. This "alphabet code" made it possible for the scholars to see how the poem was structured.

> [A] The Lord is my light and my salvation:
>   [B] Whom shall I fear?
> [A] The Lord is the stronghold of my life.
>   [B] Of whom shall I be afraid?

Once biblical scholars began using this marking system, they discovered an entirely new form of poetry which they called chiasmus. A chiasm is much more difficult to see because it doesn't follow the traditional A-B-A-B repeating sequence. Instead, it reverses it. When diagramed, a chiasm is structured like this: A-B-B-A. Some biblical scholars call this form of writing "mirror imaging." Verse 27 in chapter 2 of the New Testament book of Mark is a chiasm.

> *The sabbath was made for man.*
> *and not man for the sabbath.*

This is how the couple divided it for Tom:

> [A] The *sabbath*
>   [B] was made for *man,*
>   [B] and not *man*
> [A] for the *sabbath.*

A longer chiasm was found in Isaiah, chapter 6, verse 10:

> [A] Make the heart of this people fat,
>   [B] and make their ears heavy,
>   [C] and shut their eyes;
>   [C] lest they see with their eyes,
>   [B] and hear with their ears,
> [A] and understand with their hearts . . .

Once biblical scholars became proficient at identifying and diagraming chiasms, they made another startling discovery. Unlike other Hebrew poems, chiastic verses frequently had one line that was not repeated. This line was nearly always in the center of the poem. For example, Isaiah, chapter 55, verses 8 to 9, read:

> [A] For my thoughts are not your thoughts,
>   [B] neither are your ways my ways . . .
>   [C] For as the heavens are higher than the earth,
>   [B] so are my ways higher than your ways,
> [A] and my thoughts than your thoughts.

The words "thoughts" and "ways" were clearly repeated in typical A-B-B-A fashion, the couple told Tom. But stuck in the middle of the chiasm was line [C] and it stood completely by itself. There was no parallel line that mirrored the verse: "For as the heavens are higher than the earth. . . ."

The couple who explained all of this to Tom told him that the center line of a chiasm was the poet's "secret" message. It was the most important verse in the poem, the one that the poet had really meant to emphasize. Readers who didn't know how to diagram a chiasm would read these verses in Isaiah and interpret them to mean that God's "thoughts" and His "ways" were far superior to the "thoughts" and "ways" of human beings, which was the most common interpretation. But what the Hebrew poet was actually saying was that " . . . the heavens are higher than the earth."

In other words, the poet's cryptic message was that heaven was an actual, physical place located directly above the earth. By locating chiastic poems and diagraming them, Tom could learn the "secret" truths of the Bible that were hidden from everyone but those intelligent enough to use chiasmus.

"What I was hearing was a totally new way to read the scriptures," Tom recalled. "It was one of those rare moments when you feel that a truth has been illuminated to you."

As soon as the couple left that night, Tom telephoned Jeffrey. It was late, but he didn't care. He had to tell Jeffrey that there was a way to separate God's truth from "the church's emotional garbage."

Chapter 18

KEVIN Currie started noticing several subtle changes in the Lundgren house in April 1985, once he began turning his paychecks over to Jeffrey. "When I first moved in, I was treated like an equal, an adult, and my opinions were respected. But once I began giving Jeffrey my paycheck, he and Alice started acting more like parents to me and exercising more and more control over my life."

Kevin was the only person in the house earning a salary, yet whenever he needed money, he had to ask and explain to Jeffrey why he wanted it. The few times that Kevin did ask for cash, Jeffrey made it clear that he was taking it away from the rest of the "family" for his own selfish needs.

A few weeks after he moved in with Jeffrey and Alice, Kevin noticed another change. He was doing more and more household chores. It started when he volunteered to wash the dishes one night. All of the sudden, that became his job. So did baby-sitting for the children when Jeffrey and Alice went out, and cleaning the house. Kevin was soon cooking most of the meals at night too. "I had become the maid," he said.

Jeffrey had spent quite a bit of time studying the scriptures with Kevin at night, but during the summer of 1985, four college-age interns arrived to help give tours through the temple and Jeffrey and Alice began focusing on them. Of the four, they liked Sharon Bluntschly and Daniel D. Kraft, Jr., the best.

"The interns didn't know anyone else in town and Bill and Eleanor Lord were so much older that it was natural for them to turn to Alice and me," said Jeffrey. "Sharon, in particular, was lonely so she started coming over to our house all the time."

One of five children, Sharon had grown up in Beaverton,

a farming town of 1,100 in the middle of Michigan, where she had done well academically in high school but had always been somewhat of a wallflower. She had enrolled at Graceland College in 1977, but she couldn't make up her mind what she wanted to study so she eventually dropped out and went to work as a tour guide at the RLDS historical site in Nauvoo, Illinois. This was where Joseph Smith, Jr., had established a Mormon community after being driven out of Missouri by angry mobs in 1838. After that stint ended, Sharon had gone to Independence to work as a tour guide at the church's headquarters. The RLDS had only three historical sites, and since Sharon had worked at Nauvoo and Independence, Kirtland was the only one left, so she had arrived to complete the trio. Jeffrey considered Sharon "a complete loser."

"Sharon had never been on a date, never kissed a boy. She was short and weighed about two hundred and thirty pounds. It looked like she cut her own hair by putting a bowl over it. She acted like an old maid even though she was only twenty-seven. The only joy in her life was food. She had no self-esteem, no ambition. All she had ever done was float around the church as a tour guide."

A few days after Sharon arrived in Kirtland, Alice invited her over to the house. "I was sitting on the couch with Alice in her living room and she began talking to me about really strange things," Sharon later testified. Alice told Sharon that Joseph Smith, Jr., had appeared to Jeffrey in the temple. She mentioned that when she was in summer camp in 1969, a church patriarch had proclaimed that Alice would someday marry a man who would do great things for the church. "Alice continued telling me things and it was getting to the point where my mind couldn't handle a whole lot more when Jeff suddenly walked in," Sharon said. Jeff had been working in the visitors' center when, he said, he felt that someone was talking about him at home. Alice immediately confessed that she and Sharon had been doing just that.

"How did you know?" Alice bubbled. Jeffrey didn't reply. He just smiled.

Sharon was impressed. "How could he have known what we were talking about. . . . It was really amazing to me that he came in just at that time."

Years later, Sharon would be more skeptical. "To me now," she would testify, "it seems like it was a setup." But when it happened, Sharon thought Jeffrey had the power to "sense" things that others couldn't. Alice buttressed Sharon's thinking. "Jeffrey isn't like other men," Alice told her. "He has been chosen by God for a special purpose. Someday he will be famous."

That summer, Alice "adopted" Sharon. Alice taught Sharon how to fix her hair, how to buy clothing that complemented her figure, how to fix her nails. She was doing for Sharon what Lois Lundgren had once done for her. But Alice was adding a twist of her own to the transformation. She became Sharon's sexual adviser. "Alice wanted me to work on being carnal, sensual, and devilish," Sharon said later.

"Sharon knew nothing about sex," Alice recalled, "so I set out to educate her." Alice had Sharon watch a videotape of the sultry rock singer Tina Turner. "Tina may not be the most beautiful person in the world, but her body language makes her sexy," Alice said. She and Jeffrey also rented a variety of soft porn to show Sharon to help her loosen up. Finally, Alice asked Kevin to take Sharon on a date.

While Alice made Sharon her summer project, Jeffrey worked on Danny Kraft, Jr., a lovable nineteen-year-old wisenheimer. At age six, Danny had decided to become a musician. At age eleven, he decided to become an artist. By the time he graduated in 1982 from high school in Nauvoo, he had mastered nine musical instruments, won dozens of art awards, and maintained a straight-A average. He was skinny, energetic, impressionable, and eager to please. Jeffrey originally had opposed Danny's working as a guide. Although Danny regularly attended an RLDS church in Nauvoo, he had never been baptized. As soon as Danny arrived, Jeffrey began pushing him to join the church.

Just as they had done with Sharon, Jeffrey and Alice invited Danny into their home and quizzed him about his past. Jeffrey quickly decided that Danny's carefree attitude was a facade. Danny's parents had divorced in 1974. "He's covering up the pain," Jeffrey told Alice later. "Danny is looking for someone to love him—to take the place of his mom and dad and be his family."

A few days later when Danny dropped by the house, Alice told him that she was uncomfortable being addressed as "Mrs. Lundgren." It made her feel old, she joked. "Why not just call me 'Mom' " she told Danny. "You can call Jeffrey 'Dad.' "

Kevin had watched how Jeffrey and Alice manipulated Sharon and Danny, and he realized that neither of them realized it. "Jeffrey began using me to do reconnaissance that summer," Kevin said. "He would send me over to spy on the summer interns, and when I came back to the house, he'd grill me about what they were saying and doing. He especially wanted to know what they were saying about him and Alice. I noticed that he would use the information to his advantage. He was a master at telling one person one thing and then telling someone else another thing and keeping them both in the dark."

On Memorial Day weekend, a group of young people from Independence arrived at the temple for a tour. Shar Olson and Richard Brand were among them. They were best friends. Both of them had made a similar trip on Memorial Day in 1984 and had enjoyed it so much that they had organized this one. By this time, word about Jeffrey had filtered back to most RLDS churches in Independence. "We had heard about this man who worked at the temple and supposedly knew a lot about it so we decided to ask him to teach a special class about the temple for our group," Shar later recalled. Jeffrey quickly agreed to give the group a longer tour than usual. During it, he pointed out the symbol for man on the pulpit and mentioned there wasn't a symbol for woman. Shar and Richard had both strongly opposed the ordination of women as priests and Jeffrey's discovery intrigued them. After the tour, they stayed behind to ask Jeffrey additional questions. Before the group left, they collected a "love offering" and gave it to Jeffrey, who had mentioned several times during the tour that he didn't receive any salary from the church but instead relied on God to provide for him and his four children. The group gave him $400.

A few days after the group left, Bill Lord called Jeffrey into an office at the visitors' center.

"You can't ask for or accept money for giving tours," Bill said. One of the parents who had been chaperoning the Memorial Day tour group had complained. "You're going to have to turn that money over to the church."

Jeffrey quickly apologized and turned over the money. But he asked Bill if it would be okay if the church used the money to buy paint and carpet for the house where he and Alice lived. "Bill agreed," said Jeffrey, "so I got it anyway." He ended up getting even more. When Richard Brand heard what had happened, he became upset and mailed Jeffrey a check for $650. Jeffrey didn't tell anyone about it, but he did write down Richard's name and address. He was someone Jeff planned to remember.

By June, Sharon was spending every free moment at the Lundgrens'. She ate all her meals there too. Jeffrey mentioned this one afternoon when it was time to buy groceries, and Sharon volunteered to turn over her salary of $500 per month to the family. It was added to the $1,600 per month that Kevin gave the Lundgrens. Although Jeffrey had been warned not to solicit donations, he still did. Jeffrey bragged to Kevin about the biggest gifts—$500 from one church group and $300 from another—but no one, not even Jeffrey, kept tabs of the ones, fives, and tens pressed into his hands after he gave a tour.

Sharon decided to stay in Kirtland when summer ended. Jeffrey had convinced her that it, not Independence, was the true site of Zion. She got a job at Holzheimer's Grocery Store as a checkout clerk. The church agreed to let her continue to live in a tiny apartment near the temple that was normally reserved for student guides. But it began charging her rent. Sharon continued to turn over her paychecks to Jeffrey and Alice. In turn, Jeffrey promised to pay her bills and feed her. Danny, who had been baptized into the RLDS by Jeffrey in July, returned to art school but promised to come back to work as a guide the next summer.

After the four student interns had gone, Bill Lord told Jeffrey that it was time to audit the books for the temple and visitors' center. This was the first year that Jeffrey had been responsible for the records and when Bill examined them, he was disappointed. Donations to the temple were substantially less than what was expected. In previous years, sales of books and souvenirs and contributions at the temple had always increased. But not this year, and Bill couldn't figure out why. When he checked the visitors' log at the temple and discovered that a record number of tourists had visited the temple, Lord became suspicious. He called Jeffrey into his office.

"Something is wrong here," Lord said.

Jeffrey looked nervous.

"There is money missing," Lord continued.

Jeffrey suddenly blurted out an explanation. He said that he had been reluctant to mention it during the summer, but he suspected that one of the student interns had been stealing from the cash register. He put the blame on a student he had never liked.

"We didn't have any proof," Lord said later, "so there was nothing we could do." At the time, neither Bill nor Eleanor Lord suspected that the real thief was Jeffrey.

Shortly after that encounter, Kevin, Jeffrey, and Alice went to see the movie *Manhunter*, which is based on the Thomas Harris bestselling novel *Red Dragon*. Jeffrey and Alice both loved to watch movies and they were constantly seeing parallels between various films and their own lives. Jeffrey was mesmerized by *Manhunter*, which described a fictional FBI investigator's pursuit of a ruthless serial killer. The agent eventually caught the murderer by figuring out how he thought. In the movie, this was called developing the same "mindset." After the show, Jeffrey, Alice, and Kevin spent more than an hour discussing it in the kitchen of the house and then Jeffrey went to study his scriptures. Years later, Kevin would still recall what Alice said once they were alone.

"Jeffrey reminds me a lot of the agent in that movie," she told Kevin. "He figures out a person's mindset—what they want, how they think, what their weaknesses are—and then he uses that to get whatever he wants from them."

Chapter 19

Ɪɴ the fall of 1985, the adult Sunday school teacher at the Kirtland RLDS congregation decided to take a break, so Jeffrey was asked to teach. He immediately began showing the twenty-five class members how to diagram chiastic poems. Most of them had heard about chiasmus because of an article printed by Ray Treat in *The Zarahemla Record*. It had pointed out that the Book of Mormon, like the Bible, contained chiastic poems. Treat claimed this was significant because, in his eyes, the fact that both books contained chiasms was proof that the Mormon scriptures had been written thousands of years ago by a band of Hebrews, not by an imaginative twenty-four-year-old New York boy in Palmyra.

Jeffrey told the adults that Treat had missed the point. By diagraming chiastic poems, he explained, a reader could discover the "secret" truths in the scriptures. Chiasmus reminded Jeffrey of "hidden picture" drawings that he had seen as a child. When you looked at such a drawing the first time, you would see a picture—the face of an old woman with a big nose, for instance. But if you stared at the drawing long enough, the old woman's face disappeared and you could see a completely different drawing—the outline of a young woman wearing a feathered hat.

"Jeffrey was just phenomenal when it came to finding these chiasms," Eleanor Lord recalled. "Everyone in the class was intrigued when he first diagramed them and explained how they worked."

While Eleanor liked Jeffrey and enjoyed his classes, she often was uncomfortable about some of his claims. "Jeffrey had a habit in class of making people believe that what he was teaching was some kind of personal discovery that he had

149

made," she said. Most weeks, she and Jeffrey would talk at the
visitors' center about the scriptures and various concepts. She
was the first one, in fact, to show him Ray Treat's article about
chiasmus. She also knew that Jeffrey got many of his ideas
from Tom. "But when Jeffrey taught the class, he always . . .
gave the impression that what he was saying was based on
some great inspiration that he had received by himself."

In October 1985, Jeffrey learned that the Church was going
to hire another tour guide, so Jeffrey telephoned Tom and
urged him to apply. Tom's wife, Patti, didn't want to move.
She had a good job in Independence and Tom was still unemployed. "But if we move to Kirtland," Tom argued, "I can sit
and study and examine records all day long and I will finally
be able to learn the truth." Patti reluctantly admitted that ever
since Tom had been studying the scriptures via the telephone
with Jeffrey, the two of them had made some remarkable
discoveries. She agreed to move, and in November 1985, Tom
reported to work at the visitors' center.

That same month, Jeffrey received a telephone call from Jim
Robbins. Even though the two men had quarreled before the
Lundgrens left Independence, Jeffrey and Jim had renewed
their friendship. Jeffrey had initiated the peace process by
writing to Jim about the symbols in the temple. Jim responded
with a letter and the two men were soon writing regularly.
Almost immediately, Jeffrey asked Jim in a letter for a personal loan and suggested that he and Laura once again consider
supporting him and Alice. Jim had declined, but had continued
to write. Jim had called because he and Laura wanted to
spend Thanksgiving with the Lundgrens in Kirtland. Jeffrey
was excited about the visit. "I have many new discoveries to
share with you," he told Jim. The Robbinses planned to spend
three full days in Kirtland, but the morning after they arrived,
Jeffrey began lecturing Jim about the secret power of chiasmus
and how Kirtland was the true location of Zion. Finally, Jim
protested.

"Jeff, I just don't see it the same way as you do," he said.
But Jeffrey continued to hammer away. The next morning, Jim
and Laura announced that they were driving to Pennsylvania
to visit a friend. They wouldn't be back until late that night.
"We just had to get away from him," said Jim. When the

Robbinses returned that night, Jeff was clearly peeved. "He let me know that he didn't like us coming up to see them and then going away for a full day. He wanted us there and the reason why was because he wanted to convince us to move to Kirtland." The next day was Thanksgiving, and after Jeffrey carved the turkey that Jim and Laura had brought with them, he launched into another lecture. By the next morning, Jim and Laura were eager to leave. While they were backing their car out of the Lundgrens' driveway, Jeffrey stepped up to the car window for one last-ditch attempt to persuade Jim that he needed to move.

"Jim, this is where the action is going to be—here in Kirtland, not Independence," he said. "I expect you back here soon."

"Jeffrey," Jim replied coldly, "you will never see me back in Kirtland unless the Lord Himself tells me to come back. There will be no more friendly visits here." With that, Jim rolled up his window and left.

That was the last time that Jim and Laura ever saw the Lundgrens. Years later, when Jim recalled that final exchange, he would remember how he felt while driving away. "As crazy as it sounds, even though I had rejected everything that Jeffrey had said, while we were traveling down the road, I turned to Laura and said, 'Maybe we ought to think about moving to Kirtland.' Jeff had this magnetism about him. He never expressed any doubts and when he said something, it was like the Lord Himself had said it. To a member of the RLDS, that is very appealing. You are trained to relate to that and I did. Only after we had driven further down the road did I realize that what he was preaching was simply nuts."

Not everyone thought so. Alice would later insist that at this point in her marriage to Jeffrey, she genuinely believed that he was fulfilling the patriarch's 1969 prophecy. "I felt God was directing our lives." She and Jeffrey still argued, particularly about sex. But both of them had eased up and were getting along better than they ever had. "The feces wasn't so common. Mostly, he would just bend my body in all sorts of uncomfortable positions. He was really getting into dominance and wanting to control me—in the bed and everywhere else. But I still loved him and I truly believed that Jeff could be someone important in the church."

Jeffrey was working hard to become such a person. Besides learning everything that he could about biblical prophets, Jeffrey was poring over the history of the church. In Kirtland, he found information in the archives that he had not been taught in Sunday school as a youngster. One such account was an embarrassing moment in Mormon history in 1843, when Joseph Smith, Jr., was given six metal plates that had been discovered next to human bones in an ancient Indian burial mound near Kinderhook, Illinois. The bell-shaped plates were marked with strange hieroglyphics and Smith was asked if he could decipher them. After studying the plates, the prophet declared that he could, indeed, read them, and he translated a sample paragraph. He noted the discovery in his private journal.

Monday, May 1—I insert fac-similes of the six brass plates found near Kinderhook. . . . I have translated a portion of them, and find they contain the history of the person with which they were found. He is a descendant of Ham, through the loins of Pharaoh, king of Egypt. . . .

The discovery of the Kinderhook Plates sparked rumors of a sequel to the Book of Mormon and sent church members scurrying to their scriptures for clues that would help them identify the mysterious "descendant of Ham." Smith had always said that God showed him only a few of the records made by the ancient Hebrews.

Shortly after Smith publicly declared the plates genuine, three men from Kinderhook came forward with an announcement of their own. The entire thing was a hoax. The men had cut six pieces of copper from a strip and inscribed letters on each with acid. These "hieroglyphics" were actually characters copied from the lid of a Chinese tea box. The copper was "aged" by rust and hidden in the Indian mound. A gullible Mormon elder was later led to the site, where he unearthed the plates and was urged to rush them to Smith.

Despite the scam, Smith insisted that other plates made by the ancient Hebrews would someday be found. His claims were consistent with passages from the Book of Mormon that predicted that God would eventually reveal the history of the ancient Hebrews to a prophet [a.k.a. Joseph Smith, Jr.] but would keep part of the records "sealed" because they contained information that the world was not yet ready to receive. Among other things, the records supposedly contained "a revelation" that would explain all things "from the foundation of the world unto the end thereof."

Jeffrey had been to Chapin Forest several times trying to find an entrance to the "secret chamber" behind the strange holes that he had found along with Tom Miller and Ray Treat. But he hadn't had any luck. One morning, Jeffrey came across a passage in Section 101 of the Doctrine and Covenants that described a revelation purportedly given by God to Joseph Smith, Jr., on April 23, 1834. According to it, God ordered Smith to build a "treasury" for "all the sacred things" that God had given him. Jeffrey read the verse to Alice.

"Joseph was in Kirtland when he received this revelation," he explained, so it was only logical that the prophet would build a treasury in Ohio. "It's got to be in Chapin Forest."

Jeffrey told Alice that he was going out to the park for one final look. About an hour later, he returned and hurried Alice into the bedroom.

"I found it," he whispered. "I found the treasury!"

Jeffrey told Alice that there hadn't been anyone else at Chapin Forest when he arrived. He had walked down the path—the same one that he had seen in his dream—to where the strange holes were located. Jeffrey had knelt down and was praying when he heard footsteps.

"My first thoughts were 'Oh, gosh, some hiker is going to see me praying and think I am stupid,' but I continued to pray. When I looked up, there was a personage [angel] there and he explained that God had sent him. He was in charge of the treasury. He told me that he had never suffered death and that he had been a guardian of the treasury from when it was built."

The personage led Jeffrey to a secret opening, he said. "The guardian told me that the treasury could only be opened if God wishes it to be opened so even if other people go look, they won't be able to find it." While Jeffrey waited, the figure went into the treasury. "I looked inside and saw that it was a large chamber. The figure came out with one plate, a single plate, and I looked down and read part of what it said, and then he took it back into the treasury."

Alice drilled him with questions. Who was the personage? Was the plate that Jeffrey saw made of gold? What did the chamber look like? Had he seen the Sword of Laban? But the big question that she wanted answered was: "What was written on the plate?"

"I can't tell you everything that I read," Jeffrey replied solemnly, "because I am not supposed to reveal it yet."

But, he continued, with a flash of excitement, "I can tell *who* the writing was about."

"Who?" Alice asked.

"Alice," Jeffrey replied dramatically, "the writing on the plate was about *me and what God wants me to do*."

Alice was excited. "Jeffrey had finally found a niche in life. He was really, really good at giving tours and really, really good at interpreting scripture. It was perfect for him, and we had Kevin and Sharon supporting us financially, so for the first time in our marriage, I didn't have to worry about where the next meal was coming from. We had stability and all these wonderful things were happening to Jeffrey. He was seeing things and things were happening to him that just didn't happen to anyone else."

God had used the scriptures to direct Jeffrey to Kirtland. God had created an opening at the temple so that Jeffrey could be a guide there. God had caused Jeffrey to have visions. And God had sent word to Alice through a patriarch at the 1969 summer camp warning her about her future husband. Like pieces of a puzzle, everything was beginning to come together. As she stood there, wondering exactly what it all meant, Jeffrey told her something else.

"Take off your clothes," he said. "We are going to have anal sex."

Alice stared at Jeffrey and then quietly disrobed.

All of her life, she had been taught that every religion required its members to make a so-called "leap of faith." Alice had decided that her marriage to Jeffrey required the same.

"I had reached a point where I had to choose: Was I going to believe what Jeffrey was telling me and support him or was I going to doubt and question him?"

As far as Alice was concerned, there was no choice. "I decided that he truly was my Lord and my master."

Chapter 20

NOT many visitors came to the temple during the winter of 1985 and early 1986 so Jeffrey and Tom Miller had plenty of time to study their scriptures. Eleanor Lord would join them some days. All three had become proficient at finding chiastic verses. But Jeffrey was the champ. "Chiasmus was becoming an obsession with him," Eleanor noted.

One morning Jeffrey burst into the center and announced that he had made an astounding discovery. He had been reading the First Book of Nephi in the Book of Mormon, which is the equivalent of Genesis in the Bible, and he had found a new meaning for a phrase it contained. According to the book, the prophet Nephi explained that he had written the history of the Nephites *in the language of my father, which consists of the learning of the Jews and the language of the Egyptians.* Most Mormons felt this was a reference to "Reformed Egyptian," the term that Joseph Smith, Jr., used to describe the writing on the mystical golden plates. But Jeffrey had a different explanation.

Before Jeffrey revealed one of his discoveries, he always laid the groundwork by quoting scripture and this time he began in chapter 41 of Genesis, which tells how God caused Pharaoh dream *two* strange dreams. Jeffrey read part of verse 32 aloud:

" . . . *the dream was doubled unto Pharaoh twice; it is because the thing is established by God . . .*"

"Why did God cause Pharaoh to dream twice?" Jeffrey asked. Without waiting for a reply, he told Tom and Eleanor to turn to the Old Testament book of Job, verse 14 in chapter 33, which read: *"For God speaketh once, yea twice, yet man perceiveth it not."*

Jeffrey paused and then summarized his points. The Hebrews had written their poetry by repeating each line. God had caused Pharaoh to dream *two* dreams. And the writers of Job said that God "speaketh once, yea twice."

"What the scriptures are telling us," Jeffrey said, "is that God says everything twice—He speaks chiastically!" In Jeffrey's eyes, it made perfect sense. The reason the ancient Hebrews had used "parallelism" in their poetry is because they wanted to praise God in His *own* language, he explained. So when the prophet Nephi used the phrase the "language of my father" and the "learning of the Jews," he was referring to chiasmus.

Tom thought Jeffrey was on to something, but Eleanor wasn't so certain. "I now realize that this was a turning point for Jeffrey," she said, "because in his mind, he had found a great truth. Jeffrey felt that he had found a foolproof way to separate God's words from man's words. If a scripture was chiastic in structure, then it was of God. Otherwise, it was from man, and didn't really count."

Jeffrey was so confident that he used a red marker to cross out the lines in the Bible and his Mormon scriptures that didn't pass the test.

A few days after Jeffrey made this discovery, Eleanor asked him if he planned to discard the Lord's Prayer and Christ's Sermon on the Mount since neither was a chiastic poem. Did Jeffrey really believe that those scriptures didn't matter?

Jeffrey said he needed more time to figure it out, but he was sure enough of his theory to teach it the next Sunday to his adult Sunday school class. When the class ended, a woman took Jeffrey aside. "While you were teaching, I saw a vision of Moses standing next to you!" she told him. Another class member said that God had given him a revelation for Jeffrey. "Thus saith the Lord, you are to continue on the path that you are on, teaching the truth."

Jeffrey sent letters about chiasmus to the Patricks and the

Averys in Independence. Both couples wrote back asking for more information. At home, he explained his discovery to Kevin Currie, who still lived with him, and Sharon Bluntschly, who continued to spend most of her time at the Lundgrens' house.

But his biggest booster was Alice. "Maybe this is it!" she gushed. "Maybe this is the revelation you are supposed to bring forth—the one that was prophesied by the patriarch!"

There was one person who didn't think Jeffrey was anyone special. The Reverend Dale Luffman had become the RLDS stake president in the Kirtland area in January 1986. As such, he was supposed to make sure that the twelve congregations in his stake operated smoothly and adhered to church policy. Luffman was a full-time, salaried employee of the RLDS who answered to church officials in Independence. He was not warmly welcomed at the RLDS congregation in Kirtland. The church rolls listed 150 members, but a handful of elders really ran the brick church across the street from the Kirtland temple and they were fundamentalists who considered Luffman a "liberal" sent from church headquarters to bring them into line. In their eyes, the new stake president represented everything wrong in the RLDS. He had attended another denomination's seminary: Princeton University in New Jersey. [How, fundamentalists asked, could Luffman have learned anything by going to another religion's school, especially one that didn't believe in the Book of Mormon?] Worse, Luffman had received an undergraduate degree from an Oregon college run by the Roman Catholic Church. In the 1970s, he had helped organize a boycott of grapes on behalf of migrant farm workers and he had led student demonstrations against the Vietnam War. If that weren't enough, shortly after Luffman arrived in Kirtland, he described himself as an "ecumenicist." That meant that he didn't believe that the RLDS was God's only "true church." Within days after Luffman arrived, a rumor swept through the congregation in Kirtland. Luffman had befriended a minister from another church and was thinking about joining the local ministerial alliance. To fundamentalists, such a move was blasphemy.

Luffman hardly looked a rebel. A lanky man in his early forties, he had a closely trimmed salt-and-pepper beard and thick glasses, and spoke with a stuffed-nose twang. He had grown up poor, was well read, and didn't seem too concerned about the pomp and circumstance of organized religion. If anything, the first impression that most people had was that Luffman was pretty ordinary.

Within two weeks of his arrival, Luffman and Jeffrey clashed. It happened after Luffman preached his first sermon in the Kirtland church. He talked about how Christ's death and His love had saved the world. After the worship service, Luffman planned to attend Jeffrey's class, but he got delayed by a telephone call. Seconds later, as he walked down the hall to the class, he heard his name being mentioned. He paused outside the classroom and listened.

"You all heard the stake president's sermon today," Jeffrey announced, "and before we start, I want to talk about it." During the next fifteen minutes, Jeffrey accused Luffman of preaching "lies." "Our God is a God of vengeance," Jeffrey said, "and He expects only one thing from us—repentance. Repent, repent, repent. Those who do not repent will perish."

Luffman stepped into the classroom and took a front-row seat. Without a hint of embarrassment, Jeffrey began that day's regular lesson. Afterward, Luffman called Jeffrey into the church office.

"Your action was completely unethical," Luffman declared. "Everyone has a right to a difference of opinion. That's one thing. But you're telling people that I lied and that only *you* know the truth! Who are you to speak for God? What right do you have to tell people what is the truth?"

Jeffrey didn't defend himself. He simply listened as Luffman berated him.

"I expect an apology," Luffman finally concluded.

"I apologize," Jeffrey said, without any visible sign of remorse.

Jeffrey had never been particularly well liked in any church. Alice was the one who always made friends quickly while Jeffrey was aloof and haughty. But the fundamentalist elders at Kirtland rallied around Jeffrey. "I think Jeffrey found in the Kirtland congregation a unique climate," Luffman said later. "The few elders running the show saw in Jeffrey a spokesman for their point of view and Jeffrey liked to feel important. I think the two groups fed on each other."

During the following weeks, each time that Luffman preached at the Kirtland congregation, Jeffrey rebutted the sermons line by line in the adult class. As always, he got away with it by using his amazing memory of scriptures. Rather than attack Luffman in person, Jeffrey simply recited verses that contradicted whatever Luffman had preached.

Even though Luffman was furious, there was little he could do. Jeffrey worked for Bill Lord, who reported to the office of historical sites in Independence. Luffman reported to an entirely different office. The stake president didn't have any say over who worked at the temple.

"He's untouchable," Luffman complained after church to his wife, Judy. "I can't fire him."

There was, however, one way in which Luffman could discipline Jeffrey. The elders in the church had recommended that Jeffrey be promoted within the RLDS priesthood to the rank of elder. As stake president, Luffman got first shot at that request. He rejected it. If anything, the rejection seemed to win Jeffrey even more status.

"Jeffrey became almost a folk hero in the eyes of many fundamentalists in the church and he was gaining a tremendous following," Alice said later. "All day, every day, we had people coming to our front door, asking to see Jeffrey. Even Mormons [LDS] invited him to speak to them about the temple. People would come and ask if they could have their picture taken with Jeffrey because of his growing reputation."

It was about this time that someone noticed that Jeffrey's profile resembled a photograph in the temple of a death mask that had been made of Joseph Smith, Jr., after his murder. "I had little girls who were Mormon missionaries coming to the door asking me what it was like to be married to someone who looked like the beloved Joseph Smith," Alice said. Jeffrey found the comparison flattering and began mentioning the similarities during tours. He would tell people jokingly that he was Smith reincarnated.

As Jeffrey's popularity increased, Luffman tried new ways to undercut him. He decided to start another adult Sunday school class in the Kirtland church in the hope that it would draw members from Jeffrey's. It didn't. Jeffrey turned the tables on Luffman. Fundamentalists would come to Jeffrey's class, but would boycott church whenever Luffman preached. One Sunday, so many elders avoided the worship service that Luffman didn't have the required number to serve communion. Luffman reacted by organizing a leadership recruitment drive, an attempt to get "new blood" onto the various church committees that ran the church. He was trying to push out the old fundamentalists. But that didn't work either. "The situation deteriorated—fast," Luffman recalled.

At home, Kevin noticed that Jeffrey was spending hours talking about how he would lead a revolt of RLDS fundamentalists. He'd oust Wallace B. Smith, fire Luffman, kick the women out of the priesthood, restore the "true" RLDS church, and declare himself the new president-prophet.

At work, Jeffrey became bolder. He acted as if the temple were his personal domain. When Jeffrey felt a group of elders from out of town weren't paying attention during a tour, he belittled them. "I preached for forty-five minutes about how this temple was sacred and they had no right to come into it unless they were spiritually prepared." Afterward, one of them agreed, but others complained.

"You've got a real ego problem," an elder told him.

One Saturday morning in late April, Jeffrey mentioned that he wanted to leave work early because he and Alice were going to an antiques show. There hadn't been many visitors that morning, so Tom volunteered to stay at the visitors' center until noon by himself and then lock up. Jeffrey told him not to worry about taking the money out of the cash register. "I'll come over later and do it."

Tom knew that Jeffrey was adamant about being the only person who counted the daily receipts at the visitors' center. But when it was time to lock up, Tom didn't want to leave money in the register. He was afraid that he'd be blamed if it got stolen or came up short. So Tom counted the money and compared the total to the cash-register tape. The receipts and cash didn't match. Sixty-seven dollars was missing. Tom checked his figures again, but he hadn't made a mistake. Someone had taken sixty-seven dollars. "The only logical explanation is that Jeffrey took the cash," he told his wife that afternoon. They agreed that Tom should give Jeffrey a chance to explain before telling Bill Lord.

On Monday morning, Tom confronted Jeffrey. "Hey, the receipts show sixty-seven dollars missing." Tom didn't mean it to sound like an accusation but his old police training had kicked in and that is exactly what it sounded like. "Did you take it?"

Jeffrey turned red. "We were a little short," he replied, "so I borrowed it. I'm going to pay it back."

"Hey, that's stealing, Jeffrey. That is contrary to everything we are all about here."

"No, it's not," Jeffrey retorted. He was going to put an IOU in the cash register, he said. He took the money because he needed to buy milk for his children. Tom didn't believe him. The way he remembered it was that Jeffrey had left early Saturday to go to an antiques show. Tom didn't believe Jeffrey was hard up for cash. Once Jeffrey had showed him a three-hundred-dollar hunting knife that he had bought at an antiques store. When Tom reminded him of that fact, Jeffrey said that Alice had actually taken the money. She was the thief.

"His story kept changing," Tom said, "and it kept getting worse and worse." Finally, Jeffrey broke into tears. "He began crying, really sobbing . . . he starts blubbering like a baby about how I couldn't turn him in because he didn't have anywhere else to go. He told me that I'd ruin his family and his life and his children's lives. It was quite a tirade and it pissed me off. I told Jeffrey, 'Hey, buddy, you made the bed, you lie in it. If this is what you are about, then I got no time for you.' "

When Tom said that he was going to tell Bill Lord about the money, Jeffrey raced out the visitors' center door. "A few minutes later, Alice shows up and she starts pleading and starts crying too," said Tom. "She says, 'Oh, this will ruin our kids, please think about them,' and I said, 'Hey, lady, you think about it, you did it, not me.' And then she starts telling me about how Jeffrey didn't mean to hurt anyone and how I was going to destroy him. I was outraged that Jeffrey would send his wife over to beg me."

Despite the pleas, Tom told Bill that Jeffrey had stolen the money. Jeffrey and Alice rushed in to speak privately with

Bill as soon as Tom finished. Both were in tears. "Jeffrey told me that he had taken the money to buy bread and milk for his children," Bill said later. "Those were almost his exact words, and I felt sorry for him."

Bill asked Jeffrey why he was broke. "I thought you told me that you were receiving money each month as part of an inheritance," Bill said.

"They didn't get it to us soon enough this month, but as soon as they do, I'll pay it back," Jeffrey replied.

Bill needed time to think it over. He wanted to consult with his boss in Independence. Jeffrey and Alice left. "We had never had a tour guide who was as enthusiastic about the temple as Jeffrey was," said Bill, "and he was a young fellow and he had a family and I felt that he deserved another chance. I felt he was truly sorry and figured it was just a minor mistake." After lunch, Bill called Jeffrey into the office. "We've decided to let this go," he said. Jeffrey would have to refund the sixty-seven dollars, but that was it.

Tom was flabbergasted when he learned that Jeffrey had gotten off the hook. What was even more incredible was that Bill had left Jeffrey in charge of the books. Tom felt betrayed. Part of the reason he had moved to Kirtland was to study with Jeffrey. He had believed he was someone special and now he felt Jeffrey was nothing but a common thief. "We could have been best friends. . . . We had gotten so far in our studies . . . and yet it clearly didn't mean anything to Jeffrey. He knew how to say all the right words, but they didn't mean anything to him."

Chapter 21

HAD the Reverend Dale Luffman known that Jeffrey had been caught stealing from the cash register, he would have used that information to get him fired. But no one told Luffman. Tom Miller didn't like him and Bill Lord didn't feel it was any of the stake president's business. As a result, Jeffrey's image as a pious fundamentalist spokesman continued untarnished. A short time after the theft episode, Jeffrey was invited to speak about the temple to an RLDS congregation in Richmond, Missouri. Since the church was only a few miles from Independence, Jeffrey wrote a short letter to Richard Brand and invited him to the lecture. Cheryl Avery happened to telephone and Alice invited her too. Jeffrey's lecture and slide show went well and afterward Jeffrey sought out Richard and thanked him for the $650 that he had given him the summer before. He also began recruiting Richard. After all, if Jeffrey planned to launch a fundamentalist revolt, he was going to need someone to lead. "God's calling you to the temple," Jeffrey told Richard. "When are you moving there?" Richard demurred.

Cheryl Avery and her daughters tracked down Jeffrey and Alice at the lecture. Each was carrying a cherry pie. Cheryl wasn't that good a cook, Alice later said, and as a joke, Jeffrey had once made a big fuss about one of her cherry pies. "He had eaten one of them all by himself. So here comes Cheryl and the girls with four pies for us." Jeffrey rolled his eyes at Alice when Cheryl wasn't looking. Cheryl just didn't understand.

When they returned to Kirtland, Jeffrey wrote a letter to Richard urging him to join them. Meanwhile, Jeffrey and Alice avoided Tom at the visitors' center. Instead, they spent their time welcoming the new batch of college-age students who had come to work as summer tour guides. As promised, Danny

Kraft, Jr., had returned. He had walked into the Lundgrens'
house and yelled, "Dad and Mom—I'm home!" With Danny's
help, Jeffrey had started teaching nightly classes at his house
for the summer students as well as Kevin and Sharon.

On Memorial Day, Richard and Shar Olson returned with
another church group just as they had in 1984 and 1985. This
time, they brought Richard's best friend, Greg Winship. Shar
asked Jeffrey to give them a tour and teach a class, which he
did. Only this time, Jeffrey openly declared that Kirtland was
the real site of Zion.

"Are you listening, Richard?" Jeffrey asked in front of
everyone.

Richard had just graduated from the University of Missouri
and everyone assumed that he would find a job or attend
graduate school, but a few days after he and the others returned
to Independence, Richard announced that he was moving to
Kirtland to study with Jeffrey.

"Richard had been brought up believing that religion was
the most important part of your life," Jeffrey said later. "He
felt that I could help him understand the truth." Kevin, Sharon,
and Danny came, in Jeffrey's opinion, "because they were
losers or thrill seekers or because they thought they could get
something from me. Richard came because he loved the truth."

The youngest of three children and the only son of Wilmer
G. and Twylia Brand, Richard grew up in what authorities
would later describe as a "quintessential all-American home."
His father was an air-traffic controller, an ordained RLDS
elder, and a good provider. Twylia stayed at home to look after
her children. As a student at William Chrisman High School,
the same Independence school that Jeffrey had attended, Brand
did all the right things. He was a member of the National
Honor Society, the baseball and basketball teams, and a writer
on the school newspaper. He graduated in the top 2 percent
of the 1981 class and was later remembered by his classmates
as being an intelligent, deeply religious, handsome student
who was popular with his peers and liked by his teachers.
At college, he earned a bachelor of science degree in civil
engineering with a grade-point average of nearly 3.5 and was
later characterized by a professor as an "outstanding young
man full of potential."

Richard arrived in a new Mitsubishi pickup truck that he had just bought. He'd gotten the money, he told Jeffrey, from the estate of his grandmother. She'd left him $17,000 in cash. He had spent $13,000 to buy the truck, brought $1,000 in cash with him, and had another $3,000 in a savings account back in Independence. It didn't stay there long.

Originally, Richard planned to rent an apartment, find a job, and study with Jeffrey part time. But Jeffrey suggested that Richard move in with him for a while first and "get up to speed" on his scriptural studies. Richard agreed and fixed up a classroom area in the Lundgrens' basement. Each morning, Richard would go downstairs to study. Jeffrey had taught him how to diagram chiastic verses and he was eager to discover the scriptures' "hidden" messages. But he didn't have much luck and he became depressed.

"I told Richard that the reason he wasn't getting anywhere was because he was worshiping a false god," Jeffrey recalled. "I told him that he worshiped his truck. I said, 'You spend more time bowing down before your truck, washing and polishing it, than you do bowing down before your God,' and after a few days, he agreed that possessions had always been too important in his life."

Jeffrey suggested a solution.

"Sell your truck," he said. "Get rid of your false god."

Richard offered to sell it to Jeffrey for one dollar.

"No, you will still be driving it and worshiping it, and although we could use a dependable vehicle, the issue is that you must get rid of it because it is coming between you and God."

The Mitsubishi truck had less than two thousand miles on it and was only five months old. Richard sold it for $5,500. He gave the money to Jeffrey as evidence that he no longer intended to let possessions rule his life. Jeffrey was pleased. He told Richard that he was welcome to move in permanently with him and Alice and he said that Richard didn't need to find a job. Jeffrey would take care of him, in return, for the rest of Richard's inheritance. Richard agreed.

"I told him that he was doing the right thing in the eyes of God," Jeffrey remembered, "and his depression went away and he started making real headway in his studies."

By the fall of 1986, Jeffrey had attracted a core group of "disciples." Kevin and Richard lived with him in the house. Danny and Sharon lived across the street in student apartments that they rented from the church. About twice a week, Jeffrey would teach special classes just for them at his house. Most focused on how the RLDS Church had fallen away from the scriptures by becoming too liberal. The group studied scriptures that talked about how God would someday cause a new prophet to rise up and restore Zion.

It was during this period that Alice had a strange dream. It was dark in her dream and all she could hear at first was a whirling noise, like the sound of helicopter blades chopping the air as they began to turn. A light appeared—a spotlight illuminating a boxing ring. Alice was inside a huge auditorium, high up, away from the ring, in the cheap seats. Two men were wrestling, their muscular, well-tanned bodies dressed in skintight trunks. One of them lifted his opponent and slammed him on the mat. Everyone yelled, but Alice turned away. She knew someone was watching her. Someone was waiting for her. At that point, Alice woke up. She told Jeffrey about the dream the next morning.

"God is trying to show me something," she said. "But I don't understand."

A short time later, Kevin saw the movie *The Highlander*, and when he got home, he told Jeffrey and Alice that they had to see it. They went the next afternoon. The movie began in total darkness. Blood-red words suddenly appeared on the screen and the voice of Sean Connery vibrated through the theater.

> "From the dawn of time we came, moving silently down through the centuries, living many secret lives, struggling to reach the time of the gathering, when the few that remain will battle until the last. No one has ever known that we were among you—until now."

The screenplay, based on a story by Gregory Widen, followed the adventures of Conner Macleod, a Scot who should have died in 1536 when he was wounded in battle, but who miraculously survived and later discovered that he was a member of a rare race of immortals. These men could be killed only when they were beheaded with a sword. During the centuries that followed, Macleod and the other immortals lived like ordinary people until the time of the "gathering," when all of them met to fight. Only one could claim the ultimate prize—complete knowledge of everything in the world.

Within seconds after the movie began, Alice grabbed Jeffrey's arm. "This is it!" she announced. "This is my dream."

The first scene in the movie was shot in an auditorium where a yelling crowd was watching a professional wrestling match. The camera panned the fans and then zeroed in on the hero, who was sitting near the top of the auditorium in the cheap seats scanning the mob for his adversary.

"It is exactly like my dream," Alice whispered. During the next 110 minutes of the movie, Alice repeatedly squeezed Jeffrey's arm. She didn't have to say anything to him. He knew what she meant. He saw dozens of similarities between the film and his life.

"It was like watching our own lives being played out on the screen," Jeffrey later explained. "The term 'the gathering' was straight from Joseph Smith, Jr. . . . The prize was also scriptural. One man gets the power . . . to know everything in the world. Holiness is defined in the Book of Mormon as knowing all things, becoming one with God."

After the movie, as Jeffrey and Alice were walking to their car, Alice suddenly stopped.

"Listen," she said.

Jeffrey looked around. He was quiet.

"It's the same whirling noise that we heard in the theater," said Alice.

She looked at Jeffrey and waited for him to look directly at her.

"Why is this happening to us?" she asked. "Jeffrey, why are you so different from other men?"

Jeffrey didn't say anything.

"I want to see it again," Alice said. "The movie."

They returned to the theater. That afternoon they watched the movie over and over and over again until the theater closed.

The next day the two of them came back. They saw the show a total of seven times that weekend.

The following night, Jeffrey got out his scriptures and spread them and several other books out on the floor of the living room. He was looking for a specific story in the Book of Mormon about three Nephites whom God made immortal. These faithful saints, according to the Mormon scriptures, are still walking among ordinary humans, ministering to the faithful, unknown to everyone.

"I became convinced that God had moved the director and screenwriter of that movie," said Jeffrey. "God had moved them to make it solely because he wanted Alice and me to see it. He wanted me to know that I was truly different from other men."

Alice watched Jeffrey as he read his scriptures. "Jeffrey was totally oblivious to everything around him when he studied," she recalled. "He called it 'Becoming one with the word' and the house could be on fire and he wouldn't know it. I never knew anyone who loved to learn as much as him. It was second only to his love of sex."

Alice went out into the living room, sat beside him, put her arms around him and asked: "Jeffrey, who are you?"

"Who do you think I am?" he replied.

"I don't know, Jeffrey, but you are not like anyone I've ever known or seen."

"I think we need to find an answer to your question," he replied. "I think it is time to find out who I really am."

Chapter 22

JEFFREY went to the temple to pray. But he didn't know exactly what to ask. "Alice got real pushy after we saw *The Highlander*. She'd say, 'Are you the great last prophet that we're all looking for?' . . . The thought had hit me from time to time. I would wonder, 'Why am I the only one seeing these things?' The thought entering my mind was 'Who the heck am I even to think that I am this man?,' but Alice kept pushing and I kept wondering, 'Could it be true? Could I really be this prophet, this seer? Is God choosing me?' "

The longer Jeffrey thought about it, the more logical it seemed. He had read about all of the prophets and he thought that he had the same qualities as they had. "The most important thing is your willingness to do what God asks. I have never cared what other people thought. I had always loved the scriptures. I began to realize that it could be true. I could be the last seer. Why not?"

There was only one real glitch in his mind. Prophets were supposed to proclaim a great revelation. Joseph Smith, Jr., had brought forth the Book of Mormon. What did Jeffrey have to reveal? "I said to God, 'Okay, if I'm supposed to be this great last servant, the one like Moses, then what am I supposed to reveal to the world? Tell me, God. Show me what you want me to reveal. And I began to pray."

Five. Ten. Fifteen minutes. Nothing happened. No voices. No beams of light. No personages. No signs of any kind came to Jeffrey. After an hour, his mind wandered. He thought about *The Highlander*, about being immortal. He decided to read his scriptures, and for no apparent reason, he turned to Genesis and read chapter 6. In the standard Bible, chapter 6 contains twenty-two verses that describe the descendants of Adam and the building of Noah's ark. But Jeffrey was reading the "inspired" Bible as translated by Joseph Smith, Jr., and when Smith rewrote chapter 6, he added forty-nine verses. Most described men who later showed up in the Book of Mormon. Their names were inserted in the genealogy of Adam to prove that they were his direct descendants and not fictional characters. Perhaps the most amazing addition that Smith made, however, was a series of verses in Genesis that described the eventual birth of Jesus Christ, the Millennium, and how the latter-day saints would be raised up to rule the earth. It was these verses that Jeffrey was reading, and when he came to verse 60, a specific line caught his eye.

> . . . In the language of Adam, Man of Holiness is his name; and the name of his only begotten is the Son of Man, even Jesus Christ, a righteous judge, who shall come in the meridian of time.

By this time, Jeffrey had fallen into the habit of diagraming every verse that he read to see if it was "God's words or man's."

> [A] In the language of Adam
> [B] Man of Holiness
> [C] is his *name*
> [C] and the *name* of his only begotten
> [B] is the Son of Man
> [A] even Jesus Christ

Lines [C] clearly mirrored each other because the word "name" was in each. Jeffrey decided that the [B] lines also were parallel because "Son of Man" was synonymous with "Man of Holiness." But the [A] lines clearly didn't match. The first one talked about the "language of Adam." The second line talked about "Jesus Christ."

Jeffrey closed his Bible. He was frustrated. He tried to pray, but he couldn't concentrate. "I felt that God was telling me that He had already shown me everything that I needed to know. All I had to do was open my eyes." Jeffrey glanced around the temple. "God had directed me to Kirtland. The scriptures said that if I went to the Ohio, I would be endowed with the power. The secret had to be in the temple. What was I missing?"

He decided to read every verse in the scriptures that described the building of temples. He began in Exodus, chapter 25, where he came across these lines:

And let them make me a sanctuary; that I may dwell among them. According to all that I show thee after the pattern of the tabernacle, and the pattern of all the instruments thereof . . .

The word "pattern" had been repeated. Jeffrey continued on. In First Chronicles, chapter 28, he read several verses that quoted God telling David how his son Solomon was to build a temple. Verse 11 read:

Then David gave to Solomon his son the pattern . . .

It was in verse 12 too:

And the pattern *of all that he had by the spirit . . .*

Jeffrey found it again in verse 19:

All this, said David, the Lord made me understand in writing by his hand upon me, even all the works of this pattern . . .

Jeffrey felt that he was on to something. Like a bird eating bread crumbs dropped in a line, he continued on. He turned to chapter 43 of Ezekiel. At this point in Jewish history, Solomon's temple had been destroyed and the Hebrews had been taken into captivity in Babylon. In verse 10, Jeffrey read about Ezekiel's vision of how the temple—the house—should be rebuilt and how the Jews—the House of Israel—should construct it.

Thou son of man, show the house to the House of Israel, that they may be ashamed of their iniquities; and let them measure the pattern . . .

"Everywhere I looked, I found mention of this 'pattern' but I still didn't know what it was, only that it came from God."

In the New Testament book of Hebrews, chapter 8, verses 5 and 6, Jeffrey found the word "pattern" once again.

> . . . *See, saith he [God], that thou* make all things according to the pattern . . .

"Was it coincidence," Jeffrey asked, "that every time there was a mention of a temple, there was talk about this mysterious 'pattern' from God?"

Jeffrey decided to see if the word "pattern" was mentioned in his Mormon scriptures. In Section 52 of the Doctrine and Covenants, he found this verse:

> *And again, I will give unto you a* pattern *in all things, that ye may not be deceived; for Satan is abroad in the land, and he goeth forth deceiving the nations. . . .*

Jeffrey closed his scriptures. He knew that God had given Moses a "pattern." He knew that God had given David a "pattern." He knew that God had given Ezekiel a "pattern." According to Section 52, this "pattern" was in all things that God made and those verses also told him that he could use this pattern to tell whether or not he was being deceived by Satan.

But what was the "pattern"?

Jeffrey had an idea. God told Joseph Smith exactly how he wanted the Kirtland temple to be built, so the pattern had to be in the temple. What made the Kirtland temple different? Jeffrey looked around. Other churches usually had only one or two pulpits and they were always located at the front of the sanctuary. But the Kirtland temple had pulpits at the front and rear of the chamber. This was something that visitors frequently asked about. Why so many pulpits—more than twenty? Jeffrey knew that the pulpits were used by various priesthood members.

"I had looked at these pulpits every day, but until that night, I had not really seen them," Jeffrey said. "Suddenly my intelligence clicked in and I saw the pattern. If you cut the temple exactly in half, you would have the exact same number of pulpits on each half. You would have the exact same number of columns, the exact same number of doors, the exact same number of windows. Both sides would mirror each other. The entire building was chiastic.

"I had finally found the pattern. I realized that everything that God does is according to this mirror imaging or chiastic pattern. Everything."

Jeffrey decided to check his theory. "What was the most important thing that God has created? Man. He created man in his own image. I thought about my own body. If you cut a man in half lengthwise, both sides would be equal."

There was only one problem. It was the same nagging one that Eleanor Lord had first mentioned. What about all of the scriptures that weren't written chiastically, such as the Lord's Prayer and Christ's Sermon on the Mount? If everything made by God was chiastic, then why not these verses?

Jeffrey thought for a moment and then had the answer. Just because the verses didn't appear to mirror each other in English didn't mean that they weren't synonymous in Hebrew. "Maybe they were translated wrong." And then Jeffrey had an even more startling thought. "Why would God worry about English or Hebrew?" If God spoke chiastically, then the words were chiastic, and if they didn't seem synonymous to humans that was because "mankind really doesn't understand how to interpret God's words."

"Ordinary people wouldn't be able to interpret them because that was the job of a prophet," Jeffrey said. "Only a seer could see how the verses were chiastic."

Jeffrey opened up his Bible and looked again at verse 60 in Genesis.

> [A] In the language of Adam
>   [B] Man of Holiness
>   [C] is his *name*
>   [C] and the *name* of his only begotten
>   [B] is the Son of Man
> [A] even Jesus Christ

If Jeffrey was correct, lines [A] had to match. As he sat there studying them, Jeffrey suddenly received "the power" to see "the truth."

"The scales fell from my eyes." The line "in the language of Adam" was exactly the same as the line "even Jesus Christ," Jeffrey decided, because "Jesus Christ spoke in the language of Adam."

"It all fit."

Jeffrey began reading other scriptures. He discovered that every one of them held some new meaning that only *he* could reveal by way of the pattern. Jeffrey had found his great revelation. Now he could declare himself a prophet.

"I immediately began searching the scriptures to see what my role was." A few hours later, Jeffrey returned home and woke up Alice, who had gone to bed. He told her that he finally understood the vision that he had seen on Halloween night in 1983 when Damon ruptured his liver and had been rushed to the hospital for surgery. That was when Jeffrey suddenly had been at the foot of the cross watching Jesus die.

"I didn't imagine that," he explained. It really hadn't been a vision at all. It had been a *flashback*. "Alice," Jeffrey said, "the reason why I could see the crucifixion was because I was *actually* there when it happened."

In what sounded remarkably like the plot of *The Highlander*, Jeffrey explained that God had created eight great seers at "the beginning of time." These men had lived through the centuries without knowing that they were immortal until God needed them. At that point, God gave them the power to understand who they were.

"I have lived countless other lives before!"

"What?" Alice replied, startled.

"I had no recollection of my previous lives because my eyes were sealed by God. But now it is my time. I am the last seer. My eyes are being unsealed so that I can bring the pattern into the world and redeem Zion."

Jeffrey was so excited that he couldn't sleep. He decided to return to the temple and pray. When he walked into the lower court and looked up at the pulpits, he saw an angel. Years later, during an interview in the Lake County jail, Jeffrey would recall what he saw that night in the Kirtland temple. During the story, he would break down in tears and take several minutes to regain his composure.

"The angel was Joseph [Smith Jr.]. He didn't speak," Jeffrey said. "But I looked at him and he smiled. He smiled a big smile and all the fear that I had in my heart was pulled away and I felt the greatest joy and peace that I had ever felt. I sensed the purity of Christ's love. . . . And I understood why he was smiling. He looked at me, and in a very simple sense, there was a change of command taking place. He had waited for me a long time and now his job was finished. I was finally at the point where it could happen, where he could turn the role of the prophet over to me so that the scriptures could be fulfilled."

Chapter 23

NEITHER Jeffrey nor Alice felt it was "scriptural" for them to announce in the fall of 1986 that Jeffrey was the last seer. Christ had waited for his disciples to figure out for themselves that He was the "Son of the living God." Even so, Jeffrey and Alice decided it would be okay to drop a few hints. At the visitors' center, Alice asked Eleanor and Tom why Jeffrey had so many curious things happen to him.

"Why does he see revelations in the scriptures that no one else sees?"

Later, Tom would blame Alice for Jeffrey's belief that he was a prophet. "She pushed the ideal but she would never come out and say it. That was typical. Alice loved secrecy. She'd tell us, 'I know something you don't know about Jeffrey, but I've sworn that I can't tell anyone.' "

At home, Alice posed similar questions to Kevin Currie, Richard Brand, Danny Kraft, Jr., and Sharon Bluntschly during

Jeffrey's classes. "Isn't it strange that God is revealing all these things to Jeffrey?" she'd say.

Jeffrey was more subtle. He would describe what a prophet did and then he would describe what he was doing.

Even Eleanor, who had come to look upon Jeffrey and Alice as if they were her own children, felt the two of them were acting strange. "Jeffrey became more and more arrogant," she said. "He would never come out and say to me, 'I am a prophet of God,' but I knew that was what he thought. At first, I wanted to take him aside and say, 'C'mon Jeffrey, get real!' But then I thought, 'Who am I to say whom the Lord might raise up to be a prophet?' "

Kevin Currie felt differently. He had known Jeffrey the longest of any group member, and when Jeffrey explained the pattern, Kevin was skeptical. "Jeffrey was basically developing his own language," Kevin said. "He would diagram a verse and then he would say that the words that he had placed opposite each other were synonymous. Oftentimes, they clearly weren't. Sometimes they were antonyms. But he didn't care. He would say, 'Well, these words might appear opposite to you, but in God's eyes they are exactly the same.' I just didn't see any point in it because he had basically come up with a way for him to say anything that he wanted to say, interpret scripture any way that he wanted to interpret it, and if you disagreed with him, he told you that you were wrong and didn't understand the pattern because you weren't the seer."

Jeffrey knew that Kevin didn't believe him. One Sunday afternoon, the men in the group played a game of touch football. Afterward, Kevin complained that his shoulders were sore. Richard began to rub them. They were sitting in the living room, and when Jeffrey and Alice walked in, Jeffrey quickly called Richard into the kitchen to talk. The rest of that night, Richard avoided Kevin. "Jeffrey and Alice told Richard that I was gay and that he should be careful around me," Kevin remembered. They had told Richard that Kevin was trying to seduce him. "That's when I first began to realize that they were splitting me away from the others." Kevin felt Jeffrey and Alice were playing different group members against each other, in his words, "creating an environment of fear so the only people you felt that you could trust was them." Kevin decided to move back to Buffalo.

Jeffrey didn't try to stop him. "Jeffrey told me that it was good that I was going because I had a spirit contrary to the spirit of God and I had brought this evil spirit into the house." As soon as Kevin left, Jeffrey called Richard, Sharon, and Danny into the living room. "The real reason why Kevin left," he said. "is because he's fallen in love with another man."

At about the same time that Kevin left, Jeffrey received a letter from Dennis and Tonya Patrick. He had written to them about the pattern and his discoveries. "We're moving to Kirtland," Dennis announced in the letter. Dennis explained that he had used Jeffrey's pattern to make some exciting revelations of his own. Dennis also said that a voice had told him to move. "It was an audible voice," Dennis later recalled writing to Jeffrey. "The voice said, 'It is my will and my desire that you sell your house and move to Kirtland.' Then it told me how much I should sell my house for." Dennis had resigned from his job at Bendix Aerospace and would move as soon as he and Tonya sold their house, the letter said.

Jeffrey was outraged. "Who does Dennis think he is?" Jeffrey asked Alice. "There is only one person God speaks to and that is *His* prophet and I am that man, not Dennis Patrick." For more than two days, Jeffrey fumed. "God told me this would happen," he said. Jeffrey reminded Alice of his vision, the one where he was given gold plates to interpret. "Dennis tried to wrestle those plates away from me and that's exactly what he is trying to do now . . . seize all the glory for himself."

Jeffrey wrote the Patricks a scalding reply. "You are not welcome here. . . . You are not coming to Ohio for the right reasons."

The Patricks were devastated. Dennis telephoned their realtor and stopped the sale of their house. He called Bendix, but someone had already been hired to fill his old job. Dennis called Jeffrey, but that didn't help. "I'm not inviting you up here," Jeffrey scolded, "until you are ready to learn the truth."

Meanwhile, Jeffrey was pressing Greg Winship to join his group. He had come to Kirtland to visit his pal Richard Brand. Greg had first met Jeffrey during the Memorial Day trek that Richard, Shar Olson, and he had made earlier that year. Since then, Richard had written Greg letters about Jeffrey and his discovery of a "perfect way to find the truth."

"Greg was very sharp when it came to the scriptures," Jeffrey said. "I liked him." Greg also came from a wealthy family. During his weekend visit, Jeffrey and Alice pumped Greg for personal information. They learned that he was the middle son in a family with three boys. His father, Gerald, was a former Missouri state senator and owner of Winship Travel, a thriving travel agency, where Greg worked. His mother, Carol, had stayed at home and raised the boys. Greg had never been in any serious trouble. He had received good grades at Harry Truman High School where he had been the drum major for the marching band, a member of the school choir, and active in school plays. After graduation, he had attended Graceland College where he was co-captain of the cheerleading team and on the junior varsity volleyball squad. Greg was twenty-six years old, slender, and meticulous in his appearance and habits. Each night he faithfully recorded all of that day's activities in a diary.

Greg's life sounded idyllic. But the more Jeffrey probed, the more certain he was that Greg was unhappy. By Saturday night, Jeffrey knew what was wrong. While Greg was in college, his parents had divorced. The split had badly shaken Greg. "He thought they had a perfect marriage," Jeffrey later told Alice. Part of the reason why Greg was upset was because of his interpretation of Matthew, chapter 6, verses 35 and 36, which quoted Jesus Christ as criticizing divorce:

> . . . whosoever shall put away [divorce] his wife, saving for the cause of fornication, causeth her to commit adultery; and whosoever shall marry her that is divorced, committeth adultery.

Not only was Greg worried about his parents' divorce, he was worried about his own failing marriage. Greg had married Anna Marie Crownover in Independence after he returned from college, but the relationship was a disaster.

The next day, before Greg left, he asked Jeffrey for advice. "Greg was trying to decide whether or not he should get a divorce. What he wanted to know was . . . if he got divorced and then remarried, would he be committing adultery?"

Jeffrey told Greg that God had created Eve by taking a rib from Adam. "Flesh was taken from flesh to create flesh," he said. God had used Adam's rib to create a "perfect companion" for Adam. God had, in fact, created a perfect companion for every saint. "Greg, there is a woman in this world who is flesh of your flesh, bone of your bone," Jeffrey explained. "She was created specifically for you so it doesn't really matter if you are married or you are divorced. If the woman that you are living with right now isn't your true companion—the one that God made for you—then you are committing adultery and you will continue to commit adultery until you are paired with your perfect mate."

Was his wife this perfect companion? Greg asked.

"Greg, I can't tell you right now who your perfect companion is," Jeffrey said, "but I can tell you that the woman you are now with is not the one."

Shortly after Greg returned to Kirtland, he filed for divorce and made plans to move to Ohio to join Jeffrey's group.

Besides the Patricks and Greg, Jeffrey had notified three others about the pattern. Jeffrey had told his old college chum Keith Johnson and Dennis and Cheryl Avery. The Averys had visited Kirtland earlier in the summer, and during that visit, Jeffrey had found out something about Dennis that had made him friendlier toward him. Dennis had mentioned that his mother had died and left him several thousand dollars. Rather than spend the money on new furniture, a better car, or a vacation, Dennis had used it to pay off the mortgage on his house. Even then, Dennis still had a few hundred dollars left over, which he had used to buy a nine-year-old Toyota sedan as a second car.

"I don't owe a penny to anyone," he bragged to Jeffrey. "I consider that part of being a good steward."

Jeffrey thought Dennis was stupid. But he didn't say so. Instead, he massaged Dennis's ego and he gradually moved the conversation from the Averys' finances to his own. Jeffrey explained how he and Alice were completely dependent on the Lord to take care of them.

"We don't even have a car," he explained. The station wagon that the Lundgrens had driven to Ohio in 1984 had long ago been junked.

Dennis felt sorry for Jeffrey, and when he returned to Independence, he telephoned Jeffrey. "We want to give you the Toyota," Dennis announced. He and Cheryl had discussed it on the ride home.

Since that time, Jeffrey had gone out of his way to write letters to Dennis and Cheryl, even though he loathed them. "Jeff and Alice didn't have a phone so they would get calls at the visitors' center," recalled Tom Miller. "The Averys would call up and Jeffrey would be really nice to them, almost encourage them, and then after he had hung up, he would deride those people something terrible and make fun of them. He and Alice both would. I kept thinking, 'Well, if he really despises them, then why is he so friendly when they call?' "

Tom had met the Averys. They seemed pretty ordinary. He began to suspect that Jeffrey was scheming to get something from them. But he couldn't figure out what it was.

Chapter 24

JEFFREY would later claim that he had never encouraged Dennis and Cheryl to move to Kirtland. But they certainly felt that he did. In February 1987, an excited Dennis stopped at the home of his younger brother, Tim, in Independence. Dennis and Cheryl were returning home from a weekend visit with Jeffrey and Alice.

"I know you won't understand this," Dennis declared as soon as he walked into Tim's house, "but we are moving to Kirtland." Tim began to object, but Dennis cut him short. "We are firm on this and we're going to leave as soon as possible."

Why now? Tim asked.

The answer was simple. Jeffrey had told them it was time. Dennis had been taught by the church that he was to help build Zion. Section 6 of the Doctrine and Covenants admonished the saints to "seek to bring forth and establish the cause of Zion." Previous generations had succumbed to sin and failed. Now it was his generation's turn. As they talked that night, Dennis explained how Jeffrey had discovered the pattern, a revolutionary way to interpret scripture. Based on what Jeffrey had shown him, Dennis was convinced that Jesus Christ was about to return and he was going to appear at Kirtland.

At one point, Dennis took a piece of paper from his pocket and showed it to Tim. Jeffrey had given it to him. It was a chiastic diagram. Tim recognized a few of the lines. "Dennis tried to explain it to me." According to Jeffrey, the diagram proved Zion was in Kirtland. "Dennis said that he and Cheryl had to go to the Kirtland temple if they wanted to see Jesus." After his brother left that night, Tim got out his scriptures and looked up the verses that Jeffrey had diagramed. "Why, they didn't say anything at all like what Jeffrey said they meant. He was twisting the scripture all around."

Although Dennis was nine years older, Tim knew that he was gullible. He was afraid that he was being conned.

Dennis and Cheryl were so eager to move to Kirtland that they didn't bother listing their house for sale with a realtor. Instead, they sold it for $20,000 to some people that they knew.

"Your house is worth much more than that," Tim complained.

Dennis didn't care. "All that matters is that we get to Kirtland."

On February 19, Dennis gave notice at Centerre Bank. After seventeen years, he was resigning. In March, he and Cheryl drove to Kirtland to find a house. Realtor Margaret Mitchell took them around. Jeffrey tagged along to make certain, as he put it, "you don't get taken in." They rented a modest house just down the street from the Kirtland temple. As soon as they got back to Independence, they began packing. Dennis asked Tim if he'd help load the U-Haul truck that they had rented. Tim tried to talk his brother out of moving.

"I'm afraid you think Jeffrey is a prophet," Tim said. "I'm afraid you're making a big, big mistake."

"I'm trying to keep an open mind," Dennis snapped. "Maybe he is a prophet, maybe he isn't."

Tim knew he couldn't change his brother's mind. "He felt Jeffrey had discovered this great truth, this pattern."

It took only a few hours to load the Averys' meager furnishings. Tim waved good-bye when they drove away. In Kirtland, Jeffrey was waiting. "They came right to my house. I had all the guys in my group go to their house, help them unpack the U-Haul, and get everything into place," said Jeffrey. "Alice took them meals and helped Cheryl get their three girls enrolled at school. Dennis and Cheryl were both so helpless that if we hadn't led them by the noses they would have been lost."

During the Averys' first two weeks in Kirtland, Jeffrey and Alice stopped by to check on them every day. One afternoon when they came by, Cheryl was chatting with one of her neighbors. Cheryl introduced Jeffrey and Alice to her as "our best friends."

On May 4, Dennis opened a bank account at the National City Bank. Jeffrey had recommended it. Dennis deposited $20,532.55, which included his savings and the money that he was paid for his house.

The smiles that Jeffrey and Alice put on when they were with the Averys quickly disappeared whenever they weren't around. "Jeffrey went to great lengths at the visitors' center to say that he wished the Averys hadn't come," recalled Eleanor. "He and Alice both used to mock them something terrible behind their backs."

Inside the Lundgren house, the Averys became the butt of every joke. "The Averys were called lazy. . . . Jeff called Dennis a wimp," recalled Sharon. "Everything was backward. Cheryl was the one who made the decisions. She was the one that wore the pants."

But whenever the Averys came to see Jeffrey and Alice, everyone in the group was friendly, so much so that Cheryl invited the group over for dinner after she and Dennis got settled. Richard and Sharon refused to go, but Danny said he'd go with Jeffrey and Alice. When they arrived, Alice went into the kitchen to talk to Cheryl.

"I'm making a special pizza tonight!" Cheryl said.

"C'mon, Cheryl," Alice said, "what are you going to put on the pizza?"

Cheryl grinned and took a jar of dill pickles from the refrigerator. She diced a couple and spread them over the sauce and dough.

When Alice walked into the living room, she whispered to Jeffrey: "You aren't going to believe what's on this pizza."

Jeffrey thought it tasted terrible, but worse was yet to come. Cheryl had made rhubarb pie and she cut Danny a huge slice because she knew it was his favorite. He took a bite and nearly gagged. Alice almost burst out laughing. Danny fidgeted until Cheryl left the table to get something from the kitchen. When she returned, Danny's piece of pie was gone. Alice knew that he hadn't eaten it, but she didn't see where he could have hidden it. A short time later, Jeffrey, Alice, and Danny left. As soon as they were outside, Danny pulled off his boot.

"He had dumped the pie inside it," Jeffrey recalled. "He'd been walking with rhubarb pie in his boot since dinner." Everyone at the house thought the story was hilarious.

A few days later, Richard overheard Alice and Jeffrey talking.

"Why are the Averys here?" Alice asked.

"So I can have their money," Jeffrey replied.

Chapter 25

WITHOUT explanation, Jeffrey invited Dennis and Tonya Patrick to move to Kirtland in January 1987. He didn't mention the couple's aborted attempt some three months earlier. But he did suggest that Dennis and Tonya sell their house and bring the proceeds with them. Two weeks after they listed their home for sale, they had an offer. It was the exact price that the "voice" had told Dennis to ask for. Dennis saw it as a sign. On February 28, they drove into Kirtland in a rental truck filled with their belongings and stopped at the

Lundgrens' house. Dennis knocked on the front door. Tonya and Molly, the Patricks' six-year-old daughter, stood beside him. Jeffrey greeted them with an icy stare. "Jeff and Alice didn't want to have anything to do with us," Tonya said later. "Jeffrey had ordered Alice not to even talk to me."

"What's going on, Jeff?" asked Dennis.

"There are things you have to learn," Jeffrey replied. "Until you do, you are not part of the family."

Dennis was dazed. Tonya was in tears. Molly was confused. They got back into the truck and drove down the street to the Hilltop Apartments. That Sunday, the Patricks sat by themselves in church. The Reverend Dale Luffman was thrilled when he spotted Dennis. He had known Dennis and had been good friends with his parents when they lived in Oregon.

"We've been praying for a priesthood member to come in and help us clean up this mess at the church here," Luffman earnestly confided to Dennis after the service.

"What's the problem?" asked Dennis.

"Real simply—a man named Jeff Lundgren."

"Jeffrey is why we're here," Dennis replied.

Luffman was disappointed. "I knew right then and there that I had lost them," he said. "They were part of this group of dissenters that Jeffrey was building around himself."

Besides the Patricks and the Averys, Greg Winship had moved to Kirtland to study with Jeffrey. He had gotten a job as a tour guide at the temple. Jeffrey had also started to recruit another couple, Ron and Susie Luff, who had gone on a tour of the temple with him. They lived in Springfield, Missouri, and Jeffrey was corresponding with them.

At least once each week, Jeffrey taught a scripture class to members of his group. They included Richard, Sharon, Danny, Greg, Dennis Patrick, Tonya, Dennis Avery, Cheryl, Alice, and, on most occasions, Damon Lundgren, who was now sixteen. Jeffrey told them that they had to "erase everything" from their minds about religion.

"This is not my rule," Jeffrey explained, "it is what God is commanding you to do!"

Jeffrey told the group to open their Mormon scriptures to Section 90 in the Doctrine and Covenants, a record of a revelation that Joseph Smith, Jr., purportedly received from God on May 6, 1833. Jeffrey read part of it to them:

> " . . . [the] wicked one cometh and taketh away light and truth, through disobedience, from the children of men, and because of the tradition of their fathers. But I have commanded you to bring up your children in light and truth."

He then diagramed the verse:

[A] [the] wicked one cometh and taketh away *light and truth*
  [B] through disobedience from the *children* of men
    [C] and because of the tradition of their fathers.
  [B] But I have commanded you to bring up your *children*
[A] in *light and truth*.

Lines [A] were parallel because they both contained the words "light and truth," he said. Lines [B] mirrored each other because they had the word "children" in them. Line [C] stood alone. It was the "secret" chiastic line.

"God says light and truth are taken away because of the 'tradition of their fathers,' " Jeffrey explained. These traditions, he continued, were everything the RLDS had taught them. "You must get Satan's garbage out of your memory banks," he said. "I will teach you what to think, what to believe."

Dennis would later recall Jeffrey's presentations with a certain awe. "He was very calculated and extremely effective. Jeffrey never said anything without having scriptures to back it up and he would explain each verse and build on each verse, piece by piece, until he had constructed an elaborate foundation and proven his point. It was difficult to challenge him because when he got through, it didn't seem like *he* was telling you to do something—it seemed like *God* was telling you to do it based on the scriptures."

Dennis noticed something else about Jeffrey's classes. Everyone had to agree with Jeffrey. If they didn't, they were criticized. "He would use the pattern to tell us what a scripture actually said and then ask us if we could see it. If anyone didn't see it, he would go over it again and again and again, until everyone in the room finally agreed with what he said."

One night, Jeffrey marched into class and barked out an order. "Open your Bibles to Malachi." He read the first verse of chapter 3 aloud to the group:

"Behold, I will send my messenger, and he shall prepare the way before me; and the Lord whom ye seek, shall suddenly come to his temple . . ."

That verse, Jeffrey lectured, contained an extraordinary secret. "It tells us that Christ 'shall suddenly come to his temple.' " Where, Jeffrey asked, is this temple? And then he quickly answered his own question. "The temple is in Kirtland." And who has God sent to the temple? Again, he answered his own question. "The messenger who is preparing the way." How, Jeffrey continued, would this messenger prepare the way? This time, Jeffrey paused before answering. The last messenger, Jeffrey said, was sent by God to reveal the pattern to the world. That was how members of the group could identify him. The messenger was the person teaching the pattern.

Dennis snapped. "Jeffrey was telling us that he was the last messenger."

After several weeks of classes, Dennis and Tonya finally began to feel that they were being accepted by the others in the group. On a late summer night, Jeffrey came to their apartment. He wanted them to join the "family." The Lundgrens called their own children the "naturals," he explained. Richard, Greg, Sharon, and Danny were the "unnaturals." Everyone in the "family" called Alice and Jeffrey, "Mom and Dad." Before Dennis and Tonya could become one of the unnaturals, however, there was something they had to do. Jeffrey opened his Bible to the New Testament book of Acts and read them chapter 4, verse 32, which describes how the early Christians lived communally with "all things in common."

If the Patricks wanted to become part of the family, then Dennis was going to have to turn over to Jeffrey the paycheck that he got each week from working at a local health spa.

"I want you to submit a monthly budget to me," Jeffrey said. "I will decide how much money you need."

Jeffrey then asked Dennis what he had done with the cash that he'd received from selling his house in Independence. Most of it had gone to pay bills, Dennis replied.

"Jeffrey got angry and told me that I had wasted the money. He said I should have given it to him instead of paying off a bunch of Gentiles. He was the one who was going to build Zion. . . . Gentiles didn't matter. The only reason why God had put them on earth was so we could use them."

Dennis and Tonya agreed to give Jeffrey all of their cash and future earnings. "We felt we were going to build Zion and we wanted to do our part," said Dennis. "I was willing to do whatever it took to do this right and see Christ."

Before he left, Jeffrey read Dennis and Tonya another story from the Bible. This one was from chapter 5 in Acts, which describes how Ananias and Sapphira, an early Christian couple, held back some of their possessions from the communal pot. When the apostle Peter questioned them about it, both lied and were immediately struck dead by God. Dennis and Tonya got the point.

Now that the Patricks were part of the family, they were invited to the Lundgrens' house for scripture classes much more often than once a week. They were also privy to the private goings-on of the group. Both of them discovered that Jeffrey not only controlled the family's money, but also directed their personal lives as well.

Jeffrey claimed that all of his followers' names were hidden in the scriptures, just as his was, along with the names of their "true companions"—the spouses that God had created specifically for them. It was this claim that had helped convince Greg Winship that he should file for divorce and move to Kirtland to find the woman who, Jeffrey claimed, had been made from "flesh of his flesh." As soon as Greg had gotten settled, he had asked about the name of his future spouse.

"I'm still looking for yours," Jeffrey said, "but I have found the names of others."

Greg asked him who? But Jeffrey wouldn't say. Alice did. One afternoon, she took Sharon aside.

"Jeff and I were wondering if Richard isn't the one for you," she told her.

"Yeah," Sharon replied, "I was wondering the same thing."

Sharon was pleased to be matched with Richard, but he was not enthused when he heard what Alice had said. Although Sharon had gone on a diet and lost several pounds, she still was chunky. Richard was used to dating striking, slender, stylish women. Sharon was plain. As always, Jeffrey would later tell his followers that he really had nothing to do with matching Richard and Sharon. It was God who had ordered them to become married.

"I looked in the scriptures and they were clear about it," he said. "Sharon was flesh of Richard's flesh."

But the timing of the match happened to coincide with a conversation between Richard and Jeffrey that had irritated the "father" of the family. Richard had poked fun at Jeffrey one afternoon while the two men were lifting weights by pointing out how pudgy he was getting. "Richard had an aversion to fat," Jeffrey later said, "and my physical shape bothered him. Sometimes my weight would get up to two hundred and seventy pounds and I'd have a tummy on me. That was repulsive to Richard." As soon as the men finished lifting weights, Jeffrey hurried inside and grabbed his scriptures.

"God is fat," he declared. He showed Richard several verses that described God as being "heavy" and "stout." "Those words are synonymous with fat," Jeffrey insisted. "God has a stomach on him." Richard had laughed.

It was shortly after that exchange that Richard was matched to Sharon. While Jeffrey later denied that there was any connection between the two events, the irony of matching a "pretty boy" with Sharon did cause him to smile. Perhaps God, he later quipped, had wanted to teach Richard a lesson.

Although Richard did not find Sharon attractive, Jeffrey ordered him to begin courting her, and Richard complied.

At about this same time, Jeffrey announced that Dennis and Cheryl Avery were going through their money much too quickly. Everyone in the family knew that the Averys were never going to be fully accepted. Like the Gentiles, they were being provided by God, Jeffrey said, for the group to use. Jeffrey decided that he was going to have a special class specifically designed to get the Averys' cash. He and Alice would do most of the talking. The unnaturals would do their part by agreeing with everything they said and pressuring Dennis and Cheryl to turn over the proceeds from the sale of their house. No one balked at the idea.

On the night of the special class, Jeffrey quoted the same scriptures that he had used on the Patricks. Others in the group explained how much they were contributing to the communal pot. On June 27, Dennis Avery came to see Jeffrey. He and Cheryl had decided to give Jeffrey a check. They wanted to be "of one heart and of one soul" with everyone else. In return, Jeffrey promised to pay their rent. Dennis took out his checkbook and began to write, but Jeffrey stopped him. "Make it out to cash, not to me," he said. He did not want the Internal Revenue Service asking about the income. Dennis wrote in an amount and showed it to Jeffrey for his approval. Jeffrey nodded and sent him to a nearby bank. When Dennis returned, he gave Jeffrey an envelope filled with bills. It was $10,000. Jeffrey thanked Dennis and sent him home.

Chapter 26

WITHIN an hour after Dennis handed him $10,000 in cash, Jeffrey was at Veith Sports Supply buying a .45-caliber Interarms semiautomatic pistol. From there, he drove to Pistol Pete's, another Ohio sporting goods store, and bought a .243-caliber Ruger hunting rifle and another .45-caliber Colt semiautomatic pistol. He waited one week and then returned to Pistol Pete's and bought a Ruger .44-caliber magnum handgun. During the next few days, Jeffrey bought camouflage clothing, tents, camping supplies, canned food, and hundreds of rounds of ammunition. Jeffrey was stockpiling weapons and supplies for his "storehouse." Many saints believed in keeping a one-year supply of food and other goods needed for survival during the last days of tribulation. According to the Book of Revelation, the world would be stricken with famine, disease, and wars shortly before Jesus Christ returned. Jeffrey was going to be prepared. By the end of June, Jeffrey had added another Mini-14 Ruger assault rifle to his cache. He now had enough guns to arm all the men in his family. Richard already owned his own guns. Danny, Greg, Dennis Patrick, and Damon were issued weapons that Jeffrey had bought.

During the summer of 1987, Jeffrey and his group came to focus during their scriptural classes on one of Joseph Smith, Jr.'s best-known revelations. It had to do with the persecution of saints and the "redemption" of Zion. In November 1833, an angry mob beat and tarred and feathered several Mormon elders in Independence. The mob then forced dozens of Mormon settlers at gunpoint to leave the county. The saints' homes were looted and their property was seized. When word of the attack reached Kirtland, Joseph Smith, Jr., was outraged. He announced that God had given him a revelation, which was later recorded as Section 98 in the Doctrine and Covenants. According to it, God had commanded his saints to "redeem Zion," which, Smith said, meant that they were supposed to launch an armed attack on the Gentiles in Independence. Smith used the revelation to whip up support, and in May 1834, he set off for Missouri with two hundred armed men. He called his army "Zion's Camp." Church historians would later claim that Smith hoped that this show of force would intimidate the Gentiles, but when his band arrived at the Jackson County line, it was met by a much larger group of armed Missourians. Rather than fight, Smith appealed to state officials to avoid bloodshed by compensating the Mormons for the land and property that had been stolen from them. The governor ignored Smith's request and the two armed camps faced off in a stalemate. When cholera swept through the ill-prepared Mormon troops, the prophet was forced to retreat to Kirtland with little to show for his effort.

Jeffrey told his followers that Section 98 had been misinterpreted by Smith and the RLDS Church. It actually had nothing to do with the 1833 attack on Mormons. Rather, the revelation contained secret instructions from God to Jeffrey and his followers. These instructions were concealed in a part of the revelation known as the "parable of the vineyard."

Joseph Smith, Jr., had claimed that God told him this parable. It was about a rich nobleman who was once given a choice spot of land to use as a vineyard. He sent his servants to plant olive trees on the property and he sent watchmen to build a lookout tower there and also construct a wall around the vineyard to protect it from attack. The watchmen built the tower, but they decided that there wasn't any need for them to put up a wall so they ignored the nobleman's orders. One night, an enemy attacked, plundered the vineyard, and destroyed the lookout tower. When the nobleman heard what had happened, he sent his warriors to reclaim the vineyard and take revenge.

Smith had said the parable was an example of what can happen when the saints didn't follow orders from God [the nobleman in the parable]. But Jeffrey put an entirely different spin on the story. He diagramed each sentence in the parable and then revealed the "secret" messages that they contained. According to Jeffrey, the vineyard in the parable was actually Kirtland, the lookout tower was the Kirtland temple, and God was ordering Jeffrey's followers to guard the temple.

"I am the last messenger that God has sent to the Kirtland temple to prepare the way for Christ's return," Jeffrey reiterated, "and the reason why He has called you here is because you are going to help me protect it."

Jeffrey told his followers that major earthquakes would erupt during the final days before Christ returned and a huge mountain would rise up underneath the Kirtland temple, lifting it into the sky. This was based on Jeffrey's interpretation of verses 2 and 3 in chapter 2 of Isaiah. Jeffrey read the crucial lines to his followers:

> *"And it shall come to pass in the last days, when the mountain of the Lord's house shall be established . . . all nations shall flow unto it. And many people shall go and say, Come ye, and let us go up to the mountain of the Lord . . ."*

Once the temple was raised on this mountain, Satan's armies would swarm to Ohio in a final attempt to destroy the temple, kill the "last messenger" and thereby prevent Christ from returning to earth, he said. Jeffrey and his band would be waiting on the mountain for the onslaught.

"We will not have electricity. We won't have houses. We will have to live off the land and we will have to protect the temple by whatever means possible until Christ shows up." That was why Jeffrey was buying tents, food, and military-style weapons.

"When the armies of Satan come against us," Jeffrey preached, "when they come to kill me and to kill you, we must be ready to fight and to die. We must be ready to shed blood.

"And," he added, "there will be lots of it spilled—lots and lots of it."

It sounded gallant and everyone agreed. If they were going to have to kill in order to protect the temple, then they would do just that.

Chapter 27

In the late spring of 1987 while Jeffrey was preparing his followers for Armageddon, Tom Miller was reaching some conclusions of his own about what the scriptures said and what the RLDS Church espoused. "Everything we have been taught and everything I understood is completely false," Tom announced one morning to Jeffrey while they both were at work in the visitors' center. "I have come to the understanding that the RLDS is a church of men. There is a church of God, but to my knowledge it doesn't exist on earth as I perceive it to be defined in the scriptures."

Jeffrey agreed with him.

"Then why don't we walk out together?" Miller suddenly suggested. "I'm going to resign right now. Why don't you go with me? We'll go over to Dale Luffman's office and both quit."

Jeffrey declined.

Miller pressed him. "Why stay on if you don't believe any of this? Why preach lies?"

"I'm not preaching lies," Jeffrey replied, "because I'm not teaching what the RLDS is putting out. I'm teaching the truth." Jeffrey still planned to someday lead a fundamentalist revolt. He would restore the truth to God's "only true church."

"Sure," Miller retorted. Later when he recalled their conversation, Miller said: "I knew enough about what Jeff was teaching to know that it was erratic and illogical and not consistent with the scriptures. The reason Jeffrey didn't want to resign was because he was all puffed up about teaching his Sunday school class and he had these followers. He liked feeling important."

Miller marched across the street and tossed his priesthood card on Luffman's desk. "I told him that I had no time for him, no time for the church. . . ." Luffman was not sorry to see Tom Miller go. He had been part of the group of troublemakers. By June 1987, Luffman had been the stake president for eighteen months, but he still hadn't been able to get rid of Jeffrey nor quiet the growing feud that was splitting the congregation. If anything, Luffman was losing. The adult Sunday school class that Jeffrey taught had become an ironclad stronghold for dissidents. Not everyone in the class felt comfortable with Jeffrey's constant harping about chiasmus. But the presence of Jeffrey's group—Richard, Greg, Danny, Sharon, the Patricks, and the Averys—each Sunday stifled all debate. Even Bill and Eleanor Lord were beginning to feel intimidated.

In July, Luffman felt the conflict had become, in his words, "almost demonic." He decided to confront his critics head-on. On Sunday morning, he walked into Jeffrey's class and made a fifteen-minute plea for peace. "I want to appeal to you to join the body of Christ," he said. He talked about the need for the congregation to come together and said that it was wrong for one clique to believe it had "higher or more important knowledge" than anyone else. He complained about members who boycotted the worship service and he berated those closest to Jeffrey who had not made any effort to participate in church functions. When he finished, Luffman expected a rebuttal from Jeffrey or someone in the class. But no one said anything.

"I stood there in dead silence for what seemed like an eternity, and then after a while, Jeffrey stood up and said, 'It is time for our lesson,' and everyone opened their books. I realized that I had reached absolutely no one."

When the class ended, Luffman marched up to Jeffrey. "This is the last time you are teaching in this church. Your class is finished."

Luffman was personally disbanding Jeffrey's class. Jeffrey was usurping the power of the local church to choose its own teachers. As stake president, Luffman was recognized under Ohio law as the legal representative for the Kirtland church and if he was forced to physically bar Jeffrey from teaching by calling in the police, he was prepared to do so. Luffman had had enough.

Jeffrey didn't show up the next Sunday. Neither did members of his group. Luffman felt good. He had finally won a battle with Jeffrey. At least that is what he thought. "The next week, I noticed a whole lot of folks on Sunday morning going down the street into the home of a fundamentalist member," Luffman recalled. "After a couple weeks of this, I spotted Jeffrey walking over there too."

Jeffrey was still teaching. He'd simply moved his class into the living room of one of his supporters.

Now it was Jeffrey's turn to fight back. He ordered the members of his group to begin withdrawing their memberships from the RLDS church. "Every time Luffman baptized someone and added a name to the church rolls," he recalled, "I had one of my people resign. That way, Luffman could never get ahead." Richard, Danny, Sharon, Greg, the Patricks, and the Averys all played along. Luffman seethed.

In early August, Kevin Currie knocked on Jeffrey's front door. He was homesick, he told Jeffrey, and wanted to move back in with them. Jeffrey said it was okay, but as punishment, he made Kevin sleep for one week in the basement. Later, he joked, "I'm gaining more followers than Luffman."

If anything, Jeffrey's confrontations with Luffman made him more cocky, and less cautious. One afternoon in late August, Jeffrey was giving a youth group a tour. As usual, he mentioned the pattern and how it could be found in anything that God made or said. One of the adult leaders asked if Jeffrey had found it in the Doctrine and Covenants. Without thinking, Jeffrey replied that he had found it in all of Joseph Smith, Jr.'s revelations, but not in some of the more recent ones. Which ones? the visitor asked. Jeffrey said that Section 156, the 1984 declaration that allowed women to join the priesthood, was not chiastic and, therefore, was "man's word, not God's."

Eleanor Lord was helping Jeffrey give the tour and when she heard what he said, she knew he had made a big mistake. In effect, Jeffrey had just called the church's President-Prophet Wallace B. Smith a fraud.

"You really blew it, Jeff," she said after the tour. "Instead of hedging your bets and telling that man to determine for himself whether or not the pattern was in the Doctrine and Covenants, you had to give them your answer."

Eleanor explained that the adult sponsor who had questioned Jeffrey was a high priest in the church, one of the loftiest positions, and an obvious supporter of Wallace B. Smith.

"Jeffrey was stunned and afraid," Eleanor recalled later. "He hadn't realized until then exactly what he had done."

At the very minute that Eleanor was criticizing Jeffrey, the high priest was storming across the street to see Dale Luffman.

"Who is this Jeffrey Lundgren?" the high priest asked.

"Confidentially, he's a guy I've got a lot of problems with and I'd like to hang his butt and get him out of here," Luffman replied.

The priest told Luffman what Jeffrey had said during the tour. Luffman got excited. "Would you do me and the church a big favor?" he asked. "Write down word for word exactly what happened and give me a copy." Luffman said he would make certain that reports of the incident would be sent to Jeffrey's boss and also Wallace B. Smith.

"You bet I will," the high priest replied.

A few days later, Bill Lord received a letter from church officials in Independence. It said there were too many full-time guides at the visitors' center and that Jeffrey should be fired. The letter made Bill Lord angry. "I didn't hire Jeffrey," he told Eleanor. The director of historic sites had hired Jeffrey. Bill sent word back to Independence. If the church wanted Jeffrey fired, then the director who hired him was going to have to get rid of him. No one in Independence did anything.

Luffman became frustrated. "No matter what I tried, I couldn't get rid of this guy."

And then Luffman's luck changed. A church official, who was completely unaware of the dispute over Jeffrey, happened to notice that contributions to the Kirtland temple and sales at the visitors' center had plummeted to an all-time low. The church ordered an audit. "Over the period of time that Jeff Lundgren had been assigned the task of taking care of the financial records [two and a half years], the church calculated that he had extracted out of the till between seventeen and twenty-one thousand dollars," Luffman later said.

Although the church was certain Jeffrey had stolen the money, it didn't have any evidence. A church official was sent to Kirtland to confront Jeffrey. The two men made a deal. Jeffrey would resign as a temple guide. In return, the church would permit him to continue working one more month and would let him stay in his church-provided house rent-free until he found somewhere to move. The church also promised to keep quiet about the missing money.

Because the accusations against Jeffrey were dealt with in such a hush-hush fashion, Bill Lord wasn't told the real reason why Jeffrey was being forced to resign. He incorrectly believed that Jeffrey was being ousted because of his controversial teachings. Consequently, Lord left Jeffrey in charge of collecting donations to the temple and tallying the cash register receipts at the visitors' center, a move that even Jeffrey found to be incredible.

Jeffrey moved quickly to protect his reputation. He called everyone in his group together and explained that the church was kicking him out because, as he put it, "I am preaching the truth.

"Whenever a prophet begins to prophesy," Jeffrey explained, "the people turn against him. The scriptures say that prophets are 'cast out.' That is happening now. I am being 'cast out' of the temple. I have been told to resign."

It didn't take Jeffrey long to come up with a new scheme. Jeffrey wanted to form a commune. He and his group would create their own Zion. Jeffrey began calling realtors. A few days later, Stanley Skrbis called. Skrbis owned a five-bedroom farmhouse on a 15.07-acre tract on the southern edge of Kirtland. At one time, it had been a beautiful apple orchard with a comfortable two-story farmhouse and picturesque red barn. But the trees had been neglected and the house and barn were in bad need of repair. Skrbis was willing to rent it cheap—the entire acreage for $650 per month—if Jeffrey would fix up the property.

"This is just what I want," Jeffrey announced. Later that night, he called everyone together and explained what he had in mind. They would pool their money and rent the Skrbis property. They would repair the house and barn and work to make the apple orchard productive. Over time, they would open the barn as a combination crafts and antiques store. Jeffrey and Alice would buy and sell the antiques. Group members would provide homemade crafts. They would sell quilts, handicrafts, even homemade apple cider and apple pies. Eventually, they would buy the farm and become so prosperous that none of them would have to work anywhere else. They would wait on the farm for Christ to return.

The longer Jeffrey talked about the commune, the grander the expectations became. He even had a name picked out for the antiques business: Kristen's Kupboard, after his daughter and favorite child. By the time the class ended around midnight, everyone was enthused. "This is going to be just wonderful," Alice declared.

In mid-September, Shar Olson arrived in Kirtland to visit Richard and Greg. During the weekend visit, Jeffrey fussed over Shar. He told her about the pattern and how the group was moving to the farm. "I felt that I was being called to go," she said. Privately, Jeffrey also assured her that he could find the name of her "true companion" in the scriptures. Shar hurried back to Independence, quit her job, and moved to Kirtland. She moved in with Sharon.

Jeffrey also contacted Ron and Susie Luff and invited them to move to Kirtland. Ron had been writing Jeffrey letters since May when the Luffs first met him during a temple tour, and the Luffs were convinced that Jeffrey was someone special. Ron quit his job at the James River Power Station in Springfield,

Missouri, listing his reason for leaving as: "desired relocation and church work." He and Susie, along with their two small children, Matthew and Amy, arrived in Kirtland during September. Jeffrey sent them to stay in Greg's apartment.

As soon as Jeffrey paid the first month's rent on the Skrbis farmhouse, he and his followers went to work. They hauled away trash, gutted the interior, hung Sheetrock, painted, papered, cleaned, and polished. Within two weeks the rickety farmhouse was a showplace. By late September, it was ready. Jeffrey announced that Kevin, Richard, Shar, Danny, and Sharon would live with his family in the farmhouse. The Patricks, Averys, and Luffs would live in their own apartments but would still be required to financially support the commune. Greg had been invited to live at the farm, but had decided to keep his apartment.

Bill Lord would later recall that Jeffrey's last day at work as a temple tour guide fell on a Saturday. Even though he was being forced to resign, Jeffrey gave several tours that morning and seemed as enthused as ever when he talked about the temple. When it was time to close the visitors' center, Jeffrey emptied the cash register, tallied that week's receipts—some $1,600—and put the money into a bank bag for the last time. He told Bill that he would deposit it, as usual, that afternoon.

"Jeffrey was upset about being fired," recalled Eleanor. "He and Alice both were. They felt abused and picked on, but in their hearts, I think they knew better." It was a tearful time for the Lords. Despite the problems, they both adored Alice and genuinely liked Jeffrey.

The next Monday, Bill went over early to open the visitors' center. Within minutes after he had unlocked the front door, Jeffrey burst in. He had bad news. On Saturday, he had stopped at the post office before taking the temple's $1,600 to the bank. "I left the money bag on the front seat of my car when I went inside and must have accidentally left the doors unlocked," he told Bill. "When I came back, someone had taken it."

"Did you report it to the police?" asked Bill.

"I didn't think it would do any good," Jeffrey replied. "I'm sure the thief is long gone."

Bill simply nodded his head.

Chapter 28

LIFE on the farm seemed wonderful—at least to Shar Olson. "I felt a real sense of belonging," she later remembered. "It began when we fixed up the house." For two weeks everyone worked side by side. "We'd get off work, meet at the farm, and begin knocking down walls. We'd work until we dropped. Jeff would go buy us a bucket of chicken and we'd sit on the floor covered with plaster and eat and laugh and talk about how we were going to make this all work and how we were going to bring about Zion. I really felt like we were becoming a family."

That was something Shar craved in the fall of 1987. By her own account, she felt lonely. Born less than a mile from RLDS headquarters in Independence, Shar was the youngest of three children and an only daughter. "I was a daddy's girl and I loved it," she said. "I thought we had a perfect family." When Shar was eleven, her parents divorced. "I remember lying in bed at night listening to them argue." After her parents separated, Shar and her mom became best friends, and the church became central to their lives. "I went through all the girls' groups. I started in Skylarks, the RLDS version of Brownies, and moved up through the various programs." She spent six weeks each summer in church camps, rarely missed a Sunday service, prayer meeting, youth group. She grew up inside an RLDS cocoon, thinking everyone believed in the Book of Mormon. She found out otherwise when she went to a Baptist-affiliated college for one year. "Everyone kept asking me if I was saved." She stuck out, felt out of place.

Her father had remarried so Shar went to live with him for a few months in New Orleans. She felt just as awkward in that sultry city as she had at college. Shar returned to the center spot. She was a beautiful girl with straight blond hair that dangled to her waist, an attractive figure, an effervescent personality. Worlds of Fun amusement park hired her to work as a character escort. She guided a fellow employee dressed in an animal costume through the amusement park where they posed for photographs with children. Shar became reacquainted with Greg Winship at an RLDS meeting of young adults. He introduced her to Richard. A short time later, Shar's mother married Greg's uncle. "The church had always been the one part of my life that was rock solid," she later recalled. In 1984 that changed. Shar was in the RLDS auditorium when delegates approved the ordination of women into the priesthood. She burst into tears. "It seemed like all the foundations that I had grown up with were crumbling." Shar's mother moved to Texas. Richard and Greg went to Ohio. Following her pals to Kirtland seemed natural.

At the farm, Shar began calling Jeffrey and Alice "Dad" and "Mom." It fit. "Alice was motherly." Each night, Alice would rub lotion on Shar's feet because she had dry skin.

"Shar liked to get attention," recalled Jeffrey. "I would be sitting on the couch with my daughter Krissy curled up next to me and Shar would come over and curl up on my other side. It wasn't sexual. She just wanted someone to love her."

Late one night after the group moved to the farm, Shar knocked on the door of the Lundgrens' bedroom. Jeffrey and Alice were watching television. She sat on the edge of their bed.

"Mom and Dad, I need to know something," she said. She and Danny had been spending a lot of time together. Shar wanted to know if that was okay. "I don't want to get involved if he's not my true companion."

Alice began to giggle. "I was hoping you two would hit it off!" she exclaimed.

"It's okay for you two to spend time together," added Jeffrey.

The next morning, Shar asked Alice if Danny was the one.

"I can't say," Alice replied. "Only a prophet can answer that."

"So, like do we know any prophets?" Shar replied innocently.

Alice looked directly at Shar. "Do you?" Alice asked.

"Do I?" Shar replied, confused.

"I guess you will have to figure that out for yourself," Alice replied.

"That is when I first realized that Alice thought Jeff was a prophet," Shar said later. "She was really pushing that idea. She wanted to be a prophet's wife."

That night during scripture class, Jeffrey told Danny and Shar to sit next to each other. Although Shar didn't know it, Jeffrey had told Danny before she arrived in Kirtland that the next woman to join the group was his companion. Danny was pleased. He had quickly fallen in love with Shar.

Ron and Susie were also happy about their move to Kirtland. Like Shar, they had become disenchanted with the liberalization of the RLDS. Both of them considered themselves spiritually gifted. Ron, who was twenty-seven, had written a book of inspirational poetry. Susie felt she had the gift of prophecy. Jeffrey hadn't liked either of them when they met. "When they first started writing me, they would tell me all this spiritual nonsense," he said, "so I would write back these horrible letters and really chastise them. I thought I'd never hear from them again, but they would always write back and tell me that what I had written had been right. It was like they were saying 'Hit me! Oh, hit me more! I deserved that.' "

Ron had grown up in Independence, where he had been a weight lifter and football star at Harry Truman High School. After graduating in 1978, he had joined the navy. He had started dating Susan Edson, who was a year older and had also grown up in Independence, during a trip home. They were married February 7, 1981, by Ron's father, an RLDS priesthood member. Like Jeffrey, Ron had a weight-lifter's build with broad shoulders and thick arms. Susie was slender and a nonstop talker.

"Like most of the others," Jeffrey said, "Ron and Susie came because they wanted me to give them something. They felt I could take them to see Christ."

At the farm, Jeffrey held scripture classes every night. Everyone but the Averys was required to attend. "The classes were basically to reestablish and reaffirm very strongly in our minds that there was such a thing as the pattern and that the pattern was true," Ron later told federal investigators. "The basic precept was that if you used the pattern you could not err, you absolutely could not flaw." Once the group accepted that precept, Jeffrey moved to the next step. "Ultimately, anyone who believed in the pattern also came to believe in the seer who brought it forth," recalled Ron. "And since the pattern could not err, they came to believe that the seer could not err either."

In short, Jeffrey was infallible.

Most classes lasted two or three hours, unless someone made a mistake. "Then there would be a 'session' time," said Ron, and "sometimes those would get to be real loud discussions and they would lead to the early hours of the morning, sometimes three or four o'clock."

The word "session" was a reference that Jeffrey originally had used when disciplining his children. Damon was rather meek, but Jason, then thirteen, was stubborn. "It would take ten or fifteen licks before he finally gave in. I called them a session because they took so long."

Dennis Patrick, Susie Luff, and Dennis and Cheryl Avery received the most "sessions" from Jeffrey—and Alice. "The slightest little mistake would evolve into a whole big example of sin," said Ron. "This was continuous and basically what that evolved into was that people were taught that they couldn't do anything right." Jeffrey would tell someone to do a task and then chastise them for not doing it the way that he would have.

"But you didn't tell us how to do it," a group member would respond.

"You should have known without asking," Jeffrey would reply.

There was only one correct answer to any question, Ron said. "You had to become one heart and one mind with Jeffrey."

One night everyone was eating dinner at the farm and talking about the Old Testament prophet Isaiah, when Susie announced: "I'd like to meet a prophet face-to-face." For several seconds everyone was quiet. Susie was sitting across from Jeffrey.

"Susie," Alice replied, "you wouldn't know a prophet if he was sitting across the table from you." Everyone laughed. Susie didn't understand. But Ron did.

"It took some time and it took the classes to do it," he later told investigators, "but I came to believe . . . that Jeff was the seer of the last days, the one that Malachi speaks of . . . he was the prophet of the last days who had come to prepare the way for Christ's return."

Everyone worked at the farm except for Jeffrey and Alice. Prophets were forbidden by God to have regular jobs because that would require them to submit to another human being, Alice told the group. "Prophets only answer to God."

"Alice didn't have to work either," said Shar, "because she was the wife of the prophet."

Richard had gotten a $22,400-per-year job as a civil engineer in a nearby town. Kevin collected about $18,000 annually as a clerk at a Veterans Administration hospital near Cleveland. Sharon earned minimum wage as a cashier at a convenience store. Shar got a job as a clerk at the Makro Department Store. Danny framed pictures at Gallup's Fine Art store. Dennis Patrick worked first at Scandinavian Health Spa and later at Chemical Financial Corporation, earning $20,850 annually. Greg earned $20,275 yearly as an accountant at Astro Travel Service. Ron operated a forklift at Cleveland Electric Illuminating Company, earning $17,630 per year. Investigators would later estimate that Jeffrey and Alice were collecting between $1,500 to $2,000 per week from their followers. Jeffrey was supposed to use the income to pay everyone's bills, but he didn't. No one but Jeffrey knew how the money was being spent. The Averys were the only ones not making weekly contributions. That was because Dennis had already given Jeffrey $10,000 and because Dennis and Cheryl were now broke. Dennis had held a slew of low-paying jobs since moving to Kirtland, but none paid more than minimum wage and the family was forced to apply for food stamps.

Whenever anyone wanted money, they had to ask Jeffrey, and Shar discovered that he was tightfisted when it came to everyone's needs except his and Alice's. The Patricks were told that there was no money for such frivolous expenses as buying a pizza on Friday night. Yet, at least once a week, Jeffrey would announce that he and Alice needed some time alone and they would go out to dinner and to a movie. If Alice didn't like what was being fixed for supper, she would

send Jeffrey for a shrimp party platter from the local Red
Lobster and the two of them would gorge themselves in their
bedroom.

Everyone who lived in the farmhouse, except Alice, had
chores. Shar was supposed to dust the hardwood floors downstairs once a week, do everyone's laundry, clean the refrigerator and stove. Sharon cleaned the upstairs and was responsible
for picking up the four Lundgren children's clothing, making
their beds, and tidying their rooms. Richard took care of the
trash, Danny cleaned the bathrooms, Kevin helped cook. Even
Tonya and Susie, who didn't live at the farmhouse, were
expected to come every Saturday and help clean. "Alice mostly
slept," Shar recalled. Jeffrey began referring to the women at
the farm as "Alice's handmaidens."

Despite the inequalities, no one complained. All of them
believed in the pattern. All of them believed in Jeffrey. All
of them thought that he was a prophet.

At first Jeffrey seemed content at the farm, but his mood
soon changed. He began complaining to Alice about how the
RLDS had treated him, how unfair it was that a "fool" like
Dale Luffman was recognized as a minister while God's "last
messenger" remained anonymous, how he was once again
forced to resign from a job. "Jeffrey missed giving tours,"
said Alice. "He was used to having fundamentalists seek him
out for advice." At the farm, no one came to the door to take
his picture, no one slipped hundred-dollar bills into his hand, no
one remarked about how much he resembled Joseph Smith, Jr.
Jeffrey had once talked about overthrowing Wallace B. Smith.
Now he spent his mornings building hutches for the rabbits that
the group had decided to raise.

Less than two weeks after moving to the farm, Jeffrey
announced that he had found a startling message in the scriptures. He had been studying the "parable of the vineyard" when
he had come across this line:

> . . . the lord of the vineyard said unto one of
> his servants . . .

Jeffrey reminded the class that the "lord of the vineyard"
was God. He then pointed out that he—Jeffrey—was "one of

His [God's] servants." Obviously, he said, the parable contained a hidden message "to me from God."

To learn what this secret instruction was, Jeffrey had used the pattern to divide the parable. He had done this by putting the words that came directly *before* "the lord of the vineyard" at the top of his diagram and those that came directly *after* that phrase at the bottom. This is what he wrote.

[A] saved my vineyard from
   [B] the hands of *the destroyer*
     [C] and the lord of the vineyard
   [B] said unto one of his *servants*
[A] Go, and gather together the residue of my servants

When he did this, Jeffrey discovered that the word "servant" was synonymous with the words "the destroyer" because they were both on [B] lines and mirrored each other.

"God is giving me a new name and a new job," Jeffrey declared. "Besides being the last messenger, I am now to be called 'the destroyer.' People will die at my hands."

Whom did God want him to destroy? Jeffrey asked rhetorically.

The answer was in the [A] lines. Jeffrey explained that God wanted him to gather "the residue of my servants"—a symbolic reference to Jeffrey's followers—and with them, he was to cleanse the vineyard until it was "saved."

"The enemies that I am to destroy are the persons now in control of the vineyard," Jeffrey said. He then quickly reminded his followers that the vineyard was symbolic of the Kirtland temple.

"Dale Luffman and the RLDS Church are the enemy," he said. "They are the wicked who have seized control of the vineyard."

Jeffrey opened his scriptures and read several lines of the parable aloud to the class. He was visibly excited and his voice rose as he spoke: "Go ye straightway unto the land of my vineyard. And redeem my vineyard, for it is mine . . . avenge me of mine enemies."

Jeffrey slapped shut his book. "Ladies and gentlemen, God is commanding us to take over the Kirtland temple. I am the destroyer. We must destroy the wicked who are now in control of the temple if we want Christ to return.

"And that is exactly what I intend to do."

Jeffrey had not only found a way to take revenge on Dale Luffman but he had come up with an idea that was bound to make him famous once again.

Chapter 29

JEFFREY wanted to prepare his followers for the takeover of the Kirtland temple. He began by bringing home war movies. *First Blood,* the story of John Rambo, a Vietnam veteran who took on an entire town's police force single-handedly and won, was one of the first that he rented. Next came *Apocalypse Now.* Jeffrey canceled class so that everyone could watch it. When it ended, Jeffrey rewound the videotape and started it over. He watched it four times in a row. The next night he canceled class again. This time, he shared his experiences in Vietnam with the group. He said he had participated in covert missions in enemy territory. He'd killed untold numbers of Vietcong both with his rifle and in hand-to-hand combat. He'd cut off the ears of some as souvenirs. He was so deadly that his peers nicknamed him "killer."

"Jeffrey convinced us that if a policeman was holding one of us as a shield, all we had to do was stand perfectly still and Jeffrey could shoot him between the eyes," recalled Shar. " 'It might make you deaf for a while,' he told us, 'but otherwise you'll be okay.' "

When Jeffrey resumed teaching his nightly classes, he fed his followers a steady fare of violence from the Book of Mormon and the Bible. He talked about how Jael, in chapter 4 of the Old Testament book of Judges, had pounded a tent stake through the head of Sisera as he was sleeping. He recalled how Moses

Self-proclaimed prophet Jeffrey Don Lundgren told jurors that he executed the five members of the Dennis Avery family because God ordered him to "destroy the wicked." The Averys' biggest sin: questioning whether Lundgren was really a prophet.

CURT CHANDLER/CLEVELAND *PLAIN DEALER*

Jeffrey Lundgren is returned to Lake County in handcuffs from San Diego, California. Claiming that the prophets in the Old Testament had worn their hair long for religious reasons, Jeffrey refused to cut his before trial.　　DUNCAN SCOTT/*NEWS HERALD*

At her trial, Alice Lundgren claimed that she was a battered wife who had suffered years of psychological and sexual abuse. But Jeffrey's followers described Alice as Jeffrey's "cheerleader" and closest adviser. "If Jeffrey wants me to be his doormat, then I'll be happy the rest of my life cleaning his shoes," Alice was quoted as saying. CURT CHANDLER/CLEVELAND *PLAIN DEALER*

Kirtland Police Officer Ron Andolsek examines the pit in the barn where the bodies of the Averys were found nine months after the murders. Jeffrey selected a corner that flooded from rainwater, explaining that the Averys had to be covered with water just like the Egyptians who drowned while pursuing Moses across the Red Sea. LUCI WILLIAMS/CLEVELAND *PLAIN DEALER*

Dennis and Cheryl Avery were wooed to Kirtland, Ohio, by Jeffrey Lundgren's fundamentalist teachings. The Averys gave Jeffrey and Alice a car and $10,000 in cash. But when the Averys ran out of money, Jeffrey shunned them and eventually told his followers that God wanted the Averys murdered as a human sacrifice. Dennis, Trina, and Cheryl are pictured standing in back row. Rebecca, in overalls, and Karen are in front.

MARLENE JENNINGS

When Alice was eighteen, a church patriarch prophesied that she would marry a "companion" who would "be great" and "bring forth a marvelous work and wonder." Although Alice was certain that Jeffrey was that man, his parents opposed their marriage until she became pregnant.

RECENT PHOTO OF ALICE IN THE OHIO REFORMATORY FOR WOMEN COURTESY OF ALICE LUNDGREN

A devout church member, Shar Olson believed Jeffrey was a prophet until she caught him lying. At the time Olson left the group, Jeffrey was planning to take over the Kirtland temple by force and behead the Reverend Dale Luffman. Olson tipped off Kirtland Police Officer Ron Andolsek to the threat.

CURT CHANDLER/
CLEVELAND *PLAIN DEALER*

Follower Kathryn R. Johnson left her husband and four children after Jeffrey convinced her that she had been created from one of his ribs and was supposed to be his wife. She later gave birth to Jeffrey's child and at her court sentencing proclaimed that her only crime was "loving Jeffrey."

CURT CHANDLER/CLEVELAND *PLAIN DEALER*

Two paramedics remove a body from the barn on the farm that Jeffrey Lundgren and his followers rented outside Kirtland, Ohio.   GEORGE HEINZ/CLEVELAND *PLAIN DEALER*

Kirtland Police Chief Dennis Yarborough (left), one of the first to become suspicious of Jeffrey, confers with Lake County Prosecutor Steven C. LaTourette and Assistant Prosecutor Karen Kowall on the morning the Averys' bodies were unearthed.

CURT CHANDLER/CLEVELAND *PLAIN DEALER*

Dennis Avery's younger brother, Tim, and his wife, Lisa, suspected that Jeffrey Lundgren was a fraud but were unable to convince Dennis and Cheryl. After the murders, Tim and Lisa were escorted by Chief Yarborough through the barn where the bodies were found. CURT CHANDLER/CLEVELAND *PLAIN DEALER*

Kirtland Police Chief Dennis Yarborough kneels beside several holes drilled into a slab of rock at Chapin Forest. Jeffrey told his followers that the holes were air vents that led to a hidden treasury that contained golden tablets inscribed with holy scriptures and that the opening to the treasury was guarded by an angel.

CURT CHANDLER

Damon Lundgren begged for mercy at his trial and claimed his father forced him to participate in the murders. Testimony showed that Damon became physically ill when his father made him look at Dennis Avery's bloody body moments after he was executed. Jeffrey Lundgren reacted by giving Damon, then eighteen years old, a fatherly hug.

CURT CHANDLER/
CLEVELAND *PLAIN DEALER*

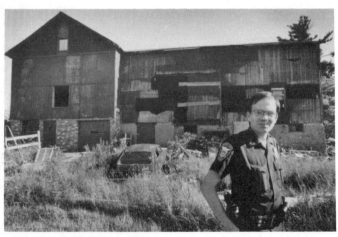

Kirtland Police Officer Ron Andolsek stands in front of the barn where the Averys were buried. He became so engrossed in the case that he suffered fits of depression. CURT CHANDLER

Kathryn Johnson was arrested by police in California shortly after Jeffrey and his family were caught. She had been living in a motel close to where Jeffrey and Alice were staying. Jeffrey had kept her presence a secret because he was afraid Alice would leave him if she knew his "second wife" was nearby.

Troubled by a painful recurring back injury, near bankruptcy and newly divorced, Debbie Olivarez proved easy prey when her cousin, Jeffrey Lundgren, invited her to join his commune. He promised her a safe harbor. Instead, Olivarez ended up cooking the Averys their "last supper" and watching as the family members were led one by one from the farmhouse to the barn where they were executed.

CURT CHANDLER/
CLEVELAND *PLAIN DEALER*

Keith Johnson told federal agents that five bodies were buried in a Kirtland barn after Jeffrey claimed Kathy Johnson as his second wife. Jealous and angry, Johnson wanted agents to find where Kathy was hiding and punish Jeffrey for the killings.

CURT CHANDLER/
CLEVELAND *PLAIN DEALER*

Dennis and Tonya Patrick were college pals of Jeffrey's and early followers, but he eventually turned against both. Jeffrey threatened to tie Dennis to a tree and shoot him in the testicles. Later, he announced that he was taking Tonya as his new wife. After several intimate weeks, Jeffrey tired of Tonya and sent her back to her husband.   SCOTT SHAW/CLEVELAND *PLAIN DEALER*

Bashful and homely, Sharon J. Bluntschly had worked as a tour guide at two other Mormon historical sites before she moved to Kirtland and met the Lundgrens. Jeffrey and Alice decided Bluntschly was too prudish so they showed her soft-core pornographic movies and told her that the Bible required women to become "carnal, sensual, and devilish."

CURT CHANDLER/
CLEVELAND *PLAIN DEALER*

Gregory S. Winship ran a chain saw outside the barn during the Avery murders to cover up the sound of gunfire. He was later praised by Jeffrey Lundgren for his cleverness in squeezing and gently releasing the chain saw's trigger so that it mimicked the noise of a saw cutting through wood. CURT CHANDLER/ CLEVELAND *PLAIN DEALER*

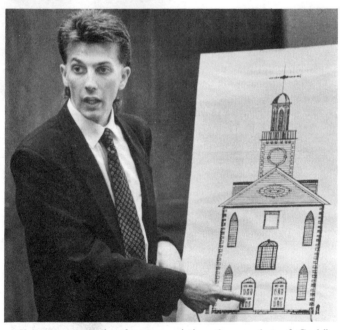

"I cannot apologize for my assisting the prophet of God," follower Daniel D. Kraft, Jr., declared during a two-hour speech at his sentencing. Unrepentant, Kraft showed jurors drawings he had made of the Kirtland temple, which, he said, proved Jeffrey was "not a false prophet." A psychologist testified that Kraft had been "brainwashed" by Lundgren.

CURT CHANDLER/CLEVELAND *PLAIN DEALER*

Richard Brand helped carry the Avery family members into the pit after they were bound and gagged so that Jeffrey Lundgren could kill them. Brand later became the state's chief witness but not without some trepidation. He told prosecutors that he was afraid Jeffrey Lundgren would simply laugh and stand up unharmed after an executioner threw the switch turning on Ohio's electric chair. CURT CHANDLER/ CLEVELAND *PLAIN DEALER*

Another shot of Damon Lundgren; this one shows a scab on his lip that was the result of a jailhouse altercation. He was cold-cocked by another prisoner while walking out of his cell in the Lake County jail. CURT CHANDLER/CLEVELAND *PLAIN DEALER*

Follower Susie Luff was considered simple-minded by others in the Lundgren group, but when Alice Lundgren told her and three other women in private that God wanted them to perform a strip-tease for Jeffrey while he masturbated, Susie was the first to question why God would make such a peculiar request.

CURT CHANDLER/
CLEVELAND *PLAIN DEALER*

A former high school football player and navy veteran, Ronald B. Luff was Jeffrey's number-two man because he knew how to carry out orders. When Lundgren told Luff to come up with a way to lure the Averys out of the farmhouse and into the barn without arousing suspicion, Luff came through. He gave the last victim, six-year-old Karen Avery, a piggyback ride to her death on the pretense that they were going to see the horses in the barn.

CURT CHANDLER/
CLEVELAND *PLAIN DEALER*

The Reverend Dale Luffman clashed with Jeffrey Lundgren during their first meeting and later succeeded in getting Lundgren booted out of the Reorganized Church of Jesus Christ of Latter Day Saints. Lundgren responded by plotting to kidnap Luffman and his family and behead them during an armed takeover of the Kirtland temple. The attack was nixed after Shar Olson tipped off the police. CURT CHANDLER/ CLEVELAND *PLAIN DEALER*

A former navy pal of Lundgren's, Kevin Currie fled the communal farmhouse at Kirtland when he discovered that Jeffrey planned to kill him. Currie warned the FBI that Jeffrey was dangerous, but agents didn't believe him. CURT CHANDLER/ CLEVELAND *PLAIN DEALER*

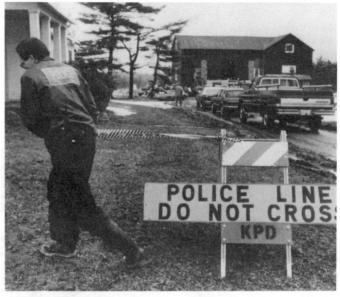

Kirtland Police Officer Ron Andolsek seals off the Lundgren communal farmhouse on the morning that the grave was first uncovered. The house is to the left and the barn where the pit was located is in the upper right corner of the photograph.

LUCI WILLIAMS/CLEVELAND *PLAIN DEALER*

had murdered an Egyptian, how Nephi had slain Laban, and then Jeffrey read everyone the story of the prophet Jacob in the Book of Mormon. Jacob was preaching when his enemy, Sherem, demanded proof that Christ had risen from the dead. Jacob said there was only one way to convince a skeptic such as Sherem and that was by asking God to strike him dead. And that, according to the Mormon scriptures, is what God did.

"God was not afraid to kill," Jeffrey pointed out.

He then reminded everyone how God had ordered him in Section 38 to "go to the Ohio . . . and there you shall be endowed with *power* from on high."

"How am I supposed to receive this power?" Jeffrey asked. Before anyone could answer, Jeffrey referred to the murder of Sherem. "When God wanted to show that He had power, God killed the wicked. If I want to show that I have God's power, if I want to be endowed with that power, then I must kill the wicked."

"I had always believed in the scriptures," said Dennis Patrick. "They couldn't be wrong and everything Jeffrey showed us came directly out of the scriptures."

Just before Christmas, Jeffrey began revealing in class specifics about how he would take over the Kirtland temple. As he did with everything, Jeffrey tied the temple takeover to the return of Jesus Christ. He said that Christ could only return if there was no wickedness in or near the temple. That meant every man, woman, and child who lived within a one-block radius of the temple, some twenty-five people, would have to be executed. This would include Bill and Eleanor Lord. The only family who would not be murdered during the first step of the takeover was Dale Luffman's. Luffman, his wife, Judy, and their three children, ages thirteen, ten, and five, would be bound and gagged and brought into the temple where they would be taken before Jeffrey. After reading several scriptures, Jeffrey would offer the Luffman family to God as a human sacrifice. He would then behead all five of them, beginning with Luffman and moving down the line. In Moses' day, the Jews made sacrifices to God to atone for their sins. Because Christ had not yet returned, Jeffrey claimed that he and his followers were still living under the same laws as Moses. Therefore, the Luffmans would serve as the blood-atonement offering from Jeffrey. They represented the wicked who had seized "the vineyard." Their blood would be spilled to "cleanse it."

Cutting off their heads was also scriptural, Jeffrey taught. Nephi had beheaded Laban, and Conner Macleod, the hero in *The Highlander*, had used his sword to behead his opponents. Obviously, the scriptures didn't actually mention Conner Macleod, but Jeffrey claimed that God had inspired the makers of the movie and that was good enough. After all, the Mormon scriptures said that the glory of God was intelligence. "What better way to cut off a man from God than to sever his head from his body," Jeffrey asked, "making it impossible for him to use his intelligence?"

Once the Luffmans were sacrificed, Jeffrey would chant a secret prayer that would cause "the mountain of the Lord," as described in Isaiah, to rise up. A great earthquake would then erupt and everyone living in Kirtland would be killed. Only the people inside the temple would be spared. Christ would appear and the Millennium would begin. Jeffrey and his followers would be Christ's new disciples.

Alice was the first to hear Jeffrey's entire plan. She would testify later that she didn't believe he was serious. She became even more suspicious when she surprised Jeffrey one morning while everyone else who lived at the farm was at work. Jeffrey was reading military manuals. After he read a page, he would rip it out and bum it in the fireplace, she said. "I couldn't figure out why he was destroying the book until later that night at class. He taught the military stuff like it was all his idea."

Jeffrey also changed the way that he taught. He had always encouraged his followers to read along with him when he quoted scripture. But now he ordered them to close their books. "Jeffrey kept his open," said Alice. "I was sitting right next to him and could see what he was doing. He acted like he was reading a verse from one book, but I could see that he was taking a verse from one book and a verse from another book of scripture and combining them. He was making up his own scriptures."

Alice confronted Jeffrey when they were alone in their bedroom that night. "I said, 'Since when do we start taking things out of context, Jeffrey?,' and he said, 'What'ya mean?,' and I said, 'Now, Jeffrey, this is Alice you're talking to and I saw what you did. You were mixing and matching those verses.' "

Jeffrey exploded in a rage, she said. "He said, 'You shut up about this. You shut up.' He started to shake me. . . . I think that's when I first began to see that Jeffrey was a con man. I believed that he was giving everyone a line of baloney and I decided the temple takeover stuff was bullshit."

If Alice felt that Jeffrey was, as she said, a "con man," she kept quiet about it. "There was never any expression of unbelief on Alice's part," Kevin later said. If anything, Alice became Jeffrey's cheerleader. The two of them reminded Kevin of a tag team in professional wrestling. Jeffrey would declare the "word of the Lord" in a class and then Alice would "rush in and convince everyone that what Jeffrey was saying was the truth."

One night when Shar and Alice were alone, Shar asked her if Jeffrey was serious about killing the Luffmans and taking over the temple. "Alice looked right at me," Shar recalled. "She said, 'Jeffrey is dead serious. If he says he's going to do it, he's going to do it.' " And then Alice added another statement that stuck in Shar's mind. "You've got to understand," Alice said. "I'm not only putting my life on the line here, but I've put my children's life on the line for this. Jeffrey is a prophet. He is who he says he is. You've got to believe it and so do I. I've got to."

Jeffrey assigned everyone tasks. Richard was told to get copies of city maps that showed where gas and other power lines were located. Danny built a replica of the temple and the houses around it and put numbers on the ones where people were to be executed. Since Dennis Patrick lived less than one block from the police station, he was told to watch it and record when the officers changed shifts. Sharon compiled a list of area gasoline stations. Jeffrey said that he might blow one up to create a diversion. The women in the group were shown different bullets and told that they would have to learn to identify them by touch in case they needed to load the men's weapons at night. Shar and Tonya practiced in a room with all the lights off. Jeffrey gave every man a code name. He called himself Eagle-One because, as he put it, "I am in charge and my eyesight is as good as an eagle's." His son Damon, now age seventeen, was Eagle-Two. Danny was Eagle-Eye; Richard, Talon-One; Dennis Patrick, Talon-Two; Ron, Falcon-One; Greg, Falcon-Two. The family farmhouse was dubbed "Eagle's Nest." The red barn was "Red Eagle." The temple was "Eagle's Mound."

No one would later remember what Dennis Avery was called. It simply didn't matter. Dennis and Cheryl still came to classes, but only about once a week. Dennis was working as a night watchman for Wackenhut Security and it was difficult for him to attend at night. Cheryl didn't feel comfortable leaving her three daughters home alone, even though the oldest was thirteen. "The Averys are so stupid," Jeffrey told the class one night, "that the first they will know about the temple takeover is when they see us on television inside the temple."

In February 1988, Jeffrey revealed that he had found the secret prayer that he was required to say in order to make the "mountain of the Lord" rise. God had hidden it in Isaiah, chapter 57, verses 13 and 14. Everyone scrambled to their Bibles. Jeffrey said the key words were "cast ye up, cast ye up."

"Why are those words repeated?" he asked. "Because that is how God talks."

A few days later, Jeffrey made another exciting announcement. God had given him a specific date to attack the temple. "He told me it was posted somewhere in the temple," he explained, "so I went to find it. I looked everywhere and then God's wisdom came to me. If you go to see a doctor, how do you know when he will be in his office? You know by looking at the front door because that is where a doctor posts his office hours." Jeffrey grinned. "God has done the exact same thing. He posted the date that His temple will be redeemed right on the front doors."

The temple doors were decorated with five circles: two large ones and three small ones. The two big circles were symbolic of the second month in the Jewish calendar, Jeffrey said. The three small ones represented days. "God is telling us that He wants us to take over the temple on May third."

Jeffrey asked if anyone knew why that date was significant. Only Alice did.

"May third is Jeffrey's birthday," she volunteered. That was another sign, Jeffrey solemnly declared, that proved he was God's last messenger.

It soon seemed that Jeffrey was having almost daily revelations from God about the takeover. Everyone in the group was getting excited. One night, Jeffrey announced that God wanted them to actually take over the temple on May 1, and then hold the police at bay until May 3 when Christ would appear. "We are going to have a shootout with the police," he said. The next day, Jeffrey showed the group six gas masks that he had bought to use if the police fired tear gas into the temple. But none of Jeffrey's revelations caused as much panic as when he announced that only twelve members of his group were going to survive the shootout and actually be there when Christ appeared. There could be only twelve, Jeffrey said, because Christ had had only twelve disciples when He was alive. Jeffrey, Alice, and Damon were guaranteed safe passage. But only nine of the remaining adults would make it. That meant four of them were going to be killed.

"No one knew if they were on the list," recalled Shar. "It became very divisive and competitive."

Shar asked Jeffrey one day in private if she would make it. "You and Danny are two of the twelve," Jeffrey assured her. Shar asked about Greg and Richard. Jeffrey wasn't certain about Richard, but Greg was safe. Jeffrey then volunteered the names of three group members who were "expendable."

"Kevin is definitely going to die," Shar later quoted Jeffrey as saying. "Even if Kevin survived the takeover, Jeffrey was supposed to shoot him with a shotgun because Kevin was unclean and couldn't be there when Christ returned." Dennis and Tonya were also going to be killed by Jeffrey. "Jeffrey was going to tell the police that we had hostages," Shar said. "He was going to kill Dennis and Tonya and Molly and throw their bodies off the roof of the temple to show the police that we were serious."

Although Shar didn't know it at the time, everyone who asked Jeffrey if they were among the lucky twelve were privately assured that they were safe. They were also told the name of someone who wasn't going to survive. Jeffrey told Kevin that the Patricks were going to die. He told the Patricks that Kevin was going to die.

Shar and Kevin commuted to their jobs in Cleveland each morning together. Most days, Shar slept while Kevin drove. But she was too nervous to sleep during February 1988. "I wanted to warn him, to tell him that he was going to be killed," she explained. "But I was afraid too because if Jeff was who he said he was, then Jeffrey was only doing what God wanted him to do. I figured that God must want Kevin dead."

Shar didn't need to warn Kevin. He had figured it out on his own. "I had picked up several signals." Still Kevin didn't get really scared until he saw how Jeffrey reacted one day when he developed a kidney stone. Jeffrey was in tremendous pain, yet when it was time for the men to lift weights, he performed his normal workout. "Jeffrey always tried to claim that he was sort of a super human, that he was immortal," Kevin said. "The fact that he had a kidney stone showed that he was no different from any other man." But there was something else that bothered Kevin. Jeffrey had been in agony, yet it was so important for him to show off that he had endured the excruciating pain. "I realized just how important all this was to him—how important being a prophet had become. I also realized that he was drawing off our energies. Each time someone new came into the group, Jeffrey gained more confidence in himself. He figured that he was right, that he was a prophet. We were feeding off his fantasy and he was feeding off our fantasy and together we were creating an even bigger and bigger fantasy that was beginning to take on a life of its own."

A few days after Jeffrey recovered from the kidney stone, he and Kevin bumped into each other in the kitchen. For a brief second, their eyes met. "It was strange, but at that very instant, we both knew," said Kevin. "He knew that I no longer believed in him and I knew that he would not, could not, allow me to doubt him. He had too much to lose."

On February 16, the group had a chocolate sheet cake for dessert after dinner.

"Whose birthday is it?" chirped Kristen Lundgren, then age nine.

Jeffrey looked at Kevin. "It's Kevin's going-away cake," he said. Everyone laughed. Kevin had run off before and come back, so everyone assumed that Jeff was kidding him.

Kevin interpreted Jeffrey's comment differently. "He was going to kill me." The next morning, Kevin left for work as usual, but when he got there, he turned in his resignation and hurried to the bus station. Kevin had driven to work by himself that morning. Shar had taken a different job and no longer rode with him into Cleveland. Everyone at the farm wondered where Kevin was that night when he didn't come home. Just before dinner, the phone rang. As always, Jeffrey answered it. A woman was on the line. She refused to give her name, but said that she was a friend of Kevin's.

"The car is parked at the Cleveland bus station," she said.

Jeffrey slammed down the receiver.

"That son of a bitch has run off," Jeffrey swore and then, in front of Alice and Shar, he declared: "Kevin's as good as dead. I'm going to track him down and kill him."

Chapter 30

FOR three days, Jeffrey stormed around the farmhouse, openly discussing how he was going to kill Kevin. "He's in Buffalo hiding. I could get up there and do him and be back overnight." He telephoned Kevin's mother but Kevin had already warned her not to tell Jeffrey where he was hiding. He telephoned the Veterans Administration hospital where Kevin had worked in Cleveland and the one in Buffalo too, but Kevin had not left a forwarding address. Jeffrey finally gave up. "Whether he dies at my hand or whether he dies because I say the prayer that raises the mountain and causes the earthquake really doesn't matter," Jeffrey told the group. "Kevin is dead to God."

In March, Jeffrey learned that Bill and Eleanor Lord had resigned as tour guides and were moving out of the Sidney Rigdon house. He and Alice insisted on helping them move. Jeffrey's group moved everything in one day. Bill was impressed. "It was swell." It reminded the Lords of an old-fashioned barn raising where everyone got together to work hard and build a barn in one day. Jeffrey and Alice refused to accept any cash so Bill took everyone out to dinner. Jeffrey was happy. The Lords had moved far enough from the temple that he wouldn't have to kill them.

By the first of April, the takeover permeated every conversation at the farm. Frequently, it was Alice who brought it up. As the "mother" of the family, Jeffrey had assigned her the job of taking care of the minor children during the temple takeover. Besides Jason, Kristen, and Caleb, she would have to watch the Luffs' two children, and Molly Patrick. She was in charge of buying food for the takeover too. The family would need food between May 1, when they seized the temple, and May 3, when Christ appeared.

"What do you like to eat when you are under stress?" Alice asked Shar one afternoon.

"I don't know," Shar replied. "Why?"

"Oh, I was thinking about the takeover. Isn't this weird? I mean, what we're talking about is the insurrection of a national historical monument!" During the next few minutes, Alice speculated about how long it would take the television cameras to arrive and whether the group would be on the national news. Would *60 Minutes* do a segment on the family? Alice's sister, Terri, had moved to Saudi Arabia with her husband. Alice wondered if the television stations in the Middle East would broadcast the story. "Everyone was getting geared up," said Shar.

One night in mid-April, Jeffrey announced that he was not going to teach his regular class nor drill the group on various military procedures. Instead, he read a passage from the Book of Mormon. It was verses 1 through 47 in the Third Book of Nephi, chapter 5, which told how Jesus Christ had appeared to the ancient Hebrews in the New World after he had been crucified by the Jews.

> . . . *They cast their eyes up again towards heaven; and behold, they saw a man descending out of heaven. And he was clothed in a white robe, and he came down and stood in the midst of them . . . And it came to pass that he stretched forth his hand, and spake unto the people, saying, Behold I am Jesus Christ, of whom the prophets testified should come into the world . . .*

By the time Jeffrey finished reading the verses, there were tears in his eyes. He had always lectured them against becoming emotional but Jeffrey couldn't control himself—or so it seemed.

"This is what we can accomplish if we follow God's words," Jeffrey concluded, his voice cracking. "We can actually see Jesus Christ." He paused and then said, "I am going to see Him. No one is going to keep me from it."

That night, many of Jeffrey's followers couldn't sleep. A few went down to the kitchen and talked about what Jeffrey had said. The idea that they were going to meet Jesus Christ and become one of his chosen disciples, just like Matthew, John, and Peter, was so fantastic that it was difficult to grasp.

The group got a new member in April. It was Jeffrey's cousin, Debbie Olivarez. Because she was from Jeffrey's "bloodline," she didn't need to undergo an orientation period as the Patricks had. "Understanding the pattern will be natural for her," Jeffrey said. Debbie's mother was Lois Lundgren's sister, and as children, Debbie and Jeffrey had frequently played together. Debbie had always been her grandmother Gadberry's favorite grandchild, a fact that had irked Jeffrey. But Debbie had fallen out of favor with the Gadberrys and the Lundgrens when she married John Olivarez in 1969 while still in high school. Debbie had thought that she was pregnant at the time. "I really didn't love John when we got married," Debbie later confided to Jeffrey. "But I felt so guilty about the sexual relationship that I was afraid no one else would want me. I felt like used merchandise."

During the next eighteen years, Debbie and John appeared to be a perfect RLDS family. They were youth leaders in their local RLDS congregation, and John held a series of important church financial jobs. Together they had four children and Debbie became a registered nurse. The two of them eventually opened a family-run Mexican restaurant in Independence. But privately, Debbie was becoming disenchanted. She never had really fallen in love with John and she didn't think that he loved her. When she confided in an RLDS marriage counselor, he told her that she was to blame. "I was the woman. If I would just do whatever my husband told me to do, then our marriage would be fine." After Debbie left the counseling session, the priest called her husband and told him everything Debbie had said in confidence.

In November 1986, Debbie filed for divorce. When the divorce became final in March 1987, Debbie became despondent. She wrenched her back at work and was put on disability. She began going on shopping sprees to boost her spirits. By the fall of 1987, she was heavily in debt and suicidal. To help cheer her up, her grandparents asked Debbie to drive them to Kirtland to visit Jeffrey and Alice. "They had just moved to the farm and it was wonderful. I felt really at peace." Debbie returned to Independence, but Jeffrey invited her back at Christmas and mailed her an airplane ticket. "Deep down I had always been looking for a knight in shining armor to carry me away and Jeffrey convinced me that he could deliver that person to me," Debbie recalled. "He had told me that he knew who my 'true companion' was. . . . He said, 'You will never have a normal relationship unless I help you. You will never find the man that you want. I am the only one who can do that for you.' I believed him and I wanted someone desperately to love and someone to desperately love me."

Debbie returned to Independence, put her house up for sale, and told her parents that she was joining Jeffrey's commune. Jeffrey helped Debbie find a job at a Cleveland hospital. Eleven days after she moved to the farm, she was working as a nurse and stealing medical supplies for use during the temple takeover. "It didn't seem wrong. Everything Jeffrey said fit into place with the scriptures that he cited."

Jeffrey told Debbie that Greg Winship was her true companion. They began dating. "I was happy," Debbie said.

On April 22, Jeffrey went over the final details of the takeover. Everyone would arrive at the farmhouse on May 1. The men would dress in full camouflage military outfits, their faces painted black. They would hike through the apple orchard behind the farm and then follow a right-of-way owned by the electric power company to the back of the RLDS church property. They would split into two groups. Ron, Dennis, and Greg would break into the temple. Danny, Richard, Damon, and Jeffrey would go from house to house killing the occupants. They would capture the Luffman family and bring them to the temple. By that time, the women and children would be safely inside with the other men. Jeffrey would behead the Luffmans. He had already bought a machete and had practiced swinging it in front of the group. Jeffrey would say the secret prayer and the men would get ready for the inevitable shootout with the police.

On May 3, the mountain of the Lord would rise up and Christ would appear and bless the twelve adults who had survived.

There was only one problem. Jeffrey wasn't certain what year God wanted the temple taken over. The front doors listed only the month and day. Jeffrey told his followers that he would get up early in the morning and go to a hill where he would ask God to appear and tell him if this was the year. Everyone was nervous and tense.

When the Patricks left the farmhouse that night after attending Jeffrey's class, Jeffrey called everyone back together. That included Ron and Susie, Greg, Debbie, Richard, Sharon, Danny, Damon, Shar, and Alice. "It was always understood that the Patricks would not make it," Shar later testified. "Jeff always said that Dennis was jealous of Jeff, that he wanted to be in Jeff's position, and that he was a doubter in Jeff's power."

On this particular night, Jeffrey added a new twist. He would kill Dennis once everyone was in the temple, he said, but God wanted someone else to murder Tonya and Molly. "Alice will do it," Jeffrey said. She was required to kill to prove that she believed in Jeffrey. He had bought Alice a 9-millimeter pistol and taught her how to shoot it, he said.

"I looked at Alice," Shar recalled later in court testimony, "because it kind of took me aback and she kind of sat back on the chair and rubbed her hand on the edge of the table and she said, 'We all have to do what we have to do.' "

Chapter 31

KEVIN spent February and March in Buffalo hiding from Jeffrey. He stayed mostly with friends. Only his mother knew where he was and sometimes Kevin didn't tell her. He'd simply call her for messages. When she told him that Jeffrey had telephoned, Kevin panicked. "Jeffrey was so much a part of my psyche," Kevin later recalled, "that I was afraid he could anticipate my moves."

Kevin hadn't taken any of his belongings when he fled Cleveland. He hadn't wanted to arouse suspicion at the farm by packing a suitcase. On the day that he escaped, he had telephoned a woman in Buffalo and asked her to buy him a bus ticket. By noon, Kevin was on his way out of town. He had less than five dollars in his pocket.

He was terrified at first. He couldn't sleep. He started smoking, a habit he'd kicked. Whenever he went outside, he would scan the license plates of approaching cars. If the plate said Ohio, he panicked. Even after several uneventful weeks, Kevin remained scared. Finally, he decided to tell the Federal Bureau of Investigation about the temple takeover. He looked up the address in the telephone book and had a friend drop him off there.

"I didn't even make it past the front lobby. An agent came out to interview me and I could tell from the questions he asked that he figured I was a nut case."

Kevin couldn't blame him. The agent didn't know anything about Joseph Smith, Jr., the RLDS, or the Kirtland temple. Talk about beheadings, the Sword of Laban, and "redeeming the vineyard" sounded fantastic. After listening to Kevin's story, the agent said that the takeover sounded like a "problem for the local authorities." He then asked permission to take Kevin's photograph. "He was more interested in investigating me than Jeffrey."

Kevin hurried out of the FBI field office. He felt foolish. He decided to forget about tipping off the police. But he couldn't shake the image of Jeffrey lifting weights even though he had a kidney stone. "I knew he was going to kill someone." Kevin dialed information and scribbled down the number for the Kirtland Police Department. Maybe there he could find someone willing to take him seriously.

April 28, 1988, was a mundane day for Kirtland Police Chief Dennis T. Yarborough and that was exactly how the forty-three-year-old, slightly balding, tobacco-chewing chief liked them. "Cops generally start working in a small city police department and then go up the ladder until they land some high-paying, big federal-agency job," Yarborough later explained. His twenty-three-year career had taken the opposite track. Yarborough started at the top—as a plainclothes army security officer stationed at the White House in 1965. Four years later, he moved to Pennsylvania as a state-highway trooper. Next came a six-year stint with the Cuyahoga County Sheriff's Department, whose jurisdiction included the Cleveland area. Finally in 1979, Yarborough was named chief of the six-officer Kirtland Police Department. From national, to state, to county, to city: to Yarborough, being police chief of a tiny town was the best possible job. There were two types of law. Hands-on-the-hood, spread-your-legs, I'm-bustin'-your-ass big-city law, where a cop made a name for himself by racking up "collars," and what Yarborough liked to describe as down-home "heartbeat" law, as in "You get so close to your people that you can hear their hearts beating." That was the sort of law that Dennis Yarborough practiced.

There had been only one murder in Kirtland since 1979. In 1987, a total of 91 serious crimes were reported. That was an average of 7.5 crimes per month, about one serious crime every four days. Most of them were not major by big-city standards. Sixty-three of the crimes were thefts, such as stolen bicycles and missing tools from construction sites. Not a single armed robbery. Not a single bank robbery. Not a single arrest related to illegal drugs. There were only five, count 'em, five, burglaries in the entire city during the entire year.

Still, Yarborough and his officers kept busy. Much of what Yarborough did as chief didn't fit into a statistical breakdown. It wasn't unusual for a drunk to rap on Yarborough's bedroom window at 3:00 A.M. looking for a ride home or for frantic parents to call and demand that Yarborough find their wayward teenager who was still carousing on the streets.

There were two reasons why Yarborough had applied for the chief's job. The first was his wife, Gail. Her family could trace itself back to the founders of Kirtland and she had never wanted to live nor been happy living anywhere else. She and Yarborough had met in sixth grade, had fallen in love in seventh, and had never been interested in dating anyone else. In high school, she was the band's majorette. He was the scrappy quarterback of the Kirtland Fighting Hornets football team, good enough to get four scholarship offers from small colleges. Yarborough chose Kent State University instead, but eventually dropped out and joined the army. He and Gail married when they were both twenty. Gail came back sixteen times that first year to visit her folks in Kirtland. It was the first time she had been away from home and she hated living in suburban Washington, D.C. It was Gail who eventually got him to apply to be police chief. Gail worked as a secretary at the high school. She knew everyone in town. On most Sundays, her parents came for supper.

Gail's folks considered Yarborough a "newcomer" even though his family had moved to Kirtland in the 1950s after his stepfather, a welder by trade, was hired at a nearby General Motors auto plant. Yarborough had grown up poor—a family of five all living in a twenty-seven-foot-long trailer. He never minded.

The other reason why Yarborough was police chief, besides Gail, was because he genuinely, some would even say naïvely at times, wanted to help other people. The way that Yarborough treated "old Edna" was typical. By everyone's standards, she was mean and nasty. Only her cats seemed to like her. She had about a dozen. The chief got stuck with handling her chronic complaints. One hot afternoon, Yarborough spent an hour listening to Edna blab about some insignificant gripe.

Finally, he interrupted and asked Edna the names of her cats. It turned out that each of her cats was named for a character from Shakespeare. Pretty soon, Edna was gabbing about the famous English playwright. When it was time to go, Edna berated Yarborough, but begrudgingly added that he was better than the last chief. It was Yarborough who later found Edna dead, lying naked on the floor of her bathroom. She had suffered a stroke. Before Yarborough called the morgue, he took a housecoat out of the closet and put it on the corpse. Several neighbors had gathered outside. "I just didn't want anyone to see her like that," he said. "She would have been embarrassed."

Yarborough recognized the name Jeffrey Lundgren, when Kevin called. Although he was a backslider, Yarborough was raised RLDS. He'd heard all about Jeffrey's ongoing feud with Dale Luffman. Gail and her parents were fundamentalists. Yarborough's mother, who lived with him and Gail, supported Luffman. The chief had gotten an earful from both about the church's problems.

Yarborough had always thought Jeffrey was odd. Shortly after Jeffrey moved to town in 1984, he stormed into Yarborough's office. People were peeking through the windows of his house at night, he claimed. Yarborough waved off the charge. It was probably youngsters, curious about their new neighbors, or tourists who had mistakenly thought the house was part of the temple. Jeffrey didn't think it was funny. A few days later, Yarborough noticed that Jeffrey had painted the glass on all the basement windows green to prevent anyone from seeing inside. All the shades in the house were kept down all day too. "I wondered what he was trying to hide."

A few months later, Yarborough had spotted Jeffrey driving a 1952 green Chevrolet. Yarborough had owned one like it as a teenager. He ran a check on the license plate and discovered it belonged to Danny Kraft, Jr. Curious, Yarborough asked a few questions and discovered that Jeffrey had attracted several young followers.

He hadn't heard much recently about Jeffrey, although his relatives had mentioned that Jeffrey had resigned as a tour guide and started a commune at the old apple orchard. And now Kevin Currie was on the phone, telling Yarborough that

Jeffrey was going to lead an armed takeover of the temple and behead Dale Luffman.

By the time Kevin finished talking, Yarborough was "ninety percent" certain that it was true. But it was so bizarre that Yarborough decided to get a second opinion. He telephoned the FBI office in nearby Painesville and asked to speak to Special Agent Robert Alvord. Yarborough considered Alvord a personal friend. A tall, lanky man in his early forties, Alvord had been with the bureau eighteen years and was an ex-F4 Phantom-jet pilot who had served two tours in Vietnam.

"This is Yarborough," he announced when Alvord came on the line. "Do I have something that is going to ring your bell!" He quickly highlighted Kevin's story. "I think he's telling the truth, Bob," Yarborough concluded. "How can you guys help me?"

Alvord wasn't sure he could, particularly since the FBI office in Buffalo had already interviewed Kevin in person and decided he was unreliable. Unless Yarborough came up with some sort of evidence to collaborate Kevin's story, Yarborough was on his own.

The chief felt trapped. If Kevin was lying, Yarborough would look like a rube for believing him, especially since the FBI hadn't. But if Kevin's story was true and Yarborough didn't respond—just the thought made Yarborough shudder. The chief sorted through the stacks of papers on his desk and eventually fished out a calendar. He had three days until May 1. "I was trying to figure out how I could possibly corroborate Kevin's story. I didn't have a clue."

Yarborough decided to quiz his six officers. Had any of them noticed anything suspicious about Jeffrey and his group? One had. Ron Andolsek, a chain-smoking, skinny thirty-five-year-old patrolman, had butted heads with Jeffrey only a few days earlier. A neighbor had complained because geese from Jeffrey's farm were running loose. Andolsek had told Jeffrey to keep the geese penned. When Andolsek told the neighbor that the geese were being rounded up, she had told him that Jeffrey and his followers were weird. Caleb Lundgren had told her daughter that on May 3 the "earth was going to open up and all of the devils and demons were going to come up." Andolsek had figured the story was the result of an overactive imagination, but now he wondered: Had Caleb overheard his father talking about the temple takeover? Kevin Currie had mentioned that there was going to be a great earthquake on May 3. That seemed to fit with Caleb's story.

Buoyed by Andolsek's remarks, Yarborough briefed Kirtland Mayor Mario Marcopoli and asked for permission to pay his officers overtime so that he could stake out the Lundgren farmhouse. The story struck Marcopoli as unbelievable, but he authorized the extra pay.

Later that night, Yarborough drove his unmarked brown station wagon to a spot near the farm where he could see the house and the route that Jeffrey was supposedly going to use in three days to reach the temple. It had been less than twelve hours since Kevin had called. Kevin said the takeover was scheduled to happen between 9:00 P.M. and 1:00 A.M. Yarborough wanted to make certain that Jeffrey hadn't moved up the date. He stayed at his post watching the house through binoculars until 1:00 A.M. and then he went home. Yarborough hoped Kevin *was* a nut.

During the next three days, Yarborough quietly talked with church officials and learned that Jeffrey had been fired for stealing church funds. He was told that Jeffrey despised Dale Luffman. With time running out, Yarborough decided to confront Jeffrey. "I didn't want to tell him that we knew about the takeover because then he would have figured out that Kevin had called us. But I wanted Jeffrey to know that he was being watched." Kevin had mentioned that Jeffrey and his group had conducted military training drills in the orchard. Yarborough telephoned the farm and asked Jeffrey to stop by the station.

"We've had some complaints about paramilitary groups being spotted in your orchard," Yarborough said. "Have you seen them?"

"No," Jeffrey replied.

"Probably guys playing war games with paint guns," Yarborough continued, trying to sound nonchalant. "We'd appreciate you keeping an eye out for them."

"Sure," Jeffrey volunteered.

"Of course, we'll be watching for them too," the chief added.

Jeffrey seemed nervous. Yarborough asked him if he owned any guns. Only a couple of rifles for hunting and some black-powder guns that he collected, Jeffrey said, lying.

Jeffrey had what the chief later called "dancing eyes." "He kept glancing around. He was like a frightened rabbit."

After Jeffrey left, Yarborough spoke to one of his officers. "How can anyone follow that guy?" Yarborough asked. "He's a real dud."

Later that day, Yarborough made a private telephone call to a friend from his days in the army. "I need a favor," he said. A few hours later, the chief picked up a .45-caliber Ingram Mac-10 machine gun capable of firing 1,200 rounds per minute.

On the night of May 1, Yarborough and three of his men staked out the temple and church. Nothing happened. They were there the next night too. Again, nothing happened. Yarborough hoped his talk had scared Jeffrey away. But he couldn't be certain.

On the afternoon of May 3, Yarborough briefed his officers. "If it's gonna happen, then tonight's the night." One of them asked if they had sufficient "probable cause" to begin shooting if they spotted Jeffrey and his squad coming toward the temple. There were seven of them and Kevin had said that they would be carrying semiautomatic weapons. Did Yarborough really plan on yelling "Stop! Police!" before opening fire?

"If we see them in military gear with weapons," Yarborough replied quietly, "that's all the probable cause we need."

At about 8:30 P.M., Yarborough drove behind the RLDS church. He positioned himself so that he would be the first to see Jeffrey, the first to confront the group, the first to begin shooting. He also would be the group's most likely target. Yarborough placed the Mac-10 machine gun in his lap. He was angry. Things like this weren't supposed to happen in Kirtland.

"I had resolved myself," he said later. "If Jeffrey came up behind the church with his followers, they were never going to make it to the temple alive."

Chapter 32

SHAR Olson got out of bed early on the morning that Jeffrey was scheduled to ask God when He wanted the Kirtland temple taken over. She walked downstairs in the farmhouse and found Jeffrey eating breakfast in the kitchen.

"Why are you up?" Jeffrey asked.

Shar had a ready explanation. "I figured if you were going to go see God, then I should get up and support you."

Jeffrey smiled and praised her for being such a devoted daughter. A few minutes later he left. Shar watched through a large picture window in the farmhouse as Jeffrey walked toward a hill that he claimed was the largest mountain in Ohio. [It wasn't but no one in the group had ever checked.]

Shar had lied. She had gotten up because she wanted to make certain that Jeffrey really did go to the "mountain." Shar had started to doubt that Jeffrey was a prophet and his comments that morning had made her even more suspicious. A real prophet would have known why she had gotten up early.

Shar sat at the window for more than an hour. Jeffrey had told his group that God always appeared in a brilliant beam of light. She didn't see any beams of light, but she noticed two clouds in the sky almost directly over where Jeffrey had gone. When Jeffrey returned to the farmhouse, he again thanked Shar for getting up with him.

That night Jeffrey told the group during scripture class that God had indeed appeared to him that morning in a beam of light that had shone down through a completely clear blue sky. Shar knew immediately that Jeffrey was not telling the truth. She had seen two clouds in the sky. But she kept quiet and continued to listen to Jeffrey's story.

God had been angry when he appeared, Jeffrey said. He was disappointed in Jeffrey's followers. Despite Jeffrey's teachings, his followers still needed to repent. "Thus saith the Lord, this is not the year for Christ to return to His temple," Jeffrey said. "You are unclean."

"The reason why it did not happen," Ron later told investigators, "was because . . . our sin would not allow us to come into the presence of God." Christ could only return to the temple if it had been cleansed. "There was too much sin in Jeffrey's household," Ron said.

That night, Jeffrey went one by one through the group and described each person's sin. Only one person was pure enough to meet Jesus. That was Jeffrey. Alice's sin was disobedience because she still did not submit her will to Jeffrey. Dennis Patrick's sin was pride and arrogance because he still attempted to interpret scripture by himself rather than blindly accepting what Jeffrey said. But Jeffrey's harshest criticism was aimed at Richard. It was his refusal to marry Sharon that was the primary reason why the temple takeover had been called off. At one point during the class, Jeffrey took out a .45-caliber pistol and placed it next to his scriptures. Looking directly at Richard, Jeffrey said: "I will get you to meet God—one way or another."

After that class, the mood at the farm changed, Shar said. Richard blamed himself for letting the group down. Everyone else felt guilty. People began to bicker. Alice and Jeffrey fought too. Shar had gotten a job as a waitress at night, which meant that she didn't have to go to work until late in the afternoon. She was generally the only group member home in the mornings with Jeffrey and Alice. One morning, Shar was awakened by the sound of Alice and Jeffrey arguing.

"When are you going to submit your will?" she heard Jeffrey holler. "When are you going to obey your Lord and master and do what I command?"

A few minutes later, Alice stormed out of the bedroom and left the farmhouse. She got as far as the gravel drive before she stopped, began to cry, and returned to the house.

"She spent three days in bed after that," Shar said. "Alice didn't come out of her bedroom and Jeffrey catered to her." He made her milkshakes, brought her shrimp platters, bought her presents. When she finally emerged from the bedroom, Alice said there was something she wanted to tell the group. "She apologized to the family and said it wouldn't happen again," said Shar. "It was pretty typical of Alice. After all of these outbursts of hers, she would calm down and she'd say that she was a broken woman now and that she was perfect and she was the submissive wife, but it wouldn't be too long before they'd be back into it again."

In May, Shar got a telephone call at work from a creditor who complained that she was several months behind on her car payments. Jeffrey had assured her that he was paying her bills. Like everyone else, she turned over all of her cash to him. That night at dinner, Shar mentioned the call. Jeffrey ordered everyone to leave the room but the two of them.

"I don't owe those Gentiles anything," Jeffrey said. "God doesn't need credit and neither should you." He then criticized her for being "rebellious."

A few days later, Jeffrey and Shar clashed again. This time it was over a Mother's Day telephone call. Jeffrey didn't allow anyone to use the telephone without his permission and he caught Shar talking to her mother. That night at class, Jeffrey said Alice was sick in bed because of Shar's disobedience. "I was told that Alice was my mother . . . and I had greatly hurt her because of my sins."

The next day when Shar went to apologize, she found Alice lying in bed with the curtains drawn.

"I'm really sorry," Shar said. "I didn't mean to hurt your feelings."

"As a mother," Alice replied slowly, "it's just a burden I'm going to have to bear."

Alice stayed in bed three days before she felt well enough to rejoin the group.

Shar decided that it was time for her to quit the family. But she wasn't going to sneak away like Kevin Currie. She wasn't going to leave all the clothing and the furniture that she had brought from Independence. She went to see Jeffrey one night while he was in an office that he had made in the barn.

"I want out," she said.

"You wait here," he replied sternly. Jeffrey rushed over to the farmhouse and when he returned, he had Alice and Danny with him. For the next two hours, Alice and Danny pleaded with Shar to stay. Alice cried. "You can't do this!" she said. Alice reminded Shar that she was supposed to marry Danny. Their names were written in the scriptures. When Alice and Danny failed to sway Shar, Jeffrey weighed in, only he was nasty.

"You will never amount to anything if you leave," he said. "God will curse you."

Shar started to cry. "I was sitting on an old ammo box and they had formed a semicircle around me with their chairs and they just kept going on and on and on and then finally Danny said, 'Hey, wait a minute.' He looked over at Jeffrey and he said, 'You said that Shar was one of the twelve who was going to make it, going to survive the temple takeover. You said her name was written in the book.' Jeffrey turned red and then he said, 'No, if she leaves, she dies.' And then he looked at me and put his finger in my face and said, 'I'll see to it that your flesh will rot if you leave.' "

Shar became hysterical. "I'll stay, I'll stay," she mumbled.

And then something strange happened. Alice became irritated and accused Shar of staging the entire evening. She claimed that the real reason Shar wanted to leave the group was because, in Alice's words, "you're just horny." No one was allowed to have sex at the farm unless they were married. "The bottom line is that you want out because you want to go get screwed."

Shar was crushed. "Sex had nothing to do with it, but for some reason, Alice fixated on it."

For two weeks, Shar stuck it out, and then one night, Alice came prancing into her bedroom wearing a sexy pair of pink silk pajamas.

"Jeffrey bought them for me," she gushed. "What do you think?"

That very morning Shar had asked Jeffrey for ten dollars to buy a new pair of tennis shoes because her only pair had a hole in them. "We don't have enough money right now," he'd told her.

"Mom," Shar told Alice, "I want out. I don't want to live here anymore."

Jeffrey was waiting the next morning when Shar came downstairs.

"Get your shit and get out," he said.

As Shar started to leave, Jeffrey came after her. He reminded her that when she had moved to the farm, he had paid to put some of her belongings in storage. He was keeping two expensive quilts that Shar had inherited to pay that bill, he said. Shar didn't care.

There was no way for Shar to move everything that morning but she didn't want to spend another night at the farmhouse. A waitress at work said she could live with her until she found her own apartment. Shar drove to the farm the next day in a small U-Haul truck to collect her belongings. Jeffrey and Danny carried Shar's furniture from the farmhouse. Neither spoke to her. When the U-Haul was packed, Jeffrey stepped up to Shar.

"You know what your problem is, Shar?" he said. "You have a real problem being submissive to men."

"Show me a man," Shar shot back, "worth being submissive to."

As Shar drove away, Jeffrey decided that Alice had been right.

"What Shar needed," he said later, "was a man to give her a good fuck."

Chapter 33

SHAR'S departure threatened Jeffrey. He knew it. So did Alice. Shar hadn't fled in fear like Kevin. She'd simply walked out and Jeffrey hadn't been able to stop her. Worse, Jeffrey had prophesied that Shar and Danny were going to be married and that Shar was going to be one of Christ's twelve disciples during the Millennium. If that was true, why had she gone?

No one in the group had said anything, of course, but Alice figured it would only be a matter of time before others began doubting Jeffrey. There were plenty of warning signs about what was ahead. Despite Jeffrey's nightly harangues, Richard still hadn't married Sharon, Greg hadn't moved to the farm as Jeffrey had demanded nor had he married Debbie, and Dennis Patrick was still questioning Jeffrey's scripture interpretations in classes. Privately, Alice suspected that one reason Jeffrey had started bringing his .45 pistol to class with him every night was because, without it, he was afraid that no one was going to take him seriously.

During the summer of 1988, Alice began drinking heavily. She would stay up until two or three in the morning watching videotapes and then sleep until one or two in the afternoon. She'd drink a beer before dinner and take a few Excedrin P.M. to quiet her nerves. Some nights she wouldn't come to class. Instead, she'd have Jeffrey buy her a six-pack or a bottle of wine and she would drink in her room and pop painkillers while watching television. Alice's drinking got to be a joke in the class because of comments that Jeffrey had made.

"Everyone knew when the beer started following Alice into the bedroom that Jeffrey had told her he wanted to have anal sex," Debbie later remembered.

Jeffrey had talked openly about it. He had decided that Alice's vagina had stretched after childbirth, making it difficult for him to achieve orgasm. As a result, he had turned almost exclusively to anal intercourse. Alice hadn't protested, at least not to anyone in the group. The beers and pills supposedly helped Alice deal with the pain of anal sex.

While that might have been one reason for Alice's drinking, pill popping, and depression, there was another. When Alice was, as she later put it, "gut level honest" with herself, she didn't really believe that Jeffrey was a prophet. Worse, after Shar left, Alice began to suspect that Jeffrey knew that his wife suspected he was a fraud. "I was expected to believe in him, that he was a prophet. If I didn't believe him, I think he felt no one would."

Alice's doubts and Jeffrey's insistence on anal sex were linked, she later claimed. "Jeffrey was always dreaming up ways for me to prove that I really loved him. I decided it was because of his childhood. The only way that he had received attention and love was by proving that he deserved it, so Jeffrey was always demanding that I do things to prove to him that I loved him. He would say, 'I'm testing you, Alice. I want to see how much you love me.' And I would say, 'Why do I have to be tested?,' and he would say, 'The Lord constantly tests the faith of his servants.' Whenever he began to suspect that I doubted him, he would become more dominant in the bedroom. He had to control me. It became an obsession with him."

"At first," Alice continued, "he used a lubricant when we had anal intercourse, but later he decided my own blood was the best lubricant."

One night in July, while Alice was lying in bed sipping a beer, she listened to Jeffrey teaching the group outside her bedroom. The four Excedrin that she had taken started to make her feel lightheaded. She knew that Jeffrey was going to cut this class short because he had already told her that he wanted to have anal sex after class. She took two more Excedrin and another swig of beer. She began to feel sorry for herself. "I thought, 'Alice, all you've ever wanted in life was a decent house and a nice family. Is that so much to ask for?' "

As she lay in bed, she thought back to the summer of 1969 when the patriarch had prophesied about her future. She had been so certain, so filled with dreams. Jeffrey hadn't lived up to any of them. The only time in their marriage when they weren't poor was when the group members supported them. How long would that last? How long before Jeffrey blew it again?

Alice wasn't certain how late it was when Jeffrey slipped into their bedroom, but by the time he got under the covers and began to kiss her, she was wallowing in self-pity and was drunk. As Jeffrey started to roll her over and pull off her pajama bottoms, Alice let loose with a string of profanity. During the next few minutes, she blistered Jeffrey in a voice that was slurred and often incohèrent. She would later not be able to recall precisely what she had said that night nor was she really certain that she had actually said all of the words that she had been thinking. But the next morning, there was one word that seemed etched in her mind: LOSER.

A short time after that encounter, Jeffrey told Alice that he wanted her to come to class. Instead of opening his scriptures, Jeffrey read a passage from Sun Tzu's *The Art of War*. It was a short story that described how the King of Wu decided to test Sun Tzu's leadership skills one day. The king asked Sun Tzu if he could take any group of people and turn them into a well-disciplined fighting force. When Sun Tzu replied that he could, the king sent him 180 women from the royal harem. Sun Tzu divided the women into two groups on the military parade ground and commanded them to "Face right!" The women burst into laughter. Some faced right, some left, others didn't move. Sun Tzu repeated his instructions, and this time when the women giggled and turned the wrong way, he ordered two of the king's favorite concubines to step forward. While everyone watched, Sun Tzu beheaded the women. He then gave the order "Face right!" and every woman did exactly that. Sun Tzu told the king that his new troops were ready to do whatever they were ordered.

Jeffrey didn't say much after he read the story and none of his followers was certain why it was important. They were to learn soon enough.

Chapter 34

DENNIS Avery had always had a terrible sense of timing and he proved it by showing up at the farmhouse to complain shortly after Shar left the group. Dennis had discovered that the $575 monthly rent for his three-bedroom house in Kirtland hadn't been paid for nearly a year. Jeffrey had promised to make the payments but he hadn't and Avery's landlord was threatening eviction. Jeffrey didn't have time to waste on Dennis Avery. "Dennis represented everything that I hated in a person," Jeffrey later recalled. "He was a physical and spiritual weakling who couldn't keep his house in order." Jeffrey's anger flashed. There was sufficient income coming into the commune to pay the Averys' back rent, Jeffrey said, but he was not going to do it. Why should he help a Gentile get rich? he asked.

Jeffrey told Dennis that he was going to have to move. If he left during the night and didn't leave a forwarding address, his landlord probably wouldn't be able to find him, and even if he did, so what? Dennis and Cheryl were broke. Taking them to court would be a waste of time.

Dennis had always been proud that he didn't have any debts, his brother Tim later recalled. In this case, Dennis didn't have much choice. Dennis went home and told Cheryl to begin packing. On July 15, 1988, the Averys moved into a three-bedroom house that rented for $450 per month in Madison, twenty-four miles east of the farmhouse. Dennis didn't leave a forwarding address nor tip off his landlord that he was going.

Investigators would later wonder why the Averys remained loyal to the Lundgrens. This is how Jeffrey explained his hold on Dennis and Cheryl: "All of their lives the Averys had been losers. They'd never fit in, never really been accepted by anyone. They were oddballs and they knew it and deep down they hated it because they believed that they were just as good as anyone else; in fact, Dennis thought that he was better. What I offered them was a chance to be exactly that. They believed that Jesus Christ wanted them to be His disciples. Can you imagine—them as His disciples? But they believed it was true because they wanted to believe it was true and as long as they believed that I could take them to meet God, then they were going to follow me."

For whatever reason, when Cheryl enrolled Trina, Becky, and Karen in the Madison school district on August 15, she identified Alice Lundgren as the person the school should notify if it couldn't find either parent and there was an emergency. And when Dennis filled out job applications, the first name that he always listed as a reference was Jeffrey's.

Trina Avery hadn't wanted to move. She was just getting settled in the Kirtland schools. Being in ninth grade was difficult enough without being the new kid, especially when you were a heavyset, awkward, self-conscious girl much more at ease with a book than with other teenagers. Most people thought Trina looked like her mother. She had shoulder-length dark curly hair and a round face. But she had inherited both of her parents' shyness. Trina hadn't wanted to leave Independence and shortly after they arrived in Kirtland, she bought a bulky hot-pink sweatshirt and had the words WHY ME? printed on the front of it in big black letters. "I put 'why me?' on everything because I hate Ohio and I put it on my sweatshirt to get other kids' reactions," she told her grandmother. "Most kids think it's crazy." The question "Why Me?" became Trina's trademark at school, where she stayed close to her younger sister Becky. Trina wrote "Why Me?" on her notebooks and included it in letters sent to a classmate back in Independence. Cheryl figured Trina would get over it. She and Dennis looked on Trina as their "brainy" child. She got good grades and often acted more like an adult than a youngster. Still, at age fourteen in 1988, Trina slept with a night-light in her room and hadn't yet gotten rid of her stuffed animals and dolls. The night-light was a gift from her mother and was a white unicorn with a bulb inside. In her sparse bedroom, Trina had tacked up a poster. It was not a photograph of a teenage heartthrob or rock-and-roll star, but a picture of three Care Bear cartoon figures hugging each other. She had gotten it during an RLDS summer camp. "Good friends are worth holding on to," it said.

The Averys' middle daughter, Becky—only her father called her Rebecca—was twelve when the family moved to Madison and was so different from Trina that strangers never would have guessed they were related. She was such a picky eater that Cheryl worried that Becky might be anorectic. A school counselor dismissed her fears, suggesting instead that Becky's poor eating habits were simply a way for her to show her independence. Becky was stubborn, always on the go, and a tomboy ready to take on any dare. Shortly after the family moved to Ohio, Becky decided to try her mother's curling iron without telling anyone. Within ten minutes, she had gotten her long stringy hair so tangled up that it took Cheryl two hours to free it. Becky's most prized possessions were her pet goldfish, which she named "Happiness," a twenty-eight-inch-tall [she had measured him twice] stuffed dog named "Big Carl," and a special white pillowcase that she had made in Independence while in Orioles, an RLDS girls' group. It was divided into six squares and each contained the outline of a human hand that had been first drawn on and then stitched with thread. Besides the outline of Becky's own hand, the prints on the pillowcase belonged to the four other girls in her Orioles group and her leader. Becky always showed her pillowcase to visitors and quickly confided that she had liked Carey, who was "really, really nice," but not another girl whose hand was on the case because she had been "creepy." Such comments would embarrass Cheryl, but Becky didn't care. She said what she thought.

Karen, who had just turned six when the family moved to Madison, was the baby. She was, in Becky's words, "a giggle-box," who was always smiling, always laughing. If Karen wasn't playing with her favorite doll—"Linda"—she was sprawled on the floor with her pick-up sticks. Once the family got to Madison, Karen went to first grade at the Red Bird Elementary School. She had enjoyed herself until a boy made fun of how she talked. Words such as "okay" and "see" came out sounding like "oway" and "thee." Trina told Karen to ignore the boy. Becky suggested that Karen kick him in the leg.

Cheryl had taught all three girls to sew and Trina and Becky were both making quilts. They worked on them after school on special racks kept in the living room. The racks weren't in the way. There wasn't much other furniture in the house. The family room contained a well-worn sofa and a folding lawn chair. The walls were decorated with drawings by the children, posters from magazines, and cross-stitch pictures that Cheryl and the girls had sewn. Karen had just finished making a bunny rabbit on a cross-stitch pattern for her father.

Jeffrey would later accuse the Avery girls of being ill-mannered and disobedient, but no one else in his group would remember them that way. Even if they had been, they were not as troublesome as the Lundgrens' own four children. Damon, who was about to turn eighteen in the fall of 1988, was a slender, rather docile boy whose goal in life seemed to be trying to please his father. Jeffrey had decided to make Damon his successor and was molding him into being a leader. In Jeffrey's mind, that meant making Damon tougher. It was a difficult job, according to Damon's grandmother, Donna Keehler, because Jeffrey had spent most of Damon's life beating the spunk out of him. "You get whipped so many times for being disobedient, and you don't be disobedient," she explained. Still, Damon tried to live up to his father's arrogant ways. When his father put him in charge of cleaning the weapons and leading the men in exercises, he strutted around the farm. "One time Damon came in the room where Richard and I were," Sharon later testified. "Damon told Richard he had to stand at attention when he [Damon] entered. Another time, he told Richard to kiss his feet or something like that." Debbie had known Damon all his life and she noticed a change. "Jeffrey made him a two-star general. He answered only to Jeffrey."

Ironically, Damon's younger brother, Jason, couldn't care less about doing what his father wanted. Yet when it came to a family pecking order, Jason was Jeffrey's favorite son. Although Jason was only fourteen, he was built like his father and could overpower Damon and give most of the men in the group a good fight if he wished. Jeffrey said Jason was too young to study with the adults and that suited him fine. "I thought all that stuff he was teaching was boring," he later said. No one at the farmhouse except for Jeffrey could tell Jason what to do, and even Jeffrey frequently had to back up his orders with physical threats to make Jason comply.

Daughter Kristen, who was nine years old, was an active, beautiful girl, but even by Alice's account she was "completely spoiled by her father." Behind her back, group members called her "prissy" rather than "Krissy." Whatever she wanted, Jeffrey made certain that she got. The Lundgrens' youngest child, Caleb, age seven, was mostly ignored by his parents. He was a sweet child, but Jeffrey had always thought him dense and he treated him with disdain.

During late July and early August, Jeffrey moved to reinstate his authority over the group. One night when Greg Winship wasn't in class, Jeffrey told everyone that they were going to have a special class designed to pressure Greg into moving into the farmhouse. Greg was an avid volleyball player, and after the temple takeover was called off, he had started to drift away from the group. Jeffrey's special class worked. On Labor Day, Greg moved in and was rewarded by Jeffrey with an expensive antique bedroom set. Other group members got rewards too. Jeffrey had just received a surge of cash. Debbie's house in Independence had sold and she had also settled the workman's compensation claim that she had filed after she hurt her back working in an Independence hospital. Combined, those two checks totaled $32,492.32, all of which Debbie dutifully turned over to Jeffrey.

Jeffrey bought clothes for Alice and together they went antiques shopping. He bought himself a .54-caliber black-powder rifle for his gun collection and he purchased a 1986 Nissan pickup truck. He took everyone to a nearby amusement park for a day, and he and the other adults went out to dinner several times. Jeffrey encouraged Richard and Sharon to go out on dates and sent Greg and Debbie dancing at the Brown Derby, a popular Kirtland restaurant-bar. Jeffrey concentrated on cementing his relationship with Ron Luff too. He bought toys for the Luff children and went out of his way to spend more time with Ron. Both of them enjoyed weight lifting, and when they worked out together, Jeffrey began sharing with Ron what seemed to be confidential information about the group and scriptures. "Basically what he told me was that I was to be the spokesman for the seer in the last days," Ron later told investigators. "That became a second-in-command type situation for me." As Jeffrey's new lieutenant, Ron was expected to help keep the group in line. Whenever Jeffrey decided to "session" someone in class, Ron would jump in.

There was only one family that didn't benefit from Debbie's cash. Jeffrey didn't do anything special for Dennis and Tonya Patrick or their daughter, Molly. "They don't deserve it," he told Alice.

In September, Jeffrey announced that he had used the pattern to discover a new revelation that had made the taking of the Kirtland temple no longer necessary. Jeffrey had discovered a way for his followers to meet God face-to-face. In fact, if the group followed Jeffrey's instructions, every one of them would not only be able to see God, but also to *touch* God. According to the Book of Mormon, an ancient Hebrew identified as the "Brother of Jared" was so righteous that God appeared before him. Jeff was fascinated by the story and claimed that he had discovered a way for the group to compel God to appear to them in the same way.

It took Jeffrey several weeks to explain how this process would work and, as always, he first laid an intricate foundation by citing dozens of scriptures and using the pattern to reveal hundreds of hidden messages. But in the end, his plan was actually quite simple. In order to take his followers before God, Jeffrey would first have to become "endowed with the power." The way for him to obtain this power was by killing the "wicked" and offering them as a human blood-atonement sacrifice to God. Jeffrey wasn't certain how many people he was supposed to kill or who they were. But once he offered God this blood sacrifice, then he would receive the "power" to take his followers to meet God.

There was only one catch. Everyone in the group had to go before God at the same time, and if any of them had any "sin" at all, God would destroy the entire group. This was because, as Ron Luff later told federal investigators, "nothing unclean can come before God."

Jeffrey told his followers that he had come up with a way for them to purge themselves of all sin. After Jeffrey made the human sacrifice, the group would isolate itself from the evils of society by going into the "wilderness." In this case, the "wilderness" would be somewhere remote where the group could camp without being disturbed and focus on becoming "of one heart and mind" with God. "I don't know where the wilderness is," Jeffrey said. "But God will lead us there."

A short time after Jeffrey explained his revelation, he called his followers together and told them to open their Mormon scriptures to Section 105 of the Doctrine and Covenants, a revelation that Joseph Smith, Jr., said he received from God on July 23, 1837. Jeffrey read them the key lines:

> "Behold, vengeance cometh speedily upon the inhabitants of the earth. . . . And upon my house shall it begin. . . . First among those among you . . . who have professed to know my name and have not known me. . . ."

Jeffrey told the group that God was telling him through these verses that he was to select someone to sacrifice from within his own "house," someone who had claimed to worship God but who really did not know Him.

Jeffrey didn't say anything else. The message was clear. The only question was "Who would it be?"

Chapter 35

WHEN Jeffrey Lundgren and his men didn't come charging up the embankment behind the RLDS church during the night of May 3, Chief Yarborough was relieved. Still, he didn't want to take any chances so he had his ambush set up on the night of May 4 just in case Jeffrey came late. He didn't. Yarborough was back to square one. Had Kevin Currie bamboozled him or had Jeffrey simply postponed the takeover because he knew that the police were watching?

Yarborough went to see Kenneth Fisher, an RLDS bishop who lived near the Kirtland temple and one of the people on Jeffrey's hit list. Fisher gave the chief a list of fifteen people who were members of Jeffrey's group. Yarborough didn't recognize any of the names. All of them were "outsiders," not from Kirtland. He turned the list over to Ron Andolsek, who immediately began checking with federal, state, county, and city law-enforcement agencies. It didn't take Andolsek long to discover that none of Jeffrey's followers had a criminal record.

"On paper they were perfect, law-abiding citizens," the chief recalled. "It just didn't fit. How could they be involved in a plot to behead a preacher and his family?"

Yarborough checked out several library books on religious cults and mind control. He found his copy of the Book of Mormon. "I'm going to figure out what makes this guy tick," he told Andolsek. "I don't want to spend every May third wondering if this is the year he's going to attack." Andolsek had a few ideas of his own. He began parking his squad car on the blacktop near the Lundgren farmhouse. He acted as if he were using his radar to check for speeders, but he was actually spying on the commune. By the end of August, both men had collected a large file on Lundgren. They had found out where Jeffrey did his banking, where his followers worked, what model of cars the group used, and had even obtained a list of the videotapes that Jeffrey had recently rented. But neither the chief nor Andolsek had found a single piece of damaging evidence that would corroborate Kevin's story. Late one hot Friday night in August, the two men went over everything in their file, piece by piece. When they finished, Yarborough shook his head in disgust. The only crime that Jeffrey had committed was a zoning violation.

"We could arrest him for having too many people in one house," the chief said. "But that would make it harder for us to do surveillance."

Andolsek agreed.

It looked as if they'd hit a dead end.

What neither of them realized was that only a few miles down the road from the Kirtland police station, the one person who could provide them with the help that they needed was busy working as a waitress at Chi Chi's Restaurant, serving platters of chicken tacos and bean burritos. Shar Olson was not on the list of cult members that Bishop Fisher had given Yarborough. Shar had arrived after Jeffrey had been fired by the church. Fisher didn't know her. During his stakeouts, Andolsek had spotted Shar's 1986 Nova at the farmhouse but she had quit the group in June, and since she never showed up at the farmhouse again, he had assumed that she had just been passing through. Shar didn't plan on contacting the police. She didn't want to get Greg, Richard, or herself into trouble. She just wanted to be left alone.

In August, a fellow waitress told Shar that her father was in the lobby waiting to speak with her.

"My dad?" she replied. And then Shar realized that it was Jeffrey.

"What do you want?" she demanded.

Jeffrey told her that Richard had received a letter from his parents, Wilmer and Twylia Brand, who were trying to get him to quit the group. Richard's parents had been suspicious of Jeffrey from the start, particularly when they learned that Richard had sold his prized truck shortly after moving to Kirtland and given Jeffrey all of the money that his grandmother had left him. In the letter, the Brands mentioned the sexual affair that Jeffrey had engaged in while at the Lake of the Ozarks Hospital. How could Jeffrey be a prophet, the Brands had asked, if he was guilty of adultery? Richard had shown the letter to Jeffrey and he had immediately known that Shar was the source. Alice had once told Shar about the affair.

"Why'd you tell Richard's parents?" he asked, "and what *else* did you say?"

"I didn't tell Richard's parents anything," Shar replied innocently. Technically, she was telling the truth. "Jeffrey had always played word games with us," she later explained. "I was turning the tables on him because I hadn't told Richard's parents, I'd told Richard's sister and she had told them."

Jeffrey seemed unconvinced. "Well, someone told them," he replied.

"Listen," Shar snapped, doing her best to sound assertive, "let's not play games. I'm not out to get you in trouble. All I wanted was out of the group. I'm not going to say anything about your teachings and plans."

Jeffrey changed tactics. "Danny loves you," he said. "Sharon and Debbie are going to pick out engagement rings. You could do that too."

"Just leave me alone," Shar repeated. She turned and walked away.

The Brands telephoned Shar a short time later and pressed her for more details about the group. Why had she quit? Shar avoided answering but they were persistent. Finally, she blurted out: "Jeffrey's threatened me. He told me my flesh will rot. I can't say anymore."

Jeffrey returned to Chi Chi's several weeks later to see Shar. The Brands had written their son another letter. This time they were threatening to report Jeffrey to the Internal Revenue Service for tax evasion since he hadn't paid any income taxes on the money he received from his followers.

"Jeffrey was furious and he accused me of telling them things," Shar recalled, "so I said, 'That's right, Jeff. I'm tired of your stupid games. I did tell them and if anything happens to me, there won't be any questions about where it came from.' He stormed out of the restaurant."

A week later, Danny's stepmother called Shar. Obviously, the Brands were spreading the word to other parents that Shar had left Jeffrey's group. On September 20, Shar got yet another call, but this time it was Dale Luffman on the phone. He was conducting his own probe, he explained, because he wanted to get Jeffrey thrown out of the RLDS. The squabble between fundamentalists and liberal factions had finally reached the breaking point in the Kirtland congregation. The church was splitting. A group of fundamentalists was starting its own "restoration RLDS" congregation. Luffman felt Jeffrey was partly to blame and wanted to bring him up on charges within the church of encouraging members to quit the RLDS. After some prodding, Shar agreed to meet Luffman at a Bob Evans restaurant in a neighboring town. After swearing Luffman to secrecy, Shar unloaded her story. He was horrified. Chief Yarborough hadn't told Luffman about the temple takeover plot nor had anyone told the minister that Jeffrey had been planning to behead him and his family. As soon as they finished talking, Luffman raced to the Kirtland Police Department. Ron Andolsek happened to be on duty.

"Jeffrey Lundgren is running a cult," Luffman announced, "and is planning on killing me and my family."

Ten minutes later, Andolsek telephoned the chief. "I got something you need to hear," he said. "We got another informant."

Shar was angry when Andolsek telephoned her early the next morning. She had told Luffman not to tell anyone about the plot. But she finally agreed to meet Andolsek a day later, on September 23, at 11:30 P.M. at Maxx Doogans Tavern, a popular college hangout about fifteen miles west of Kirtland.

Shar was nervous during the meeting, but she told Andolsek everything that she knew about the plot, and then Shar pulled out a spiral notebook. She had kept detailed notes during Jeffrey's classes.

"When he started talking about killing people," she told Andolsek. "I paid real close attention."

Andolsek flipped through the pages. Written in flawless script were descriptions of various types of bullets, instructions for how to use gas masks, lists of military terms. Instructions for dismantling an AR-15 semiautomatic rifle were followed by scriptural notations about ancient Hebrew warfare.

The next morning, Andolsek typed a nine-page single-spaced account of his interview with Shar and gave it to Yarborough. As soon as he finished reading it, the chief dialed Special Agent Robert Alvord's number. This time, the chief was certain that he could get him to listen.

Across the street at the RLDS church, the Reverend Dale Luffman was putting the finishing touches on his own report about Jeffrey. He had already telephoned various church officials in Independence and briefed them. He'd also warned them—if Jeffrey did something crazy, it was going to reflect badly on the entire RLDS denomination.

"We've got to get this guy out of the church," Luffman had said. "Fast."

In his letter, Luffman had asked the church to take the extraordinary step of excommunicating Jeffrey. On October 10, Luffman received a package of documents from the church. According to the church's bylaws, Jeffrey was entitled to a formal hearing, similar to a court trial, before he could be excommunicated. If he wished, he could argue his case in person before a church council. Jeffrey would have three days to reply to the charges that Luffman had filed.

Luffman had been careful not to mention the temple-takeover plot in his formal charges against Jeffrey. Yarborough had asked him to keep that hush-hush until the police could get more evidence. Jeffrey was being accused of teaching doctrines contrary to the church's beliefs and of encouraging members to quit the church.

Luffman telephoned an elder in the Kirtland congregation and asked if he would ride with him to the farmhouse. Luffman needed a witness from the church to prove that Jeffrey had been served the excommunication papers. Luffman also figured it would be safer if someone went with him to the farm when he confronted Jeffrey.

When Luffman turned his sedan into the farm's driveway, he spotted Jeffrey working outside in the yard. Neither man wasted time with social niceties. Luffman walked up to Jeffrey and stuck out the excommunication papers.

"Do us both a favor, Jeff," Luffman said. "Don't bother fighting this."

"I'll think about it," Jeffrey replied coldly.

Luffman turned around and left.

At about six o'clock that same day, a thunderstorm rolled through the Kirtland area. It left a beautiful rainbow behind. Jeffrey noticed that it was really two rainbows side by side, and he began yelling to everyone in the farmhouse to "come and see—come and see." There was a reason why he used those particular words. After everyone saw the double rainbow, they hurried back inside and grabbed their scriptures. They wanted to discover what significance the rainbow had since it had appeared on the same day that Jeffrey was served with excommunication papers. Jeffrey sat at the kitchen table watching Greg, Richard, and Danny searching their scriptures. He already knew what they were going to find and if they didn't, he would nudge them toward it. He had known from the moment that he spotted the rainbow exactly what the scriptural importance of it was—or at least, what he would tell them it was. That night in class he would announce that God had sent them a sign. It was time for them to make preparations to go into the wilderness. It was time for them to make a human sacrifice. Jeffrey was certain of it and he knew exactly who he was going to kill.

Chapter 36

MARTIN Luther, the German theologian and leader of the Protestant Reformation, didn't believe the Book of Revelation belonged in the Bible because of its graphic accounts of how God would someday torture and kill the wicked. The book was written at a time when the Roman Emperor Nero was setting Christians on fire in his garden to provide light for his evening meals, and Luther claimed that its message of retribution was aimed more at building up morale among the suffering Christians than establishing some long-lasting Church doctrine. The angry bloodletting in Revelation certainly didn't fit with Christ's turn-the-other-cheek teachings.

It was Jeffrey's favorite New Testament book.

No one would later remember who was the first to turn to the Book of Revelation shortly after the double rainbow appeared. But someone mentioned chapter 6 of the book and within minutes everyone in the kitchen was reading the story of the Four Horsemen of the Apocalypse and the seven mystical seals that were to be opened just before Christ returned to rule the earth for one thousand years. Verse one read:

> *And I saw when the Lamb opened one of the seals, one of the four beasts, and I heard, as it were, the noise of thunder, saying, Come and see.*

Everyone in the group saw the similarities:

• The verse contained the words "the noise of thunder." Just after Jeffrey received his excommunication papers, a thunderstorm had just rolled across Kirtland.

• The verse contained the words "Come and see." That is what Jeffrey had called out.

"Is it possible," one of the men said, that God opened the first seal today?"

Jeffrey was enjoying himself. "Read the second verse," he told them.

> *And I saw, and behold a white horse; and he that sat on him had a bow; and a crown was given unto him; and he went forth conquering; and to conquer.*

• The verse said the man on the horse had a "bow." A rainbow had appeared after the storm.

Jeffrey was quick to tell the group that the word "bow" also had a secret meaning. It could be used to describe a pair of eyeglasses, he explained, because the piece that connects the two lenses and holds the glasses on a person's nose is shaped "like a bow." That was significant, Jeffrey continued, because eyeglasses were invented to help people see. "Helping people see is also the job of the seer or prophet," Jeffrey said. Accordingly, the word "bow" could also mean "seer or prophet."

"What this verse is telling us is that God has given the rider of the white horse a bow or the ability to prophesy."

That night at class, Jeffrey told his followers that the similarities between what had happened that day and chapter 6 in Revelation were not a coincidence. He told them that God had opened the first seal and that now it was up to the riders on the four horses to begin opening the other seals that would eventually bring about the earth's destruction. Jeffrey then announced that he was going to reveal to them, by using the pattern, the identity of the riders.

During the next few nights, Jeffrey led his followers on an incredible, intricate trip through the Bible, Book of Mormon, and Doctrine and Covenants that was designed to ultimately lead them to one inescapable conclusion: God had chosen Jeffrey to be the rider not only of the white horse but of the next three as well.

"I am God's prophet. I am the last messenger. I am the destroyer. I am the rider of the white horse. God has chosen me to open the seals."

Now that Jeffrey had made that declaration, he told his followers to continue reading the story of the opening of the seven seals. The next verse read:

> And when he had opened the second seal, I heard the second beast say, Come and see.
> And there went out another horse that was red; and power was given to him that sat thereon to take peace from the earth, and that they should kill one another; and there was given unto him a great sword.

Jeffrey told his group that God had opened the first seal by causing the rainbow to appear. Now it was up to Jeffrey to open the remaining ones.

"The rider of the red horse is required by God to show blood," he declared. "His job is to kill."

Jeffrey continued. "This verse in Revelation is another sign from God that my job is to destroy the wicked."

As far as Jeffrey was concerned, everything that he had learned by using the pattern to interpret scripture was beginning to fit together and it all pointed to one event.

God had told him in the "parable of the vineyard" to kill.

God had told him that if he wanted to be endowed with power, he had to kill.

God was now telling him to kill if he wanted to open the seven seals.

"I checked and checked the scriptures over and over and they all kept coming back to the same thing," Jeffrey said. "There was absolutely no doubt whatsoever about what God was commanding me to do."

Chapter 37

ONCE the first seal was opened, the clock was running. Richard Brand would later tell federal investigators that Jeffrey was required to perform the human sacrifice within six months. The rainbow had appeared in October 1988. That meant Jeffrey had until April 1989 to, as he liked to put it, "show blood." The remaining seals would have to be opened during the six months that followed the human sacrifice if Jeffrey wanted to successfully bring the world to an end.

This one-year deadline for opening the seals was based on scriptures. Jeffrey had taught that a Hebrew named Enoch had taken one year to accomplish a task that God had given him. Jeffrey was expected to do the same. While Enoch was not a major character in most Protestant Bibles, in the RLDS inspired version, Enoch was a monumental figure. Most of his exploits were described in sixty-one verses that Joseph Smith, Jr., added to chapter 7 of the Old Testament book of Genesis. Although Enoch lived in the days described in Genesis, God had allowed him to see the crucifixion of Christ and the Millennium. Jeffrey told his followers that God had shown him Jesus dying on the cross and the earth's final days, too. No one in the group had missed the similarities between Enoch's life and Jeffrey's claims, but rather than suspect that Jeffrey was imitating Enoch, they assumed God was treating Jeffrey in the same way.

Picking someone to kill had been easy for Jeffrey. He had always detested the Averys and he felt that he could prove to the group that Dennis, Cheryl, Trina, Becky, and Karen Avery were "wicked." The Averys had stopped attending Jeffrey's classes shortly after they moved to Madison. Because of this, they didn't have any idea that Jeffrey was going to offer God a human sacrifice. Jeffrey made certain that they didn't find out. He instructed everyone in the group not to tell the Averys what was going on. At the same time, he began wooing them back to class. When the Averys did attend, Jeffrey taught token classes. He told them that the group was going into the wilderness to see God and he assured them that he wanted them to go too, but Jeffrey never mentioned that he planned to sacrifice them or anyone else.

By March, *everyone* in the group knew for certain that the Averys were to be killed, Richard later told investigators. Talk of a human sacrifice preoccupied the group whenever the Averys weren't around. "We constantly talked about shedding of blood," Debbie later testified. "That it had to be done, that we were going to the wilderness, we were going to see God there."

Later, in interviews, Jeffrey would repeat much of what he told his group about Dennis and Cheryl and why God wanted them killed. He cited verse 17, in chapter 9 of the Book of Alma in the Book of Mormon to prove that the family was wicked.

> "And therefore he that will not harden his heart, to him is given the greater portion of the word, until it is given unto him to know the mysteries of God, until they know them in full.
>
> "And they that will harden their hearts, to them is given the lesser portion of the word, until they know nothing concerning his mysteries.
>
> "And then they are taken captive by the devil, and led by his will down to destruction."

"By not attending my classes, the Averys have 'hardened their hearts,' to the word," Jeffrey told his followers. "They are not interested in learning the 'greater portion of the word.' Instead, they have chosen to receive 'the lesser portion.' " Accordingly, the Averys had been " 'taken captive by the devil and led by his will down to destruction.' "

"I told my people that they should thank God for the Averys. You see, God had provided the Averys to us to be used as sacrifices."

The only question in Jeffrey's mind by mid-March was how he would kill them. Debbie would later recall a conversation that she had one morning in March while sitting in the kitchen with Alice. Jeffrey had come in with his scriptures and announced that he had discovered how to kill the Averys. Wicked men were supposed to be beheaded, according to the Old Testament. Women were supposed to be stripped naked and then split open so that their internal organs could be pulled out. Children, meanwhile, were supposed to be picked up by their feet and swung against a wall until their heads were smashed. Jeffrey was perplexed because he wasn't certain whether Becky, who had just turned thirteen, was a woman or a child, Debbie testified later. It was Alice who came up with a solution.

"Alice said that it would depend on whether or not Becky had started her period," Debbie recalled.

Jeffrey quickly agreed and asked if either of them knew if Becky had started menstruation. Neither did. Jeffrey put it on his list of things to find out.

As April approached, Jeffrey started assigning his followers different roles in the murders. He sent Debbie and Greg to a local library to find out how hot a fire had to be in order to cremate a body. At the time, Jeffrey was thinking about killing the Averys in their home in Madison and then setting their house on fire. Debbie told him that a house fire wouldn't be hot enough to destroy incriminating evidence. Jeffrey rejected the plan. Damon, meanwhile, was told to familiarize himself with explosives. Danny was asked to forge birth certificates in case the group decided to change their identities.

While the murders were being planned, Jeffrey was also getting his group ready for the wilderness trek. He told his followers that each of them would be expected to learn a special survival skill. "Sharon liked to study plants so her assignment was to figure out what we could eat if we lived off the land," Jeffrey said. "I would provide the meat by hunting, Sharon would provide the foliage." One night during their scriptural class, Sharon served the group deep-fried dandelions. "They were delicious," Jeffrey said.

Besides such duties, every man was to be a soldier in Jeffrey's "Army of Israel." Jeffrey declared himself the four-star general. Alice made him a flag. It was purple with a white star and a red eagle. By mid-March, Jeffrey had amassed more than four thousand rounds of ammunition and had added to his arsenal a forty-eight-pound, handmade .50-caliber rifle that cost $2,700. He bought it because he wanted a gun capable of shooting down a helicopter.

On March 16, Jeffrey's buddy from his college days, Keith Johnson, and his wife, Kathy, arrived in Kirtland. Jeffrey had been busy recruiting Keith for months. He'd even paid during February to fly Keith from Missouri to Kirtland for a three-day visit. Jeffrey had told Keith then about the opening of the first seal and had urged him to join the group when it went into the wilderness. Jeffrey needed Keith, he later said, because the scriptures required the rider of the four horses in Revelation to have seven servants. At the time, Jeffrey had only six—Danny, Richard, Greg, Dennis Patrick, Ron, and Damon. Keith and his family moved into the apartment rented by the Patricks. There was no sense in getting a place of their own since the group was scheduled to go into the wilderness during the week of April 17.

Jeffrey announced that everyone would be allowed to take six sets of warm clothing and six sets for summer weather with them. The rest was to be sold at flea markets. Jeffrey also ordered everyone to apply for as many credit cards as they could. Ron and Susie got the most—four. Running up large bills on credit was a way for the group, in Jeffrey's words, to "spoil Babylon" by sticking the Gentiles with unpaid bills.

As March came to a close, everything seemed to be on schedule. And then Jeffrey made another discovery. It happened while he was teaching a scripture class. He was in the midst of diagraming a verse from the Book of Mormon when he came across a passage that told how a great Mormon general had lost ten of his men in combat. They had died fighting to protect the mysterious golden plates that Joseph Smith, Jr., would later find. Jeffrey didn't say anything to his followers, but later that night, he reviewed the scriptures and interpreted them to mean that he was supposed to kill ten persons—not just five. Jeffrey mentally ranked each group member according to their "sins." He decided that he would sacrifice Dennis and Tonya Patrick and their daughter, Molly, and Richard and Sharon as well as the Averys.

During the next few days, word that Jeffrey had decided to kill ten, not just five, leaked out to everyone but those who were slated to be murdered. The Averys had never been liked, but the Patricks and Richard and Sharon were. Debbie Olivarez would later recall a conversation that she had with Alice while the two of them were driving to a local grocery store.

Why, Debbie asked, were Richard and Sharon to be killed? "I said, 'None of us is perfect and I don't understand what makes their sin different than my sin.' And Alice said that they were ripened in iniquity and they couldn't change. They were so sinful there was no help, no hope that they would change and repent."

During the first week of April, Jeffrey began pressuring Greg to marry Debbie, and Richard to marry Sharon. He had told them earlier that they had to be married before the group left for the wilderness. On April 4, Greg and Debbie were married by Jeffrey. The next day, Richard married Sharon. The only difference in the ceremonies came when Jeffrey asked Richard why he was marrying Sharon.

"Because you want me to," Richard said.

On April 10, Jeffrey took Ron Luff and Keith Johnson out into the barn at the farm. He had decided that it wasn't practical to kill ten people by beheading the men and splitting open the women. Instead, he had found a verse in his Mormon scriptures that said: "I will make thy horn *iron*, and I will make thy hoofs *brass*." Jeffrey interpreted the verse to mean that he could shoot his victims with bullets because a .45-caliber cartridge had a *brass* shell and an *iron* slug. He planned to shoot all ten after they were put into a pit. Jeffrey showed Ron and Keith where to dig and told them how big to make the hole. Damon volunteered to help. The location of the pit was also scriptural, Jeffrey claimed. Moses had freed the Jews from captivity by leading them from Egypt across the Red Sea into the wilderness. Jeffrey was going to lead his people into the wilderness after murdering ten of his followers. "The barn was red," Ron Luff later explained, " . . . and the barn has an area that floods every spring when it rains . . . so the area within the barn that floods was to be where the people were to be buried so they would be covered over within the Red Sea."

Alice would later claim during testimony that she really didn't believe Jeffrey was serious. She had simply been playing along. "I didn't think he would kill anybody," she testified, "because he would come up with these wild-haired plans all the time and he didn't carry through with them. I thought this was just another one of his insane ideas. Like the Kirtland temple takeover, or like the obtaining of the golden plates, or obtaining the Sword of Laban, saying words and making an earthquake happen."

Jeffrey knew that Alice doubted him. He suspected that others in the group did too. "I made it clear that I was serious about this and I was not joking, but I could tell that some of them didn't take it serious. No matter how many times I warned them about God's wrath and fury, they just didn't get it. Even Alice didn't understand that this was not a joke. That I was going to do exactly what I said."

Chapter 38

CHIEF Yarborough was two steps behind Jeffrey. During the fall of 1988, while Jeffrey was busy deciphering the mysteries of the Four Horsemen of the Apocalypse, Yarborough was still investigating Jeffrey's plans to take over the Kirtland temple.

Yarborough had telephoned FBI Special Agent Alvord in September when Shar Olson had come forward. The chief had told him that there were now two informants willing to testify that Jeffrey had planned an assault on the temple. The fact that Shar Olson corroborated Kevin Currie's story interested Alvord, but he still felt the case was a local matter. The chief was investigating Jeffrey on charges of "conspiracy to commit murder," and that was a state crime, not necessarily a federal one. There was another reason why Alvord was reluctant. Both informants had told Yarborough about Jeffrey's plans to overthrow the temple on May 3, 1988. That was nearly four months ago. More important, Jeffrey hadn't done it. If the chief wanted to make an arrest, he was going to have to come up with new evidence that showed Jeffrey was still planning an attack. Alvord wasn't certain Yarborough could do that.

Still, Alvord wanted to help. He trusted Yarborough's judgment, and if the chief felt that Jeffrey was dangerous, then Alvord wanted to get him locked up. But Yarborough was going to have to come up with some hook that would justify the FBI's entering the investigation. Otherwise, Alvord knew his bosses wouldn't go for it.

In October, Yarborough called Alvord with an idea. Instead of investigating Jeffrey on charges of "conspiracy to commit murder," Yarborough suggested that the FBI go after him for possible violations of "domestic security" statutes and alleged violations of his followers' "civil rights." Both of those were federal crimes that fell under the purview of the FBI. Alvord liked it.

On October 13, Alvord telephoned Yarborough—the FBI was officially entering the investigation. Alvord had convinced his bosses that Jeffrey was a potential domestic terrorist.

Now that Alvord was authorized to investigate the cult, he told Yarborough that he wanted to talk to Shar as soon as possible. Ron Andolsek, who had befriended Shar, set up the meeting. Alvord was impressed with Shar. She was smart and articulate. She'd make a good witness. She was also cooperative.

During the interview, Shar mentioned that she still spoke regularly with Greg Winship. In fact, Shar and Andolsek had talked about the possibility of her wearing a concealed microphone to lunch one day with Greg. She felt that Greg would tell her if Jeffrey was still planning on taking over the temple in May. Andolsek was in the process of trying to borrow a "wire" for Shar to wear. The Kirtland Police Department didn't own one. It had never needed such a device.

Alvord quickly nixed the idea. If anyone in the group thought that Shar was helping the FBI, she might be harmed. Instead, Alvord suggested that Shar give the FBI permission to monitor her telephone calls. She agreed, and on October 27, Shar telephoned Greg. At this point, Jeffrey had not completely discarded his plan to take over the temple, so Greg talked about it as if the group still might launch an attack.

At one point, Shar asked Greg if he really was willing to kill someone.

"If God can tell Nephi to go slay Laban, then He can tell me to go kill whomever," Greg replied. He said, however, that he wanted to make certain that it was God giving the directions. "We're talking ten years to life and I'm not ready to do that. I'm not ready to run out and kill somebody, but I'm definitely thinking about it, whereas I wouldn't have even thought about it before."

Did Greg know when Jeffrey might take over the temple? Shar asked.

"This May, who knows?" Greg replied.

Alvord had heard enough. He sent a reconnaissance team to fly over Jeffrey's farm and take photographs of the route that Jeffrey and his group were supposed to use when they made their way through the apple orchard to the RLDS church. He dispatched a surveillance team to take pictures of Jeffrey and members of his cult. Alvord also contacted the FBI field office in Buffalo and asked that an agent there be sent to interview Kevin Currie. This time, the agent was to take whatever Kevin said seriously. Alvord then arranged to meet with Dale Luffman.

Within a matter of weeks, Alvord had become as engrossed in the case as Chief Yarborough and Andolsek. One night, he found himself driving by the farmhouse. He just wanted to see it. Like Yarborough, Alvord was trying to figure out how Jeffrey thought. He wasn't having much luck.

Just before Christmas, the FBI set up another telephone call between Shar and Greg. But this time, Greg was guarded on the phone and refused to discuss the takeover. Jeffrey had told everyone that he had seen a strange van parked outside the farmhouse for long periods. He figured Yarborough was watching him.

On February 24, 1989, Alvord wrote a confidential report for his superiors. He concluded that Jeffrey was dangerous and was most likely planning to attack the temple on May 3, 1989. But, Alvord said, there was not sufficient evidence to file charges against him. The statements by Kevin and Shar were too old and they were about an event that hadn't happened.

The FBI generally gives an agent sixty days to complete an investigation. After that, there has to be a good reason to continue spending an agent's time and the government's money. Alvord's sixty days would end on March 3. He asked for an extension into April and got it. But Alvord was told that unless he came up with something concrete, he'd be ordered to close the case.

Alvord drove to Kirtland and conferred with Yarborough. They decided to ask the U.S. attorney in Cleveland for permission to search Jeffrey's farmhouse. Maybe they'd get lucky and find something that would provide them with enough "probable cause" to arrest Jeffrey. Both men felt that if Jeffrey was taken out of the group, his followers would most likely scatter.

Alvord typed up a detailed memo and submitted it to the U.S. attorney. He also sent a copy to the FBI's legal-review department. Both offices told Alvord that there was insufficient evidence to justify getting a search warrant.

Once again, Alvord drove to Kirtland to talk to Yarborough. "We both knew the guy was dangerous, but we couldn't touch him," the chief recalled. "It was frustrating as hell."

The two investigators decided to take a risky step. They would confront Jeffrey at the farm without a search warrant. They would flood the area with officers: sixteen from the FBI and all six members of Kirtland's police force. They had been told that they didn't have enough probable cause to get a search warrant, but Jeffrey didn't know that. There was always the chance that he might *assume* that they could get a warrant and simply give them permission to search in order to avoid a hassle. "To be truthful about it," Yarborough later admitted, "we were going way, way beyond our authority." Even so, both men wanted to do something.

If nothing else, Alvord and Yarborough agreed that their plan would show Jeffrey that he was being watched. He'd been scared off before. Maybe he'd be scared off again.

"So when do we do it?" asked Yarborough.

Alvord wanted to wait until the last possible moment. "April eighteenth," he said. It was a Tuesday. That would be good because he and the chief could brief their men on Monday.

Yarborough agreed.

Neither knew that Alvord had picked a date that was exactly one day too late.

Chapter 39

DIGGING the pit in the barn was much harder than Jeffrey had expected. Although the floor in the room frequently flooded, the ground had been packed down after years of use. When Ron and Keith took a break to eat lunch on April 10, a Monday, they told Jeffrey that it would take them at least five days to dig the pit. That was okay with Jeffrey. He had plenty of other tasks to complete.

"It was time for me to inquire of the Lord to see if He had changed His mind," Jeffrey recalled. He went to the mountain near the farm and knelt down.

"I said to God, 'What is thy will? Give me a sign. Tell me what to do.' And then I opened my scriptures and began looking. I quickly realized that all I was getting were 'go' statements."

On Tuesday, April 11, Keith took a break from digging the pit and went with his wife, Kathy, to buy two horses. Jeffrey said he needed to take horses into the wilderness because he was, after all, the rider of the four horses in Revelation. He bought an ATV [all-terrain vehicle] too because, as he put it, "the scriptures told me that I was to have a chariot in the wilderness."

On Wednesday, April 12, Jeffrey bought a .44-caliber Smith & Wesson revolver. There wasn't any particular verse that told him to buy the gun. He simply wanted another one.

Later that night, he and Alice went to the Averys' to eat dinner. After the meal, Alice helped Cheryl sort through the family's possessions and decide what could go to the wilderness and what was being left behind. Jeffrey played with Karen. As she giggled, he bounced her up and down on his leg. When they got home, Alice told the group that the Averys had a microwave and some Corelle dishes that they could take with them.

On Thursday, April 13, Jeffrey told officials at Kirtland Elementary School that he was taking Kristen and Caleb out of their classes for one week because the family was going to Disneyland.

By Friday, April 14, all of the group members had quit their jobs, and Ron and Susie and their two children had moved from their apartment into the laundry room at the farmhouse. Jeffrey wanted his second in command at the farm to help plan the executions. That same day, Richard and Dennis Patrick drove to the Averys' house and started moving the family's belongings into the barn at the farm, where they were quickly picked over by group members. At one point, Cheryl showed up and asked Jeffrey why she and Dennis and their girls hadn't been invited to stay at the farm like the Luffs. "I told her we didn't have room," Jeffrey said, "but the truth was I didn't want them in my house because they were evil." Instead, Jeffrey issued the Averys five sleeping bags and told them to stay in their now-empty house until he sent someone for them.

On Saturday, April 15, the pit was nearly ready, but Jeffrey wasn't. "My intelligence told me that what I was doing was right," he later said, "but my flesh was weak. I was still struggling with the thought of killing ten people. These were not strangers. I wanted to wait at least one more day to make certain that I was absolutely right in what I was doing."

That morning, Dennis Patrick came to the farm to see if he could help pack supplies. Jeffrey sent him to the barn to help

Ron and Keith. Dennis didn't know that he was digging his own grave.

Later that night, Dennis Avery called Jeffrey. He had forgotten to mention it earlier, but he had been issued a credit card with a $1,500 limit that hadn't been used. Jeffrey told Dennis that they would go shopping the next day.

On Sunday, April 16, Jeffrey decided to check his scriptures one last time. "I was looking to see if there was some way to extend mercy to any of the ten," he later said, "and as I looked, I suddenly said, 'Ah-ha! I can extend mercy.' "

The verse that Jeffrey found was in the New Testament book of First Corinthians, chapter 7, verse 14, which read: "For the unbelieving husband is sanctified by the wife . . ."

"Tonya and Sharon were doing the best they could and God was telling me that because of the women, their husbands had been ransomed from the pit."

Jeffrey looked for a scripture that would save the Averys. Instead, he found the opposite in Isaiah, chapter 30, verse 17. The crucial part read: "at the rebuke of five, shall ye flee."

"God was telling me to get on with it," he said. "The verse clearly said that I was to rebuke [kill] the Averys and go into the wilderness."

After Jeffrey finished his studies, he picked up Dennis Avery and drove to Chagrin International Arms Company where they used Dennis's MasterCard to buy a .30-caliber M-1 carbine, another .45-caliber automatic pistol, and a .380-caliber Colt pistol for a total of $1,349.

While Jeffrey was buying guns, Alice was driving Greg to a local auto-repair shop to retrieve his car. "Alice asked me how I felt about people such as the Averys having to die for my sin. My response was that I would that no one would have to die for my sin: I would that all men would repent and come unto Christ."

Later that night while several of the men at the farm were playing basketball, Jeffrey turned to Richard and said, "Tomorrow is D day."

On Monday, April 17, Jeffrey was confident that he was supposed to execute the Avery family, but he claimed that he once again asked God if they could be spared.

"I said 'Lord, show me, show me, speak to me in your word. Don't let me be blind. Let me see.' "

Prosecutors would later argue that Jeffrey really didn't have much of a choice on April 17. If he didn't kill the Averys, his followers would stop believing in him. He had ordered them to quit their jobs. He had told them that the Averys had to be sacrificed. He had already lost face because he had backed down from taking over the Kirtland temple. That was the pragmatic view.

Jeffrey later offered a different one. "I was being asked to cross a line. . . . I could lose everything precious to me in this world: my wife, my children, my life. But if what I was teaching was real, if the pattern existed and if there was a God and there was a Bible and there were golden tablets, then I was being offered something no other man on earth was being offered.

"I was going to set into action events that would make the world as we know it come to an end—events that would bring about the return of Jesus Christ.

"What it all came down to was, did I *really* believe I was teaching the truth or was I going to shrink away? . . . Either I was teaching a lie and I was a false prophet and none of it was true or I was teaching the truth, in which case, my path was clear. Those were the two choices. God was saying, 'Okay, Jeffrey, do you really believe? Are you willing to step across the line?' And at that instant, I understood. I knew what I had to do."

On the morning of April 17, Jeffrey told Alice that the Patricks and Richard and Sharon had been spared. Jeff and Alice drove into Kirtland to the Patricks' apartment. Dennis was gone. Because Keith and Kathy Johnson were still living there, Jeffrey and Alice hurried Tonya to an upstairs bedroom to talk in private.

"Jeff told me that Dennis was not getting his act together," Tonya later recalled. "That he was sinful but that I was doing all right and he had no problems with me and because of that, Dennis wasn't going to be killed. He told me that he had planned to kill Dennis, Molly, and me that night but not now. I was in shock."

Once Jeffrey finished talking, Alice jumped in. "Alice told me how worried she'd been about it and how happy she was that

I was saved," Tonya said. Jeffrey told Tonya not to tell Dennis about their talk. He would tell him personally that night.

Meanwhile, back at the farm, Greg was making a reservation at the Red Roof Inn in Kirtland for the Averys. If the police, for some reason, ever went looking for them, Jeffrey wanted the Averys' last known address to be a motel, not the farmhouse.

After Greg made the motel reservation, he drove into Cleveland and bought a stun gun for $59.99.

At 11:30 A.M., the Averys were picked up at their house and brought to the farm for lunch. Jeffrey and Alice, as well as Debbie and Ron and Susie, ate sandwiches and leftovers with them and then Ron drove the Averys to the motel.

There are conflicting stories about what happened next. Sharon Bluntschly later testified under oath that she and Alice went on an errand to a nearby bank, and while en route, Alice told her that she and Richard were not going to be sacrificed that night because of Sharon's efforts and subservience. When they returned to the farm, Alice told Jeffrey what she had done and he got angry because she had upstaged him. Alice claimed that Jeffrey had told Sharon that she and Richard had been saved. Regardless, by late afternoon on Monday word had spread through the farmhouse that only the Averys were to be killed.

At 3:00 P.M., Jeffrey left the farm by himself and drove to Tom Miller's house. The police would later speculate that Jeffrey went to recruit Tom. That was wrong. Jeffrey wanted to tell Tom that God had chosen him—not Tom—to be the rider of the horses in Revelation. The two men had once talked about leading a revolt of fundamentalists in the RLDS. That was nothing compared to what Jeffrey was about to do.

"Jeffrey was totally unkempt when he arrived," Tom Miller said later. "His hair was dirty and he was very rushed and he said, 'I didn't come here to convince you to follow me,' and I interrupted and said, 'Jeff, that's great 'cause I wouldn't follow you anywhere.' "

Jeffrey stopped speaking. "His face went blank and his mouth fell open and he just sat there for the longest time," Miller said.

"I decided that there was no point in trying to share the truth with him," Jeffrey later recalled. "He'd made it clear that he was not interested in knowing who I was."

Jeffrey got up to leave.

"Jeff, are you running from something?" Miller asked. "Are you running drugs or in trouble? Maybe I can help you."

Jeffrey hurried out to his truck and drove away. He was angry. Who did Tom Miller think he was to offer to help him?

When Jeffrey returned to the farm, he went into his bedroom and got one of his .45-caliber pistols. He chose the stainless-steel Combat Elite semiautomatic and took enough bullets for twenty-seven shots. He could smell dinner being cooked. He quickly loaded the gun.

Jeffrey had told Debbie that he wanted roast beef, mashed potatoes with gravy, corn, and a salad with bread for dinner. A few minutes after six o'clock, Richard arrived with the Averys. He had driven past the front door of the Kirtland Police Department en route to the Red Roof Inn.

As soon as Karen Avery came into the room, she ran toward Alice and gave her a big hug. The little girl said that she had drawn Alice a picture, but had forgotten and left it at the motel.

"That's okay, honey," Alice said reassuringly. "We'll get it later."

Karen was wearing a shirt with a rainbow and ponies on it. Alice recognized it. She had given it to Karen.

Dinner was served at exactly 6:30 P.M., but Debbie didn't eat. She was too upset. "I couldn't eat with them, knowing they were going to die." She went upstairs. The Patricks and the Johnsons were the only ones not at the farm. Jeffrey didn't want them there. He didn't believe Keith and Dennis had enough guts to kill anyone. During the meal, Danny, Richard, Sharon, and Greg tried to avoid the Averys. Jeffrey, Alice, and their children, and Ron and Susie Luff and their children, were friendly.

While everyone was eating, Dennis Avery noticed that Karen hadn't tried everything on her plate. He told her to eat some corn.

"Daddy, I don't want to," she replied.

Jeffrey would later cite that exchange as a sign from God. "She was a rebellious and wicked child," he said.

Ron Luff was amazed, not because of what Karen had said but because the Averys clearly had no idea what was going to happen. He would later tell federal investigators that he had tried to warn the Averys several times during scripture classes. "I would say, look, this is what the wicked do—but that's exactly what you are doing. And this is what happens to the wicked." It was clear to Ron, as he watched the Averys eating their "last supper" that they simply didn't realize how serious Jeffrey was about destroying the "wicked." They really were like sacrificial lambs. "I believe we could have come out . . . and told them exactly what was going to happen and they still wouldn't have known."

As soon as Alice finished eating, she popped up from the table and announced that it was time for her and Jason, Kristen, and Caleb to leave. Jeffrey had told her that she was to go buy some picnic tables after dinner for the group to use in the wilderness.

"Call before you come back," Jeffrey told her.

Alice was about to walk out the front door when Jeffrey stopped her. He needed some paper and envelopes. Jeffrey had told all of his followers that they were supposed to write letters to their parents telling them that they had left Kirtland. Everyone was supposed to give their parents a fictitious forwarding address. He had just learned that Cheryl hadn't written a letter to her mother, Donna Bailey. Jeffrey handed Cheryl a sheet of paper and dictated the letter.

Dear Mom and Dad—Just a hurried note to let you know that things have happened very fast and Dennis has accepted work in Wyoming and we needed to get there fast. We will let you know address and details when we get settled. . . . Thanks. Love Cheryl.

After Cheryl finished, Jeffrey took the letter and went into his bedroom. All of the men except for Dennis Avery, who was still eating, followed him there. He shut the door and picked up his .45 pistol. "Everyone had done their part," he said later. "Now I wanted them to know that I was going to do mine."

Jeffrey looked at each of them, including his eighteen-year-old son, Damon, who was still a senior in high school.

"Are you in or are you out?" he asked solemnly. One by one, Ron Luff, Greg Winship, Richard Brand, Danny Kraft, Jr., and Damon nodded.

"Okay," Jeffrey said, "let's do it."

Chapter 40

DENNIS Avery had always been a slow eater. Behind his back, the others had cruelly joked that he was so lazy that even chewing was a chore. But now that he was finished eating, Dennis noticed that he was the only man still in the farmhouse. All the other men had followed Jeffrey outside. None of them had said anything to Dennis.

Dennis was about to ask where the men had gone when Ron came into the kitchen from the back door. Jeffrey was in the barn, Ron explained, and he wanted Dennis to come show him what he and Cheryl wished to take with them into the wilderness. Dennis started toward the door but stopped. He couldn't decide whether or not he should wear his glasses because it was misty and he hated to get water spots on the lenses. He took them off, then put them on, and then asked Cheryl what she thought he should do as Ron waited patiently, the 50,000-volt stun gun hidden in his pocket. Cheryl suggested that Dennis take them off, which he did. It was just before 7:30 P.M.

"When Dennis walked through the door of the barn," Ron later recalled, "I lifted his shirt and tried to use the stun gun a couple of different places." Jeffrey had told Ron that the gun would work only if it hit certain nerves on the hip, neck, and chest, so Ron tried all three.

"What are you doing?" Dennis screamed as Ron zapped him. "Goddamn it. This isn't necessary!"

"All the stun gun was doing," Ron later said, "was causing a lot of pain."

Greg, Richard, Danny, and Damon knocked Dennis onto the ground. They quickly taped his hands, feet, and mouth with two-inch-wide gray duct tape. "We were not supposed to apply tape to his eyes," Richard later testified, "because he was supposed to see Jeff when Jeff shot him."

Although Jeffrey was waiting in a room in the back corner of the barn where the pit had been dug, he could hear what was happening and he had heard Dennis yelling.

"Dennis had cursed God," Jeffrey said later. "He was clearly under Satan's power."

Once Dennis was bound, Richard lifted him by the shoulders and Danny raised his feet. They carried him through the barn into the room at the back of the barn and slid him into the muddy pit. Jeffrey would later tell his followers that Dennis had managed to climb onto his knees in the pit. He had looked up from the hole at Jeffrey, who was standing over him with the .45.

"I looked him in the eyes," Jeffrey said later, "because I wanted him to know who was sending him before God for his wickedness." The scriptures required him, Jeffrey explained, to look Dennis face-to-face and then "pierce his heart."

Greg was supposed to run a chain saw outside the barn during the shootings to cover up the sounds, but for some reason he hadn't started and Jeffrey decided not to wait. As Richard and Danny bolted toward the exit, Jeffrey fired his first shot. Ron, who was standing guard outside the room, slammed the door closed just as Richard and Danny reached it.

"Got to keep this door shut," he yelled.

He was worried that the noise might be heard by neighbors. Trapped inside, Richard turned his head just in time to see Jeffrey standing at the edge of the pit firing his second round. The noise reverberated inside the barn.

"I fired two shots directly into his heart," Jeffrey told everyone later.

Ron opened the door. "Is it done?" he asked.

"All right, everybody, come look at this," Jeffrey said. "Come see what death is."

Ron, Richard, Greg, Danny, and Damon walked over to the lip of the pit together, as if each were afraid to go by himself.

"When I looked in," Damon later recalled during testimony, "Dennis was laying there on the ground . . . you could see blood all over his shirt. I started crying—I couldn't believe it. I'd never seen anything like that before. It was my own father that had just did that."

Everyone was quiet for several seconds and then Jeffrey realized that he hadn't gotten the key to the Red Roof motel room from Dennis before he was shot. Jeffrey planned to clean out the motel room to make it look as if the Averys had left town.

"Damon, get the key out of his pocket," Jeffrey ordered.

Damon didn't move. He was crying.

"I can't do it," he said. "I can't believe he is dead. I can't believe he is dead."

Jeffrey walked over to his son and put his arms around him. He still had the .45 in his hand.

"It's okay," he said, "you're growing up at a young age."

Jeffrey glanced around. It was dark except for the lone light bulb that Damon had hung earlier. He still needed the motel key.

"If nobody else will do it," said Ron, "I will."

He jumped down into the pit and grabbed Dennis by his belt. When he lifted up the body, there was a loud "sigh" as air escaped from the corpse. Everyone flinched.

"That was his last breath of life," Jeffrey said.

Ron fumbled through Dennis's pockets with his free hand, but he couldn't find the key, only a driver's license and library card. He dropped Dennis back in the mud.

"We've got to have that key," Jeffrey said.

No one moved. Jeffrey walked out of the room, leaving the others alone with the body. As soon as Jeffrey was gone, they hurried out.

Jeffrey went inside the farmhouse and asked Cheryl for the key. She gave it to him. Jeffrey silently chided himself. He should have known that Dennis would have given his wife the hotel key. That was the sort of guy he was. Jeffrey returned to the barn and removed the .45 from its hiding place under his shirt. Damon was crying so Jeffrey told him to climb into the loft and stand by the window. He could be a lookout.

"Okay, Ron, bring out the next one," Jeffrey said. He had not said "Bring out Cheryl." He had not wanted to say her name.

Ron walked to the farmhouse. Cheryl was inside with Debbie, Susie, and Sharon.

"Ron told Cheryl that Dennis needed her help in the barn," Debbie later testified, "so she left with him."

Greg, Richard, and Danny surrounded Cheryl as soon as she stepped into the barn.

"Be calm," Ron said, "don't struggle—just give it up."

Confused and frightened, Cheryl stood perfectly still as the men wrapped tape around her hands, ankles, mouth, and eyes. Jeffrey didn't want Cheryl's eyes uncovered.

In the farmhouse, Debbie paced across the kitchen floor. She heard Greg start the chain saw.

"You can't have that," someone said. Debbie spun around. Trina and Becky were arguing in front of the refrigerator. They were looking for dessert. Debbie told them to take whatever they wanted and then snapped: "Close the door!" As soon as she said it, she felt bad. She hadn't meant to be sharp. Susie walked over to her.

"Do you think it's happening?" Susie whispered.

"I hear the chain saw," said Debbie. "I think so."

Dennis had been almost too heavy for Danny to carry, so once Cheryl was taped and lying on the barn floor, Richard asked Ron if he would help carry her into the pit. They lifted up Cheryl and lugged her across the barn into the back room where Jeffrey was waiting. Ron and Richard gently eased Cheryl into the pit. The mud quickly soaked through her baggy sweatpants. Ron stayed inside the room this time to make certain that no one opened or closed the door. Richard stepped out into the main portion of the barn.

Jeffrey got up and moved to the pit. He raised his gun and started pulling the trigger. Cheryl's body smacked into the side of the pit when hit by the slugs. The autopsy would later show that Cheryl was struck twice in the right breast and once in the abdomen. All three bullets were later recovered, and unlike the soft-pointed hollow-points that were fired into Dennis, these were full-metal-jacketed rounds designed to penetrate, not mushroom. Jeffrey had switched shells intentionally. He was experimenting.

"According to the scriptures, I was going to kill again. I wanted to learn as much as I could from this experience."

Jeffrey would later recall that at one point he had talked to Ron about going into the pit after the murders to stab the corpses: "Just to see what it would feel like." But Jeffrey had decided against it.

No one came to look at Cheryl's body. After she was shot, Jeffrey and Ron left the room and went outside into the night air. The autopsy would later show that despite the wounds, Cheryl hadn't died instantly. A coroner would estimate that she had been alive in the pit for up to five minutes after being shot.

Jeffrey had waited this time for Greg to run the chain saw, and when Jeffrey and Ron stepped out of the barn, he was squeezing the trigger hard so the engine would rev and then slowly releasing it. He was trying to mimic the sound of a saw cutting wood. Jeffrey and Ron walked around the barn, checking the highway and the lights at neighbors' houses to see if anyone had become suspicious. Lee and Lois Myers, who lived east of the barn, were coming in from their patio when Lois heard the chain saw and what sounded like a gunshot. Dorothy Green, who lived across the street from the barn, heard the chain saw and at least one gunshot. But neither woman thought it was odd. It wasn't uncommon for people to hunt in the area even at night.

"Bring out the next one," said Jeffrey.

Trina Avery was in the living room reading a magazine when Ron told her that her mother needed her in the barn. The fifteen-year-old sighed and obediently followed him outside.

"Here she comes!" yelled Damon.

The men swarmed around her as soon as Trina stepped inside. Ron told Trina that they were going to play a game. Most of the children had played hide-and-seek in the barn at one time or another. The previous Halloween, the kids had used the barn for skits and a spook house. Trina didn't ask any questions. Ron told her to relax. It was going to be fun. The men taped her feet and hands, and wrapped the tape around her face.

"It's just like the three monkeys—see no evil, hear no evil, say no evil," one of them said.

No one could tell if Trina was smiling. Her head was wrapped like a mummy. Ron and Richard lifted her up and started to carry her through the barn, but as they were walking, Richard accidentally tripped on the extension cord that led to the light over the pit. The bulb fell and broke, leaving Jeffrey in the dark.

"Get a new bulb!" Jeffrey yelled.

Ron and Richard put Trina down on a mound of dirt and trash. Ron stayed with her and told her not to worry, while Richard hurried to another part of the barn to get a bulb. Within a few minutes, the light was restrung and the two men picked up Trina and carried her into the room. They lowered her into the pit next to her parents. Jeffrey stepped up and took aim. Since he had shot her parents in the upper body, Jeffrey decided to shoot Trina in the skull to see, as he later put it, which caused death more quickly—a "head shot or by shooting them in the heart." Just as he squeezed the trigger, however, Trina turned.

"Ouch!" the teenager shrieked, even though her mouth was taped.

Thinking he'd missed her head or just grazed it, Jeffrey quickly lowered the barrel and fired two shots into Trina's back. She slumped forward. He looked down at her. She wasn't moving so he decided that he didn't need to shoot her again.

Just as they had done before, Jeffrey and Ron walked around the barn to see if any of the neighbors were watching. It didn't look like it.

There were only two children left now. Becky and Karen. Ron found them playing video games in the house.

"Who wants to see the horses in the barn?" he asked cheerfully.

Both girls dropped the video-game controls, jumped up, and rushed toward the back door.

"I can only take you one at a time," he announced.

Karen, the smallest, returned to the video game. She was used to being the last in line. Ron told her that he'd be right back.

"Oway," she replied.

After Becky left, Karen noticed that her mom and dad and sister Trina were missing.

"Where's my mama?" she asked.

"It's okay," Susie answered automatically, "she'll be right back."

As Susie watched Karen return to her video game, she suddenly realized what she had said. She turned away from the child. She couldn't stand to look at her.

By this time, each man had found his own specialty. Damon was the lookout, Ron escorted the victims, Richard and Danny handled the taping, Greg ran the chain saw, Jeffrey did the killing.

Unlike her obedient sister, when Becky got to the barn and saw the duct tape, she asked: "What's going on?"

"We told her that we were just playing a game and that she was going for a ride," Richard recalled later.

Within seconds, Ron and Richard had carried her into the room and put her in the pit. Jeffrey shot her, but he didn't think that his first shot killed the feisty thirteen-year-old. She was still breathing. The impact of the bullet had knocked her over and she had hit her mother's corpse.

"I fired again," Jeffrey later said, "and when this shot hit her, her hands, which had been in her lap, went forward as if she was reaching to touch her mother's body—as if she instinctively knew that her mother was there beside her."

Ron went to fetch Karen while Jeffrey reloaded. As soon as Ron stepped inside the farmhouse, Karen was on her feet, eager to see the horses. Ron scooted down and the six-year-old rushed over to him and climbed onto his back. He had given piggyback rides before. His son, Matthew, was the same age as Karen; his daughter, Amy, was four. Karen put her arms around his neck and laughed as Ron bounced her on his back and walked outside.

Like her sisters, Karen didn't resist when the men wrapped her with duct tape, although she was clearly frightened when they put it around her eyes and mouth. She only weighed thirty-six pounds, so Ron picked her up by himself and carried her into the room and pit.

Jeffrey had already fired hollow-points, full-metal-jackets, and silver-tipped 184-grain bullets. He had shot his victims in the back, breasts, skull, and legs. Because Karen was so tiny, he didn't want to risk missing her. He also wanted to try a different angle of penetration. This time, Jeffrey chambered a .225-grain hollow-point slug that he had loaded himself. He stood directly over Karen, who was sitting in the mud. Since her eyes were taped, she had no idea that her parents and sisters were sprawled dead around her.

"I fired straight down into her skull," Jeffrey recalled. "I was less than two feet away and I pulled the trigger, bang, bang."

He was trying to put both shots into the same hole. Karen's body jumped when hit and then slumped over.

It was now almost 11:00 P.M. Jeffrey told Richard and Ron to dump bags of lime on the bodies. He thought that the lime would help them decompose. Richard carried a bag to the pit and slit it open. He tried to pour it on the bodies without looking at them.

"It didn't seem real," Ron said later. He would later not be able to recall Becky and Karen's names when he eventually described their murders to police. "I'm kind of foggy on this business," he'd say.

Once the lime was spread, they began to cover the bodies with rocks. They would then refill the hole and fill the room with trash.

Jeffrey took his pistol and left the other men to do the work.

"Before I went into the farmhouse," Jeffrey later recalled, "I walked into the apple orchard and looked up at the heavens and said a prayer. 'God,' I said, 'I have been thy sword of judgment this day. May my offering be acceptable. May all I've done be acceptable to you this day.' Then I went inside and cleaned up."

Chapter 41

ALICE had driven directly to the Patricks' apartment when she and three of her children left the farmhouse after dinner. She dropped Kristen and Caleb there to play with Molly Patrick and drove to Makro, a large discount department store in a nearby town, where she bought two picnic tables. Jason tagged along to help load them into the truck. A clerk had to get the tables out of a storeroom, and by the time Alice had paid and bought two one-pound bags of chocolate candy for her kids and a bag of cashews for herself, it was 10:30 P.M.

Alice returned to Kirtland and hurried inside the Patricks' apartment without knocking. She went directly to the telephone and called the farmhouse. Debbie answered.

"Can I come home now?" Alice asked.

It had been about five minutes since Karen Avery had been taken into the barn.

"You'd better wait for about fifteen minutes," said Debbie.

After Alice hung up the receiver, she went into the living room and sat on the sofa. Keith and Dennis sat on each side of her. They could tell she was upset. Dennis took her hand. Keith would later testify that Alice had a strange look on her face.

"The fog is bloodred over the barn tonight," Keith quoted Alice as saying.

Shortly after eleven o'clock, Alice returned to the farm with her children. She went into the bedroom to talk to Jeffrey. Kristen, Caleb, and Jason were supposed to go upstairs to bed, but Jason came down a few minutes later.

"I asked Sharon where the men were," Jason recalled. He was fond of Richard and wanted to see what he was doing. Sharon told Jason that all of the men were in the barn and Jason started toward the back door. Sharon rushed into the bedroom.

"Jason—Jason is heading out to the barn," Sharon stammered.

"Stupid!" Alice screamed, "How could you let him do such a thing?"

She raced out and yelled at Jason to get back into the house. Once Alice made certain that he and the other two children were in bed, she rejoined Jeffrey.

Jeffrey told Alice and Damon that he wanted them to come with him to the Red Roof Inn. He took along two green trash bags. When they got there, all three of them hurried upstairs to the Averys' room. Once inside, Jeffrey handed Alice and Damon trash bags and told them to start collecting the Averys' possessions. Purses, toothbrushes, the girls' dolls, Becky's pillowcase from Orioles with the outline of hands on it—everything was thrown into the bags as the three carefully swept through the room.

Suddenly, Alice gasped. On the counter in front of her was the picture that Karen had drawn of the rainbow.

It said: "To Alice—I Love You—Karen."

Alice picked it up and slipped it in the trash bag.

Before they left the room, Jeffrey had Damon mess up the double beds and the rollaway to make it look as if they had been slept in. The room had been paid for in advance with cash so the Averys weren't expected to check out. Jeffrey tossed the motel key on the television and pulled the door shut so that it locked automatically. They hurried down to the truck and drove home.

By the time they reached the farmhouse, the men had finished filling in the pit in the barn. Keith and Kathy Johnson and Dennis and Tonya Patrick had arrived at the farm for scripture class. Jeffrey had telephoned them before leaving for the motel and told them to come out. One by one, the adults filed into the living room and waited as Jeffrey took the trash bags from the truck into his bedroom.

"It was stone cold silent," Alice recalled.

When Jeffrey returned, he opened the Book of Mormon and began to read:

"Behold the Lord slayeth the wicked to bring forth his righteous purposes."

It was the verse from First Nephi that described how God had ordered Nephi to behead Laban.

Jeffrey shut his scriptures and looked up at the group. Everyone in the room, except for him, appeared to be in tears.

"Ron," Jeffrey said, "did my servant Richard serve me well tonight?"

Ron replied; "Yes, your servant Richard served you well."

Jeffrey went through the entire list of names and Ron's answer was the same until he reached Damon. When Jeffrey asked about his son, Ron replied; "Your servant Damon served you the best that he could."

Jeffrey told everyone that he was proud of how Damon had performed.

"Damon is a man now," he said. "He served me well."

Jeffrey turned and stared at Dennis and then at Richard. "We were told that we were lucky to be alive," Richard later said, "that Sharon and Tonya, because of their obedience to Alice, had pulled our cookies out of the sand."

Jeffrey berated both men for several minutes for being rebellious and he warned them that they could still end up like the Averys. Dennis was shaking. Richard lowered his head and bent down in his chair, his hands dangling lifeless between his legs.

There was no doubt whatsoever that Dennis Avery was under Satan's power, Jeffrey announced. "Even his last words were rebellious." Jeffrey explained that just before his mouth was taped shut, Dennis Avery had said, "This isn't necessary."

"He was still trying to tell me what to do," said Jeffrey. "He was trying to be the seer, the prophet."

Dennis Patrick felt physically ill. He looked around the room. "Knowing how close we had come to being in the pit with the Averys, I couldn't believe what he was saying. This was not the Jeffrey that I had known in Independence. This was someone else."

Tonya couldn't stop sobbing.

"I kept thinking about Karen," she said. "The last time I'd seen her, Jeffrey had been holding her on his lap. He had been playing with her and now he had just killed her."

Tonya would later quote Jeffrey as asking the group: *"Is this real enough for you?"*

Jeffrey wanted to know how everyone felt. He asked Richard first. "Nobody should have to die like that," Richard said. "That's just no way to go."

When it was Keith's turn to respond, he simply said, "Shit, shit, shit."

"There is no going back now," Kathy Johnson said.

This is what Alice remembered telling everyone. "Our lives are over. Life as we know it is gone. We are wanderers and strangers in a strange land."

Debbie Olivarez would later quote Alice's remarks differently. "Alice told us, 'You need to be thankful for this man.' She was talking about Jeff. She said, 'He is going to take you to see God. He did this for you. He killed these people so you could see God.' She was playing the role of cheerleader just as she always did for him."

Jeffrey told the women that they should "comfort" their men that night. "This is just the beginning," he reminded them. "The scriptures say we will have to kill many, many more."

For several minutes it was completely quiet except for the sound of crying.

"Now that the sin is gone," Jeffrey concluded, "we can go into the wilderness and see God."

Class was dismissed.

It was after 1:00 A.M. when everyone went to bed. Jeffrey started a fire in the bedroom fireplace and carried the trash bags with the Averys' belongings over in front of it. He began going through them, taking whatever he wanted, burning whatever he didn't. When he got to the drawing of the rainbow that Karen had made for Alice, he tossed it into the flame.

Neither of them could sleep when they first went to bed.

"At one point during the night," Alice later recalled, "Jeffrey asked me if I were asleep and I said, 'No,' and then I said, 'Oh, Jeff, why did you have to do it?,' and he was quiet and then he said, 'It was the will of God.' "

Alice didn't reply.

"Jeffrey truly believed. He thought he was becoming divine. There was never any show of doubt. He genuinely believed that he was exactly who he said he was based on his reading of the scriptures."

Alice lay next to him in the morning darkness with her eyes wide open and then she reached over and took his hand into her hand and held it. He gently squeezed it and fell asleep.

Chapter 42

At precisely 9:00 A.M. on April 18, FBI Agent Robert Alvord and Chief Dennis Yarborough began briefing the sixteen special agents and six police officers who were going to descend on Jeffrey and his followers. Alvord explained that the FBI would handle the interviews, the police officers would secure the area. The agents were shown photographs that had been secretly taken of Jeffrey, Sharon, Danny, Ronald, Greg, and Damon. Agents also were given profiles of Jeffrey and some key group members that were done by the FBI Behavioral Science Unit. Alvord and Yarborough had identified eight people to interview. They were: Jeffrey, Alice, Greg, Richard, Ron, Danny, Sharon, and Debbie. Of course, anyone else at the farmhouse would be questioned, but Alvord and Yarborough felt the list covered the most important group members.

There were three families not mentioned. They were the Johnsons, the Patricks, and the Averys. No one knew anything about Keith and Kathy Johnson. Ron Andolsek had spotted their yellow Chevrolet Sierra station wagon parked at the Lundgren farmhouse on April 3 and had gotten their names by tracing their Missouri license plates, but nothing else was known about them. Shar and Kevin had talked about Dennis and Tonya Patrick. Both said that the Patricks were disliked and were considered by Jeffrey to be untrustworthy. The Avery family was on the bottom of the suspect list. When Alvord wrote a synopsis of the case on February 24 for his supervisors, he mentioned the Averys in only two sentences.

> Dennis Avery, wife Cheryl, are members of the group, however, the Averys do not participate in the paramilitary activities of the group. Avery is also considered expendable by Lundgren, in as much as both of them are considered to be "doubters."

Andolsek had tried to find out more about the Avery family, but he hadn't been successful. Seven months earlier, Andolsek had gone to the house that they rented in Kirtland but it was empty, and when he checked with the post office, he found that the Averys hadn't left a forwarding address. No one was even certain that they were still in the area.

Near the end of the briefing, Alvord reminded the agents that Jeffrey had a large number of weapons, including assault rifles. If Jeffrey or any members of his group began shooting, the agents were to pull back and wait for help from the Cleveland FBI office. By 10:00 A.M., everyone was ready to go.

There was no one in sight at the farmhouse when Alvord and Yarborough arrived. As soon as the men stepped from their cars, Yarborough put his right hand inside his jacket. He had a snub-nosed .38 pistol there. He planned to keep it pointed at Jeffrey through his coat the entire time that he was being interviewed.

When Alvord knocked on the door, Alice answered in her bathrobe.

"We need to talk to Jeffrey," Yarborough said.

"He's in the barn," she replied. "I'll get him."

She shut the door in their faces and ran through the house to the back door. Yarborough and Alvord raced around the side of the house. They turned the back corner just as Alice was hollering from the doorstep for Jeffrey. The two men looked away from the house toward the barn.

"I saw the fifty-caliber rifle, the huge gun, sitting out next to the window," Alice later recalled. "So I grabbed it and carried it into our bedroom and put it under the bedcovers and made the bed real fast so you couldn't tell it was hidden there."

Jeffrey, Alvord, and Yarborough came into the house. Other agents, who had been told to stay away from the farm until Alvord and Yarborough had found Jeffrey, now swarmed onto the property. Richard, Danny, Damon, Dennis Patrick, and Keith Johnson were herded into the front yard and ordered to sit on the porch. "Don't talk to each other," an agent barked.

Sharon and Susie were in the house. Greg had left the farm earlier that morning to dispose of several trash bags that contained property from the barn that belonged to the Averys. He was dropping the bags at random in Dumpsters around suburban Cleveland. Ron and Debbie had left the farm earlier to do some last-minute grocery shopping. Kathy and Tonya, meanwhile, were at the Patricks' apartment.

An agent hurried Alice outside and put her in a car. While she was waiting, Andolsek slid into the front seat. He had a list of questions on a clipboard. He began by telling Alice that she and Jeffrey were under suspicion for a crime that could end up with both of them receiving the death penalty.

"I froze," Alice later said. "I thought, 'How did they find out about the Averys!'"

Andolsek said that the FBI knew "everything."

Alice felt faint. "I kept thinking, 'How did they find out!' "

And then Andolsek said, "Alice, what does 'Redeeming the vineyard' mean?"

Alice suddenly relaxed. "I realized that he didn't know anything about the murders the night before. He was talking about the temple takeover. I about laughed."

Inside, Jeffrey was drawing that same conclusion based on the questions that Alvord and FBI Agent Lloyd N. Buck were asking him. "It was clear that Shar had talked to them," he said. "I knew they didn't have a clue about the Averys being in the barn."

The agents asked if Jeffrey would show them his guns. Jeffrey paused. "They didn't have a search warrant, otherwise they would have shown it to me, so I knew I could refuse to show them my guns. But I figured they'd just go get one and I had planned on leaving for the wilderness that day. I wanted them out of the house as quickly as possible."

Jeffrey took the men into his bedroom and got out the bag with the pistols in it. They checked the weapons and then told Jeffrey that they wanted to see his rifles, including the ones that he had hidden on the second floor behind a false wall in a bedroom. Now Jeffrey was certain that Shar was the informant because she had known about that hidden chamber. Jeffrey led Alvord upstairs and opened the false wall in the closet. He took out the rifles and the agents checked to see if he had altered any of them so that they would fire automatically, a violation of federal gun laws. He hadn't.

While the agents questioned Jeffrey, other group members were being quizzed outside. Once the group members realized that no one except them knew about the murders, the mood turned almost lighthearted.

"Yes, we have firearms," Damon said. He volunteered that his father also had a lot of rabbits. "We are not violent people. We kill our rabbits when they are sick . . . but wrestling in the backyard is the most violent thing we've ever done."

FBI agents later quoted Danny saying that he "could never kill anything, including animals." The movie *The Highlander*, he added, didn't have anything to do with Jeffrey's teachings.

Richard told agents that he believed Jeffrey was "very knowl-edgeable" about the church, but said that he could never be considered a prophet because a prophet had to be able to per-form great acts or miracles and Jeffrey hadn't done anything like that.

Susie said that she and Ron were leaving Ohio to look for work elsewhere.

Alice also played dumb. The only guns in the house, she said, were black-powder rifles. When Andolsek asked her if Jeffrey had ever seen Christ in a vision while the couple was visiting Niagara Falls—a tidbit that Kevin had told the FBI—Alice laughed. "That's a new one," she said. Andolsek realized that he was wasting his time and left Alice in the car with a woman officer. Alvord had specifically assigned an FBI agent who was a member of the LDS church to interview Alice, and he took over, but he didn't get anything useful from her either.

Shortly after the agents began questioning the group, Greg drove by the farm and spotted the police cars. His first instinct was to keep driving, but he didn't want to look suspicious, so he parked his car and walked to the farm. Before he reached the house, he realized that he had Dennis Avery's credit cards in his back pocket. He had thought Jeffrey might want to keep them. It was too late for him to dispose of them now. He hoped no one searched him.

Alice glanced out the window of the car and saw Greg coming. She looked over to where the FBI had lined up the men. "Dennis Patrick and Keith Johnson were in la-la land," she recalled. "They were in total shock and scared to death. But when I looked at Richard, he gave me the thumbs up. He and Damon and Danny were acting like really cool dudes."

Alice announced that she wanted a glass of water and a woman agent escorted her from the car into the kitchen. The agent opened the cupboard and gave Alice a glass. Greg came in to get a drink too. "Greg opened the refrigerator and said, 'Gee, Mom, we're almost out of milk. Don't you think I should go get some for lunch?' I didn't catch on at first, but then I said, 'Yes, you'd better go.' They let Greg leave and he immediately went looking for Debbie and Ron to warn them not to come home."

Greg flagged them down a few miles from the farm and warned them. "Ron and I just started driving around," Debbie recalled. Greg, meanwhile, dropped Dennis Avery's credit cards into a trash bin behind a convenience store.

Alvord wasn't learning anything useful from Jeffrey. Nor had he or Yarborough seen any maps, drawings, or anything else that might give them probable cause to arrest him. They had found the stun gun, but had no way of knowing that it had been used the night before on Dennis Avery. They had also found camouflage uniforms and gas masks. But there was nothing illegal about either. At 11:51 A.M., Alvord conferred with Yarborough and both agreed that it was time to call it quits. Alvord would later file a written report about his conversation with Jeffrey.

> Lundgren advised that he believes that a judgment day is at hand, but it is at the hand of the Lord and not his, and Lundgren finds no justification in the scriptures for violently taking the temple or killing other individuals.
>
> He advised that he does not consider himself a prophet, but does consider himself a teacher.
>
> Lundgren advised that the camouflage uniforms were for hunting and the stun gun was purchased for his wife for her own personal protection. The gas masks are used for spray painting and refinishing.
>
> Lundgren advised that he does a great deal of hunting and his father was a collector of guns and he has just continued the tradition.

When the officers returned to the Kirtland Police Department, Yarborough told Alvord that they had "blown it."

"Bob, we didn't do what we were attempting to do out there today," Yarborough said. "We wanted to break them up and put the fear of—" he suddenly stopped because he didn't want to say the word God. He continued—"the fear of law enforcement in them. I'm afraid we actually tightened the cohesiveness of the group." If anything, Yarborough continued, Jeffrey probably now thought that he was invincible.

Alvord debriefed his agents. All of the suspects had denied that Lundgren was a prophet, except for one. Keith Johnson had been clearly nervous and had told FBI Agent John Powers and Kirtland Police Lieutenant Edward A. Dodaro a bizarre story. Keith said that the group was about to go to the "wilderness" because God was going to appear to Jeffrey on May 3, 1989, and bestow tremendous powers on him. Lundgren would be able to call fire down on his enemies, as well as lightning, and be able to cause earthquakes that would shake the earth and destroy most civilizations. After this was done, the Russians would take over the world and on May 4, 1990, Lundgren would lead an armed assault on the RLDS church in Kirtland, which he would rescue from the Russians. Lundgren would have the "Sword of Laban" when he did this. Keith told the officers that he believed Lundgren could do these things, but if God did not appear to Jeffrey on May 3, 1989, he would leave the group.

Keith's story was as strange as the ones that Shar and Kevin had told, and because of that both Alvord and Yarborough suspected that some of it was true. But Keith hadn't said anything that would justify the FBI's continuing to keep its investigation of Jeffrey going. Alvord knew that he had run out of time.

When Alvord left the police station that afternoon, he told Yarborough that he still wanted to help. Although the FBI's probe would be officially closed in a few days, he would personally be willing to check out any leads that the chief might develop. Yarborough thanked him.

Back at the farmhouse, everyone gathered in the living room as soon as the agents left. Jeffrey quizzed each person: "What did they ask you? What did you say?" Keith listened to what the others said and quickly realized that he had said too much. When Jeffrey asked him, Keith claimed that he hadn't told the officers anything. Greg didn't want to talk out loud. He grabbed a pad and pencil and wrote messages. The FBI, he scribbled on his pad, had bugged the room. Jeffrey doubted it.

Jeffrey turned to Alice. "Now do you have any doubt that I am who I say I am?" he asked.

"Jeffrey considered the fact that the FBI didn't know about the Averys a direct confirmation of the fact that he could do anything he wanted," Alice later said, "and do it right under their noses."

"God has promised me that he will protect my back," Jeffrey said. "We don't have to worry. The Lord is with us."

Just the same, Jeffrey decided that he wanted to leave the farm as soon as he could. But first, he wanted everything in the house that had anything to do with the temple takeover destroyed. The city maps that Richard had stolen were burned in the fireplace. The replica of the temple that Danny had made was smashed and burned too. At one point, Jeffrey had talked about disguising Damon and Danny as paramedics during the temple raid. He had bought them white outfits and Debbie had stolen some paramedic patches from the hospital where she worked. The outfits and patches were tossed into the fire. Jeffrey had bought several old police badges at gun shows and those were dropped into the septic tank. Sharon, meanwhile, stood in the bathroom burning notes that she and others had taken during Jeffrey's classes. She flushed the ashes down the stool. The group burned so many items that they had to stop and clean out the fireplace. Jeffrey sent Damon into the apple orchard with ashes. "Break them up and spread them out," he ordered.

By 2:30 P.M., all the evidence about the takeover had been destroyed. The group got back to packing. At 3:00 P.M., Keith went to Tom's Sunoco Station, which is located next to the police department, to pick up his Sierra, which was having its clutch repaired. Andolsek had seen the distinctive school-bus-yellow truck parked there earlier, and when he spotted Johnson at the station, he called to Yarborough and the two of them hustled over to speak with Keith. They hoped he would feel free to talk now that he was away from the farmhouse. But Keith wouldn't comment. He was still going to the wilderness, he said. But if he ever left the group, he would contact the police. Back in the station, Yarborough and Andolsek agreed that Keith was the "weak link." Over time, both felt that he could be turned into an informer. The only question was whether the officers would get another chance to turn him.

Counting the children, there were twenty-four people making the trip to the wilderness. Debbie had bought over $2,000 worth of food that was spread all over the kitchen floor. There were

still things in the barn that had to be sorted. Jeffrey decided that
everyone was taking too long. He announced that he and his
family, and Susie and her children, were going to leave. The
others would load the U-Haul truck and leave as soon as they
could. Jeffrey put the bag of pistols and all of the rifles into
the Nissan truck that he was driving. He told his children and
Alice to get in. Susie would drive the Luffs' 1978 Plymouth
sedan. The others would ride in the U-Haul, Greg's Honda,
and the Johnsons' Sierra that was going to be used to pull a
horse trailer. Jeffrey appointed Greg to be in charge.

"I had no idea where I was going," Jeffrey said later. "The
scriptures just said to drive in a southbound east direction."
He and Greg looked at a map. Jeffrey pointed toward West
Virginia. They chose a highway. Jeffrey said that he would
stop at a motel at around eleven o'clock. He would stay in one
that could be seen from the road. Greg's group should keep
driving until they spotted Jeffrey's truck. In case they missed
each other, Greg and Jeffrey agreed on a place to meet farther
down the highway the next morning. Whoever got there first
would wait for the others.

At dusk, Jeffrey and his family, and Susie and her children,
left the farmhouse. Alice looked back as they drove away. She
would later recall that only one FBI agent had asked about the
Averys and he had asked only one question about them before
switching the subject. The agents had no idea that the bodies
of Dennis, Cheryl, Trina, Becky, and Karen had been buried
less than twelve hours earlier.

Fifteen minutes after Jeffrey left the farm, he signaled Susie,
who was following his truck, to turn in to a Burger King
restaurant. The kids were hungry and so was he, but Alice
couldn't eat.

It was nearly midnight by the time the others at the farm finished getting everything packed. A heavy fog had come over the
farm. It was so thick that it was difficult to make out objects that
were more than five feet away. The group decided that God had
created the fog to make it difficult for the police or FBI to see
them loading the truck. God was helping them escape. Debbie
was excited when the caravan finally left the farmhouse.

"I was a bit nervous about who was on our tail at first," she
said later, "but once we got out of Ohio, I began to relax."

Jeffrey had told Debbie that she and Greg were going to have a baby, even though Debbie had undergone a partial hysterectomy. He had told her that she would be healed and when she was packing for the trip, Tonya had given her some of Molly's old baby clothes to take. She wanted to have Greg's child. She loved him. She also believed in Jeffrey.

"He was going to take us to see God face-to-face. And I was really looking forward to that moment."

Part Three

Killer

And that prophet, or that dreamer of dreams,
shall be put to death; because he hath spoken to
turn you away from the Lord your God . . .

—*DEUTERONOMY 13:5*

Chapter 43

> And the Lord spake unto Moses, saying, Send thou
> men that they may search the land of Canaan, which I
> give unto the children of Israel . . . (Numbers 13:1–2)

LIKE Moses, Jeffrey was leading his followers into the wilderness, so it seemed fitting that after two days of traveling southeast on various state highways, they arrived in the Canaan Valley of West Virginia. When Jeffrey pulled into Davis, a town of 950, and spied a motel called The Highlander, he declared that he had arrived at the spot where God wanted them. While the family relaxed at a motel, Jeffrey left early each morning to search for a suitable campsite.

His choice of the Canaan Valley almost did seem divinely inspired. Tucked in the Appalachian Mountains, Davis is located on a jagged sliver of West Virginia caught between the states of Maryland and Virginia like a finger slammed in a car door. Settlers were drawn to the valley in the 1880s because of its abundant timber, clear streams, and coal. Today it is the Canaan Valley Ski Resort and the Smoke Hole Caverns, both south of Davis, that attract crowds. Neither interested Jeffrey, but two miles east of town, he found exactly what he was looking for—a huge undeveloped and isolated tract known locally as Yellow Creek Hollow. Officially, the miles of pine forests were owned by the Monongahela Power Company, but the hollow was a virtual no-man's land, open year-round without charge to the public for camping, fishing, and hunting. Best of all, Jeffrey learned, there was little supervision.

By April 23, Jeffrey had moved the group to a campsite in the hollow, but after some fishermen wandered through, he decided to go deeper into the forest. He settled near a stream and organized his camp "chiastically," with a group of tents on one side of the water and another group on the other. The sites were supposed to mirror each other "just like verses in the scriptures." Danny Kraft, Jr., designed a fifteen-foot bridge, which the men made out of logs, to connect the sites.

Jeffrey wanted his camp to be as comfortable as possible. A kerosene-powered generator supplied sufficient electricity to operate a deep freeze, a microwave oven taken from the Avery household, an electric fence used to pen the two horses, and a pair of televisions and videotape players. One television and VCR was kept on a picnic table for the group. The other was in Jeffrey's tent for his private use. There were more than two dozen movies including *The Highlander*.

Jeffrey and Alice lived in the largest tent. It was divided into three sections. One was used as a living room, the other two as bedrooms. Jason, Kristen, and Caleb had mattresses in one; Jeffrey and Alice slept in the other. Damon lived in a separate tent with Danny. Each family had its own tent. There was also a tent for supplies and one filled with toys for the children. A tarp strung over picnic tables served as an outdoor dining area and there was another tent for use as a kitchen.

Because Debbie Olivarez had worked as a cook at summer church camps, she made all the meals. Kathy Johnson tended the horses. Tonya Patrick oversaw the laundry, which was washed in water from the stream and rinsed in big plastic trash cans. Susie Luff and Sharon Bluntschly took care of the supply tent, watched the children, and cleaned the Lundgrens' tent. As was the case at the farm, Alice didn't have specific chores.

Jeffrey assigned each man a job. Richard Brand emptied the toilets—trash cans lined with plastic bags—and built a shower using a lawn sprinkler as a shower head. Greg Winship and Damon Lundgren helped care for the horses. Dennis Patrick was in charge of the firepit where trash was burned. Keith Johnson, Ron Luff, and Danny Kraft collected firewood and did the countless other chores that arose during the day. Jeffrey's job was hunting game in the mornings and teaching at night. Each of the men, except Jeffrey, also took turns standing guard. When they were on sentry duty, they were armed with a semiautomatic assault rifle. Most days, Jeffrey wore a .45-caliber pistol on his belt. By this time, he had promoted himself to the rank of five-star general in the Army of Israel. His army's ammunition and most of the guns were stored in a locker at the foot of Jeffrey's bed. The trunk had belonged to Cheryl Avery, who had saved her babysitting money as a teenager to buy it for her trip to college.

On May 3, Jeffrey arose early and announced that he was going to the top of a nearby mountain to meet God. It was Jeffrey's birthday, and now that he had sacrificed the Averys, it was time for him to be "endowed with power." He returned at midmorning, riding into camp on the ATV. Everyone swarmed around him.

"Jesus Christ appeared to me," Jeffrey proclaimed. Christ had descended from heaven in a beam of light and had told him that He was pleased with the blood atonement of the Averys and the group's trek into West Virginia. Because of Jeffrey's faithfulness, Christ had bestowed a new title on him. Jeffrey told everyone to open their Bibles to verse 5 of chapter 54 of Isaiah:

> For thy Maker is thine husband; the Lord of hosts is his name; and thy Redeemer the Holy One of Israel; the God of the whole earth shall he be called.

"I have taken on Christ's name," Jeffrey announced. "I am not Jesus Christ, but because I have taken on the task that He has commanded me to do, I can be like Jesus Christ and He has given me the title of 'God of the whole Earth.' "

Christ had made him immortal, Jeffrey said. He could no longer be "pierced" by bullets, knives, or any other objects. Christ had also made him divine. "I am the law," said Jeffrey. "There is no other law." No one in the camp was to question any command that he gave. "Would you question Jesus Christ?" Jeffrey asked them. "Then do not try to tell the God of the whole earth what to do." Anything less than total subservience was a "sin" and a sign of "rebellion" that would block the group from being able to stand before God.

During the next few weeks, a routine developed at camp. The women worked in the mornings while the men either hunted or studied their scriptures. Afternoons were reserved for family time when parents were supposed to teach their children the pattern and how to use it. Jeffrey taught a scripture class each night. There were two new concepts that Jeffrey promoted after he declared himself the "God of the whole earth." He called them "peradventuring" and "delusion."

Peradventuring was a word that Jeffrey had derived from the story of Sodom and Gomorrah, found in chapter 18 of Genesis. God had decided to destroy the town of Sodom because it was wicked, but Abraham bargained with Him and got God to promise to spare Sodom if "peradventure there may be fifty righteous within the city." Abraham couldn't find 50, so he asked God to make the number 45, then 40, 30, and 10. God finally ended up destroying the city, just as He had planned. Jeffrey said that Abraham's bargaining with God was "peradventuring." Abraham was trying to second-guess the Lord. Whenever anyone in Jeffrey's group made a suggestion or even used the phrase "Well, I just thought . . ." Jeffrey and Alice would accuse them of "peradventuring." The only person in the group who was supposed to think was Jeffrey. Everyone else was to "submit" their will to his.

The second concept that Jeffrey taught was called "delusion." According to the New Testament book of Second Thessalonians, chapter 2, verses 10 to 13, people who rejected God's truth were given "a strong delusion" by God so that "they should believe a lie." Jeffrey interpreted that verse to mean that he could lie whenever he wished. "If someone is wicked, then he is your enemy, he is under Satan's authority and you do not tell your enemy what you are doing," Jeffrey explained. "There is nothing wrong with deceiving your enemy—military generals do it all the time." Jeffrey said that if he told anyone in the group an obvious lie, he wasn't really at fault—he was giving them a delusion because *they* didn't want to hear the truth. They were to blame.

Greg Winship and others took notes during Jeffrey's classes. The police later confiscated some of these records and discovered that Alice acted as Jeffrey's cheerleader after most classes. She would jump up and lecture or chastise the class. Here is a sample of what the police found:

> Alice on July 9 [Explaining how women are to be sexually subservient to their husbands]: "Ladies, give till they can't take any more!"

Alice on July 22: "It's my observation you get into trouble when you start using your own thoughts. Always ask what would Dad [Jeffrey] do? What has Dad said to do? Every situation you're in is an open-book test and you forget to use the books."

Alice on August 5: "If the rest of us think we will skirt by without judgment—we're wrong. If Jeff says there is rebellion and the thought comes 'I have no rebellion,' that's rebellion."

From the moment the group arrived in West Virginia, Dennis Patrick was a problem. "I fell into a total depression after the Averys' murders," he said later. "I didn't talk to anyone. I didn't eat. I couldn't sleep. I was just numb." Tonya became frustrated. "I needed Dennis and he wasn't there for me," she said. "Dennis was a complete zombie."

Dennis's depression irked Jeffrey. "I told Dennis to get his act together. Everyone understood that God had ordered me to destroy the wicked. Why then would Dennis mourn their destruction? Why would he be upset that the wicked had been destroyed unless he too was under Satan's influence?"

Despite Jeffrey's repeated warnings, Dennis couldn't shake his depression. He was appalled by the murders. Jeffrey decided to have a special class specifically about the executions to "shake up" Dennis. Jeffrey wanted to remind him that he too would be sacrificed if he didn't do what the "God of the whole Earth" demanded. "I related to the class that I saw Cheryl and Trina being killed," Richard Brand said later. "I told Dennis Patrick that was no way for anyone to die. It was not even an option to consider—to be executed like that."

The most exhausting account of what happened in the barn on April 17 was provided by Jeffrey, who described in incredible detail, without any hint of emotion, exactly how he had killed each member of the Avery family. After class, he told Dennis that he was going to meet a similar fate if he continued to show remorse over the "destruction of the wicked."

Terrified, Dennis managed to put on a happier face, but he soon found himself in trouble. It began when he and Tonya drove into Davis to wash the group's clothing at a Laundromat because it had been raining for a week, making it impossible to wash and dry the clothes outdoors. Although wives were supposed to be subservient to their husbands, Jeffrey had put Tonya in charge of the laundry. Dennis was merely sent along to help. Yet when they reached the Laundromat, Tonya found that she had only enough cash to wash and dry half the laundry. Jeffrey hadn't given her enough money. She decided to wash and dry half the load so that the group would have some clean clothing to wear, but Dennis told her that it would be better to wash all of the clothing and then take it back to camp wet where it could be put out to dry. After a brief but hot argument, Tonya relented. When they returned to camp, Jeffrey asked Tonya why none of the laundry was dry and she explained what had happened.

Jeffrey accused Dennis of peradventuring. Jeffrey had put Tonya in charge. By upsurping her power, Dennis had tried to second-guess Jeffrey's will.

Everyone in the group began chastising Dennis. "It may sound like a minor thing," Kathy Johnson said later, "but if Dennis couldn't obey a simple command, how could anyone count on him to obey a big one? The goal of the group was to become one heart and one mind with Jeffrey so we could see God. Dennis was keeping us from that."

That night at class, Jeffrey turned to Debbie. "How long would it take for Dennis to die," he asked, "if I strapped him to a tree and shot him in the balls?"

Dennis's face lost its color. The group became silent. Without waiting for Debbie to reply, Jeffrey slowly removed his .45 pistol from his belt. Dennis thought he was going to be killed.

"Jeffrey said that I wasn't being a man because I wasn't taking responsibility for keeping the commandments of God," Dennis Patrick recalled, "so if I were to have seed, that seed would be bad seed. He said he was going to destroy my seed by shooting off my balls, and then he was going to let me die a slow and agonizing death."

Jeffrey pointed his pistol at Dennis's crotch and for several tense seconds, everyone watched, fully expecting Jeffrey to pull the trigger. "I was going to shoot him," Jeffrey said later. "I had thought that my people had learned their lesson but Dennis still didn't get it. I was not joking around. God had ordered me to destroy the wicked and Dennis was clearly one of them."

Dennis begged for another chance "to get it right." He groveled.

"Okay," said Jeffrey. He lowered his pistol.

Dennis would get a final chance, but as punishment, Tonya and Molly were going to be taken out of Dennis's tent. He needed to be alone so that he could concentrate on his sin. Tonya and Molly were told to move in with Jeffrey and Alice. Dennis was forbidden to speak to his wife and daughter without permission from Jeffrey. The other men in the group were told to take away Dennis's weapons and instructed to stand guard at night over Dennis's tent to make certain that he didn't try to escape. "Every second after that," Dennis remembered, "I was being watched and my every move, my every comment was reported directly to Jeffrey."

During the next few days, Jeffrey talked openly about killing Dennis. At one point, Jeffrey said he was going to order the men to dig a pit for Dennis "just like the one that was dug for the Averys." Another time Jeffrey told Dennis that he would be killed while he was sleeping. "Jeffrey said he was going to have all the men surround my tent at night and simply open fire."

Alice encouraged Dennis's fears. "Jeff's got the same look in his eyes as he did on the day that he killed the Averys," Tonya later quoted Alice as saying.

"I lay awake for hours at night in the quiet and every time I heard a twig break or a leaf rustle," said Dennis, "I'd wonder if they were coming to kill me." He thought about getting a gun and shooting Jeffrey, but decided that he couldn't. "I'm not capable of killing someone." He thought about trying to escape, but rejected that thought too. "I didn't want to leave Tonya and Molly behind. Besides, if I went to the police and told them what kind of weapons Jeffrey had, there was going to be an armed attack and I didn't want Tonya and Molly killed." He thought about suicide, but didn't want to do that either. "Deep down, I still believed Jeffrey was a prophet and I really wanted to do everything right. I believed that Jeffrey could lead me to the Lord."

Dennis decided to keep his mouth shut. He didn't argue, didn't make suggestions, he simply did what he was told.

Jeffrey had always taught that if a man was so wicked that he had to be destroyed, then the rest of his family also had to be murdered. While Tonya was worried about Dennis's fate, she was also angry because she felt that he had put her and Molly into a precarious position.

"One night Tonya asked me if she and Molly were in danger," Jeffrey said, "and I told her that she was completely safe." That was not all Jeffrey told Tonya. Three days after she moved into his tent in early May, Jeffrey said that he was in love with her.

"He was very tender at first," Tonya said later, "very caring and kind." Jeffrey told Tonya that he had always felt a special "tenderness" toward her even during their college days before she had married Dennis, when all of them used to hang out at the RLDS student center in Warrensburg. Because of his warm feelings toward her, Jeffrey had asked God what role Tonya was to play in his life. The answer, he said, had dumbfounded him. Tonya was to be his second wife. "You are flesh of my flesh, bone of my bone," she later quoted him as saying. Jeffrey had come up with a new scriptural interpretation. He had already told everyone that God had created a "true companion" for every man. This companion was made by God out of the man's rib—just as Eve was made from Adam's rib. Jeffrey was now telling Tonya that God actually created two "true companions" for every man. "The rib cage is chiastic. There is a rib on each side, so God really takes both of them, not just one." Jeffrey told Tonya that she was his Bathsheba, that she was his "missing" second rib.

Tonya believed Jeffrey. She was also frightened of him. Within a week, the two of them were having sex. Tonya was worried that Alice would find out. Jeffrey assured her that Alice wouldn't know and if she did, he'd come up with an explanation to satisfy her.

Despite Jeffrey's assurances about Alice, she began suspecting within a month. "Tonya was a very prim and proper person when she first moved into our tent," Alice recalled. "She always wore a bathrobe, and then all of the sudden, she wasn't wearing one and wasn't being careful at all around Jeff."

In early June, Alice had one of her recurring migraine headaches. She didn't attend that night's scripture class but at one point, she walked outside the tent to use the bathroom. On her trip back, Alice spotted Jeffrey and Tonya walking hand in hand across the camp. "They stopped and kissed."

Alice fretted for more than a week and then she finally confronted Jeffrey. He denied everything, and with each denial, Alice became more convinced. "You're lying," she yelled. "You're nothing but a liar."

Jeffrey refused to change his story. Instead, he fell back on his scriptures. "Jeffrey had a habit of doing something and then looking for scriptures to justify his actions," Alice said later. "And that was exactly what he did when I confronted him."

By early July, Jeffrey had figured out a scheme. He told Tonya that it was time for him to announce that she was his second wife, but he cautioned her not to tell anyone that they had already been sexually active for two months. "He told me that he'd found a way to deal with Alice."

One morning, Jeffrey took Alice for a walk and when they stopped to rest, he told her that God was angry at her because of her rebellion. Opening his Bible, Jeffrey turned to chapter 54 in Isaiah. He read the first two verses to her. The key phrase was:

> . . . for more are the children of the desolate than the children of the married wife, saith the Lord. Enlarge the place of thy tent . . .

Jeffrey diagramed the passage and told Alice that it contained a secret message to him from God. This is what he wrote:

> [A] the married wife
>   [B] saith the Lord
> [A] enlarge the place of thy tent

"The Lord is ordering me to 'enlarge my tent' by taking a 'married wife,' " Jeffrey said. "Who is 'the married wife'? Obviously, it is Tonya."

"No!" Alice shrieked. "You can't do this, Jeffrey!"

"It is your fault," he replied. Jeffrey explained that God had grown tired of Alice's constant quibbling and had decided to show her that it was not easy being the "God of the whole earth."

"You are always trying to second-guess me and be like God," Jeffrey said, "so God has decided to let you make a life-or-death decision."

God had ordered Jeffrey to "pierce" Tonya. He could do it with his penis by taking her as his wife and having sexual intercourse with her, he explained. Or he could shoot her with his .45 pistol. It was up to Alice to choose which it would be.

"Jeffrey said it didn't really matter to him which I chose," Alice said later, "and I believed that he was ready to shoot Tonya and Molly."

Falling to her knees, Alice begged him not to make her choose. "Jeff just stood there with his arms crossed across his chest. I cried and cried and cried."

"Choose ye this day," Jeffrey proclaimed. "You have to pay the price for your disobedience."

Alice stood up. "I guess you have another wife," she said, amid sobs.

When it was time for scripture class that night, Jeffrey told Tonya to stay in the tent. After his followers were seated, he opened his Bible and read the verses from Isaiah about the "married wife." He then took out his .45 pistol and held up a bullet so that the group could see it. He loaded and cocked the handgun.

"I'm only going to say this once," Jeffrey said solemnly, "so everyone listen. When I'm finished, I don't want any objections."

Jeffrey explained how God had become angry at Alice and had made her choose how Tonya would be "pierced." As Jeffrey spoke, Alice sat next to him staring at the ground.

"Rather than taking Tonya's life, Alice has agreed to my taking Tonya as a wife," Jeffrey announced. He raised the .45 pistol and pointed it directly at Dennis's forehead.

"Do you have any problems with this, Dennis?" he asked.

"I knew what my response was supposed to be," Dennis said later. "I answered, 'No, sir.' "

That night, Alice began crying when it was time for bed. Tonya was soon in tears too. The two women sat on the bed sobbing. "Tonya said to me, 'Alice, please don't hate me,' and I said to her, 'I could never hate you, Tonya.' And then Jeff came in and told me that he was going to go help Tonya take a shower and I said, 'Oh, Jeff, do you have to do it now?,' and he sat down and said, 'Okay, I won't do it tonight.' " Jeffrey told Tonya to sleep in the children's room that night with Molly.

The next morning, Jeffrey told Alice that he wanted her to go for a ride with him on the ATV. They rode several miles away from camp until they came to a stream. Jeffrey stopped the ATV and told Alice that there were two parts to her punishment. God had required her to make a life-or-death decision, which she had done. But since Jeffrey was Alice's personal "lord and master," he too had a right to punish her for her rebellion. Alice was going to have to prove to Jeffrey that she would obey his every command. She told him that she would.

Jeffrey told Alice to strip, and when she was standing naked in the woods, he ordered her to remove his clothing. "I thought we were going to make love," said Alice, "but instead, Jeffrey had a bowel movement and he instructed me to cover him with his own feces, leaving just enough for him to use to masturbate with. I did as he commanded and then he told me to tell him how beautiful he was, how wonderful he looked with all of this feces on him. I did this while he masturbated."

Jeffrey couldn't achieve ejaculation, Alice later said, so he commanded her to help stimulate him. "He took some of the feces and put it in his own mouth," Alice said later, "but he didn't swallow it. A lot of saliva come out and . . . he pulled me up and made me kiss him on the lips and then he . . . told me to perform oral sex on him without washing any of the feces off."

Alice did what he asked, but after several minutes, she became physically ill and began to gag. "He grabbed me and pushed his penis into my mouth and told me not to stop again for any reason. He told me to swallow everything—told me that I couldn't spit. I went on with it until he had obtained orgasm."

Afterward, Jeffrey led Alice to the creek. "I was told to give him a bath and he told me that I had been obedient and that I was forgiven and he thanked me for being a pure wife and I said, 'Okay.' And then he told me that he loved me."

They got dressed and returned to camp.

A few days later, Jeffrey announced that it was time for God's commandment to be carried out. He ordered Alice to "prepare the bed" in the tent for Tonya. He intended to "pierce" her. While Alice did what she was told, Jeffrey raced over to the camp's makeshift bathroom and surprised Tonya, who was inside. Grinning, he watched her for several seconds as she sat on the toilet and then announced that he wanted her back in the tent immediately.

When Tonya got there, Jeffrey ordered Alice to leave. She closed the tent flap behind her and hurried over to the kitchen where Debbie and Kathy were baking bread. "Alice was talking a mile a minute about funny things that her children had done," Kathy said later. "It suddenly dawned on me what was happening." All the other adults also figured out what was going on and they began gathering around Alice to give her moral support.

Jeffrey and Tonya were in the tent for only a few minutes when Jeffrey came scurrying outside. He rushed over to Alice.

"I couldn't do it," he announced in a voice that everyone could easily hear. Jeffrey explained that he had been unable to have sex with Tonya because she was not, as he put it, "flesh of my flesh.

"I was undressed and Tonya was undressed. I saw her and she saw me. I touched her and tried to find something to focus on that was arousing. I'm not trying to belittle her, but she is not my flesh and . . . I couldn't obtain an erection so I got dressed and said, 'I'm sorry, but if you want any satisfaction, you're going to have to do it by yourself.' "

That story is similar to the explanation that he first gave Alice when she discovered ten years earlier that he had spent the weekend in a motel with a fellow employee from Lake of the Ozarks Hospital. Despite the similarities, Alice appeared overjoyed.

"Oh, Jeffrey," she squealed, throwing her arms around him. "I knew you couldn't betray me."

The rest of the day, Jeffrey strolled through camp making jokes about his own inability to have sex with Tonya. He told everyone that he had been forced to "pierce" Tonya with his finger because he found her so unattractive that he simply couldn't obtain an erection. Kathy Johnson would later recall that Jeffrey had told her and Keith that Tonya had given a new meaning to the biblical phrase "withering away."

Tonya, who had been told to stay inside the tent all day, could hear what Jeffrey was saying and she was confused and hurt. She knew that he was lying. Why, she wondered, was he belittling her? That night, a completely different Jeffrey from the "loving" one who had wooed her, came into the tent. He briskly told Tonya that she was filled with sin. He had been studying the scriptures, he announced, to see what he was supposed to do with her. "Jeffrey had been telling me for weeks that I was pure and free of sin and now he was telling me I was wicked—just like that. All I could think was that he was setting the stage to get rid of me. He was tired of me and wanted someone else." Jeffrey told Tonya that she could remain in his tent, but he wasn't going to sleep with her and he warned her against telling anyone about their sexual encounters.

At scripture class a few nights later, Alice once again jumped to her feet and lectured the women about how they should do whatever their husbands demanded. Debbie would later recall Alice's comments. "She said, 'If Jeffrey wants me to be his doormat, then I'll be happy the rest of my life cleaning his shoes. He is my master and I live only to serve his desires.' "

Shortly after Alice made that declaration in late July 1989, Jeffrey told her that God had caused him to dream a strange dream.

"Jeffrey told me that God had shown him a woman's vagina in this dream," Alice later said. "He said that God had ordered him to find this vagina."

Chapter 44

THE day after FBI agents and the entire Kirtland police force descended on Jeffrey's farmhouse outside Kirtland, Patrolman Ron Andolsek telephoned a Cleveland-area psychologist for advice. The therapist confirmed Andolsek's fears. Now that

Jeffrey had been confronted by police and had avoided arrest, he would probably claim that he was being protected by God, the therapist said. He might even tell his followers that he had become divine.

Andolsek drove by the farmhouse later that day and noticed that it seemed deserted. A short time later, a neighbor complained about rabbits, chickens, and other animals running loose at the farm. When Andolsek drove up to the house and peeked in the windows, he could tell that Jeffrey and his followers had fled.

"Damn!" Chief Yarborough said when he learned that Jeffrey was gone. "At least when he was at the farm we could watch him. Now we got to find him."

For four days, both men worked the telephones. They called Jeffrey's bank, the post office, the different places where group members worked. When that failed, they began calling various relatives of group members. No one knew where Jeffrey had gone. Shar and Kevin had both mentioned that Jeffrey was friendly with Tom Miller so Andolsek telephoned him. At first, Miller was reluctant to talk. He thought the RLDS was behind the probe. But when Andolsek explained that Jeffrey was suspected of conspiring to take over the temple, Miller cooperated. He recalled how Jeffrey had come to see him on April 17 and had acted weird. "He's gone off the deep end," Miller said. Like the others, however, Miller didn't have a clue where Jeffrey had gone.

On April 28, Andolsek got his first lead. He learned that Greg Winship had used his credit card to buy several items at a local store. Andolsek called Robert Alvord at the FBI office in Painesville and gave him the number of Winship's credit card. Alvord notified the bank that issued the card and officials there promised to send the FBI a list of Winship's recent purchases.

Meanwhile, Chief Yarborough urged Dale Luffman and RLDS Bishop Ken Fisher to leave town between May 1 and May 4. "We don't know when that idiot might come storming back with guns blazing." Both took Yarborough's advice.

There are few secrets in a small town, particularly after nearly two dozen FBI agents and police officers are seen swarming around a farm. By May 1, nearly everyone in Kirtland had heard about Jeffrey's plan to take over the temple on his birthday. People figured there was a fifty-fifty chance that he might show up.

Just before 9:00 P.M. on May 1, Yarborough and Andolsek drove to the same posts near the temple that they had manned one year earlier. But this time, they were not alone. Curious townsfolk cruised past the temple all night long looking for the chief. A few waved. Yarborough felt as if he was part of a circus sideshow.

On May 2, Andolsek got a call from the FBI. Special Agent Alvord said that Greg Winship had used his credit card on April 18 to rent a twenty-four-foot-long U-Haul truck. Greg had picked up the vehicle within hours after the FBI and police had finished questioning Jeffrey and left the farm. Andolsek telephoned the local U-Haul dealership, which had rented Greg the truck, and learned that Greg had dropped off the truck six days later at a U-Haul dealership in Falls Church, Virginia, a suburb of Washington, D.C. When Andolsek called the manager there, he was told that Greg had driven the truck a total of 603 miles and had returned it "full of red mud."

Andolsek got out a map of the eastern United States and drew a red line from Kirtland to Falls Church. He then began writing down the names of all the state and national parks along both sides of the line within a six-hundred-mile radius of Kirtland. After compiling the list, he telephoned the U.S. Park Service and asked if there were any parks in particular where red dirt was common. Most parks on his list, he was told, had spots where red soil could be found. Discouraged, Andolsek decided to try a different approach. After obtaining Chief Yarborough's permission, Andolsek asked the federal park service to send a Teletype to all of its rangers. He also sent the Teletype to state park officials and local sheriff's departments in a five-state area. The message described Jeffrey and his group.

Lundgren contends to be a prophet and . . . advocates the use of deadly force . . . One member told FBI/Police that they were going to leave for the "wilderness" to find the "sword of Laban" which will be used to decapitate people. . . .

The Teletype contained the telephone number for the Kirtland Police Department and asked rangers to call immediately if they had any useful information. That night, Andolsek and Yarborough returned to their temple posts, but neither felt an attack by Jeffrey was likely.

"I figured Jeffrey had gone off somewhere trying to find the Sword of Laban," Yarborough said. "At first, I was relieved and then I thought, 'Oh, Lord, May third comes around every year.' Am I going to be sitting in the church parking lot every year waiting for that asshole?"

When May 3 passed without incident, Yarborough found that he was being criticized by some townspeople and had become the butt of several jokes. A few fundamentalists, who had attended Jeffrey's classes, claimed that Dale Luffman and the RLDS hierarchy had used Yarborough to unfairly persecute Jeffrey and drive him from town. Others claimed the chief had been taken in and had overacted to the insane ravings of a frustrated blowhard. Even Kirtland's mayor began to openly wonder if Yarborough hadn't become obsessed with Jeffrey, making him into a much bigger threat than he really was. Yarborough began to feel pangs of self-doubt. After all, there was still no proof that Jeffrey had broken the law. "Maybe I was wrong to spend so much time worrying about him since he and his group were gone—that's what I began to wonder."

Weeks passed without any word about Jeffrey's whereabouts. No one whom Andolsek had notified had seen the group. And then on June 5, Yarborough and Andolsek got lucky.

West Virginia Game Warden Harold "Rocky" Spencer had been on a routine patrol in Yellow Creek Hollow when he decided to check a remote area for turkey hunters. Turkey season had just opened and Spencer wanted to make certain that anyone hunting in the hollow had bought a valid license. Spencer had been going through the woods when he spotted Jeffrey's camp. As soon as he saw an armed guard standing watch, he became suspicious and ducked behind some bushes. The game warden crept close enough to copy down the license numbers on the cars parked in the camp. He then carefully retreated and contacted Sheriff Hank Thompson. At age twenty-nine, Thompson was serving his second year as sheriff of Tucker County, a 465-square-mile area that he patrolled with the help of only two deputies. A big man with boyish good looks, Thompson had grown up in Davis and had spent eleven years as a deputy before running for office. He was so well known in the county that he really hadn't needed to put his last name on his campaign posters. All it took was "Vote for Hank."

Thompson had seen a copy of the Teletype that Andolsek had sent to sheriffs offices and he rummaged through the pile of paper on his desk and retrieved it. He compared the license numbers that Spencer had given him with the ones on the flyer, and when they matched, he dialed Yarborough's number.

"So Jeffrey's in West Virginia," Yarborough said. "Well, I'm glad you have him and not me." The two lawmen spoke for nearly an hour. "My first concern," Thompson later said, "was keeping a lid on who they were. Ninety percent of the people in my county are coal miners and if they found out some religious cult was camping up there, the first thing they'd do is grab their guns and move them out. I'd have a massacre on my hands."

Since Jeffrey hadn't been accused of committing any crimes, there wasn't much Thompson could do except watch the group and keep Yarborough posted. He volunteered to do that. The next day, Yarborough called again. Yarborough called again the following day. The next day, Yarborough called again. Thompson, who had other problems to solve, began to wonder if Yarborough was investigating anyone besides Jeffrey Lundgren.

Thompson assured Yarborough that he was keeping an eye on Jeffrey, but the sheriff didn't feel that it made sense for him to go into the heavily armed camp and begin questioning group members without some legitimate reason. Jeffrey had started driving into Davis three or four times a week to buy kerosene for the camp's electric generator, and even though he was guarded in his comments, he seemed friendly enough when the sheriff spoke to him.

By the end of July, Yarborough was insisting that Thompson visit Jeffrey's camp. Yarborough had started receiving telephone calls from the worried relatives of various group members and he wanted to know for certain who was living in the camp. Even Alice's mother, Donna Keehler, had called and demanded to know where Jeffrey had gone.

In early August, Thompson decided to visit the camp on the pretense that school would be starting soon and West Virginia required all children to be enrolled. He decided, however, that before he hiked into the camp, he was going to buzz over it in a state-owned helicopter. That way he could see how Jeffrey and his band were going to react before landing. If the group started shooting, then Thompson could retreat and call in reinforcements.

Thompson telephoned Yarborough and explained his plan. The next day, Yarborough called Thompson. The chief had discovered that before Jeffrey left Kirtland, he had bought a .50-caliber rifle capable of shooting down a helicopter.

"I just wanted to warn you," said Yarborough.

"Oh, Christ," Thompson replied sarcastically. "That's just what I wanted to hear."

Chapter 45

BY the end of July, the group had been in the wilderness for nearly four months and everyone was becoming depressed. No matter what they did, Jeffrey claimed that there was still too much sin for his followers to go before God. Jeffrey was still meeting God on a regular basis. He would ride the ATV off to a nearby mountain and return several hours later with a new revelation or commandment. But he always told the others that they would be destroyed by fire if he took them along.

The biggest problem, Jeffrey said, was the women. They were "filled with pride." During the first week of August, all of them were hustled into the Lundgren tent for a private meeting with Alice. They were told that Jeffrey had decided that they had to be literally "stripped" of their pride. Kathy Johnson, Debbie Olivarez, Sharon Bluntschly, and Susie Luff were each going to have to humble themselves by performing a striptease in front of the "God of the whole earth." Because Tonya was Jeffrey's second wife, she did not have to perform. Neither would Alice.

Alice warned the women not to tell their husbands about the dances. No one was to know but them and Jeffrey. Alice would tell them when they were to come into his tent and perform.

Susie Luff was upset after the meeting. She was devoted to Ron and didn't understand how taking her clothes off in front of Jeffrey was going to free her from sin. Within an hour, she had told Ron everything that Alice had said.

Of all the men in the group, Ron was the strongest. He was also not afraid of Jeffrey. Ron found Jeffrey lifting weights and demanded to know what Alice was talking about. Jeffrey assured him that Susie had misunderstood Alice's instructions. He had no intention of asking the women to perform a strip show for him. He promised to explain everything that night at scripture class.

When the group got together later that evening, Jeffrey put a completely different spin on the story. He said God was disappointed with the group, so much so that He had even considered destroying everyone except for Jeffrey and starting over. But Jeffrey had come up with a way to appease God.

With his scriptures firmly in hand, Jeffrey explained that in Moses' day, a wife could "intercede" on her husband's behalf whenever he fell into disfavor with his lord and master. "The wife could beg the lord to spare her husband and family." That was still true today, Jeffrey said, and that was what God wanted the women in the camp to do. They were to "intercede" on their families' behalf with God's representative on earth—Jeffrey.

Jeffrey then moved on to the next part of his explanation. He told everyone to read verse 21 in chapter 28 of Isaiah, which said that the "Lord" would perform a "strange act." Jeffrey explained that he was the "Lord" mentioned in this verse and that God had ordered him to perform this "strange act."

Once again, Jeffrey referred everyone to the scriptures, this time chapter 32 of Isaiah, verse 11. It read:

Tremble, ye women that are at ease; be troubled, ye careless ones; strip you, and make you bare, and gird sackcloth upon your loins.

Jeffrey said that this verse defined the "strange act." Each woman in the group was to come into Jeffrey's tent and strip. They were to dance in front of him completely naked for one hour. That was scriptural, Jeffrey said, because the word for "tremble" in verse 11 also meant "to dance" in ancient Hebrew, and the verse clearly stated that the women were to strip and be bare when they danced.

While the women were dancing, they would become humble and their sins would be transferred onto Jeffrey because he was the "God of the whole earth."

"Christ took on the world's sin when he shed his blood for us on the cross," Jeffrey said. "I will do the same thing for you. I will take on your sins."

Jeffrey had already told everyone that he was immortal. "Obviously," he said, "I can't be crucified or shed my blood, but God has shown me a way that I can shed my blood symbolically and wash away your sins.

"In a rape case," Jeffrey continued, "a man's semen can be used to identify him, just as his blood type can be used to positively identify him."

In God's eyes, Jeffrey proclaimed, "blood and semen are the same."

While each woman was dancing naked in front of him, Jeffrey would masturbate and ejaculate his semen into each woman's panties, he said. "This will be the same as when Christ shed his blood."

After he had "soiled" each woman's panties with semen, he would hand them back and she would be required to wear them the rest of the day. This would fulfill verse 11, which said that the women were to "gird" their "loins" in "sackcloth."

Jeffrey said that he would be "loaded down" with the sins of the group after the dances. He would ride the ATV up to the mountaintop, where he would meet God and be purified by His presence. The group's sins would then be wiped clean.

There was only one catch, Jeffrey announced. If he did not ejaculate during a dance, then that woman's sins could not be cleansed and she and her family would have to be destroyed.

It took Jeffrey nearly two hours to explain his scheme. When he finished, no one objected. "Once everyone understood the scriptural basis for it," Jeffrey later recalled, "then no one had any trouble with it because they could see that it was not a sexual act at all and not some weird fantasy of Jeffrey's. Instead, it was a very loving and a highly spiritual undertaking."

Even so, Ron and Keith approached Jeffrey after class and told him that they were worried about sending their wives alone into his tent to strip while he masturbated. While neither wanted to come out and say it, Jeffrey knew why they were upset. They were afraid that Jeffrey was going to take their wives away from them just as he had taken Tonya away from Dennis. Jeffrey assured Ron and Keith that the scriptures said a man could have only two wives, no more. To further calm their fears, Jeffrey announced that Alice would be beside him during the entire ritual and that he would keep a sheet in front of him so that the women wouldn't see his penis while he masturbated. Alice, he said, would be in charge of preparing the women. "I wanted them to know that this was all aboveboard," Jeffrey later explained, "so I put Alice in charge and they accepted that."

Alice was certain that Jeffrey had concocted the entire "intercession" scheme that afternoon after he had been questioned by Ron about having all of the women perform stripteases. "He was using the scriptures to get what he wanted," Alice said, "which was to see all of the women's vaginas so he could find the one in his dream."

Later, when she was asked why she hadn't debunked Jeffrey, Alice claimed that she was scared. "Jeff made it perfectly clear to me that if this was not successful . . . children were going to die," she testified.

Others in the group would recall Alice's demeanor somewhat differently. "Alice said that Jeff was afraid that we were going to mock him," Sharon later testified, "that we were going to make light of it, and Alice said, 'You're not going to do that to him.' She said, 'If I have to, I'll beat you to make you do this and I don't care if it takes hours and hours, you're going to get through it.' "

Debbie described Alice as an enthusiastic partner when Jeffrey first explained intercession. She quoted Alice as saying that women were "created with three holes in which they could be pierced by men—orally, vaginally, and anally." The women were to show Jeffrey each of these areas during their dance. Alice also suggested songs that were Jeffrey's favorites for the women to play while dancing.

On August 14, Tonya took all of the children out of camp so they would not know what was going on. Susie reported to Jeffrey's tent at 9:00 A.M. As instructed, Ron stayed in his own tent, reading scriptures and praying. Alice, who was wearing the sexy pink pajamas that Jeffrey had bought her, greeted Susie at the entrance and hugged her. She slipped Susie's hour-long tape into the stereo player, flipped it on, and then sat down beside Jeffrey. He was perched on the bed and was completely naked but was covered from the waist down by a sheet. Jeffrey nodded and Susie began to slowly undress. Alice had told the women that they were supposed to be cheerful and seductive. The striptease was supposed to be pleasing to Jeffrey and their panties were supposed to be the last piece of clothing to be removed. The women were also to be nude by the time the first song on their tape finished.

After Susie had removed her clothing, she handed Jeffrey her panties. He quickly wrapped them around his penis and began to masturbate while Susie went through the various moves that Alice had told her were required. Alice would later claim that each woman was also told to masturbate while she danced. This was a new twist that Jeffrey had added that morning.

"The night before the dances, when we were having sex, Jeffrey told me that he wanted to fantasize, and he asked me to tell him what Susie was going to do when she danced in front of him the next day," Alice said. "I said Susie was going to masturbate, and then the next day, he made me tell each woman when they came in that they were going to have to 'come unto the Lord' literally."

After Susie had danced for about forty-five minutes, Jeffrey ejaculated into her panties. He waited for several minutes and then slipped on his purple sweatpants and stood up.

"Are you stripped of pride, my daughter?" he asked.

As instructed, Susie replied: "Behold!" She then fell on the tent floor, facedown at Jeffrey's feet.

"Arise and come forth," Jeffrey declared.

Still naked, Susie stood and walked to Jeffrey, who was bare-chested. He opened his arms and while he embraced her, Alice darted behind Susie and held up a statement for Jeffrey to read. Alice had written it.

"Unto thee, I have shed my blood for thee," Jeffrey read. "I have bought you with a price. I have washed thee and sanctified thee. This day, thou has preserved thyself, and thy seed through my blood forever."

Susie had been told by Alice to reply by saying: "Yea, Lord, I know that thou speakest the truth."

Jeffrey then released Susie and handed her the panties. "Susie was told that she could get dressed," Alice recalled. "All of the women were to dress slowly in front of Jeff because you neither rushed into the presence of the Lord or rushed out of His presence." Before Susie left, Alice gave her a short statement that was nearly identical to the ones that she and Jeffrey had exchanged. Susie was told to go directly to her tent and read the first statement to Ron. He was then to come to the Lundgren tent, dressed in full military gear, and swear his allegiance to Jeffrey, which he did.

After Susie's dance, the adults had lunch. Later that afternoon, it was Sharon's turn. "When Sharon was completely undressed," Alice said later, "Jeffrey whispered to me: 'Richard's got nothing to complain about.' There was one song on the tape, I think it's called 'Only for You,' and Sharon sat down naked on the floor and spread her legs open wide and held her breasts in her hands and the singer was saying, 'Only for you, only for you,' and Sharon leaned back and began to masturbate but Jeffrey didn't find her stimulating so he signaled me to go under the sheet. I got under the cover and began licking and kissing him on the testicles while he masturbated."

Sharon later testified that she had watched Alice go under the sheet and that Jeffrey had ultimately ejaculated. After going through the same ritual that he had with Susie, Jeffrey sent Sharon back to her tent and Richard appeared in full military gear and swore his allegiance to Jeffrey.

Kathy danced the next morning at ten o'clock. From the moment that she entered the tent, Alice was jealous. Kathy rarely wore dresses, but had one on that morning. She had fixed her long brown hair so that it was on top of her head. As she danced, she undid her hair, letting it fall to her shoulders. Alice quietly started to smolder.

"This feeling washed over me as I watched Kathy dance," Alice later claimed, "and I looked at Jeff and he was totally enthralled by her dancing and when she got to the point where she was completely naked, she turned her back toward us and bent over at the waist and I heard Jeff say in the faintest whisper, 'There it is.' I knew he was talking about the vagina in his dream—the one that God had ordered him to find—and I said to myself, 'Take a good look, Alice, because this is your competition.'

"When it came time for him to masturbate," Alice continued, "Jeff obtained it rapidly and when he was all done, and she had fallen on her face on the tent floor, he told her to arise and come forth, and Kathy looked up from the floor and said, 'My Lord, may I kiss your feet?,' and he said, 'Yes,' and she kissed his feet and he took her in his arms and read her the message, and then she got dressed—but she stayed in the tent like they were old college buddies, just chatting away."

That day at lunch everyone in camp knew something had happened during Kathy's dance to irritate Alice. "Alice was pissed and I began to worry," recalled Debbie, "not about Jeffrey, but about what Alice would do if Jeffrey really liked my dance. I was more afraid of her than him at that point."

Debbie's turn to dance came that afternoon. She had dressed in several layers of clothes and each was a completely different outfit, including one with suspenders. Even Alice later admitted that Debbie's dance was "really cute" but she remained irked after Debbie's performance. "I was still angry about Kathy," Alice recalled, "because I knew that Jeffrey was going to come up with some reason to bed her."

Jeffrey stayed in his tent for two days after the dances. Alice told everyone that he was physically ill because of the sins that he had taken on from the group. Only on the third day was he strong enough to come out of his tent and ride the ATV to the nearby mountain where he met God. When he returned to camp later that day, Jeffrey was chipper and in perfect health. God had cleansed all of the sins.

Shortly after he returned to camp, Jeffrey approached Keith in private. "He told me that Dennis had to die," Keith recalled. "I asked how much time Dennis had, and Jeffrey said, 'Not long.' " Jeffrey told Keith that Dennis was doomed because he didn't have anyone to dance on his behalf; therefore, he was still filled with sin. Tonya couldn't "intercede" for Dennis because she was now Jeffrey's wife. All of the other men in the group had been saved, he explained. Susie Luff had danced for Ron. Sharon had danced for Richard. Debbie had danced to save Greg. Kathy had danced on behalf of Keith. Jeffrey had told the group that his son, Damon, and Danny Kraft, Jr., were okay because Alice was their mother. [Although Danny was not part of the Lundgren family, he had never been married; therefore Alice was his true 'mother,' Jeffrey said.] That left Dennis Patrick.

Months later Keith would look back on his conversation with Jeffrey and realize that he was being set up, but at the time, he didn't sense what Jeffrey was pulling into play.

As soon as Jeffrey left him, Keith hurried to his tent and told Kathy that Dennis was going to be killed. "I didn't want Dennis to be destroyed," Kathy said later, so she told Keith that she was willing to dance naked again on Dennis's behalf if that would save him.

Keith and Kathy went to see Jeffrey. They found him exercising in the weight-lifting area. Alice was sitting next to Jeffrey reading scriptures out loud as he lifted weights.

"Kathy wants to know if she can intercede for Dennis," Keith said.

Jeffrey bolted upright from the weight bench. He appeared angry. Dennis's fate was none of Keith's business, he said. "You are peradventuring!"

Alice was just as outraged. "Why are you asking questions about Dennis?" she demanded. "Don't you know that you can't just throw out a question like that? You know Jeffrey will have to act on it. He'll have to do something."

The penalty for trying to second-guess God was death, Jeffrey declared. Keith was going to have to be "pierced" either with a sword or bullet. Keith was dumbfounded. He immediately began apologizing.

"There is an alternative," said Jeffrey. Kathy could intervene on Keith's behalf once again. But this time, dancing naked in front of Jeffrey wasn't going to be enough. "Someone must be pierced. God demands it," Jeffrey said. Rather than shooting Keith, Jeffrey could use his penis to pierce Kathy.

"Alice was livid," Kathy said later. "She said, 'Didn't you realize what you were setting yourself up for?,' and I said, 'Well, no, I thought if anything it would be another dance experience.' "

"Well, now that you understand what you must do," Alice asked Kathy, "how do you feel?"

"Alice, if it saves a man's life, then I'll do it. I don't hold this flesh that precious," Kathy replied.

Alice stormed off to her tent. But Jeffrey stayed at the weight bench. He would give Keith one week to consider his options.

Chapter 46

WORD spread quickly through camp about Jeffrey's ultimatum, and on August 25, Keith told Jeffrey that Kathy had agreed to have sexual intercourse with him in order to save Keith and Dennis. Jeffrey hurried over to talk to Kathy. "He wanted me to know that he wasn't going to hurt me," she said. "Jeff said that if I had any fears, or any questions, I should ask. . . . I told him that to be quite frank, my concerns were with Alice and Keith, I wasn't afraid of Jeffrey at all."

There weren't many things that Kathy Johnson was afraid of. At age thirty-six, Kathy had given birth to four sons, raised prizewinning goats, horses, and cattle, run a thirty-acre farm by herself, sold insurance, and done hard physical labor nearly every day of her life. Kathy was considered a "tomboy"—even as an adult. In a dress and nylons, she looked awkward. But in blue jeans, cowboy boots, and a wool shirt, Kathy was radiant. Of all the women in the group, she was the one most suited to the rugged outdoor life. She was strong, smart, and fiercely stubborn. She was also, the group discovered, extremely gullible. At times, Kathy herself would even joke about how she was a naïve "Iowa farm girl."

The oldest of five children, Kathy had grown up near Woodbine, a town of 1,400 just north of Council Bluffs. When she was eleven, her parents decided to convert their four-hundred-acre farm into a dude ranch. Each summer, as many as seventy children would fill the ranch's bunkhouses. They came to learn how to ride horseback and it was Kathy's job to teach them. By the time she was in high school, she was an expert rider, experienced rodeo racer, and shrewd horse trader. She was an honor-roll student and an outstanding distance runner on the school track team. When she graduated in 1971, Kathy held school records in three track events.

Kathy had met Keith at Central Missouri State University where she planned to study nursing. She had enrolled at CMSU because her parents were both active RLDS members and they wanted her to attend a school near the center spot. Keith was a senior, she was a freshman, and when they were introduced at the RLDS student union, Kathy was instantly smitten.

Keith was handsome, with jet-black hair and engaging eyes. He was confident, funny, clever. They went out a few times and Kathy was soon deeply in love, but Keith decided to marry someone else. Heartbroken, Kathy left college after her freshman year, returned home, and eventually wed a boy who had worked for her parents at the dude ranch. Three years later, Kathy got a divorce, and Keith, who had got a divorce himself by then, began writing her. They were married on May 7, 1977.

It was Keith who had first introduced Kathy to Jeffrey and Alice. When they met, Kathy felt uncomfortable. She didn't like Jeffrey's sexual jokes and Alice seemed mousy.

The newlyweds didn't really see much of the Lundgrens. The Johnsons were too busy. Kathy and Keith had bought a thirty-acre farm not far from Warrensburg. Keith worked as a machinist during the day. Kathy sold insurance and ran the farm. Their social life revolved around the church. After she got pregnant, Kathy quit the insurance business. She had three more sons in quick succession. When the first reached school age, Kathy founded Zion's Hope Country School. Later, she taught her boys at home rather than expose them to public schools. "Our goal was to seek the Lord," she recalled. "It was the center of everything that we did."

Keith worked hard in the church and moved up its ranks. At first glance, the Johnsons seemed to have everything—a good income, a nice home, a loving family, and status in their church and community.

But in 1983, Keith was laid off from his job and was unemployed for eighteen months. He and Kathy were forced to sell their farm and move into a house owned by Keith's relatives. They went into debt and their financial stress took a toll on their personal relationship, they both later said. Still, they stuck it out. It was during this same time that the RLDS decided to ordain women. At the RLDS worldwide conference in 1984 and later in 1986, Keith introduced numerous ill-fated motions aimed at preventing women from serving as priests. He soon found his fundamentalist viewpoint unwelcome among the church hierarchy.

Like most others in Jeffrey's group, Keith and Kathy had sought out Jeffrey and his teachings as an alternative to the liberalization of their church. It didn't take much prodding to convince both of them that the RLDS was being led by a fallen prophet. Their decision to join Jeffrey's group was supposed to be a rebirth for the Johnsons. They saw it as a chance to start over.

On the day that Kathy reported to Jeffrey's tent to be "pierced," Alice went for a walk away from camp. Keith read his scriptures. "I told Kathy to do whatever she had to do to keep us from being killed," Keith said later. Kathy found Jeffrey eagerly waiting in his tent.

"All it was supposed to be was intercession," Kathy said later, "but what actually transpired was something of a whole lot bigger magnitude. We both sensed that this was an incredible experience."

During intercourse, Jeffrey announced that he loved her.

Afterward, he told Kathy that he had always felt a "tenderness" toward her. He wasn't certain why, but he had felt it from the time that they first met. He was going to check the scriptures to see why she was different from other women.

Kathy had no way of knowing that Jeffrey was using exactly the same lines on her that he had used on Tonya four months earlier.

"I wasn't sure what was happening," Kathy recalled. The "God of the whole earth" had told her that she was special and she believed him. She had become convinced that Jeffrey was a prophet.

That night, Alice attempted to reclaim her turf. Greg, Sharon, and Debbie all had good voices and Alice asked them to sing several love songs to Jeffrey. "They were supposed to be from Alice to Jeffrey," Kathy recalled, "but I was sitting right across the picnic table from Jeff and he was staring at me and I knew he was thinking of me."

Worse, so did Alice.

The next morning, Jeffrey stopped by Kathy's tent while Keith was out hunting.

"I have a problem," he said.

"Oh," Kathy replied.

"You ruined me. I don't want anyone else sexually but you. All I can see and feel is you."

Kathy later recalled her feelings that morning. "Maybe I never lost the Iowa farm girl in me," she said, "but I was in love. I was totally in love with this man."

"How do we deal with all this?" Kathy asked Jeffrey.

"I'll look in the scriptures," he said. "I'll find a way."

That night, Alice once again tried to please Jeffrey. This time, she told the group that she was going to dance for him. "She had a dress on and heels and hose and she climbed up on one of the picnic tables and began to dance seductively," Debbie remembered. "She didn't strip and she didn't have any rhythm and Jeffrey ended up just getting really disgusted and pissed off because he didn't want his wife doing that in front of the other men. He said, 'What the hell are you doing this for?,' and that was the beginning of a world war because Alice had this big erotic thing planned and she had looked totally ridiculous."

Everyone in camp could hear Alice screaming that night at Jeffrey. The next morning, Alice stayed in her tent until noon and then she suddenly emerged and raced over to where the women were doing laundry.

"I hope all of you are happy," she said sarcastically. "Because of you and your stupid intercession, I haven't had a good fuck all week."

She then glared at Kathy and marched back into her tent.

Jeffrey had decided even before the intercession dances that he no longer wanted Tonya Patrick as his wife, and once he decided to seduce Kathy, he moved quickly to get rid of Tonya.

One morning shortly after the dances he abruptly announced that he was sending her back to Dennis. "He didn't want a sinful woman like me in his tent, he said." Jeffrey told Dennis that he was no longer in danger of being destroyed because he had reformed and because of Kathy's intercession. Tonya and Molly were moving back into his tent.

"Is she coming back as my wife?" Dennis asked, rather startled.

"Yes," Jeffrey said. "She is your wife, not mine."

That night at class, Jeffrey told the group that he had searched the scriptures and learned that Tonya was not really flesh of his flesh. Rather, she had been his "captive wife." Under the law of Moses, Jeffrey explained, a lord was allowed to take as many wives from his enemy as he wished. Tonya had been "captured" from Dennis in May because Dennis had been sinful. But now that Dennis had reformed, he was no longer an enemy and Tonya was being "restored" to him. Tonya felt foolish. "I thought to myself, 'What am I, the wife-of-the-month?'" But she didn't question Jeffrey and neither did anyone else. "All of us were playing roles by that point," Tonya later explained. "Jeffrey had become so crazy that we all just simply acted like we were supposed to. You couldn't tell who really believed in him and who was afraid."

Tonya had decided that Jeffrey was a "sham," but when she reported to Dennis's tent, she didn't share her feelings with him. She was afraid that he would report her to Jeffrey.

Over time, the group had become so paranoid that they were all suspicious of the others.

Tonya's sudden return worried the other men. Most realized that Jeffrey could do the same thing to them that he had done to Dennis—simply accuse them of being sinful and claim their spouse as a "captive wife."

"After the dances, everything got real strange, real fast," Debbie recalled.

Jeffrey was beginning to make bolder and bolder statements about his divinity and powers and he seemed fixated on sex. One night after a scripture class, Jeffrey told Greg that they needed to talk in private. After swearing Greg to secrecy, Jeffrey explained that he had been studying First Samuel, chapter 18, which described how King Saul's son, Jonathan, had loved David. Jeffrey told Greg that when the chapter was divided by the pattern, the verses revealed that David and Jonathan were homosexual lovers. Although he wasn't certain, Jeffrey said the verses seemed to suggest that he and Greg were destined to become homosexual lovers as well.

Greg was so alarmed that he told Debbie that same night what Jeffrey had said. "Greg was not interested in Jeffrey at all," she recalled, "and he was worried about what Jeffrey might demand. It was like no one was safe from Jeffrey's sexual fantasies."

Debbie noticed that Jeffrey was making more pointed sexual remarks around her too. She was worried that she was next on his "conquest list." She wasn't alone.

Ron began to pick up hints that Jeffrey was on the prowl. It seemed to him that Jeffrey was picking on Susie, criticizing her in an attempt to drive a wedge between them in a thinly veiled attempt to free Susie for his advances.

Richard also began to wonder about Jeffrey's sexual obsessions. Before the group left the farm in Kirtland, Richard had found hidden in the barn a dildo and a magazine that contained explicit photographs of homosexual acts. He was certain that both belonged to Jeffrey.

After the intercession dances, Jeffrey began talking about sex more openly in his scriptural classes at night. During one such session, Jeffrey announced that the Old Testament prophet Isaiah was a "cross dresser" who frequently wore women's clothing: Another night, Jeffrey claimed that the pattern had revealed to him that Jesus Christ had engaged in sex with various women and had even masturbated as a boy. But the strangest sexual interpretation came when Jeffrey interpreted verse 16 in Isaiah, chapter 3, which described the haughty "daughters of Zion." Jeffrey said that Isaiah had wanted to humble the "daughters of Zion" because they were filled with pride. Verses 17 through 24, Jeffrey said, told how Isaiah had examined the women's "secret parts" and made them "stink" instead of smelling "sweet." Because Jeffrey didn't go into detail, no one in the group was certain what he had meant, but Alice understood. Jeffrey was talking about smearing feces on women.

About ten days after Jeffrey and Kathy engaged in sex, Jeffrey announced that the two of them needed to go on a short trip together. During the summer, Jeffrey had sold the group's horse trailer to raise money for supplies. He had moved the horses from the camp, where they were having trouble living in the open, to a stable about thirty miles away. The stable owner was supposed to sell the animals, but instead he had been renting them to tourists for rides. Jeffrey had decided to retrieve the horses, and he said that Kathy was the only member of the group who was in good enough physical shape and smart enough about horses to help him walk the animals back to camp.

They began their trek through the mountains on September 5. Both later claimed that they got lost and had no choice but to spend the night together in the woods. It was during that night that Jeffrey told Kathy what he had found out about them in the scriptures. Just as he had done with Tonya, Jeffrey told her that she was his Bathsheba and that she was his missing "second rib."

"Does that mean that I am not flesh of Keith's flesh?" Kathy asked innocently.

"Yes, you are flesh of my flesh," he replied. "God made you from me exclusively for me."

"I didn't expect him to say that," Kathy later recalled.

Jeffrey told Kathy that he wanted her to move into his tent, but she said she needed time to think about it.

When Jeffrey and Kathy didn't return to camp that night, Alice became suspicious. The next morning, she sent Greg and Richard to look for them. They found Jeffrey and Kathy a few miles from camp. Jeffrey said one of the horses had become lame, but Greg and Richard didn't see anything wrong with it. Alice was furious.

The next day, Kathy signaled Jeffrey from the woods. She was willing to leave her husband and four children to become his wife, she said. "It really didn't make any sense for me to deny the truth," she later explained. "If I was flesh of Jeff's flesh, then I wasn't doing Keith any favors by living with him in sin."

Now that Kathy had made her commitment, she wanted to know when Jeffrey intended to tell Keith and Alice. Jeffrey wasn't certain, but he assured Kathy that he would find a way.

On September 15, Sheriff Hank Thompson swooped over the camp in a helicopter. Everyone ducked for cover. Thompson buzzed the camp again, but didn't land. He was checking to see how the group would react. As soon as the helicopter was gone, Jeffrey rushed over to Alice. Jeffrey announced that it was getting too dangerous for Alice and the children to stay in the camp. The police might arrive any minute and arrest everyone for the murder of the Averys. The group was also running low on cash and the weather was becoming frigid. Obviously, Jeffrey and his band were not going to be able to spend the winter camping in the hollow. Jeffrey told Alice that he wanted her to leave that very day for her mother's house in Macks Creek. He would join her later and they would find somewhere new for the group to live. He told her to take Jason, Kristen, and Caleb with her. Jeffrey also wanted Susie Luff and her two children to go. Alice agreed.

Jeffrey helped Alice pack the truck and then suggested that she take a nap so she wouldn't be tired when she made the thirteen-hour drive. After Alice retired into the tent, Jeffrey wandered over to Kathy's tent. It had been more than a week since she had agreed to be his wife and Kathy was irritated that Jeffrey hadn't told the group that she was flesh of the "God of the whole earth." Jeffrey knew that he'd be rid of Alice by nightfall, but he figured that he could slip into town with Kathy and be back before Alice woke up.

A few hours later, when Alice came out of her tent, she asked Ron where Jeffrey had gone. Ron said Jeffrey was in town cashing a check and making some telephone calls.

"Don't you think two and a half hours is a long time to make phone calls?" Alice asked. "Did anyone go with him?"

Ron tried to dodge the question, but Alice pressed him. "Kathy Johnson went with him," Ron finally said. Alice turned around and stomped into her tent.

"I knew that Jeffrey had taken her into town to some motel so he could fuck her," she said later.

A few minutes later, Alice heard the ATV coming through the woods. Jeffrey slowed down and Kathy jumped off the back of the vehicle as soon as they got near the camp. Kathy ducked into her tent and Jeffrey continued into the compound. As soon as he stepped off the ATV, Alice attacked. She slapped Jeffrey across the face.

"You son of a bitch!" she screamed.

All the adults, except Kathy, watched as Alice slapped Jeffrey again and again.

"Here is your almighty God," she yelled. "You can have him!"

With that, Alice marched into her tent. Jeffrey ran after her. "Don't say anything to me, Jeffrey!" Alice hollered. "You've gone too far this time! You're a lying son of a bitch." Within seconds, Jeffrey came backing out of the tent. Alice was hitting him again.

"I came unglued," Alice later recalled. "I totally lost it. I hit him. I slapped him. I kicked him. I pulled his hair. I did everything I could do to hurt him."

When she finally stopped and returned to her tent, Jeffrey looked at the group. He was beaming. "It was a big thing to Jeffrey," Dennis said, "because he wanted everyone to see that she had attacked him and he had taken all of her blows without fighting back or hitting her."

Several minutes later, Alice emerged from the tent and yelled to her children that it was time to leave. They scrambled into the truck and Susie hustled her son and daughter into the vehicle too. Jeffrey walked up to the window. Alice was still fuming.

"When you move that whore into the tent tonight, have her bring her own pillow," Alice said. "I'm taking mine."

Jeffrey had tears in his eyes.

"You're wrong about Kathy and me," she later remembered Jeffrey telling her. "Alice, you're the only woman I will ever love."

As soon as Alice was gone, Jeffrey hurried over to talk to Kathy. He intended to announce that night in scripture class, he said, that she was his second wife.

Chapter 47

WHEN the operator asked if Donna Keehler would accept a collect telephone call from Jeffrey Lundgren, she immediately shouted, "Yes!" As soon as they were connected, Donna quizzed her son-in-law. "Where are you?"

"I'm not at liberty to say," he replied.

"What's happening?"

"I'm not at liberty to say," he repeated.

Donna tried several more questions and each was greeted by the same response. Finally she gave up. Jeffrey told her that Alice and the children were on their way to Macks Creek. They were bringing a friend and her two children with them. No problem, Donna said. She'd make room. Alice drove straight through. Donna was shocked when she saw her. "The Alice who came home to see me wasn't my Alice," Donna later said. "She was like a different person."

Alice had gotten fat—nearly one hundred pounds heavier than when her mother had last seen her one year earlier. Her face was marred by three open sores that she constantly picked. And she was foul-mouthed. Alice had also become a faithful beer drinker.

Donna had heard about the temple-takeover plot from Chief Yarborough whom she had telephoned earlier that summer. She'd also talked to Dennis Patrick's parents, who, in turn, had spoken with Dale Luffman in Kirtland. Donna began grilling her daughter.

"What in the world is going on?" she demanded. Alice lied to her about everything.

The next morning after Donna went to work, the telephone rang and Alice answered. It was Dennis Patrick's mother. She mistakenly assumed that she had reached Donna and she began talking. Alice played along. The sheriff in West Virginia had flown over Jeffrey's camp and was going to go in and question the group, Mrs. Patrick explained. She promised to call again when she had more details. After Alice replaced the telephone receiver, she began searching her mother's cupboards. Neither Ralph nor Donna was a drinker, but Alice's sister, Terri, had left several bottles of liquor behind when she and her husband moved to Saudi Arabia. Alice found some wine and rum. By midnight, she had drunk two bottles of wine and started on the rum.

Within an hour after Alice left West Virginia, Jeffrey began meeting individually with all of the men except for Keith. He explained that Kathy was his Bathsheba. Greg, Richard, Danny, Damon, and Dennis didn't seem surprised or that concerned. But Ron was troubled. He didn't believe in polygamy. Jeffrey had expected Ron to be distressed. That was why he had sent Susie along with Alice back to Macks Creek. He wanted Ron to know that Susie was safe. Jeffrey wasn't going to claim her as a wife.

Jeffrey had found more than a dozen scriptures that, when diagramed by the pattern, seemed to say a man could have two wives. He gave them to Ron to study, figuring that they would keep him busy for several days.

By 8:00 P.M., Jeffrey had finished his rounds and was ready for scripture class. Jeffrey had told the men that he wanted them to sit near Keith during class, in case he decided to challenge Jeffrey's decision to take Kathy as a wife. Meanwhile, Jeffrey tucked the .45 pistol that he had used to kill the Averys in his belt where everyone could see it. Jeffrey got right to the point.

"Kathy is now my wife," he proclaimed.

Keith thought Jeffrey was joking. He looked around the group. No one was smiling. Keith realized he was surrounded. He saw Jeffrey's .45. He glanced at Kathy. She was sitting next to Jeffrey where Alice usually sat. Jeffrey was serious.

"Do you have a problem with this?" Jeffrey asked Keith.

Keith tried to seem calm. He wanted to ask Jeffrey a question, he said. Keith reminded Jeffrey of the promise that he had made before the intercession dances. Jeffrey had said that he wouldn't take Kathy as his wife. Everyone in camp had heard him.

"How can any of us trust you if you lie?" Keith boldly asked.

"I didn't lie," Jeffrey snapped. "Kathy was never your wife."

Jeffrey said he had searched the scriptures and had discovered that Kathy was flesh of his flesh—not Keith's. "You were never married in God's eyes," he said. "If Kathy continues living with you, you will both be guilty of adultery."

Keith appeared unconvinced. He and Kathy had been married for twelve years. They had four sons. He wanted to speak to her in private.

"How do I know you won't hurt her?" Jeffrey asked. Keith agreed to speak to Kathy out in the open where Jeffrey could see them. Jeffrey said that would be okay. The estranged couple walked about thirty feet away from the group.

"Keith was stunned," Kathy recalled. "He had no idea about what had been going on right under his nose or how I felt about Jeffrey. I told him, 'This is what is right, Keith. . . . ' "

Keith said that she was his wife. He didn't want her to go with Jeffrey.

"I want to be with Jeff," Kathy said. "I am flesh of his flesh." She turned and returned to Jeffrey's side.

Now that everyone knew that Kathy belonged to Jeffrey, he had another announcement. He was going to split up the camp in case the helicopter returned. He and Kathy would move deeper into the woods. Ron, Damon, Greg, and Debbie would go with them. Dennis, Tonya, Keith, Danny, Richard, and Sharon would stay behind in the original camp. The reason Jeffrey wanted Ron, Damon, and Greg with him was because they were his "three witnesses." Joseph Smith, Jr., had produced "three witnesses" when people questioned him about the mysterious golden plates. Jeffrey had told the group that God would give him golden plates similar to the ones that He had given Smith. When that happened, Jeffrey wanted his three witnesses standing by to verify the event.

After class, everyone began moving tents. By midnight, the move was complete and Jeffrey and Kathy had the large

Lundgren tent all to themselves. They spent the next three days on a "honeymoon."

Sheriff Thompson and Game Warden Spencer landed a few hundred feet from Jeffrey's original camp on the day after it had been split. As soon as they got out of their helicopter, Thompson noticed that several tents were missing. Dennis Patrick and Danny Kraft greeted the lawmen.

"The women just stood there and stared at us," said Thompson. The folksy sheriff asked Dennis why the group was camping in such an isolated area. "Our religious beliefs are different from most people's," Dennis replied. "We like the privacy." Thompson asked if the group planned to spend the winter in the hollow. Dennis didn't know, but he doubted it. He thought they might be moving to Missouri. At about that time, Sharon appeared with a tray of chocolate-chip cookies.

"Have one," she said. Thompson glanced at Spencer. Both were afraid that the cookies were poisoned.

"I don't think I need a cookie right now," Thompson said. "You want one?" he asked, looking at Spencer. The game warden shook his head.

Dennis Patrick picked one up and ate it. Thompson reminded Dennis that all of the children in camp had to be enrolled in school. Dennis nodded, but again explained that the group was probably going to move. A few minutes later, Thompson and Spencer got back in their helicopter and left. When Thompson returned to his office, he telephoned Yarborough. The first question that Yarborough asked was "Did you see Jeffrey?" They talked for several minutes. Neither of them brought up the Averys. Yarborough assumed that Dennis and Cheryl had gone with everyone else to West Virginia. Thompson figured that Yarborough already knew who was part of Jeffrey's group.

Keith Johnson decided to turn the tables on the prophet. Jeffrey had said that Kathy was his Bathsheba, so Keith went through the story of David and Bathsheba line by line. He then used the pattern to diagram several verses, and when he did, Keith made a shocking discovery. Two of David's sons had died, Keith told Dennis Patrick, so it seemed logical that if Jeffrey claimed to be David and Kathy was Bathsheba, then two of Jeffrey's sons would have to meet the same fate as David's sons. Dennis immediately raced over to Jeffrey and told him what Keith was preaching.

Jeffrey called all of the men together and had them bring Keith out into the woods. They formed a circle around him. Keith was unarmed. Jeffrey had taken away his guns. But Jeffrey had his .45 automatic.

"If you are threatening me, Keith," Jeffrey said, "then say so and let's deal with it right now."

Keith said that he wasn't threatening anyone. He had simply been studying the scriptures.

"It's not me," he explained, "it's the pattern."

Jeffrey looked at the scripture. "You've done this wrong," he declared. "It says that you should die and two of your sons will die too."

"There can be only one prophet," said Jeffrey, paraphrasing a line from the movie *The Highlander*. "I am that seer and the price for looking in the record for yourself is death."

Keith apologized and begged Jeffrey not to kill him. He talked about his four sons. Who would raise them if he was dead?

"I was prepared to execute Keith," Jeffrey later said. "The only reason why I didn't shoot him was because I had promised Kathy that I wouldn't harm him."

Just the same, Jeffrey ordered Keith to move his tent up to the new camp. Ron moved in with Keith to watch him.

After Sheriff Thompson visited the camp, Jeffrey decided it was time for the group to leave West Virginia. But he was broke. Reluctantly, Jeffrey drove to a flea market in Elkins, West Virginia, and began selling some of the group's rifles and pistols. He raised enough to buy a week's worth of groceries and enough gasoline for a round-trip to Missouri. Once there, Kathy would invite several fundamentalists to a special class on the pattern that Jeffrey would teach. Afterward, he would solicit money which he would use to move the rest of the group back to Missouri. Jeffrey, Kathy, and Damon left for Missouri the next day. Jeffrey left Ron in charge of the camp.

En route, Jeffrey stopped at a pay phone and told Alice that he was coming. When she asked about Kathy, Jeffrey used "delusion." He told Alice that Kathy was living with Keith back at the camp. He also told Alice that he had something exciting to show her. God had given him another revelation.

Alice was excited after Jeffrey called. She raced around the house like a schoolgirl getting ready for her senior prom. Alice fixed her hair, put on a dress, and eagerly waited. As soon as Jeffrey arrived, she darted out the door and threw her arms around him. Less than an hour before, Jeffrey had dropped Kathy at her mother's house outside Warrensburg. She was supposed to telephone her fundamentalist friends and relatives and arrange a place for Jeffrey to hold a class.

As soon as Jeffrey was alone with Alice, he told her about God's newest revelation. "Jeff said that he had gone up on the mountain in West Virginia and God had appeared and told him that He wanted Jeffrey to take a second wife. God had made a book appear and it had come down out of heaven and God had showed him the name of his second wife in this book."

Alice was furious.

"She hit me and threatened me. 'I'll turn you in right now. I'm going to call the sheriff on you. I'm going to tell about the Averys,' she said. Then she asked me if I knew who 'it' was, meaning my second wife, and I said, 'Yes,' and she said, 'Do you love her?,' and I said 'Yes,' and she said, 'I'll kill it! I swear I'll kill it. Who is she?' Alice was serious about her threat so I refused to tell her."

Alice already knew. "Who else could it have been but Kathy?" she later asked rhetorically. Then she added, sarcastically, "After all, it was her vagina that he had seen in his dream."

Jeffrey stayed in Macks Creek for two days, and then he told Alice that he had to hurry back to West Virginia. He left Damon behind with orders to watch Alice and make certain that she didn't tip off the police about the Averys. As soon as he left Alice, Jeffrey met Kathy and they went to Kingsville, a nearby town, where a friend of Kathy's had offered to let Jeffrey teach his class. Kathy had managed to get about a dozen friends to attend. One would later describe Jeffrey as a "wild man." His shoulder-length brown hair was dirty and matted. His face was badly sunburned, his shirt was dirty and half buttoned. For nearly an hour, Jeffrey rambled on about the pattern. He announced that he had personally seen Jesus Christ and had spoken to God. Michel Vick, a longtime friend of the Johnsons, later told a reporter for the *News Herald*, a Cleveland suburban newspaper, that she didn't believe anything Jeffrey said. If Jeffrey had been permitted to meet Christ and talk to God, Vick reasoned, then he would have been happy and exuberant. "One of the fruits of it would be joy," Vick explained. Instead, Jeffrey and Kathy looked like two fugitives on the run.

Jeffrey's spiel for money was a bust. No one was willing to help move Jeffrey's group from West Virginia back to Missouri. Jeffrey and Kathy returned to West Virginia with less money than they had left with.

Donna Keehler had grilled her son-in-law during his short visit, but he had not told her anything. As soon as he left, Donna began pressuring Alice to tell her the truth.

"Your father and I will protect you," she told Alice.

Alice would later testify that the reason she never told the police about the murders was because Jeffrey made certain that at least one of their children was with him at all times. "I never was allowed to have all of them with me at one time," Alice said. "I was afraid that he would hurt them if I called the police."

But that was simply not true. "There was a time when Alice had all of her children here," Donna said, "and Alice could have told us what was happening. I did my best to get her to tell us the truth. I pleaded with her. I told her that I would stand by her no matter what she and Jeffrey had gotten involved in. I promised her help, but Alice wouldn't tell me the truth."

Donna would later suggest that the reason Alice was reluctant to talk about the murders was not because she was scared of Jeffrey, but for another reason.

"Alice still loved Jeffrey. She was devoted to him."

Having failed to learn anything from Jeffrey and Alice, Donna began to pepper Susie Luff with questions. One morning when Alice was still in bed, Donna cornered Susie. The older woman stepped in front of the door to the utility room where Susie was doing laundry. "I blocked her way so she couldn't get past me."

"Look, Susie," Donna later recalled saying. "I want to know what is going on."

Susie began to cry. She looked as if she were going to tell

Donna the truth, but then she caught herself.

"We are a deeply religious group," Donna later quoted Susie as saying. "Jeff is our teacher. We believe what he teaches us and we have done nothing wrong."

"Susie, if you're such a religious group," Donna asked, "then why do you use the filthy language that I've heard around here? Why does my Alice drink? Why is Jeffrey smoking? This is not religion."

"Jeffrey is our teacher," Susie repeated, as if on automatic pilot. "We believe he is a prophet and we believe strongly in what he is teaching."

Donna looked directly at Susie. At least she had gotten her houseguest to admit that she thought Jeffrey was a prophet. "Susie," Donna said, "I'm Jeff's mother-in-law. I've known him longer than you. Now, I can't tell you what to believe, but if you think that Jeffrey Lundgren is a prophet, then you are a complete fool."

By October, life in West Virginia was miserable. The air became bitter cold. Jeffrey and Kathy had a portable heater in their tent, but the others went without. There was no money for food. Some days, Debbie would serve rice and cream gravy three times a day. "I wanted people to at least get some protein."

There were other problems as well. Richard had stopped talking to Sharon. Marrying her had been a big mistake, he had decided. Greg and Debbie were having marital problems too. Jeffrey had promised Danny that Shar Olson would eventually rejoin the group, but she hadn't and he was lonely. Ron missed Susie, who was still in Macks Creek. Keith was brooding over his loss of Kathy. Dennis and Tonya were still estranged.

In order to raise cash, Jeffrey ordered his followers to begin selling everything that they didn't need. He sent Dennis, Danny, Greg, and Richard to a nearby town in Maryland to look for work. As soon as they raised enough cash to rent a truck, they would move, he told them. But when the men were paid for a variety of minimum-wage jobs, Jeffrey collected their wages and drove into town with Kathy. He treated her to dinner. When, they returned, Jeffrey announced that he was going back to Missouri to find a house where they could all live together. He left Kathy in charge and took Ron with him.

Months later, group members would recall with irony that life at the camp had started to deteriorate shortly after Alice left the group. Jeffrey had preached that women were "weaker vessels" than men and not as intelligent or strong, yet without Alice, Jeffrey didn't seem to know what to do.

Once again, Jeffrey spent only a few days at Macks Creek. He had brought Ron along, in part because he hoped that he could convince Alice that polygamy was not wrong. By this time, Ron had studied the scriptures that Jeffrey had showed him and become convinced that it was okay for Jeffrey to have two wives.

"Ron was always someone I could talk to," Alice said later, "and I told Ron that this was just not right. But he looked at me and said, 'Alice, we have to obey the will of the Lord.' "

Later, when Alice and Jeffrey were alone, she confronted him.

"Who is this person? Who is supposed to be your second wife? Or is it your third wife?" she asked. "How many more are you going to have?"

When Jeffrey refused to tell her, Alice slapped him. This time there was no one else watching, no one for Jeffrey to impress by absorbing Alice's blows. He smacked her and punched her in the stomach. She fell down and he reached over and slapped her face hard, rupturing her eardrum.

"We had a go at it," Jeffrey admitted later. "I told her that all I wanted to do was help her accept the truth, but she got angry and slapped me and that started it."

Jeffrey left for West Virginia the next morning. The day after he arrived at the camp, he went into town and called Alice. He wanted to apologize. She wasn't in the mood.

"You better get back here right now," she declared.

"Alice told me that she was turning me in for the murders if I didn't move back to Macks Creek immediately," said Jeffrey, "and stay with her."

The next morning, October 12, Jeffrey drove to a pawnshop in Elkins and sold both his .45-caliber pistols, including the one that he had used to kill the Averys. He had tried to switch the barrel on the murder weapon with another pistol that Damon owned. That would have made it difficult for police to link the handgun through ballistic tests with the Averys' deaths. But the two barrels were not interchangeable.

Selling his pistols gave Jeffrey enough cash to finance a return trip to Macks Creek. This time he took the Patricks with him and once again left Kathy behind. She was livid. He was running home to Alice and she was stuck dealing with Debbie, Greg, Richard, Sharon, Danny, and worst of all, Keith. The group was completely out of money and Kathy was on her own.

After Jeffrey was gone, Kathy rode on the ATV into Davis and began calling friends in Missouri. She finally found one who was willing to drive his semi-trailer truck to West Virginia and haul her and the others back to Kathy's mother's house. She returned to camp and told everyone to begin packing the tents.

On October 15, the group arrived at Kathy's mother's house in the back of a truck, like cattle. Everyone was crabby. Kathy had sent word to Jeffrey and he was waiting. He told Kathy that he and his children would continue living with Alice at the Keehlers' until the group could find a place to stay. Ron, Susie, Dennis, Tonya, and their children were sleeping in tents pitched in the Keehlers' backyard.

"Have you told Alice?" Kathy asked.

Jeffrey had told Alice that God wanted him to take Kathy as his second wife. But, he added, he'd given Alice the impression that he and Kathy hadn't started sleeping together.

Kathy, who was exhausted, was irritated. She had given up Keith and her four children to be with him. Now it was his turn to make a commitment, particularly since Kathy was now certain that she was pregnant. "We hadn't taken any precautions," Kathy explained later. "We both knew that there was a good chance it would happen." Kathy didn't intend to be kept hidden in the background.

"Alice is just going to have to face reality," Kathy said. "You are going to have to deal with her, Jeff."

He promised he would, but said he needed more time. He and Kathy would face Alice together once the group found a permanent place to live, he promised.

Once again, Kathy began telephoning her friends and relatives. She found one willing to let the group stay in an abandoned dairy barn on his farm near Chilhowee, a rural community south of Warrensburg. On October 21, the group moved into the abandoned and drafty barn. Ron, Susie, Dennis, Tonya, and their children rejoined the others. Everyone pitched their tents inside the barn. Kathy supervised setting up Jeffrey's tent and moved her belongings inside it. When Jeffrey arrived that afternoon, he assured everyone that he would soon find a house for them. "It will be just like it was in Kirtland," he promised. His followers would get jobs and support Jeffrey while he continued to search the scriptures. Meanwhile, he would divide his time between the dairy barn and Macks Creek.

Now that Kathy had found shelter for everyone, she once again confronted Jeffrey about her status as his wife, and he agreed to take her to Macks Creek with him. He had already told Alice that he would be bringing Kathy home with him. He wanted the three of them to live together. In fact, he was going to take Kathy back to Macks Creek that very night.

"I was nervous," Kathy recalled, "because I was going into *her* home. I also had to get over my own feelings. I didn't want to share him with Alice."

As they drove down the state highway toward Macks Creek, Kathy tried to reassure herself. "If God has truly ordained this," she said, "then I am certain that it will work out."

Jeffrey agreed. But he didn't sound nearly as confident as he had when the two of them had been sleeping together in the mountains of West Virginia and Alice was a thousand miles away in her mother's house.

Chapter 48

FROM the moment that Jeffrey and Kathy rode up the gravel driveway at the Keehlers' house, Alice was annoyed. "Jeff walked around and opened her car door," Alice recalled. "He never opened a car door for me."

Jeffrey had told Donna and Ralph that Kathy needed someplace to stay. She and Keith were having marital problems, he said. Donna, who had no idea what was actually going on, said Kathy was welcome to stay in the guest bedroom across the hall from Alice's room. Donna and Ralph slept in the master bedroom at the opposite end of the house.

Alice hugged Jeffrey when he walked in and gave him a passionate kiss. Jeffrey motioned toward Kathy. With obvious disdain, Alice hugged her and grunted a welcome. Alice showed Kathy where her bedroom was.

It was nearly 11:00 P.M., and the Keehlers and the Lundgren children were all in bed. Jeffrey told Alice that he'd join her in her bedroom after he helped Kathy unpack. Alice slipped into her nightgown and perched herself seductively on the bed. After ten minutes of waiting, she crept into the hall and quietly opened the door to the guest room so that she could peek inside.

They were sitting on the bed kissing.

Alice hurried back into her bedroom and began to sob as loudly as she could.

"Are you all right?" Jeffrey asked a few minutes later when he came into the room.

"Oh, sure, Jeff, I'm fine," Alice replied bitterly. "This is my idea of a fun time!" He started to kiss her, but she pulled away.

"I could smell the residue of her kissing him," Alice later recalled. "I said, 'At least wash her off before getting in bed with me.' He got angry and accused me of being rebellious. He rolled me over on my stomach, pulled my gown up over my head, and began having anal intercourse with me."

The next morning, Jeffrey decided to take Alice, Kathy, and the children shopping. Alice had borrowed some money from her parents. All of the kids jumped into the back of the truck while Alice hurried outside and slipped into the center of the seat in the truck's cab. "Even when it came to something that little," Kathy recalled, "Alice wanted me to know that she was number one, that sitting next to him was her place."

As he drove down the highway, Jeffrey put his right arm on the back of the seat so that it touched both women. Alice noticed that he was playing with Kathy's hair.

It was almost lunchtime so Jeffrey stopped at a Taco Bell, and this time it was Kathy who hurried inside and scooted next to Jeffrey in a booth. Alice sat across from him and began handing out the food to her children.

"Jeffrey, you didn't get enough drinks," Alice announced. There were only six cups and there were seven people.

"Yes, he did!" Kathy retorted. "We *always* share *our* drink."

Alice left the table and hurried into the women's bathroom. "Jeffrey never, ever let me drink out of the same cup as he did," she said later. "It was humiliating." After about twenty minutes, Alice emerged to find everyone waiting for her in the truck.

When they got to the grocery store, Kathy started pushing the cart. Once again, Alice was angry. By the time the two women had reached the meat counter, Alice exploded.

"You whore!" she screamed at Kathy as other shoppers stared. "It was simply too easy for Kathy," Alice later said. "She was stepping into twenty years of marriage and it wasn't bothering her one little bit." Alice lunged at Kathy with her fingernails but Jeffrey grabbed her before she reached Kathy. Alice aimed her knee at his groin and Jeffrey pushed her back. She tried to kick him.

"I caught her leg," Jeffrey later said, "and swung her around and then I slapped her. I'm not proud of that, but I lost it. The scriptures say that it is better to slap someone than to have them perish for being unsubmissive so what I did wasn't wrong, particularly since Alice was asking for it. She always tries to look like she is poor and helpless, but she was going to hurt Kathy and I had to stop her."

Alice burst into tears and ran out of the store. As soon as she was gone, Kathy and Jeffrey finished shopping. Alice waited for them in the truck—in the center seat.

On the way home, Jeffrey decided to buy some shampoo at a Wal-Mart store. This time, he walked between the two women and pushed the cart.

"Since this is your first night together," Alice said cattily, "maybe you should buy something to make you feel feminine, Kathy." It was a thinly disguised slap at Kathy's tomboy manners.

"Don't worry about me," Kathy replied icily. "Jeffrey finds me feminine enough."

When they got back to Macks Creek, Kathy and Alice avoided each other. After Ralph, Donna, and the Lundgren children went to bed that night, Jeffrey ordered Alice to prepare his bath. Kathy went into the guest room and closed the door. "Jeffrey was my lord and master," Alice said, "so one of my jobs was giving him his nightly bath. I washed his body and his hair and dried him off. It was all scriptural. Christ was anointed by Mary so it was my job to anoint Jeff. I put his favorite perfume on him and he kissed me on the cheek and said, 'I'm going to spend some time with Kathy.' He said, 'Alice, I'm not on a timetable. I'll be back when I get back.' He then went into Kathy's room."

Jeffrey and Kathy would later claim that they did not have sex that night. They simply talked for a while, but Alice recalled that evening much differently.

"I went to bed, but I just laid there staring at the clock. At about fifteen till two, I went out into the hall and I could hear him snoring, then I heard him wake up and he and Kathy had sex. I went into my room. Finally, he came in and I acted like I was asleep and he shook my shoulder and said, 'Hey, you awake?' He told me that he and Kathy were really hungry and he wanted me to fix them hamburgers. I got up and cooked them hamburgers like he wanted and then I fixed him a big glass of Pepsi because I know Jeff likes to drink a big glass of Pepsi after he makes love. He usually kept one by the side of our bed just for that. I put the cup down and Kathy leaned over and she took a drink out of it. I don't know why but that was the ultimate insult. Here I was fixing that bitch hamburgers and she had just fucked my husband. I ran into the bedroom and started crying and Jeffrey came in and sat on the bed and then Kathy came in and I was in the fetal position and he was sitting at my knees with his hand rubbing my back and she was sitting on the floor stroking my hair and they were holding hands while they were doing this. Kathy says, 'It's okay to cry,' and then he moved me over on the bed and laid down and he put my head on one shoulder and Kathy laid her head on the other shoulder so that he had both of us in his arms. I wanted to die. I wasn't going to spend my life that way. The whole thing was so awful to me, I went into the bathroom and threw up. When I came out of the bathroom, she had gone to her bedroom and he had gone to sleep."

The next morning, Jeffrey announced that he needed to go

to the dairy barn and get the ATV. Alice's brother, Charles, had offered to sell it and the electric generator. As they had the day before, both women hurried outside, both hoping to sit in the center of the cab next to Jeffrey. Alice won out, but before they reached the dairy barn, Kathy began to cry and Jeffrey pulled the truck to the side of the road.

"It's Kathy's turn to ride in the middle for a while," Jeffrey said. Alice traded places with Kathy.

When they got to the barn, Jeffrey left the two women alone in the cab.

"This isn't going to work," Alice said coldly.

"Of all the women in the world," Kathy replied, "I thought we could make this work out."

"Over my dead body," Alice replied.

The two women's eyes met. Both were furious.

That night after dinner, Jeffrey decided to take everyone to play miniature golf. Damon, Jason, Kristen, and Caleb piled into the back of the truck and Alice and Kathy argued about who was going to sit next to Jeffrey. Alice won and when they got to the course, Kathy decided to stay behind in the truck. She needed a break from Alice, she told Jeffrey.

The Lundgrens went on without her, but Alice had reached her limit too and she blistered Jeffrey with profanity while he and the children tried to play golf. Halfway through the course, Jeffrey quit and ordered everyone back to the truck. None of the children said a word. Kathy climbed into the back of the truck and rode with them. All the way home, Alice screamed at Jeffrey. She never mentioned Kathy by name. She simply called her "the bitch."

Alice went directly to her bedroom when they finally got home. Jeffrey suggested that Kathy go into the guest room while he tried to get Alice cooled down. He went into Alice's bedroom and told her that he was ready for his bath.

"There's the bathroom," she shrieked. "Do it yourself." Jeffrey walked across the hall to be with Kathy. Alice cried for several minutes and then went into the kitchen and retrieved a bottle of rum that she had hidden there. By 2:00 A.M., she was drunk.

"I could hear them horsing around next door," she recalled. "So I decided to join them." Alice swaggered across the hall and pushed open the door. She marched inside and pulled the sheets off Kathy.

"Get up!" she screamed. "Get out of here!"

"What the hell do you think you're doing?" Jeffrey yelled.

"The bitch is gone," said Alice. "The party is over, Jeffrey."

"Alice," he snapped. "Get control of yourself."

It was at this point that Alice would later claim that Jeffrey attacked her. Jeffrey would later insist that Alice attacked him. Kathy would claim that she had been asleep alone in the bedroom when Alice barged in and attacked her. Regardless, the noise woke the Keehlers and Donna hurried out of her bedroom. She found Damon and Jason, who had been asleep in the living room, fully dressed and standing near the back door of the house.

"What's wrong?" Donna asked.

"Mom's throwing us out," said Damon. "She told us to leave."

At that point, Jeffrey emerged from Alice's bedroom. "His face was bleeding and big pieces of hair had been torn out of his head," Donna recalled.

"My God!" Donna exclaimed.

"Alice is drunk," Jeffrey said. "She's throwing a fit. We're leaving."

"Wait a minute," said Donna. "Get those kids back in here. You can't leave in the middle of the night like this. It's cold out there."

Damon and Jason had already sent Kristen and Caleb outside to the truck. Jeffrey called them back into the house and told them to go back to bed. Kathy, meanwhile, came out of the guest room, carrying her suitcase. Jeffrey told Damon and Jason to drive her to the barn in Chilhowee. Kathy looked upset as Jeffrey escorted her outside.

Donna, meanwhile, hurried down the hallway to Alice's bedroom. She found her daughter sprawled on the bed.

"I told him to leave," Alice screamed. "I'm through, Mom! I've been cheated on and lied to and I'm not going to put up with it any longer."

Donna was mad. "What's he done this time?" she asked. "I'm going to talk to him."

Alice panicked. She shot up from the bed. "Don't interfere in this, Mama," she warned. "You don't know what he is capable of doing."

Donna went back to the kitchen to wait for Jeffrey. As soon as she left the room, Alice grabbed a bottle of extra-strength Excedrin. "I took all fifty pills," she later said. "I washed them down with rum. I wanted to kill myself."

Donna told Jeffrey that she wanted to talk to him, but he hurried past her, went into Alice's bedroom and shut the door. Donna decided to go back to bed.

"Jeffrey walked in and backhanded me," Alice claimed, "and then he saw the pill bottle."

"What have you done now?" he asked.

"I don't want to live anymore," Alice said. "I'm going to kill myself."

Jeffrey dragged her into the bathroom and forced her to vomit. He put her head under the shower and splashed her with cold water. Finally, he forced her to go outside into the chilly air and walk around.

"I remember him telling me, 'Live for me, Alice! Live for me! Don't die!' "

The next morning Alice felt sick and dizzy when she woke up. Her arms were bruised. Her head hurt and she was alone in bed. Jeffrey was loading the truck. He had decided to move into the dairy barn with Kathy and he was taking the children with him.

When Jeffrey came into the bedroom to tell Alice what he had decided, she began to weep.

"Don't take my children," she whimpered.

"You're an unfit mother," he replied. "You're a drunk."

"You can't leave me," she continued. "I can't live without you."

Jeffrey told Alice that he was tired of her rebellion and disobedience. She began to nod. "I'm sorry. I'm sorry. I'm so sorry," she said. "I know I've been bad, but I can change. I can stop being bad."

"Jeff told me that I needed to be punished," Alice later said. "He told me to go into the bathroom and take off my clothes. I did. He told me to lay down on the floor and when I did, Jeff squatted over me and had a bowel movement on my face. He rubbed it all over my face and then he turned me over and had anal intercourse with me. After he came, he lifted me up and put me in the tub and then he washed me very gently. He washed my hair and face and everything. He told me that I was purified now and I told him that I was no longer rebellious. He dressed me and put a coat on me to hide the bruises on my arms. He told me that he had decided to take me to the barn with him. I thanked him and he told me that he loved me."

Donna was waiting when Jeffrey and Alice came out of the bedroom.

"Alice, you don't have to go," she said, stepping between them and the back door.

"Yes, I do, Mother," Alice replied.

Donna put her hands on the sides of Alice's face. She made her daughter look directly into her eyes. "Alice looked so beat up, so sad," Donna later remembered. "It was breaking my heart."

"Alice, your father and I will do anything for you. You don't have to go with Jeffrey. You can stay here with us."

Jeffrey didn't say a word. Alice looked at her mother. "Yes, I do have to go, Mother," she said. "I want to go. I want to go with Jeff."

Donna stepped out of the way. As soon as Jeffrey and Alice drove down the driveway, Donna burst into tears.

When they got to the barn, Jeffrey told Alice to stay in the truck. He went inside and called everyone together. He told them that Alice had suffered a nervous breakdown and had tried to kill herself. Ron and Greg went outside to help bring Alice in. Everyone watched.

"Alice was shuffling her feet and she looked helpless," Debbie later recalled, "but I thought it was theatrics. Her eyes were bright and sharp. I asked Dennis what he thought because he had worked in a mental-health unit and we both decided that Alice was playing it for all she could. I really doubted whether she had even tried to kill herself."

When Alice got inside the tent, she noticed the bed was draped with a red-and-white quilt with lambs on it. It was Kathy's. "Get that rag off my bed!" she said. Ron grabbed it. Alice got undressed and crawled under the covers.

At dinnertime, Kathy made a cup of soup for her and went into the tent. Alice stared up at Kathy. She acted as if she didn't recognize her. Kathy couldn't tell whether Alice was playacting or had actually suffered a breakdown.

"Hello," Alice said. "These are from my husband." She was clutching a poem that Jeffrey had written her and other love notes from the past. "Do you know Jeffrey?"

Later that night, Kathy and Jeffrey put a pad on the floor in the section of the tent next to where Alice was sleeping. Although it was dark, Alice could see them through the slit in the partition that divided the tent into sections. They had turned on a portable heater and it cast a red glow on their bodies. Jeffrey and Kathy would later claim that they had simply gone to sleep that night. Alice insisted that they had sexual intercourse while she watched.

"They thought I was asleep, but I could see them," she said later. "They began making love. I turned away but I could hear the sound of his body going in and out of her body. I felt like I could feel the entire floor vibrating and I could hear everything that they were saying to each other. I felt sick so I decided to interrupt them and Jeffrey got angry. I kept calling to him every few minutes—'Jeffrey'—'Oh, Jeffrey'—'Jeffrey, I need you.' Kathy had an orgasm but he couldn't and he got off her and he began to cry because he couldn't do it because I was calling to him. She was saying, 'It's okay. I understand.' But he was crying because he wanted to come and he couldn't come and I was glad that he couldn't come. I was glad that I kept him from coming."

When it was morning, Jeffrey came into the portion of the tent where Alice was lying in bed. Jeffrey was angry about her antics during the night. He began to scold her and Alice immediately became submissive. "I said, 'What is my lord's bidding?' " Within a few minutes, she was performing oral sex on him. When she finished, Alice announced that she was going back to Macks Creek. He was welcome to come with her, but he had to choose between her and Kathy.

"Don't do this, Alice," he said. "I'm not leaving Kathy."

Jeffrey figured Alice was bluffing. He stepped out of the tent and told everyone that Alice was leaving. She got dressed. By the time she walked out of the tent, everyone was waiting to tell her good-bye. Jeffrey told Alice that Ron was going to drive her back to Macks Creek. He walked into another part of the barn to be with Kathy. Tonya and Susie both gave Alice a hug and said good-bye. Danny refused to speak to her. Greg told her that he loved her. Sharon came over and hugged her. "Mom," Sharon said, trying to cheer Alice up, "you look so pretty."

"It didn't keep my husband in my bed, did it?" Alice replied.

Everyone followed Alice out of the barn to the truck. When she got to it, she stopped and said she wanted to talk to Jeffrey. He and Kathy came out of the barn.

"You win, Kathy," Alice announced, and then she turned and looked directly at Jeffrey.

"I told him that I had always loved him and always would love him. I said I was sorry that I didn't make him happy and had disappointed him. And then I said, 'Some day, Jeff, when it's too late, you will realize that I am the only person who has ever truly loved you.' "

After Alice finished her speech, she got down on her knees in front of the group and kissed Jeffrey's feet. A few seconds later, she was gone.

Chapter 49

RICHARD and Greg wanted out. They had been plotting an escape for more than three weeks. Richard had first mentioned leaving back in West Virginia when Jeffrey had been on one of his trips to Macks Creek.

"I think it's time for me to get out of here," Richard had said offhandedly to Greg one morning when they were away from the others.

"Well, if you're leaving," Greg had replied with a chuckle, "take me with you."

Both men had intentionally made their comments sound like jokes because neither fully trusted the other. It was Richard who decided to risk telling the truth.

"You serious?" he asked Greg.

"Are you?" Greg had replied.

"Yes," Richard had said. "I want out."

Richard and Greg had been best friends most of their lives, but after they joined the group that had changed. Jeffrey had made certain of it. He had told Richard that he was going to eventually be asked by God to kill Greg with a shotgun. Jeffrey said he had seen Richard shoot Greg in a vision. Meanwhile, Jeffrey had told Greg that he shouldn't trust Richard because he was rebellious and most likely would end up being killed like the Averys.

On the day that Richard and Greg admitted that they both wanted to quit, they once again began to feel like friends.

On October 29, Greg's father drove to the dairy barn in Chilhowee and asked his son to leave with him. Greg refused. He figured he had a better chance of hiding from Jeffrey if he left on his own, rather than going directly to his father's house. The next day, Greg and Richard decided that they would escape on Halloween night. They weren't going to tell anyone, not even their "wives." Neither of them felt their marriages were legally binding. Not only were they rejecting Jeffrey as a prophet, they were divorcing themselves from Sharon and Debbie too.

Debbie was fixing chicken for dinner on October 31 when Greg and the other men returned to the dairy barn from work. The men had all found minimum-wage jobs as laborers at a nearby company that manufactured mail-order Christmas supplies. Greg had promised to help Debbie pluck and clean the chickens, and when he didn't come to the kitchen, she decided to look for him. When she went into their tent, Debbie noticed that Greg's suitcase was gone. Suspicious, she hurried to the barn's front door just as Greg and Richard ducked through it. She caught them as they were walking toward Greg's car.

"Where's your suitcase?" she demanded.

Greg told her that he was "airing it out."

Debbie looked over at Greg's car and saw the suitcase next to it. "I started screaming at him," said Debbie. "I knew he and Richard were going to sneak away."

Greg hustled Debbie into a field where they could talk without being overheard. "I love you," she said. Debbie reminded Greg that Jeffrey had promised them that they were going to have a baby. How could he leave her?

"I've just got to get away for a while," Greg said.

Debbie knew he was lying. Once he left, he would never come back. She started toward the barn to tell Jeffrey. Richard stepped in front of her. "I was going to hit Richard and I'm sure he would have hit me right back," Debbie said. "But Greg jumped in the way. He said, 'Debbie, get yourself under control. If you're going to hit someone, hit me.' So I decked him right in the jaw and he couldn't believe I had hit him and I couldn't believe it either."

Debbie ran between the two men.

"Richard and Greg are leaving," she yelled. "They're leaving. You've got to stop them!"

Richard and Greg didn't want Jeffrey running after them, so they walked back into the barn. "We told Jeff that we'd like some time alone away from the group to get our heads on straight," Richard recalled. Jeffrey asked them what they were going to do. They said they didn't know. Then Greg asked if it would be okay for them to leave.

"Richard," Jeffrey said, ignoring Greg, "there is nothing out there for you. I need you here with me."

"You don't need me," Richard said. "You can do this without me."

Jeffrey grabbed Richard by his shirt and pinned him against the barn wall. Jeffrey's face was bright red. He was angry.

"Don't you ever tell me what I need and don't need," Jeffrey yelled. "Do I make myself clear?"

"Yes, sir," Richard replied.

Jeffrey released him.

"I wanted Richard to know, I wanted all of them to know, that no one counsels their lord," Jeffrey later explained. "A prophet never tolerates people telling him what to do. Only God has that right."

"Get out of here," Jeffrey said.

Debbie couldn't believe he was going to let them leave. She grabbed Greg's arm. "Don't leave me," she shrieked. He jerked loose and hurried to his car. Debbie burst into tears. As soon as Richard was inside, Greg hit the accelerator. He checked the rearview mirror as the car sped away from the barn. He wanted to make certain Jeffrey wasn't going to shoot them or follow them.

As soon as they were gone, Sharon turned to Jeffrey. Did he think that they would tell the police about the Averys, she asked.

"If I thought they would," Jeffrey said, "I would have slit their throats."

Debbie had smoked in high school, but had stopped shortly after that. She bummed a cigarette from Ron and within an hour she had gone through an entire pack. "I was devastated."

Back in the barn, Jeffrey called everyone together and told them to open their Mormon scriptures to the Third Book of Nephi, chapter 13, verses 46 and 47.

And woe be unto him that will not hearken unto the words of Jesus, and also to them whom he hath chosen and sent among them. For whoso receiveth not the words of Jesus, and the words of those whom he hath sent, receiveth not him; and therefore he will not receive them at the last day; and it would be better for them if they had not been born.

"Richard and Greg have rejected me and my teachings," Jeffrey said. "It would be better for them if they had not been born. They are damned just like the Averys."

Everyone understood. Leaving the group was the same as denying Jesus Christ. But Debbie didn't care. She felt abandoned. All she could think about that night was Greg and her children from her previous marriage. She had asked Jeffrey for permission to visit them in Independence and he'd promised to arrange it, but Jeffrey had been preoccupied with Kathy and Alice. As she lay in her tent that night, Debbie decided that she was going to see her children even if it meant being condemned by Jeffrey just as Richard and Greg had been.

Every Wednesday, Jeffrey drove to Macks Creek to visit Alice. Debbie knew he generally left the barn before 6:00 A.M. The closest pay telephone was four miles away. Debbie had measured it one day on the truck's odometer when Jeffrey drove her into town to buy groceries. The back injury that she had suffered years ago while working at an Independence hospital still caused her considerable pain and made her limp. But she was determined to see her three children. Debbie began walking around the barn each night after dinner to build up her endurance. No one thought anything of it. By the second Wednesday in November, Debbie was ready. As soon as she heard Jeffrey leave the barn, she pinned a note on her pillow and quietly left the barn. She had already dressed and packed a few of her belongings. Debbie figured it would take her forty-five minutes to walk to the pay phone. Ron usually got up at 6:30 A.M. He would wonder why Debbie wasn't fixing them breakfast since that was her job. She was afraid that Ron would come after her once he realized she was gone. If he did, he'd intercept her before she made it to the telephone. Debbie quickened her pace and listened for the sound of a car engine.

Back at the barn, Ron had noticed that Debbie wasn't in the kitchen. He had told Susie to go into Debbie's tent and check on her. But Susie was scared. She was afraid that Debbie had killed herself. Ron finally decided to check for himself.

"Debbie," he hollered. "Debbie, are you all right?"

He pulled back the tent flap and spotted the note that she had left. Within minutes, everyone knew that Debbie had fled. "Are you going after her?" someone asked Ron, who was in charge whenever Jeffrey wasn't with the group. He paused.

"No," he said softly. "Let her go."

When Debbie reached the pay phone, she telephoned a friend. "Sure I'll come get you," the woman said, "but at seven in the morning? What's the rush!"

"Just come now!" Debbie said. "Right now!"

Alice was spending her days in Macks Creek drinking peppermint schnapps mixed with iced tea and feeling sorry for herself. She had chosen schnapps because she figured Donna wouldn't be suspicious of the smell of peppermint. Despite repeated pressure from her parents, Alice refused to tell them what was going on. Deep down, she figured that Jeffrey would come back. He had before. The first week after Alice left him, Jeffrey telephoned her every day. The second week, he had come down twice to see her, but he had refused to stay past 2:00 P.M. Even though she was willing to have sex with him, Jeffrey refused to spend the night. In mid-November, Jeffrey told Alice that she was "well" enough to be around her children. He brought Jason, Kristen, and Caleb for a visit. They went to a state park for a picnic even though it was cold. At one point, Jeffrey and Jason ran an errand and Alice grilled Caleb. The eight-year-old innocently mentioned that Kathy had gone with him and Daddy to Wal-Mart.

"So we're still playing house with Kathy, huh?" Alice asked when Jeffrey returned.

Jeffrey slapped her, she said later. He took her back to Macks Creek and drove with the kids back to the dairy barn.

On November 15, 1989, Sheriff Hank Thompson telephoned Yarborough. "They're gone!" Thompson announced. The sheriff had stopped by Jeffrey's camp in Yellow Creek Hollow and found the site deserted. The group had left behind one tent, a sewing machine, and a Bible that had Keith Johnson's name in it. Thompson had also found several garbage bags hidden near the camp. They were filled with animal bones. He figured the men had been killing deer illegally. Thompson told Yarborough that Dennis Patrick had mentioned something about returning to Missouri.

Nearly seven months had passed since Jeffrey had fled Kirtland. The FBI had closed its case. People had finally stopped kidding Yarborough about his obsession with Jeffrey. The chief was busy with other investigations. But Yarborough still was curious about Jeffrey. He decided to make a few phone calls. Within a few days, Yarborough had discovered that Alice was living in Macks Creek while Jeffrey and the others were camping in a dairy barn. He'd learned that Jeffrey had taken Kathy as his wife. It sounded as if the group was beginning to disintegrate. "There didn't seem to be much point in keeping tabs on Jeffrey," Yarborough recalled. Yet the chief just couldn't let go. He still wasn't certain who was in Jeffrey's group. He was particularly concerned about Keith Johnson. Why had Thompson found Keith's Bible in West Virginia? Had something happened to Keith?

Yarborough called Kevin Currie's mother in Buffalo and asked her to have Kevin call him. He was still hiding from Jeffrey. When Kevin called, Yarborough told him that the group was back in Missouri. Kevin would later remember asking Yarborough the names of the group members who had gone into the wilderness. The chief began reciting names but when he said Dennis and Cheryl Avery, Kevin stopped him.

"Are you sure the Averys went with him?" Kevin asked.

"Yeah," Yarborough said.

"I seriously doubt that, chief," said Kevin. "Jeffrey would never take the Averys with him. . . . There are certain things that Jeffrey just won't change. He might change scriptures and change his interpretations, but Jeffrey is convinced that the Averys are vile creatures and Jeffrey never changes his emotional judgments of people."

After talking to Kevin, Yarborough looked through his notes. No one had interviewed the Averys when the FBI questioned group members on April 18 at the farm. No one had seen the family since then either. Yarborough called Sheriff Thompson. Were Dennis and Cheryl Avery living at Jeffrey's camp? he asked. Thompson couldn't be certain. He knew that the Patricks had been there and that Danny Kraft had been in the group, but that was it.

"Damn!" Yarborough said, when he put down the telephone receiver.

The weather in Missouri turned so frigid just before Thanksgiving that Ron Luff contacted his brother, Rick, who owned a farm outside Warrensburg and asked him if the group could move onto his property. Rick had a loft in his house where the children could sleep at night. He had a barn that was just as big as the one in Chilhowee, but in better condition, and there was a small trailer on the property that Rick usually rented out. Rick said the group was welcome. Like Ron, he was deeply religious and he was curious about Jeffrey and his teachings.

No one missed the significance of the move. It had been Ron—not Jeffrey—who had made the decision. Ron had slowly taken over more and more control of the group. It was more by default than choice. Jeffrey simply wasn't around, and when he was, he didn't seem to care.

It took the group only one day to move. Jeffrey claimed the more comfortable trailer for himself, Kathy, and his children. Everyone else pitched their tents in the unheated barn. A rumor soon spread through the group: Jeffrey and Kathy were watching hard-core pornographic movies at night. Jeffrey was also using the group's money to take Alice shopping at Bannister

Mall in Kansas City during the day. One of the Lundgren children had accidentally let slip that Jeffrey had bought his family all new clothes but had made them leave them in Macks Creek so no one in the group would know.

Jeffrey didn't care about the rumors. "I knew as soon as we left West Virginia that my people would turn against me," he said later. "The Lord was really telling me that it was time for me to start over. These people were too impatient and soft."

In mid-November, Jeffrey told Alice during one of his visits that he was making plans to shed his followers. The only one that he wanted to continue following him was Ron, he said. Jeffrey had decided to move to California once Alice was "well" enough to travel and he had collected enough money to finance the trip.

"What are you going to tell everyone?" Alice asked.

"I will tell my people that from time to time, prophets take a rest," Jeffrey said. "A prophet needs someplace to go where he doesn't have to deal with everyone's problems. I'll tell them that one reason why Christ had to leave his disciples was so they could bear witness to Him and now it is time for them to bear witness for me."

"How about Kathy?" Alice asked.

Jeffrey didn't answer so Alice pressed him. "I will not abandon what God has given me," Jeffrey replied. But, he said, God had shown him a vision about Kathy. "Jeffrey told me that God had told him that Kathy was going to die before the mountain of the Lord was raised," Alice recalled. "He told me that she wasn't going to make it. It was just going to be the two of us and our children."

Chief Yarborough wasn't the only person curious in late 1989 about the whereabouts of Dennis and Cheryl Avery. Dennis's brother, Tim, also wanted to know where they were. Tim had gotten married and he and his bride, Lisa, had sent Dennis and Cheryl a wedding invitation. Tim thought they'd come or at least send a card, but they had done neither. He thought it was strange that no one had heard from Dennis and Cheryl since April. Tim had called Cheryl's mother, Donna Bailey, and asked if she had heard from them. She hadn't. It was as if they had disappeared.

Through their contacts at church, Tim and Lisa had managed to piece together stories about Jeffrey. They knew that he'd declared himself a prophet and had taken his band to West Virginia. At first, Tim and Lisa didn't believe that Dennis and Cheryl had actually gone with Jeffrey. "They weren't the kind who would want to live in the wilderness," Lisa recalled. "Cheryl had a frog phobia." But Tim had pointed out that his brother and Cheryl weren't the sort who usually joined cults either. Anything seemed possible.

At one point, Tim and Lisa discussed driving to West Virginia to check on Dennis and Cheryl, but they decided against it after they learned that Danny Kraft's father had gone into Jeffrey's camp during the summer and had been unsuccessful at convincing Danny to leave. "We felt Dennis and Cheryl were old enough to run their own lives," Tim said. "What were we going to tell them? That they couldn't stay?"

Shortly before Thanksgiving, however, Lisa had a strange experience. "I was praying, asking God to protect them and the children," she recalled, "and I suddenly felt that God was telling me that it was okay, that Dennis and Cheryl and the children were okay, and I didn't need to be praying for them anymore."

That struck Lisa as odd. "I asked myself, 'Why wouldn't I need to be praying for Dennis's family? Why would God tell me that they were okay?,' and then it hit me. Maybe they're dead. Maybe that is why they are safe now—because they are with God."

Lisa didn't share her thoughts with Tim. She didn't want to alarm him. But she asked God in a prayer if Dennis and Cheryl and the children were with Him in paradise. Is that why she didn't need to worry about them anymore?

When Lisa Avery finished praying, she felt certain that God had given her an answer. And she was even more disturbed than before about her in-laws.

Jeffrey had told all of his followers that they would never be able to make it on their own if they quit the group. About a week after Debbie left, she telephoned Jeffrey at Macks Creek.

"Can I come back?" she asked.

Debbie had visited with her children in Independence and also talked to a few friends. But she had spent most of her

time searching for Greg. His parents wouldn't tell her where
he was hiding. Now she was desperate. "I didn't have anyone
else to turn to but the group," she said. "I didn't care if Jeffrey
killed me. I just didn't want to be alone."

A friend drove her to Rick Luff's barn the day before Thanksgiving. Everyone was happy to see her, particularly Sharon.
Debbie was still the group's nurse and Sharon had discovered
that she was pregnant. Sharon was going to have Richard's baby.
Debbie had never seen a more forsaken lot. "All of us had staked
our lives on Jeffrey. We had believed he was a prophet and now
we were all beginning to realize that we had been deceived,"
she recalled. "It was a gloomy Thanksgiving."

Jeffrey had promised to spend Thanksgiving Day with Alice.
Donna and Ralph were going to their son's house for dinner.
Alice told Jeffrey to bring the kids around two o'clock. She
got dressed and fixed a big dinner, but Jeffrey didn't arrive
until nearly eight. He and Kathy had been quarreling, he said.
Things at the barn were not going well.

"It's almost time for us to go to California," he told her.

Four days after Thanksgiving, Rick Luff and his father
knocked on the door of the trailer where Jeffrey and Kathy
were living. Rick had discovered that Jeffrey had two wives.
He didn't believe in polygamy. He told Jeffrey to get off his
property. The others in the barn were told that they were no
longer welcome either if they were sticking with Jeffrey. Otherwise, they could stay until they found somewhere else to go.

Jeffrey and Kathy packed their belongings and then Jeffrey
went to talk to his followers. He told them that they should each
find somewhere to live during the winter. He was going away
for a while, but he would contact them and tell them where
to send him money. In the spring, they would get together. By
then he would have new revelations and they would return to the
wilderness and work on opening the third seal in Revelation.

With no show of emotion, Jeffrey got into the truck with
Kathy and his children and drove away. He had decided to
take Kathy to live with one of her girlfriends. He and the
children would return to Macks Creek. As soon as Alice's
brother sold the ATV, generator, and camping equipment, he
would be ready to leave Missouri.

Debbie was astounded when Jeffrey left. She looked around.

Dennis, Tonya, Keith, Ron, Susie, Sharon, and Danny were all
standing in the chilly outdoors with absolutely no idea of what
they should do next. Debbie had given up her career as a nurse,
sold her house, and cut herself off from her children all because
she had believed in Jeffrey. Sharon was pregnant and was now
without a husband. Keith had lost his wife and his four sons
no longer had their mother. Danny had given up a promising
career in art. Dennis had almost been killed in the wilderness
and there was no guarantee that his marriage to Tonya would
survive. Tonya had been "claimed" by Jeffrey and then kicked
out of Jeffrey's tent. Jeffrey had tried to drive a wedge between
Susie and Ron in the wilderness. Greg and Richard were in
hiding somewhere. All of the women had been humiliated by
Jeffrey during his so-called "intercession" dances. Worst of
all, he had killed Dennis, Cheryl, Trina, Becky, and Karen
Avery and dragged the group into those murders. They had
either participated or kept quiet about it afterward. And now
Jeffrey was simply driving away.

"I realized at that moment that Jeffrey hadn't only killed five
people," Debbie said later, "he had really destroyed all of us
too. Our lives were ruined because of this man."

As Jeffrey's truck turned onto the road and left Rick Luff's
property, Debbie quietly swore.

"Jeff," she whispered, "you can rot in hell."

Chapter 50

WITHIN twenty-four hours, everyone but Ron and Susie
moved away from the barn. Dennis and Tonya called Tonya's
parents in Independence and went to live with them. Dennis
also called a friend in Higginsville, a tiny town north of
Warrensburg, who agreed to take in Danny. Debbie moved
into a friend's apartment in Independence. She took Sharon

along because she didn't have anywhere else to go. Keith Johnson and his four sons went to his parents' farm southwest of Warrensburg. Greg and Richard were still in hiding somewhere in Independence.

It took Rick Luff two days of nonstop counseling, but he finally convinced Ron that Jeffrey really wasn't a prophet. Ron still believed in the pattern, but he decided that Jeffrey had misused it for his own personal gain. Ron called Jeffrey at Macks Creek and told him that he was quitting the group. Jeffrey didn't argue. "The scriptures had told me that I would be betrayed," he said later.

As soon as Debbie learned that Ron and Susie had quit the group, she telephoned Dennis and Tonya.

"Ron and Susie are out," she announced. "Ron even told Jeff."

"And they're still alive?" Dennis asked.

"I'm quitting too," Debbie said.

Dennis telephoned Ron and asked if he'd really quit. They spoke for nearly an hour and when they finished, Dennis asked Tonya what she thought they should do. Tonya hadn't believed in Jeffrey for a long time. "Let's quit," she said. Dennis agreed. He telephoned Debbie. "We're out too," he said.

Debbie began working on Sharon and by nightfall had convinced her that Jeffrey was a fraud. Ron, meanwhile, telephoned Keith and told him that everyone was dropping out.

By December 6, a Wednesday, Kathy and Danny Kraft were the only two group members still loyal to Jeffrey. Everyone figured Kathy was a lost cause, but Ron and Dennis decided to visit Danny personally the following day.

That night, Keith telephoned Jeffrey and threatened to turn him in to the police for murdering the Averys unless he ended his relationship with Kathy by nine o'clock the next morning. "I told him to be a little rough on Kathy, to tell her that he never loved her and had only used her," said Keith, "because I wanted her back and I wanted her to know exactly what he was."

Jeffrey sounded nervous as they talked. "Now, Keith," he said, "there are other people to consider in this. Everyone has something to lose if you go to the police."

"Do as I say," Keith replied, "because I'm mad enough to do it."

Keith said he had written a letter about the murders and had given it to his attorney in a sealed envelope. If anything happened to him, the attorney was to open the letter and notify the police.

"Okay," said Jeffrey. "I'll tell her. I'll send Kathy back to you but I need another day."

"Just tell her," said Keith, "to come home."

As soon as they finished talking, Jeffrey telephoned Kathy in Odessa and told her about Keith's threat. The next morning, Jeffrey announced to Alice that he needed to run some errands. He drove to Odessa, picked up Kathy, and took her to a motel in a suburb of Kansas City where he was certain that Keith couldn't find her. They spent the day together and then Jeffrey drove to Higginsville to talk with Danny. He arrived shortly before Dennis and Ron were scheduled to meet him. Jeffrey realized that he was going to need someone to support him in California and Danny was the only wage earner they had left. "Danny's artistic skills were such that I knew he could find a job anywhere we went." As always, Jeffrey used his scriptures to convince Danny that God wanted him to go with the "God of the whole Earth" to a city by an ocean. Danny packed his bags and went with Jeffrey to Macks Creek. "We missed saving Danny by only a few hours," Dennis said later. "If we'd only got to him, I think we could have gotten him out."

The next morning, a Friday, Ralph and Donna Keehler left their house early for Independence where Ralph was scheduled for a routine checkup at a VA hospital. As soon as the Keehlers' car drove away from the house, Jeffrey and Alice packed up their belongings. Jeffrey no longer felt safe in Macks Creek. He figured that by this time, Keith would realize that Jeffrey was calling his bluff. Alice left her mother a note. "We may never see each other again," she wrote. "I'm sorry things turned out this way."

Jeffrey couldn't leave for California for at least one more day. Charles Keehler had found a buyer willing to pay $6,000 for the ATV and electric generator, but he wouldn't have the cash until sometime Saturday. Jeffrey drove to Osage Beach and checked his family and Danny into a motel there. Alice would later recall that it was one of the same motels that

Jeffrey had stayed in ten years earlier when he had his first sexual affair with his fellow hospital worker.

On Saturday morning, Jeffrey met Charles and collected $5,400 of the $6,000. Charles kept $600 as a commission. Still worried that Keith might be hunting him, Jeffrey returned to Osage Beach and told everyone that they were moving to a different motel, this time in Springfield. On Sunday morning, December 10, Jeffrey informed Alice that he had to run a few more errands. He drove to Kansas City by himself, met with Kathy and gave her some of the cash. They agreed that she would stay behind in the Kansas City motel until Jeffrey sent for her. Somehow, he would force Alice to accept Kathy as a fellow wife.

Jeffrey was nervous when he returned to Springfield that night. "Whenever Jeffrey is under extreme pressure, he absolutely and totally engulfs himself in his sexual fantasies and shuts out the real world," said Alice. "It's how he copes." Jeffrey asked Alice to take him shopping. They bought a bra, panties, nylons, a dress, and low-heeled women's shoes, Alice said. Back at the motel, Alice gave Jeffrey his bath, shaved all of the hair off his body except for his head and put curlers in his shoulder-length hair. She spent nearly an hour applying makeup to his face. When she was finished, Jeffrey dressed in the women's clothing and they drove to a grocery store. "He had me walk with him up and down the aisle, but he was afraid to go through the checkout stand." Instead, Jeffrey hurried out to the truck and when Alice joined him, he hiked up his skirt and ordered her to perform oral sex, Alice said later.

On that same Sunday night, Jeffrey's ex-followers were meeting in the apartment where Debbie and Sharon were staying. By this time, Debbie had found Greg, and he and Richard were at the meeting. Greg had told Debbie that he cared about her as a friend, but he no longer considered them married. Richard had not been as cordial to Sharon.

During the meeting, everyone looked to Ron for guidance. He began by talking about how Jeffrey had duped them, but the conversation quickly turned to the murder of the Averys and their culpability. Everyone was optimistic at first. After all, it was Jeffrey who had done the actual shooting. None of the women had been in the barn. Tonya hadn't even been at the farm during the killing; neither had Dennis or Keith. The only thing that those two men had done was help dig the pit in the barn and they could claim that Jeffrey had told them it was a baptismal font. They could claim that they really didn't know what Jeffrey had planned. Greg, Richard, and Ron were going to have a tougher time since they had participated in the murders, the group decided. But all they had done was follow Jeffrey's orders. In fact, just before the men had gone into the barn, Jeffrey had called them into his bedroom at the farmhouse and shown them the .45-caliber pistol that he was going to use. He had asked them one by one if they were "in or out." That questioning could be interpreted as a death threat if the right spin was put on the story.

The longer the group talked about it, the better their rationalizations sounded. But when Keith suggested that they all march down to the police station and report Jeffrey, the room suddenly fell silent. Reality hit. Dennis, Cheryl, Trina, Becky, and Karen had been dumped into a pit and murdered. No one had stopped Jeffrey. No one had gone to the police before or afterward. Most of them had lied to the FBI on April 18 when questioned at the farm. Clearly, Jeffrey wasn't going to be the only person prosecuted. Some of them were going to be punished.

Why not lie? someone suggested. If they all stuck together, they could blame Jeffrey, Alice, Damon, and Danny. It would be their word against the others'. Dennis and Keith opposed that idea. Why should they commit perjury when they clearly weren't in as much trouble as everyone else? Self-preservation had kicked in.

About halfway through the meeting, Keith told everyone that he had already given a letter to his lawyers that described the killings. "Everyone told Keith that he had to get that letter back," Debbie said later. What if Keith was killed in a car accident driving home that night? The police would inadvertently find out about the Averys.

"We have to do something," Keith said, "or else Jeffrey is just going to go down the road and do this all over again."

Debbie finally made a plea. "I need some time with my children," she said. "I want a couple of months with my kids in case we all go to jail." All of the others except for Keith openly agreed. Keith didn't say another word. "It was clear that they didn't want to go to the police, but I wasn't going to promise that," said Keith. Not hearing any objection, Ron made it official. No one would go to the police without first alerting the group, he said. That way, they could get their stories straight, hire attorneys, and cut some sort of deal so the blame would be put where it belonged—on Jeffrey and Alice.

On Monday morning, Jeffrey, Alice, their children, and Danny began their four-day drive to California in the Nissan truck. Jeffrey had decided to go to San Diego because that is where he had been stationed while in the navy and he was familiar with the city. As they drove, Jeffrey asked Alice to read him the entire book of Isaiah. He was looking for clues, he explained. He wanted to know what God desired from the "God of the whole earth."

Jeffrey and the others arrived in San Diego on December 14, according to the registration card at the Traveler Motel Suites, an eighty-five-room motel located five miles from downtown San Diego. Alice had used their actual names on the card. Their room contained a bedroom, kitchenette, and living room with foldout sofabed. During the ride west, Alice had asked Jeffrey where Kathy was. He'd lied and told her that she had returned to Iowa. The morning after Jeffrey and the others arrived at the motel, he urged Alice, Damon, and Danny to take the children outside to play. He needed to be alone to study his scriptures, he said. Alice suspected that Jeffrey was trying to get rid of her so she waited outside the motel room for five minutes and then flung open the door.

"Jeff was sitting naked on the bed masturbating while talking on the phone. I knew it was her. He was talking to the bitch."

Jeffrey slammed down the receiver and accused Alice of being rebellious. She started screaming. He pushed her into the bathroom and slammed the door. He refused to let her out for three hours.

The next morning, Jeffrey drove Alice to the local welfare office, where she spent the day applying for financial aid. Once again, she used Jeffrey's real name on all the forms. Twice, she called the motel on a pay phone, but both times the operator told her that the line to the room was busy. "I knew he was talking to Kathy again. I knew he was figuring out a way to get that bitch out to California." Alice collected some $300 in food stamps that day and another $938 through a program designed to help homeless families find housing to rent. When she got back to the motel, Jeffrey ordered pizza for everyone to celebrate her "looting" of the Gentiles. He and Alice then went to a nearby Laundromat where they played video games until 2:00 A.M. "Jeffrey got the highest score on the machine," Alice gushed later. "He was just a tremendous player."

During the next few days, Jeffrey sent Danny to find a job. He put Damon in charge of baby-sitting for the other Lundgren children. Alice slept during the day and watched television. Jeffrey, meanwhile, spent his mornings and afternoons exercising in a nearby gym and playing video games at the Laundromat. At night, Jeffrey taught Damon, Danny, and Alice various new scriptural interpretations. At one point, Jeffrey talked about recruiting motorcycle-gang members as followers. They would be tough enough to perform the killing that God was about to order, he said. Jeffrey told Alice that gang members frequented striptease bars in San Diego and he said that God wanted him to begin visiting all of the nude nightclubs to search for new disciples.

Jeffrey also announced that the third seal in Revelation had been opened while the group was in West Virginia, although no one except for him realized it. The third seal read:

> And when he had opened the third seal, I heard the
> third beast say, Come and see. And I beheld, and lo
> a black horse; and he that sat on him had a pair of
> balances in his hand . . .

The "pair of balances," Jeffrey explained, was a cryptic reference to Alice and Kathy. "The rider of the black horse is carrying a pair of balances—in other words, he has two wives." That verse, Jeffrey told Alice, was additional proof that God wanted him to be married to both women.

Alice didn't believe him, but instead of challenging Jeffrey's interpretation, Alice asked him about the one-year deadline that he had imposed for opening all of the seals. He had told everyone that God expected all seven seals to be opened within twelve months once the Averys were murdered. It had been nine months since the sacrifice and Jeffrey was still on the third seal. Jeffrey had a ready explanation. Because he was divine, like God, he spoke chiastically. "In order for you to really understand what I am saying, you have to use the pattern to diagram my exact words," he said. Had anyone done that while the group was in the wilderness, they would have discovered that his words didn't always say what they seemed to say. They contained a hidden message and, in this case, that message was that there was no deadline for opening the seven seals.

Near the end of their first full week in San Diego, Jeffrey told Alice that God had instructed him to spend three nights on the beach. During one of those nights, the Mormon prophet Nephi would appear and tell him how to open the fourth seal. He announced that he was going out that very night to see if Nephi would appear. He took Damon with him to a nearby public beach. They stayed out until 3:00 A.M. and then returned to the motel to sleep. The next night, Jeffrey said that God wanted him to go alone. He didn't come back to the motel until nearly noon on the next day.

"Did Nephi appear?" Alice asked, when Jeffrey dragged in.

"No," Jeffrey replied. "I have to go out again tonight. It must be the night."

Alice hurried outside and looked in the back of the truck. "I found a mattress in the back and it was covered with sand."

Returning to the motel room, Alice asked: "Did you and Nephi roll around in the back of the truck?"

Jeffrey said that he had gotten tired and had taken the mattress along so that he could rest.

"Jeffrey," she replied, "you're lying again. It's Kathy. You brought her out here! You're hiding her somewhere. Now where is that bitch?"

Jeffrey denied that Kathy was in San Diego. "She's in Iowa," he insisted. But Alice wouldn't believe him. They argued until Jeffrey finally left the room. When he returned, he announced that God had spoken to him. God was so infuriated by Alice's constant rebellion that He had decided not to send Nephi to meet with Jeffrey. Instead, God wanted Jeffrey to humble Alice.

"You must sleep on the floor for the next three nights at the foot of your lord and master," Jeffrey announced. "This is what God demands."

That night, while Jeffrey slept on the motel bed, Alice lay on the floor, without a blanket or pillow.

"It was at that time that I became completely and totally, absolutely convinced that there was no validity to anything that Jeffrey said or taught," Alice said later. "Everything was a lie from the time we had met in college twenty years earlier."

The next morning, Alice challenged Jeffrey. "I told him pointblank that I didn't think he had ever had any revelatory experience, that I thought he'd made up everything in his mind and that the only god that he listened to was Jeff Lundgren.

"I began telling him what a lousy provider he had been for me and the kids, and all of a sudden, he became extremely kind and compassionate and he started crying. He said, 'Alice, I haven't treated you as I ought. I haven't provided for you as I ought.' And he began to beg me for forgiveness. He said, 'Please let me make love to you.' That was the first time since we had left West Virginia that he had asked to do anything for me. I said, 'No, Jeffrey, it's too late.' I got up and I walked out the motel door and he came running after me. He followed me the entire time that I was walking and he begged me not to leave him.

"He said, 'Alice, if you ever left me, I'd die. You've got to believe in me. You've got to believe I am who I say I am, otherwise I can't go on. I need you.' "

Chapter 51

CHIEF Yarborough was at home helping Gail get ready for a New Year's Eve party when the telephone rang at 3:30 P.M. on December 31, 1989. Most of Gail's relatives were coming over later that afternoon to begin celebrating. But within seconds after Yarborough picked up the receiver, he forgot about the night's festivities. An agent for the federal Bureau of Alcohol, Tobacco, and Firearms was on the line calling from Kansas City with quite a story. Richard Van Haelst had just spent more than two hours interviewing a man who claimed that five murder victims were buried in a barn outside Kirtland.

Who, Yarborough asked, was Van Haelst's informant?

"Keith Johnson," the agent replied.

Who was supposedly buried in the barn?

A family named the Averys, Van Haelst said. Dennis, Cheryl, and their three daughters.

Yarborough didn't have to ask who the alleged murderer was, but Van Haelst volunteered the name. The triggerman, he said, was Jeffrey Lundgren.

"I felt sick," Yarborough later remembered. "I hoped like hell that Johnson was lying."

Van Haelst told Yarborough that a friend of Keith's had contacted another BATF agent, Larry Scott, that morning and had arranged for them to meet just before noon. Keith had told Van Haelst and Scott up front that one of the main reasons why he had come forward was because he wanted the BATF to track down his wife and to arrest Jeffrey. There was a chance, the agent said, that Keith had concocted the entire murder story just to find Kathy and get Jeffrey into trouble. At least that was the theory of the Cleveland BATF field office. Before contacting Yarborough, Van Haelst had called an agent there who had quickly dismissed Keith's story as the rambling of a jilted spouse who was simply bored on New Year's Eve. Van Haelst had called Yarborough, in part, out of frustration. He was trying to find someone willing to go out to the barn and at least do some snooping around.

As soon as Yarborough finished talking to Van Haelst, he telephoned Ron Andolsek and asked him to contact the Averys' relatives. Before anyone scurried out to the barn, Yarborough wanted to make certain that Dennis and Cheryl were definitely missing.

"I really hoped Keith was lying," the chief said. "I hoped it was nothing but a hoax."

The next morning, New Year's Day, Andolsek told Yarborough that none of the Averys' relatives had heard from the family since April. No one was certain where they had gone, although Cheryl Avery's mother had gotten a note that mentioned Wyoming.

Yarborough's first impulse was to race out to the barn and begin digging. But he held himself back. He wanted to move cautiously. If there were five bodies buried in the barn, the Kirtland Police Department was going to be involved in the biggest investigation in its history and Yarborough didn't want to do anything spur of the moment that might result in Jeffrey or anyone else being found not guilty later because of a legal technicality. The chief told Andolsek that before either of them could search the barn, they had to get written permission from its owner, Stan Skrbis, Jeffrey's former landlord. That was going to take much of the day.

There was another reason why Yarborough wasn't in a rush. "I didn't want those bodies to be there. I blamed myself. I thought, 'Damn, Jeffrey turned on his own group. We stopped him from hitting the temple so he turned on his own people.' I kept thinking, 'What if I'd done this or done that?' We'd never really paid much attention to finding the Averys. They didn't seem like they were part of Jeffrey's plan."

By the time that Andolsek got all of the paperwork signed it was 10:30 P.M. He and Yarborough met outside the empty farmhouse. The last time that both of them had been at the farm together was April 18, the day after the alleged murders. That fact grated on the chief. *One day! One stinking day late!*

No one had rented the farm since Jeffrey had fled owing Skrbis several months' back rent. The front yard was overgrown with weeds. The apple trees needed tending. Yarborough and Andolsek flipped on their flashlights. The electricity in the barn had been turned off months earlier. The door creaked when they pulled it open. Their lights spotlighted a miscellany of junk abandoned inside the barn. Jeffrey and his followers had discarded everything they couldn't take with them to West Virginia, tossing it aside like litter carelessly dropped from a fast-moving car. Cardboard boxes overflowing with books, green plastic trash bags bursting with clothing, letters, coats, toys, pieces of furniture—the scene reminded Andolsek of a giant Goodwill box that hadn't been emptied for months.

Keith had told the federal agents that the Averys were buried on the east side of the barn. It took Yarborough and Andolsek several minutes to make their way through the debris and several more to clear a spot so they could see if there were any signs of digging. When they had at last removed enough trash to investigate the floor, Yarborough reached down and swept away a layer of straw.

"Hey, Ron," he announced, "this is concrete under here. He couldn't have buried anyone under this."

Yarborough felt a quick elation. Maybe Keith was lying. Maybe he had concocted the story. The two men shone their lights across the barn. Something moved. Yarborough flashed his light in the direction of the sound. A terrified chicken flew toward him. The chief jumped and then laughed.

Andolsek wondered: Could Keith had been confused? Or had Van Haelst given them the wrong directions? Maybe the bodies were buried in the west corner. The two men worked their way through the debris. Yarborough counted three abandoned cars piled with boxes. In the western portion of the barn, they found a room that was packed with so much junk that neither of them could squeeze inside to look around. The hope that Yarborough had felt dissipated. There was *too* much garbage piled inside. It looked as if someone was intentionally trying to hide something there.

They were going to need help clearing the room of debris. They'd have to wait for daylight, Yarborough said. "We'll come back tomorrow." As they walked back toward the door, Andolsek shone his flashlight on a box and spotted a formal-looking document. He picked it up. High School Diploma, it said. Cheryl Clisby. Class of 1965.

BATF agent Scott telephoned Yarborough the next morning to see if he'd found the bodies. The barn's floor was concrete, the chief explained. Scott offered to send a drawing that Keith had made of the barn. It showed exactly where the grave was located. Even if the bodies had been removed, there should still be some sign of digging.

"What's your fax number?" Scott asked.

Yarborough paused. The Kirtland Police Department didn't own a fax. The chief said he'd find someone else in Kirtland who could receive it.

Yarborough was waiting in his office for the diagram to be delivered when he looked up and saw Dennis Patrick walk into the police station.

"I just stopped by to let you know my wife and I aren't in Jeffrey's group anymore," Dennis volunteered. "Neither is Debbie Olivarez."

The three of them had quit, Dennis said, and had returned to Kirtland with a U-Haul truck because they wanted to retrieve some of their belongings from the barn. Would it be okay, he asked, if the three of them went onto the property to reclaim their things?

Yarborough could tell from Dennis's demeanor that he didn't know that Keith Johnson had tipped off the BATF to the murders.

"Why don't you come back later this afternoon?" the chief suggested. Yarborough said that he'd have an officer escort them onto the property so they wouldn't be accused of trespassing.

Dennis thanked him, offered the chief his hand, and walked out of the station without any clue about what was happening. The chief grabbed his telephone and called FBI Agent Robert Alvord. Once again, Yarborough was covering himself. He wanted Alvord to be there when Dennis returned later that day.

Alvord and the drawing from the BATF arrived at about the same time. Yarborough and Andolsek had been right. The grave was in the western half of the barn in the room strewn with trash.

At 3:00 P.M., Dennis returned to the station with Tonya and Debbie, who waited outside. The three of them had contacted Shar Olson and were planning on spending the night at her apartment. As soon as Dennis entered the police station, Yarborough and Alvord began questioning him about the Averys. Dennis panicked. He didn't want to appear uncooperative, but he didn't want to tell them the truth either. He was soon tripping over his own lies. Thirty minutes later, Tonya came looking for Dennis. When she saw him, she knew something was wrong. He looked terrified. Hurrying back outside, Tonya raced over to Debbie.

"They know!" she said.

"Oh, my God!" Debbie replied.

Dennis was shaking when he came out of the station. "We've got to find an attorney," he said. "We've got to talk to a lawyer." The trio rushed back to Shar's apartment, but they refused to tell her what was going on. Dennis telephoned a local attorney who belonged to the RLDS Church. The attorney told them to get back to Missouri as quickly as they could. They left immediately, leaving Shar completely bewildered. None of them had mentioned the murders to her. Once they were a few miles outside Kirtland, Dennis stopped at a pay phone and called Greg. "They know," he said. Someone had tipped off the police without warning everyone else.

"Keith!" Greg said. It had to be Keith.

Greg promised to alert the others. They'd meet at Minsky's, a pizza place just outside Independence. The Patricks and Debbie drove all night. They met Ron, Susie, Greg, and Richard at the restaurant. No one invited Keith. Sharon wasn't there either. By this time, she had returned to her parents' house in Michigan and had just given birth to a daughter. Greg had called her and told her that Keith had squealed. He'd promised to call after the meeting and tell her what everyone was going to do. Once again, the group discussed what might happen to them, and then Ron suggested that they each contact an attorney. No one spoke for several minutes. As they looked around the table, each of them realized that once they left the pizza parlor they were on their own. Keith had been the first to jump ship. Who would be next to cut a deal?

Back in Kirtland, Yarborough, Andolsek, and Alvord arrived at the barn at 9:00 A.M. on January 3 and began removing junk from the room where the grave was located. By four o'clock, they had removed enough for Andolsek to crawl inside. He made his way to one side of the room, where he spotted chunks of dried clay on several boxes.

"Someone's been digging here," he yelled.

All three men returned to the police station. Yarborough was now convinced that Keith's story was true. He telephoned the chief of Kirtland's Volunteer Fire Department and asked for his help. At seven o'clock that night, nearly a dozen firefighters assembled at the farm. They set up large floodlights to illuminate the barn and they began clearing debris from inside the room. Ron Andolsek had a firefighter videotape the entire operation. Within an hour, the room was clean. It was obvious where the grave was located. Everywhere else, the floor was hard clay, but the ground was soft where the bodies were buried. With Yarborough and Andolsek overseeing the exhumation, two firemen began digging. As soon as they overturned the first shovel of dirt, a stench rose from the ground. Within minutes, a putrid odor permeated the room. One of the men gasped for air, dropped his shovel, and rushed outside. Yarborough, Andolsek, and the others fought back the urge to vomit. The stench became so vile that the volunteer firemen began digging in shifts. Some could work only for a few minutes. Shortly after 9:00 P.M., one of the men unearthed a swatch of blue denim. He climbed into the hole and reached down with his hands to clear away the dirt. It was a hip turned sideways. The firefighter removed about twelve inches of dirt, revealing a man's belt and what looked like the bottom of a faded plaid shirt.

"That's enough," Yarborough said. There was no question now that Keith had told the truth. They had found one body. Yarborough ordered the firemen to stop digging. His small police department and the volunteer firefighters were unprepared for the job that Yarborough knew lay ahead. He told Andolsek to get everyone out of the barn and close off the area. Yarborough wanted an officer stationed at the barn round the clock. As soon as the chief was certain that no one would disturb the grave, he began calling various county officials. The Lake County Sheriff's Department had a lieutenant, Daniel Dunlap, who had received special schooling from the FBI on how to process a crime scene. Yarborough wanted his help. Lake County Prosecutor Steven C. LaTourette needed to be notified too. He would be in charge of filing charges against Jeffrey and the others. He'd also be the person responsible for making certain that they were convicted. Besides LaTourette, the county coroner needed to be contacted.

By midnight, all of the various officials who would play some role in the case had been notified. The county coroner drove to the barn to look at the grave. It was beginning to fill with water. While digging, the firefighters had accidentally cut through a drain. The coroner and Yarborough agreed that it would be better to resume the exhumation in the morning, after Dunlap arrived. That way there wouldn't be any more mishaps.

It was well after 2:00 A.M. when Yarborough walked over to his car. Before getting inside, he looked around. No one was watching him. He turned and vomited into the grass.

"I wanted to retire right then," he later said, "because I knew what we were going to find in the morning."

Lieutenant Dunlap and Rick Kent, a supervisor at the Lake County Regional Forensic Laboratory, took control of the site on January 4. Dunlap arrived just in time. Some of the volunteer firemen had returned to the barn with a hose that they wanted to use to drain the water from the grave. Dunlap ordered the men to bail out the hole with buckets. Each was then dumped through a sieve to check for evidence, such as bullets. Once the water was cleared, Dunlap and Kent began using hand trowels to remove the clay from around the hip of the partially uncovered corpse. Every scoop of clay was put into a bucket and carried outside to the sieve. The clay was so thick that the firemen had to use water to break it apart.

Because the body in the pit was badly decomposed, it was impossible to tell at first if it was Dennis Avery, although it seemed to be a man because of its size. As Dunlap and Kent continued to unearth it, they found another body at the feet of the first. It was Cheryl. When they started to unearth the head, both men grimaced. Gray duct tape was wrapped around the face, like a mummy.

As the two men continued digging, Steven LaTourette stood away from the grave next to the barn door where he leaned against an old washer and dryer. The thirty-five-year-old prosecutor had intentionally chosen to stand in a spot that prevented him from seeing directly into the grave. He felt that it was important for him to be present during the exhumation, but LaTourette had a daughter the same age as six-year-old Karen Avery and he was having trouble watching the grisly proceedings. An aide made trips back and forth from the grave to LaTourette, filling him in on what was happening.

"They found the first two bodies rather quickly and then there was quite a bit of time before they found the third," LaTourette said later. "You could feel the deflation in the room among the people working when the third one was found. All of us had hoped that the Avery girls weren't in the pit. That just the parents were buried there."

The third body was clearly a child, resting on her mother's corpse. It would later be identified as Becky. As they began uncovering it, they found a fourth body, smaller still, with its head touching the hips of Becky's corpse. It would later be determined through dental records that this fourth body was Karen Avery. Because of the location of Karen's body, Dunlap and Kent decided to remove the remains of the thirty-six-pound girl first. Her body was held together mostly by her blue jacket and jeans. Water had again seeped into the pit, turning the clay into a thick muck. It was bitter cold in the barn. A light rain was falling outside. The stench remained almost unbearable. Dunlap and Kent were becoming exhausted. As they gently began lifting the small corpse, the mud and air made a sucking noise and created a vacuum that pulled on the remains. From a distance, LaTourette and Yarborough watched as Kent and Dunlap finally freed Karen's tiny remains from the pit. As they lifted the body from the mud, the girl's left foot fell off.

"When I saw that little girl's foot fall off," LaTourette said later, "I began to feel nothing but pure, unadulterated hate for Jeffrey Lundgren."

To prevent the other bodies from breaking apart, Dunlap suggested that each one be wrapped in a sheet before it was lifted from the grave. He and Kent could then lift the sheets, rather than touching the delicate corpses. Becky's body and the remains of Cheryl and Dennis were removed in sheets and loaded into body bags.

Fatigued, Dunlap climbed out of the muck and turned his digging trowel over to Deputy Ronald Walters. A few minutes later, the fifth body was found, curled in a fetal position. This child, identified later as Trina, had been a few steps away from the others, facing her father's corpse. After Kent and Walters gingerly cleared away the mud from Trina, they gently lifted the corpse so that they could slip a sheet under it. As Walters raised Trina's head, the girl's scalp and braided hair came loose in his hand.

At a news conference held after all of the bodies had been taken away by ambulances, LaTourette became so emotional that he abandoned the traditional "they are innocent until proven guilty" role that legal protocol demanded. Instead, the prosecutor angrily denounced Jeffrey and his followers. "These people are . . . the cruelest, most inhumane people this county has ever seen," he said. "They're going to die in the electric chair for these crimes."

It was well after midnight when Chief Yarborough finally got home that night. Gail was already in bed asleep. Yarborough took a shower, tucked his clothes in the washing machine, and crawled in beside her. As he lay there, he could still smell the stench from the barn, and despite his best efforts to block it out of his mind, all he could visualize was Karen being lifted from the grave and seeing her foot fall off. Finally, exhaustion brought sleep, but he was jarred awake minutes later. His entire body had started shaking. "It was that damn smell," he said later. "I just couldn't stop smelling it." The image of Karen returned and within seconds, his mind's eye called up the sight of Walters holding a young girl's ponytail and scalp in his hand.

Yarborough felt ill. He got up and walked through his dark house into the living room, where he found a tin of Copenhagen. Tucking tobacco between his lip and front teeth, he stepped over to the front picture window in his home. It had gotten even colder outside and the drop in temperature had changed that day's gloomy drizzle into a light snow that drifted down, reflected in the moonlight. As he peered outside at the pristine beauty, he shook his head. Things like this weren't supposed to happen in Kirtland.

Yarborough thought about Jeffrey. He was out there somewhere. Maybe he was awake, staring outside. Yarborough wondered: What sort of man can put three children into a pit and kill each one? What sort of man can then claim that God told him to do it? And what sort of people could follow such a cold-blooded killer? Only two days earlier, Yarborough had confronted Dennis Patrick. From all appearances, he seemed like a decent guy, not someone who would knowingly participate in such a crime. Why had he followed Jeffrey?

As he stood there alone in the darkness, Yarborough felt a sudden urge. There was something that he needed to do, a promise that needed to be uttered. It didn't matter that he was alone. Someone had to say it. Someone had to react to the insanity of that day, to Jeffrey's cruelty. Someone had to react to the stench of death. Someone had to care enough to not be able to sleep. God was a witness, maybe Karen was too, and maybe Yarborough was just talking to himself. Later, he wouldn't be certain why he had felt the need to speak. It didn't matter. He just did. Someone had to.

"He'll pay." Yarborough said. Jeffrey Lundgren was going to pay for what he had done.

Chapter 52

"DAD! Mom!" Danny Kraft yelled, bursting into the motel bedroom that Jeffrey and Alice shared. "The barn is on television!"

Both of them scrambled out into the living room of their motel suite. On the screen, the bodies of the Avery family were shown being carried by ambulance attendants from the barn. An old photograph of Jeffrey appeared, followed by a film clip of LaTourette promising that Jeffrey and his followers were going to "fry." It was 11:30 P.M. in San Diego on January 4.

"Get the stuff packed!" Jeffrey told Danny. Turning to Alice, he announced, "Let's go!"

Alice and her children hurried out to the truck. Jeffrey told Danny that he'd come back for him later. With their four children in the back of the Nissan, Jeffrey pulled out of the motel parking lot as Alice looked up and down the street, half expecting a squad of police cars.

Jeffrey drove to National City, another suburb of San Diego, and cruised a strip of cheaper hotels. He was looking for one that wasn't part of a national chain. He was afraid that the police might have sent his photograph and description to the better-known motels.

"There's one," Alice said, as they approached the Santa Fe Motel. Fearing that he might be recognized, he sent Alice to register. "Use fake names," he warned.

Alice was nervous. She had chosen the name Anna for herself and planned to use James for Jeffrey. But as she filled out the registration, she couldn't think of an appropriate last name so she simply wrote: Anna James, and handed the clerk a fifty-dollar bill. He took the card without examining it and handed her the key to Room 29.

As soon as everyone was in the room, Jeffrey said he was going back to get Danny. "Don't wait for me," he told her. Alice suddenly felt angry. She suspected that Jeffrey was going to warn Kathy. She was certain that he had brought her to San Diego by bus and was hiding her somewhere. But as Jeffrey started toward the door, Alice called out and then ran up to him. She kissed him and they hugged. She was scared, really scared.

Jeffrey found Danny waiting in the room. Together, they drove to a nearby motel where Kathy was living. Jeffrey told Danny that he wanted him to stay with Kathy. He'd figure out some way for them to get out of town. It was after 2:30 A.M. when Jeffrey returned to the Santa Fe Motel. Alice didn't ask where Danny was. She didn't want to know. She was too preoccupied even to question Jeff about Kathy. Alice had been watching Cable News Network. "It's been on every hour," she told Jeffrey. "The prosecutor says we're all going to fry." Jeffrey tried to calm her, but Alice was too frightened.

"I want you to kill the children and me," she announced. She began to cry. "Do it now, while they are asleep, but kill me first."

Jeffrey looked at Alice. More than anyone, he knew that she had a habit of being melodramatic. But she was serious this time. "She really wanted to die and she wanted me to kill the children."

"Jeffrey was aghast," Alice said later. "He told me that he couldn't harm his own children. I said, 'Okay, let's call my mom, she'll come get them, but then I want you to kill me.' I just wanted to get it over with."

Jeffrey agreed that they needed to call Donna Keehler about the children. As far as killing Alice, that was something that he would have to consult God about, he said. The next day, Jeffrey and Damon walked to a pay phone. Damon dialed the number and asked for Donna. That had been Jeffrey's idea. He thought the police might recognize his voice, but not Damon's. As soon as Donna answered, Jeffrey got on the phone.

"Can you come get the kids?" he asked.

Donna was furious, but she didn't want Jeffrey to hang up. "Of course I'll come," she said. "Where are you?"

"I can't say, just start driving west; call us at nine o'clock and we'll give you more directions," Jeffrey said. He gave her the number of a pay phone to call.

Donna was incredulous. How could she simply start driving west? she asked. But Jeffrey was afraid to stay on the line any longer. Even Donna was worried that it could be tapped.

As soon as she put down the phone, Donna grabbed a telephone directory. Jeffrey had given her a number with a 619 area code. According to the directory, 619 was in southern California. Donna knew Jeffrey was hiding in San Diego. It made sense that he would run to a city where he'd lived before. As she was closing the directory, the phone rang a second time. It was Jeffrey. He had given her the number of a pay phone that didn't accept incoming calls. He told her another number with a 619 prefix and reminded her to telephone him the next evening at nine o'clock based on Kansas City time.

Donna called her sister and brother-in-law. She didn't want to drive to California alone and she knew that Ralph couldn't make the trip. They agreed to go along. The next morning was a Saturday, January 6. As soon as Donna pulled out of her driveway, a car carrying BATF agents slipped in front of her, another car pulled up behind. The agents told Donna that they knew all about her conversation with Jeffrey. Worried about the fate of her grandchildren, Donna agreed to cooperate. She was, in fact, a bit relieved. "I wanted to get those kids out of there safely in case Jeffrey began shooting. They were what was most on my mind. Jeffrey had gone too far and I wasn't certain that Alice could be helped either."

The BATF had already traced both of the numbers that Jeffrey had given Donna. One was a pay phone outside a 7-Eleven store; the second was at a restaurant not far from the Santa Fe Motel. With her federal-agent escort, Donna drove southwest toward Springfield and then on to Tulsa, Oklahoma. Just before 9:00 P.M., she stopped in Oklahoma City at a restaurant and dialed the number that Jeffrey had given her. Damon answered and told his grandmother that she should keep driving west and call him on Sunday at noon Kansas City time for new instructions.

Agents from the San Diego BATF office had staked out the telephone and they watched as Damon completed the call. A plainclothes agent followed Damon as he walked back to the Santa Fe Motel, but the agent didn't see which room he went into. The stakeout was moved from the phone booth to the motel.

Inside Room 29, Alice was becoming more and more depressed. Caleb had started to cry. Kristen was sucking her thumb. Jason refused to speak to anyone. Damon was trying to comfort them but wasn't having much luck. Jeffrey had left the motel earlier that day and driven over to see Danny and Kathy. They were frightened too. Jeffrey had taken his family's laundry to Danny and told him to get it washed and dried. He had left Danny the Nissan truck so that he could bring the clean clothes back to the Santa Fe Motel when he finished. On his way to the Laundromat, Danny had taken Jeffrey back to his motel.

Damon told Jeffrey that Donna was in Oklahoma City and that everything was going as planned. Later that night, after Alice was certain that everyone was asleep, she asked Jeffrey if he had talked to God and learned whether it was okay for Jeffrey to kill her.

"The Lord says it's okay for you to die," he told her. But Jeffrey said that God expected Alice to take her own life and that He wanted her to wait until after the children were gone before she did it. Jeffrey figured the FBI would tail Donna to San Diego, but he told Alice that he had come up with a way to deliver the kids to her mother without being arrested. They would put them on a bus and then direct Donna to the next stop on the line. Once they said good-bye to their children, Jeffrey and Alice would come back to the motel and he would stay with her while she took an overdose of pills. Jeffrey had already sent Damon to buy two bottles of Excedrin P.M., two six-packs of beer and a bottle of Jack Daniel's whiskey. That would be sufficient to kill her, he said. Jeffrey still hadn't told Alice about Kathy. After he was freed of his children and Alice committed suicide, Jeffrey and Kathy would find somewhere to hide and he would start finding a new group of followers.

Alice decided to write a letter for her mother. "I told her not to question anything that she had done. I told her that I knew when I married Jeff that he was different from anyone I had ever met. I told her that I had already talked to Krissy about menstruation. I told her things about each of the children."

When Alice finished the letter, Jeffrey told her that he wanted to make love. Alice agreed. What began as a tender session soon turned violent, Alice later claimed. "I was on the bed with my head laying on the side and Jeffrey was thrusting himself into my mouth and he began doing it so hard that it began to hurt and I couldn't breathe," she said. "I began to gag and I began to vomit but he was so caught up in it that he refused to stop until he was finished.

"I went into the bathroom and threw up and I climbed in the shower and Jeff came in and got into the shower and I said, 'Jeff, why do you have to do that? Why do you always have to hurt me? And he said, 'Because it felt so good.'

"He began to cry and he cried and cried and cried and begged me to forgive him. He told me that he loved me and there was no one in the world that he loved as much as me and he was sorry. I held him in my arms and told him that it was okay. When we went to bed, he curled up next to me and said, 'Mommy I'm afraid.' I said, 'It's okay. It's okay.' And we went to sleep."

A few minutes before ten o'clock, which would have been noon in Kansas City, Donna stopped outside Holbrook, Arizona, and called the pay phone in San Diego. She told Damon that she'd be in San Diego late that night. Damon told her to call that same number at midnight. Jeffrey had decided to send the children to her by putting them in a taxi, Damon said. Donna told him that everything was still okay.

BATF Agent Van Haelst watched Damon as he talked to his grandmother. Van Haelst had flown to California to supervise the arrest and he was sitting in an unmarked car across the street. Damon seemed nonchalant when he left the phone and started walking toward the motel. He didn't pay any attention to a woman who was jogging through the motel parking lot. She was an undercover agent, and when she saw Damon enter Room 29, she stepped into a telephone booth on the sidewalk directly in front of the motel and dialed a number that connected her with Van Haelst.

"He went into room twenty-nine," she said.

As she was speaking to Van Haelst, Jeffrey came out of the motel room and walked up to the pay phone next to the one that the undercover agent was using. He was calling Kathy.

Agent Van Haelst quickly asked the jogger if she could tell whether or not Jeffrey was armed.

"No!" she said, trying to hide her excitement.

Van Haelst decided to nab Jeffrey before he could get back into the motel and alert Damon and Alice. He ordered everyone to close in. Five agents raced up to the telephone booth and jerked Jeffrey outside. They shoved him onto the sidewalk where Van Haelst stuck his revolver next to Jeffrey's head and announced that he was under arrest.

Within seconds, another team of agents led by Agent Lanny Royer burst through the door of Room 29. "Mommy! Mommy!" Caleb yelled. Kristen screamed. An agent knocked Alice down on the bed and hurried past her to Damon, who was standing near the bathroom. He was shoved down on the floor. Another agent pointed his gun at Alice, "Move, bitch, and I'll blow your brains out!" They handcuffed Damon and dragged him onto the balcony. Alice was hustled out next. Inside, the agents found an AR-15 assault rifle, two .44 magnum revolvers that belonged to Damon and Jason, another pistol, and boxes of ammunition.

Just as Jeffrey was being put into the backseat of a car, he spotted Alice on the balcony.

"Good-bye, Alice!" he yelled.

Jeffrey, Alice, and Damon were taken to jail, strip-searched, fingerprinted, and issued white paper suits to wear. They were then taken to the BATF office where Van Haelst was waiting to question them.

At 6:50 P.M., Alice agreed to make a statement about the murders. She would later claim that Van Haelst had duped her into talking by threatening to send her children to a juvenile home if she didn't cooperate. He denied her accusation.

During the short videotaped confession, Alice told the agent that Jeffrey had killed the Averys. "The more Jeff learned," she said, "the more he felt he had authority to do things. The more knowledge he attained, the more he thought it made him"—Alice paused, searching for just the right word. Van Haelst offered her one.

"Divine?" he said.

Alice nodded.

Alice put all of the blame on Jeffrey. She said he honestly believed that he was doing what God had commanded him to do, and when Van Haelst asked her why she hadn't gone to the police, Alice said she was afraid that Jeffrey would kill her too.

After they finished, Van Haelst told Alice that Damon and Jeffrey wanted to speak to her. Damon came into the room first.

"It's going to be okay, Mom," he said. He kissed her cheek.

Jeffrey came in after Damon was gone. He bent down and looked at her. He told her that he loved her and that she should not lose faith in him. He was the last messenger. God would soon free him and he would free her. All she had to do was trust him, believe in him, not lose faith.

Jeffrey stood up to leave, and when he turned around, Alice noticed that the seam in the crotch of his jail-issued white paper overalls was torn. Jeffrey's naked buttock peeked through the tear. As she watched him walk away, Alice couldn't help herself. She suddenly began to laugh.

Chapter 53

ON the morning of January 4, while the bodies of the Avery family were being extracted in Kirtland, Keith Johnson telephoned Greg and Ron and urged them to turn themselves in. Keith would later claim that he had been told by agent Larry Scott that anyone who surrendered voluntarily *before* the bodies were exhumed would be given immunity from prosecution. But after the Averys were removed from the pit, there would be no deals made.

Greg's father, Gerald Winship, had already hired a well-known Kansas City criminal attorney, John P. O'Connor, to represent his son, so Greg quickly disregarded Keith's advice. Besides, what Keith said didn't make sense to Greg. What difference would it make if someone confessed before the bodies were taken from the grave?

Ron was not nearly as skeptical. He and Susie had spoken to an attorney and had been warned repeatedly not to make any statements. But both of them trusted Keith. More important, they thought that turning themselves in was the right thing to do. Ron had been praying about it.

What they would not discover until much later was that Keith himself was worried about being prosecuted. Keith had assumed when he first came forward that the BATF would automatically grant him immunity in return for his help. Much to his horror, Keith discovered that Lake County Prosecutor Steven LaTourette was the only official who could make such a deal. The only thing that Scott and Van Haelst could do was to lobby LaTourette on Keith's behalf, and they were going to do that only if he continued cooperating.

Regardless of Keith's prodding, chances are Ron and Susie would have surrendered and confessed anyway. They thought of themselves as being righteous, godly people. Society and its laws were not as important as God's commandments, and now that both of them realized they had been duped by Jeffrey, they wanted to clear their consciences. As children they had been taught that confession was the first step to receiving forgiveness. Shortly after 12:00 noon, Ron and Susie arrived at the BATF office in Kansas City ready to repent.

As required, Van Haelst explained Ron's constitutional rights under the Miranda decision and asked him to sign a waiver of those protections. At 1:22 P.M. Ron did, and Van Haelst and Larry Scott immediately began grilling him. After two hours, Ron agreed to confess before a video camera in the BATF conference room. Van Haelst and Scott quickly set up their gear. At the beginning of the tape, Van Haelst *twice* warned Ron that anything he was about to say could be used against him in court.

"We've not made any promises and no threats have been made against you—is that correct?" Van Haelst asked.

"Yes . . . this is completely voluntary," Ron said.

Van Haelst wanted to make certain that jurors understood Ron was not being misled. The agent knew that once Ron was formally charged, his attorney would try to keep the tape from being introduced as evidence.

During the next two hours, Ron gave a detailed account of Jeffrey's teachings and how he had convinced the group that the Averys were wicked and needed to be sacrificed. In a nasal monotone, between puffs on cigarettes, Ron candidly recounted his actions on the night of the murders and those of the other group members. Only once did he show any emotion. When he recalled how he had jabbed Dennis Avery with the electric stun gun, first in the hip, then in the neck, and finally in the chest, Ron's voice cracked.

"He [Dennis] was in a lot of pain," Ron said, looking down at the floor, fighting back tears.

"Take your time," said Van Haelst sympathetically.

Agent Scott leaned forward with some tissues.

Ron sat upright, as if he were offended. "Well," he said, quickly regaining his composure, "that's fine." He pushed the tissues out of the way and continued in his southern Missouri twang.

As soon as Ron finished, the two agents interviewed Susie Luff, who proved just as candid and equally composed. Until the two of them confessed, neither Van Haelst nor Scott had known exactly what had happened inside the barn on the night of the murders. Keith had told them what he thought had happened based on comments that Jeffrey and other group members had made after the killings. But Keith hadn't been at the farm when the murders took place. More important, Keith hadn't given them a clearheaded narrative. "The message that came through from Kansas City," LaTourette said later, "was that Keith Johnson was a knucklehead. . . . He couldn't tell the same story twice in the same way."

After interviewing the Luffs, Van Haelst telephoned LaTourette and told him that a copy of their video confessions would be delivered to his office by 10:00 A.M. the next day. In return, LaTourette sent Van Haelst warrants over a fax machine so that he could arrest Ron and Susie. That night, a SWAT team from Independence arrested Dennis and Tonya Patrick, and Debbie Olivarez. Hoping to avoid a similar spectacle, Sharon turned herself in to the police in Bay City, Michigan. By this time, Richard Brand's family had hired him an attorney, Charles Atwell. He and Greg's lawyer arranged for their clients to surrender the next day at the BATF office.

LaTourette slipped the Luff videotape into a player on January 5 when he received it and called in the top members of his staff to view it. What he saw sickened him. "What always bothered me about Luff and the others who eventually confessed and made videotapes was their total lack of emotion," LaTourette said later. "They would become real teary-eyed and boohoo when they talked about how Jeff had pimped them and led them down the path, but there was no show of emotion when they talked about killing these little kids."

A few hours later, LaTourette showed the Luffs' confessions to a grand jury meeting in the Lake County Courthouse located in Painesville, the county seat, about twelve miles east of Kirtland. The jury immediately issued indictments charging Jeffrey, Ron, Greg, Richard, Damon, and Danny with aggravated murder, punishable by death in Ohio's electric chair. Because Dennis Patrick hadn't taken part in the actual killings, he was charged with complicity to commit aggravated murder, the same charge levied against Alice, Susie, Tonya, Debbie, Sharon, and Kathy. That charge carried a penalty of up to life in prison. LaTourette had planned on indicting Keith Johnson on a complicity charge, but Van Haelst urged him to grant Keith immunity because of his help. LaTourette resisted at first, but finally agreed. It was the first of several controversial decisions that the young prosecutor would make.

LaTourette had been the prosecutor in Lake County for only fourteen months when the bodies of the Averys were discovered. But he had already earned a reputation as a tough and shrewd courtroom fighter. Born and reared in Cleveland Heights, one of Cleveland's more posh neighborhoods, La-Tourette had grown up in a rock-solid Republican family where politics dominated afterdinner conversations and being a member of the high school debate squad was more prized than being a star athlete. When LaTourette was just a toddler, his grandmother had taken him with her to deliver campaign literature for a Republican congressional candidate. He would later remember how he had walked up and down his neighborhood in 1960 pulling his red wagon filled with pamphlets for Richard Nixon's ill-fated race against John Kennedy. Politics came naturally. After high school graduation, LaTourette followed his girlfriend, much to his parents' dismay, to the University of Michigan. She was Jewish; he was Methodist. But the romance eventually faded, and after he graduated in 1976, LaTourette returned to Cleveland where he got a job as a shipping clerk and attended law school at night, earning his degree from Cleveland Marshall College of Law in 1979. LaTourette had worked briefly for a prestigious Cleveland firm, but he found civil law tedious, and in 1980, he joined the Lake County Public Defender's Office in Painesville at an annual salary of a mere $13,000 per year. He was hired by its chief attorney, R. Paul LaPlante, who quickly became LaTourette's mentor and close personal friend.

At the time, the office was a struggling, shoestring operation. Funded with just enough taxpayers' money to make do, the public defenders service got all of the cases that no one else wanted. "Our clients were the pains in the asses of the court system," LaTourette recalled: the four-time losers, the poor, and the rapists, child molesters, and murderers that private attorneys refused to represent. When his grandmother asked how LaTourette could represent such "scumballs," her grandson proudly declared that everyone was entitled to a fair trial. His stint as LaPlante's right-hand man was LaTourette's walk on the wild side. On Sunday mornings, he and the other underpaid public defenders would play softball and then pile into the 'blue eagle,' LaTourette's gigantic 1977 Chrysler Newport, and drive to Fitzpatrick's, a Cleveland bar, where they would thumb their noses at the establishment over mugs of cheap beer.

In 1982, LaTourette got married, resigned as a public defender, and took a job in a private firm in Painesville. Still, civil law bored him, so in 1984, he ran as a Republican in an overwhelmingly Democratic district for the job of Lake County prosecutor. LaTourette lost by 15,000 votes out of the 47,000 that were cast. The local newspapers characterized it as a dismal effort, but LaTourette was amazed that he had collected 16,000 votes, considering that he had campaigned with only a handful of volunteers and $5,000 of his own money. During the next four years, LaTourette unmercifully hammered the incumbent in letters to the editor and worked at building alliances with the county's few Republicans. When the prosecutor's office mistakenly let an accused murderer go free, LaTourette publicized the blunder on billboards that proclaimed criminals were "getting away with murder" in Lake County. Although he was still considered an underdog in the 1988 race, LaTourette waged a fierce campaign by attacking the prosecutor for plea-bargaining cases rather than taking them to trial. On weekends, LaTourette stuffed campaign brochures into mailboxes and went door to door soliciting votes. To everyone's surprise but his own, LaTourette won the $70,000-per-year prosecutor's post by a 4,400 vote margin.

From the moment the Averys' bodies were unearthed, LaTourette understood that his political future hinged on how well he prosecuted Jeffrey and his followers. LaTourette also knew that Jeffrey's case was so controversial that he would be represented by the Lake County Public Defender's Office, and that meant LaTourette would be facing his former boss, teacher, and friend, Paul LaPlante, in the courtroom.

At age forty-seven, Paul LaPlante was a bone-thin, white-bearded, scholarly man, who favored logic to courtroom hysterics. Born in rural Ontario, LaPlante had been rebellious as a teenager. "I didn't get along with authority figures," he recalled. Some said he still didn't. As a teenager, he dropped out of high school, married, and supported himself by working as a meter reader. LaPlante soon realized that he was in a dead-end job, so he earned his high school diploma and went on to college. By 1966, LaPlante was working as a salesman for a Cleveland-based wire and copper company. Without any real reason, he decided to attend law school at night at Cleveland Marshall, the same college that Steven LaTourette would eventually attend.

It was there that LaPlante first was introduced to the U.S. Constitution and Bill of Rights, and he became fascinated by the delicate balance between the state and each individual's civil liberties. Before he could practice law in the United States, LaPlante was told that he had to renounce his Canadian citizenship, a move that the thirty-year-old thought unfair. "Once again, it made me look hard at what rights an individual in our society should have." Despite his liberal bent, LaPlante joined the Lake County Prosecutor's Office in 1973. One of his first big trials was the prosecution of two men who had murdered a gas-station attendant during a late-night robbery. LaPlante asked for the death penalty and got it. That case was one of the last successful death-penalty trials in Lake County.

Although he was an effective prosecutor, LaPlante felt uncomfortable in the role. When the county opened the Public Defender's Office in 1979, he moved to the other side of the legal street by becoming its leading defense attorney. "I quickly discovered that most of my clients were guilty," said LaPlante, "but the question was 'Has the state done its job—can it prove that they are guilty?' " Over the years, LaPlante had become convinced that the role of his office was not to get criminals set free, but to protect the individual rights of "the guilty *and* the innocent," so that no matter what they were accused of, each defendant got a fair trial.

The morning after Jeffrey was arrested, LaPlante was on the telephone conferring with a public defender in San Diego about Jeffrey's case.

Three days later, on January 10, San Diego Sheriff's Deputy Jimmy Sims spotted Jeffrey's blue Nissan truck with Missouri license tags speeding down state highway 79 about forty miles northeast of San Diego. Sims motioned the truck over to the side of the road and arrested its occupants: Kathy Johnson and Danny Kraft, Jr., who each claimed to be someone else. They had been living in a tent in the mountain community of Santa Ysabel. After Jeffrey's arrest, neither had known where to go. Kathy and Danny were taken to the same San Diego County jail where Jeffrey, Damon, and Alice were being housed.

A short time later, Paul LaPlante arrived at the San Diego jail with his chief assistant, Charles R. Grieshammer. They had come to meet their new client. "Jeffrey was clearly very intelligent and very sincere in his religious convictions," LaPlante recalled. During their first meeting that day, LaPlante didn't mention the murders. LaPlante was used to his clients' claiming they were innocent. He wanted Jeffrey to get to know him before they discussed the killings. He figured Jeffrey was more likely to tell the truth that way. The next morning, when LaPlante brought up the Averys, Jeffrey candidly admitted killing them. But he insisted that God had ordered him to do it. As they talked, LaPlante realized that if Jeffrey was asked in court about the murders, he would, as Jeffrey put it, "not deny what God had ordered me to do."

LaPlante and Grieshammer returned to Ohio convinced that their client was going to be found guilty. But that didn't mean that Jeffrey had to be sentenced to death. In Ohio, defendants facing the death penalty automatically received a two-stage trial. In the first, jurors decided whether or not the defendant was guilty. In the second, those same jurors decided whether the defendant deserved to be executed or, because of "mitigating" circumstances, should be granted mercy and receive a sentence of life in prison without parole. "We decided to focus all of our energies on the mitigating phase of the trial," said LaPlante. "There was no question Jeffrey would be found guilty of killing the Averys."

While LaPlante was returning from San Diego, his courtroom opponent, Steven LaTourette, was deciding how to prosecute the thirteen "cult cases." LaTourette concluded early on that he needed someone from Jeffrey's group to testify against the others. "I needed an eyewitness who had actually been in the barn during the killing." His first thought was Ron Luff. Obviously, Ron knew what had happened. But LaTourette was reluctant to negotiate a plea bargain with Ron for several reasons. In effect, Ron had already hanged himself with his videotaped confession. It would make more sense to offer some other follower a deal, especially one who might be difficult to convict otherwise. Ron also didn't have an attorney representing him and LaTourette didn't want to negotiate directly with a defendant. Finally, LaTourette had been genuinely repulsed by Ron's demeanor during his confession. The prosecutor couldn't get the image out of his mind of Karen Avery's foot falling when her corpse was lifted from the grave. Nor could he forget that it had been Ron Luff who had given Karen a piggyback ride to the barn on that night so that she could be murdered.

LaTourette's need for an eyewitness was quickly solved. Two days after their clients surrendered, attorneys representing Greg and Richard independently telephoned LaTourette and told him that their clients were willing to negotiate. "The first guy to the courthouse door always does better with a plea bargain than anyone else," LaTourette recalled, "and these attorneys knew that." Both lawyers had been former prosecutors, LaTourette said, and they understood that their clients were not going to get off lightly. "They understood that their clients were going to have to plead guilty to substantial charges to avoid the death penalty."

LaTourette decided to interview both Greg and Richard personally before deciding which one would make the better witness. He flew to Kansas City and met Richard first. "He was clearly still under Jeffrey's spell. He was starting to come out of it, but he really thought that Jeffrey was capable of simply walking through the jailhouse walls and coming after him." During their conversation, Richard told LaTourette that even if Jeffrey was convicted, he still might seek revenge. "Richard said his biggest fear was that we would strap Jeffrey into the electric chair and throw the switch and nothing would happen. He was afraid Jeffrey would just stand up."

LaTourette met Greg Winship on January 19. He found Greg ill with a 104-degree temperature. "Greg was convinced that Jeffrey had caused the fever because he knew that we were talking that day."

During the next few days, LaTourette flipflopped over whether to use Richard or Greg. "Both said they would testify against each other, but they made it clear that they really would rather not, and I would not get their best testimony if they did."

LaTourette decided to cut deals with both. "Winship was emotional. He cried through the whole interview. Brand was matter-of-fact; he laid it all out. Together they made a strong team."

Richard Brand agreed to plead guilty to murder and Greg promised to plead guilty to complicity to murder. Both charges carried prison terms of fifteen years to life. Of the two charges, Richard's was the more serious. This was because he had carried the Averys into the pit, while Greg had not directly been involved in the actual killing, but rather had been outside the barn operating the chain saw.

Now that LaTourette had two eyewitnesses, he felt confident that he had sufficient proof to convict all of the other men: Jeffrey, Damon, Danny, Ron, and Dennis. He now turned his attention to the women.

In February, LaTourette got a telephone call from one of the attorneys appointed to represent Alice. She was willing to plea-bargain. She was angry at Jeffrey.

After her arrest, Alice had refused extradition from California to Ohio. So had Jeffrey and Damon. Christ hadn't helped his accusers prosecute him and Jeffrey wasn't going to make things easy for LaTourette. But Alice had changed her mind and returned to Ohio on January 20, because of Kathy. Alice had suspected that Jeffrey had been hiding Kathy in San Diego, but until she was arrested, Alice hadn't been certain. She was enraged when Kathy was brought into her cellblock. "She kept coming to my cell trying to speak to me," Alice said later. "I would close the door and she would press her face up to the glass and say, 'I love you, Alice.' The bitch!"

An inmate approached Alice a few days after Kathy arrived. "Did you know she's pregnant? She's carrying your husband's baby?" the inmate asked.

Alice ran into her cell and began to cry. A few hours later, she told her attorney that she would waive extradition. She couldn't stand being in the same jail as Kathy.

"Alice wanted a deal in the worst way," LaTourette said, "But I wasn't sure that was a good idea." Based on his interviews with Richard and Greg, LaTourette had become convinced that Alice had played a crucial role in the murders even though she hadn't participated in the actual killing. "I came to believe that Jeffrey, all by himself, couldn't have gotten the others to commit the murders. Alice knew that he had never had a job, that he had committed adultery, that he was stealing from people, that he was lazy as dirt, basically. And for her to all of a sudden say, 'Hey, I've been married to this asshole for nineteen years and now he is a prophet of God'—for her to be his cheerleader and convince everybody that he was a prophet and to chastise them and so forth—was wrong."

Just the same, LaTourette knew that his case against Alice was flimsy. "She wasn't at the farm when the murders took place and I knew jurors might have a problem with that." LaTourette decided that it would be better to negotiate a deal with Alice that required her to serve time in prison than to bring her case to trial and lose.

After meetings with Alice's court-appointed attorneys, Mark

A. Ziccarelli and Joseph Gibson, a deal was struck. In return for LaTourette's reducing the charges against Alice, she would plead guilty to a charge that carried a maximum sentence of fifteen to fifty years, making her eligible for parole in as few as five years compared to a life sentence. Everyone involved seemed satisfied, except for the one court official who mattered most. All of the charges against Jeffrey and his followers had been filed in the Lake County Common Pleas Court, where they had been divided among three judges, each an elected official. Alice's case had been put on judge Paul H. Mitrovich's docket. A no-nonsense, often blunt, and stern former prosecutor, Mitrovich was considered to be the harshest judge on the Lake County bench. Behind his back, he was referred to as "Maximum Mitrovich" because of his tendency to impose the maximum prison terms possible.

Cutting a deal with Alice was politically risky for LaTourette and Mitrovich. The 250,000 residents of Lake County had been deluged with sensational stories about Jeffrey and his cult, and if letters to the editor printed in local newspapers and the callers who jammed the switchboards of local radio talk shows were any indication, the 16,500 residents of Painesville were eager for blood.

After some deliberation, Judge Mitrovich nixed Alice's plea bargain. She was going to be held accountable in a public courtroom for her actions. The public demanded it.

Once Mitrovich rejected Alice's deal, LaTourette quickly turned his attention back to finding a woman in the group who could testify against the others. By chance, Sharon Bluntschly was the first group member scheduled for trial. Her case was scheduled to start in May. LaTourette knew that she was valuable and vulnerable. She had been the first woman to join Jeffrey's group. She was also still in love with Richard, even though he made it clear to prosecutors that he despised her. Only a few months earlier, Sharon had given birth to Richard's daughter. Obviously, Richard would be the state's main witness against her and that would be emotionally difficult for Sharon. As her trial date got closer, Sharon's attorney negotiated a plea bargain with LaTourette. In return for her cooperation, the prosecutor agreed to drop ten of the fifteen charges against her. She would plead guilty to five counts of conspiracy to murder, a charge that carried a sentence of five years.

Debbie Olivarez was in the Lake County jail when she heard about Sharon's plea-bargain deal. Debbie was irritated. She didn't think it was fair that Sharon was going to get special treatment. Debbie had her attorney contact LaTourette. She'd testify for the prosecution if he gave her a deal identical to Sharon's. LaTourette agreed. A short time later, Dennis and Tonya Patrick also agreed to cooperate in return for reduced charges.

By the end of spring, LaTourette had negotiated deals with six of the group members. The only ones left were Jeffrey, Alice, Damon, Danny, Kathy, and the Luffs. As far as the public was concerned, Jeffrey, Alice, and Damon were the most important cases.

"I wanted to bring Jeffrey to trial first," LaTourette said. "There was tremendous pressure being applied by the community that I was beginning to feel. There was a feeling of 'Okay, you made these plea-bargain deals, now let's see if they were worth it.' The public was demanding that someone pay for this horrible crime—that justice be done."

No crime in Lake County's history had sparked as much revulsion as the Averys' deaths. Unlike the bedroom communities that sprouted along the shores of Lake Erie east of Cleveland during the 1960s, Painesville was an established town with a strong sense of community pride. It was one of the first settlements in northern Ohio, dating back to 1800 when General Edward Paine and his sons bought one thousand acres and led sixty-six settlers from Connecticut into the area. By 1832, it was one of the few towns with its own newspaper, *The Painesville Telegraph*, founded by Eber Howe, a crusading editor who was later credited with coining the word *bogus* to describe the activities of a group of counterfeiters who operated there briefly before being caught and severely punished. When Joseph Smith, Jr., arrived in nearby Kirtland, Howe became his most vocal critic. In 1834, Howe wrote a book entitled *Mormanism Unvailed* [sic], considered by many to be the first exposé of the new religion, and when Smith was forced to flee, Howe cheered. Although Painesville had mellowed over the years, it remained a tough, largely blue-collar community where criminals were dealt with sternly.

Public Defender Paul LaPlante was well aware of the local feeling in the community and the building pressure to bring Jeffrey to trial. He also knew that his staff of seven employees was no match for LaTourette's office with its seventeen lawyers and twenty-four support personnel. Hoping to better the odds, LaPlante called in reinforcements from the Ohio Public Defender Commission, the better-financed state version of his county office. It immediately dispatched four investigators to help LaPlante. "I had decided that we needed to find out everything that we could about Jeffrey," said LaPlante. The investigators began searching for a sign of physical or mental abuse in Jeffrey's past that would win sympathy from jurors. Besides probing Jeffrey's past, LaPlante had two criminal psychologists evaluate him. Both told LaPlante what he already knew. While Jeffrey suffered from a severe personality disorder, he was not insane, at least not by Ohio's criminal standards. There was no way that LaPlante could mount a "not guilty because of insanity" defense.

Under Ohio's speedy-trial act, all defendants must be tried within ninety days unless they request a delay. LaPlante assumed that Judge Martin O. Parks, who had been assigned the case, would automatically grant him a series of continuances. He was wrong. Parks had a full docket and he saw no need to drag out Jeffrey's trial. He scheduled it for June. LaPlante strenuously protested, so Parks agreed to delay it until July. But that was it. LaPlante was unhappy, but he felt he could meet the July deadline.

And then in May, LaTourette's office completely disrupted LaPlante's schedule. Karen Kowall, an assistant prosecutor, convinced LaTourette that he could undermine LaPlante's defense by demanding copies of all the investigative reports that LaPlante had received from the Ohio Public Defender Commission. Kowall shrewdly pointed out that the commission was financed by tax dollars and therefore fell under the state's "sunshine laws," which required public agencies to make their records available to the public on demand. In effect, Kowall's scheme would force the commission to release all of the background material on Jeffrey that its investigators had compiled for LaPlante. LaTourette demanded the documents, catching LaPlante completely off guard.

The move outraged LaPlante and the director of the state commission. Both claimed that the investigators' reports were protected by lawyer-client privilege. But LaTourette refused to back down and filed a writ before the Ohio Supreme Court demanding that the commission produce its confidential records.

As soon as LaTourette filed the writ, the four investigators working for LaPlante immediately stopped helping him. They were afraid that they might be forced to turn over their reports. "We were left with absolutely no one to help us," LaPlante complained later. "Everything we were doing came to a complete halt."

Three weeks before the trial, LaTourette dropped his request, but by then the damage had been done.

On July 12, LaPlante and LaTourette reported to Judge Parks's courtroom to review how jurors would be selected the next day for Jeffrey's trial. When the judge entered the chamber, LaPlante stood to be recognized. Once again, he asked Parks for a continuance. Once again, the judge denied it.

"Your Honor," LaPlante calmly replied, "I will not participate any further in this case. Regardless of how anyone may perceive Jeffrey Lundgren, he is entitled to be cared about, he is entitled to have the best defense possible, he is entitled to have the best preparation and vigorous presentation of the case. . . ."

In effect, LaPlante was backing Judge Parks into a corner. The defense attorney felt his client's rights were being trampled. He wasn't going to stand for it. The judge had to either grant the continuance or find a way to force LaPlante to do his job. Parks adjourned court. When he reconvened it later that afternoon, he found LaPlante guilty of contempt of court and sentenced him to ten days in jail. He then suspended all but eight hours of LaPlante's sentence and announced that Jeffrey's trial would be postponed until August 13 so that LaPlante could have more time to get ready.

While LaPlante's gutsy stand had won the defense more time, the continuance proved to be the worst possible move for Alice. Her trial was scheduled to begin one week after Jeffrey's. Now the spotlight shifted onto Alice. She would be the first group member to actually go to trial. With emotions running high inside and outside the courtroom, Alice's case gained a new prominence. LaTourette, who only a few weeks earlier had been criticized in the Cleveland *Plain Dealer* for the plea bargains that he had struck, was being forced to put his weakest case on first. The young prosecutor knew that he had to win Alice's case or his political career would be seriously weakened.

Alice's trial was to become the most sensational in Lake County history. What no one knew at the time was that it was also going to become one of the most vicious and melodramatic.

Chapter 54

JUSTICE in Lake County is dispensed in a red-brick and stone courthouse built in the 1840s directly across the street from the Painesville town square. There is a clock in the courthouse tower and on top of it is a large metal dome. A cupola rises from the dome and at its peak there is a statue of a gold-plated eagle with outstretched wings. Two quotations had been carved into the courthouse's front facade. THE RIGHT TO A FREE GOVERNMENT PRESUPPOSES THE DUTY OF EVERY CITIZEN TO OBEY THAT GOVERNMENT, says one. THAT REGARD BE HAD FOR THE PUBLIC WELFARE IS THE HIGHEST LAW, says the other.

On the morning of July 25, the first day of Alice's trial, dew still clung to the dark-green grass in the town square. The iron-and-wood park benches were damp to the touch. Two squirrels chased one another across an empty whitewashed gazebo before scampering up an ancient oak. In one corner of the park, a stone monument honored the militia, men who had volunteered to fight "the Rebs" in the Civil War. A brass plaque nearby explained that Abraham Lincoln had passed through the

Painesville rail station twice. The first time the train carried him to his presidential inauguration; the second time it carried his body in a coffin back to Illinois. No one had ever been tried before in Lake County as an accomplice to mass murder.

Prosecutor LaTourette had decided early on that his main job would be prosecuting Jeffrey, so he had intentionally appointed two women to present the state's case against Alice. He had selected Karen Lawson and Sandra Dray, in part because he thought they could, in his words, "outbitch" her. Both women were tough-talking, hard-driving, bleached blondes who had specialized in prosecuting men accused of sexually abusing women and children. Weeks before the trial, Alice's attorneys, Mark Ziccarelli and Joe Gibson, announced that their client was a battered wife who had been emotionally and physically abused. In an ironic twist, Lawson and Dray, who usually championed the cause of abused women, now found themselves on the attack.

The first legal skirmish came when Ziccarelli and Gibson asked the judge in a pretrial motion for permission to use "battered women's syndrome" as part of Alice's defense. Only a few months earlier, the Ohio Supreme Court had ruled that women accused of killing their husbands could cite long-term physical abuse by their spouses as a legitimate defense. If a woman could prove that she had killed her husband during a moment of fear and in self-defense, then she could be found innocent of murder. Although Alice had not killed Jeffrey, her attorneys claimed that he had emotionally abused her for so many years that Alice had been incapable of stopping Jeffrey from murdering the Averys. They asked Judge Mitrovich for permission to bring in experts who could testify about the effects of long-term physical abuse. "There is sufficient evidence surrounding the circumstances of this case to indicate that the defendant believed herself to be in imminent danger of death or great bodily harm," Ziccarelli told reporters, "should she not submit to the demands of her overbearing, insistent, and often violent husband. . . . She was suffering from battered women's syndrome." Alice was a victim, the attorneys argued, just like the Averys.

The prosecutor's office objected to the request. In their court brief, Lawson and Dray argued that Ohio law permitted "battered women's syndrome" to be used by defense attorneys only when a woman was accused of murdering her husband, not when her husband was on trial for killing a third party.

Judge Mitrovich agreed. He denied Alice's request for expert witnesses, but told her attorneys that he would permit them to introduce a limited amount of testimony about how Jeffrey had treated Alice during their marriage.

From the start, Alice's trial was explosive. One of the first witnesses called by Lawson and Dray described the exhumation of the Averys' bodies in such horrendous detail that Alice's attorney jumped to his feet in objection. They accused the prosecution of trying to inflame the jury. Seconds after that exchange, Lawson and Dray introduced photographs taken during the autopsies. One photograph showed Cheryl Avery's face, which was amazingly well-preserved, in part because of the duct tape that had covered it. Her mouth was frozen in what seemed to be a scream. The photograph was so horrible that Mitrovich ruled that it was too grisly to be shown to the jury. The prosecution's next witness methodically showed jurors each article of clothing that had been removed from the corpses. As soon as the first plastic bag was opened and a garment was removed, a stench permeated the room. The odor was so repulsive that Lawson held a tissue filled with Vicks VapoRub against her nose.

In contrast to such graphic testimony, Dray and Lawson called a friend of Cheryl's, who described the Averys in loving terms. "We wanted to make certain," LaTourette later said, "that the jurors realized that five human beings had been destroyed. We wanted them to see them as people, not just faceless victims."

On the second day of Alice's trial, Lawson and Dray began introducing evidence about Alice and her role as "mother" of the group. Debbie Olivarez was that day's star witness. She recalled how Alice frequently chastised Jeffrey's followers, how she was his personal spy, how she constantly pushed the idea that Jeffrey was a prophet. "Alice was," Debbie testified, "Jeff's right-hand man in a lot of things. She was his confidante. . . . She would clarify things for Jeff. . . ." It would have been impossible for Alice not to have known about the murders, Debbie said. She recalled how Jeffrey had talked about the best way to kill the Averys and how Alice had suggested that they find out whether Becky had started menstruation so Jeffrey would know whether to rip her guts open or bash her head against a wall. Debbie recounted how Alice had hurriedly left the farm on April 17 after eating dinner with the Averys before the murders. She had taken Jason, Kristen, and Caleb with her to buy picnic tables, Debbie said, but had called the farm before coming home to ask if "the company was gone." Debbie had talked to Alice on the telephone that night and she said that Alice knew exactly what was happening in the barn.

"Who, if anyone," Lawson asked Debbie, "could have prevented the murders?"

"Alice," Debbie replied, looking directly at her, "could have."

Alice grabbed her mouth and announced that she was ill. Mitrovich recessed court.

On the third day of testimony, Sharon Bluntschly told jurors that Alice was lazy and expected to be "treated like a queen" by the group. On the day that the Averys were murdered, Alice was almost gleeful, she said. "Tonight's the night for the Averys," Sharon quoted Alice as saying.

The prosecution felt jurors had heard enough. Dray and Lawson rested their case.

The defense's main witness was Alice. Looking frail and weighing barely 100 pounds, some 120 pounds less than when she had been arrested only six months earlier, Alice testified for four hours. She told jurors that Jeffrey had lied to her repeatedly during their nineteen-year marriage. She talked about his sexual affair when he worked at the Lake of the Ozarks Hospital and told how he had pushed her so hard that her spleen had ruptured. "I was afraid of Jeff," she said, "because I knew he had the potential to be very violent. But I also was very much in love with him." But Alice did not go into great detail about her marriage and she mentioned nothing at all about her sexual experiences with Jeffrey. She had been too embarrassed to reveal the details of sex life with Jeffrey to her two male attorneys, she later said. She wasn't certain that anyone would believe her.

When Jeffrey first mentioned killing ten of his followers, Alice said she had confronted him.

ALICE: I went to him and I said, "Are you really saying that you're going to kill people?" And he said, "No, no, no, this is just a test of faith. I'm not going to do anything, don't worry about it." He said, "This is an Abraham and Isaac situation."

QUESTION: What do you mean by Abraham and Isaac situation?

ALICE: Abraham was a prophet who was commanded to sacrifice his only son. He took his son up on the altar and was going to sacrifice him, and at the last moment the Lord said, "You don't have to sacrifice him." That's what Jeff was telling me. Nothing was going to happen. This was just a test of faith like Abraham's faith had been tested . . .

QUESTION: And at that time did you believe that Jeffrey would kill ten people?

ALICE: No, I didn't think he would kill anybody.

The fact that Jeffrey had decided to spare the lives of Dennis, Tonya, Molly, Richard, and Sharon further convinced her, Alice testified, that Jeffrey wasn't serious about killing the Averys.

When asked by her attorney to explain why she had left the farm on April 17 after eating dinner with the Averys, Alice insisted that she had simply gone to run an errand. She had called the farm later that night—not because she was afraid to come home until after the murders were done as Debbie implied—but because she wanted to see if Jeffrey needed her to bring him anything from town. She was completely unaware, she testified, that Jeffrey was actually going to murder the family. Alice's attorneys were happy with her testimony. They felt that she had made a good impression. As soon as they finished their gentle questioning, prosecutor Dray was on her feet. "Mrs. Lundgren," she declared, "you're a liar!"

If Alice had been terrified of Jeffrey, why hadn't she turned him in on April 18 when FBI agents and Chief Yarborough arrived at the farm to ask about the temple takeover? If Alice was a battered wife, as she claimed, then why did Sharon and Debbie testify that they had never seen Jeffrey physically abuse

Alice, but they had seen Alice hit, scratch, kick, and punch him? Finally, Dray asked, how was it possible that Alice was the only adult at the farm on the night of April 17 who didn't know what was going to happen after the Avery family finished their "last supper"?

> **DRAY:** Yes or no, nobody told you?
>
> **ALICE:** No one told me.
>
> **DRAY:** Nobody told the group's "mother" on April seventeenth, "Holy schmoly, mom, do you know what dad's planning to do tonight?" Nobody told you that, right?
>
> **ALICE:** No, nobody told me . . .
>
> **DRAY:** Let me run through this again. Richard Brand, Sharon Bluntschly, Deborah Olivarez, Greg Winship, Susie and Ron Luff . . . Of the people who were there when the Averys came to eat dinner at your table, everybody knew it was going to be their last supper but you. Is that what you're telling us?
>
> **ALICE:** (no response)
>
> **DRAY:** Yes or no?
>
> **ALICE:** Yes, everyone knew but me.

Mocking Alice, Dray began duck-walking toward the courtroom door, shouting her next question over her shoulder.

> **DRAY:** And so after dinner when you left to go to the Makro Department Store, you said, "I'm just going to Makro. I'm just going to buy picnic tables. I'll see you in a little while." Is that right?
>
> **ALICE:** Yes.

In his closing arguments to the jury, defense attorney Gibson reminded jurors that Alice hadn't been at the farm when the murders took place. He claimed that Alice had been mentally and emotionally abused by Jeffrey to the point where she was his pawn. "I didn't know Hitler, but I think Jeffrey was right up next to him," he said.

Prosecutor Lawson picked up on that theme when it was her turn to speak. If Jeffrey resembled Hitler, she told jurors, then Alice mirrored Josef Mengele, the notorious "angel of death" at the Nazi concentration camp of Auschwitz. "She was just as cold and calculating and wacko as her husband," Lawson charged.

The seven women and five men on the jury deliberated two days. Alice felt that was a good sign. She hoped that they were deadlocked. But on August 1, when the jury reached a verdict and filed into Judge Mitrovich's courtroom, Alice's hopes were quickly destroyed. The jurors found Alice guilty of all fifteen charges filed against her. Not only did the jury decide that Alice had "conspired" to commit aggravated murder, they also found her guilty of "complicity." Conspiracy meant that Alice had agreed with others to kill the Averys. Complicity meant that she had actively helped commit the murders even though she wasn't at the farm. The final five counts filed against Alice were for kidnapping. Alice's actions, the jury said, had deprived the Averys of their freedom to leave the farm on April 17 by use of deception. Dray and Lawson had won a complete victory. They hugged each other and cried when the verdict was read. Alice remained stone-faced.

In a last-ditch attempt to help their client, Alice's attorneys offered Judge Mitrovich a psychological evaluation of Alice before sentencing that said "Alice's involvement in criminal behavior was entirely secondary to her subservience to her husband." But Mitrovich was unmoved. On August 29, he sentenced Alice to the maximum prison term possible, a total of 150 years. She would not be eligible for parole until she served 115 years of the sentence.

"Good luck," he told her.

As Alice was being taken out of the courtroom, she suddenly stopped in the hallway and was quickly mobbed by reporters and television crews. During the next ten minutes, she read a statement that she had written the night before.

"My name is Alice Elizabeth Lundgren," she said. "I am not Josef Mengele and I am not the angel of death." Alice insisted that she was innocent and she lambasted Judge Mitrovich for not permitting her attorneys to call expert witnesses who could describe battered women's syndrome. "This whole process has not been so much about law or justice or truth," she said, "it has been about political fame and fortune. . . ." She accused LaTourette of cutting deals in order to get "the bigger fish—

plea bargains that will allow for the women, who last had the opportunity to save the lives of Cheryl, Trina, Becky, and Karen, to serve very little prison time if any for saving themselves rather than the children." Alice's most heated criticism, however, was directed at Dray and Lawson. "The departure of accepted courtroom decorum displayed by the prosecutor as she screamed and shouted in my face: 'Holy schmoly, mom!' or 'Mrs. Lundgren, you are a liar' gave the jury a perfect example of a woman realizing that she had only exchanged batterers. . . . No matter how much pain or destruction or peril that has filled my life—no matter how tragic the deaths of Dennis, Cheryl, Trina, Becky, and Karen—that was not, nor ever could it be reason for me to accept the prosecutors's suggestion that 'Alice should have blown Jeff's brains out' as was offered in the closing remarks by the prosecutor. I find it ironic that the suggestion of aggravated murder was offered as an acceptable course of action to have prevented aggravated murder. That would have made me equal to Jeff Lundgren which can never be because I am not a cold-blooded murderer—*he is*."

Alice broke down once while reading the statement when she mentioned Karen Avery. But she quickly regained her composure, and when she came to the end of her text, she smiled and said, "My life has taken on a whole new definition over the past several months. In a very real sense, I have known more freedom within the walls of the Lake County jail than I have known for years. . . . The correctional officers . . . have treated me with fairness and human dignity, which is a new and refreshing experience as compared to the dynamics of the group that I came out of."

As soon as she finished, deputies hurried her to jail.

During the next few days, reporters questioned jurors about their verdict and "Maximum" Mitrovich's sentence. They learned that the deciding factor in the jury verdict was not the judge's actions, the prosecutors' verbal attacks, or even the witnesses' descriptions. The jury had convicted Alice because of Alice's own words.

Alice had insisted that she hadn't known Jeffrey planned to kill the Averys on April 17. Yet after Alice was arrested in San Diego on January 7, she had made a statement to agent Van

Haelst during her thirty-eight-minute videotaped conversation that had come back to haunt her. The complete video was shown during her trial, and it was Alice's own voice, her own words, reverberating inside the darkened courtroom that jurors later said convinced them that she was a liar.

"Did you know why the Averys were coming to the farm that night?" Van Haelst had asked.

"I suspected that it was the sacrifice," Alice had replied.

"Had he talked to you about that?"

"Not—Yes and no. It was like—not directly, but indirectly."

And then Alice had said the words that few in the courtroom would ever forget.

"You had to be stupid not to know what he was up to."

Chapter 55

STEVEN LaTourette had been halfway through Scott Turow's novel *Presumed Innocent* when the bodies of the Averys were discovered, and on August 23, LaTourette followed the advice of his fictional counterpart Rusty Sabich, who explained in the opening pages that all successful prosecutors looked a defendant directly in the eye when accusing them of a crime. During his opening statement to the jury in the case of *State of Ohio* v. *Jeffrey D. Lundgren*, LaTourette pointed his finger at Jeffrey's face and called him a con man and murderer. Jeffrey flinched, looked away, and avoided eye contact with LaTourette during the rest of the trial.

"The evidence in this case will reflect," LaTourette declared, "that during the spring of 1989, in or near Davis, West Virginia, Jeffrey Don Lundgren turned to a woman by the name of Deborah Sue Olivarez . . . and said, 'You know, death stinks, but I guess I will have to get used to it.'

"The evidence in this case, ladies and gentlemen," LaTourette continued, "will bring home the smell of death. . . . Unfortunately, it will bring it within the four walls of this courtroom."

For forty minutes, LaTourette dramatically explained how Jeffrey, "through a series of sideshow and medicine-show miracles and tortured scripture, set up schemes and manipulated good, God-fearing people in a way that would have made Jim and Tammy Faye Bakker swell with pride.

"Over time, he conned these people into supporting him and his family financially," LaTourette thundered, "into permitting him to act out his sexual fantasies, and ultimately in participating with him in the death of five people."

LaTourette's oratory, which his fellow attorneys and local reporters later described as the best that they had ever heard him deliver, was followed by a flat, three-minute response by assistant public defender Charles Grieshammer. Yet it was Grieshammer's brief comment that led the five o'clock newscasts that night.

"Jeffrey Lundgren did shoot and kill Dennis, Cheryl, Trina, Rebecca, and Karen Avery," Grieshammer said, declaring his client's guilt before the prosecution had called even a single witness. "We're not going to dispute that."

It had been Paul LaPlante who had decided to tell the jurors upfront that Jeffrey was a killer. "We weren't going to insult anyone's intelligence by pretending that Jeffrey wasn't guilty," he later said. LaPlante's plan was to hurry through the first stage of the murder trial. He had seen how Dray and Lawson had sensationalized the Averys' deaths in Alice's case, and he hoped to avoid the grisly details of the murders. Instead of focusing on the Averys, LaPlante wanted jurors to pay attention to Jeffrey. During the second phase of the trial, LaPlante hoped to convince the jury that Jeffrey had been emotionally abused as a child to the extent that he deserved the jurors' pity.

Just as in Alice's trial, the first day of testimony began with ghastly accounts of how the bodies were exhumed. At one point, jurors were taken in a bus to the farm and shown the pit where the Averys had been killed. Jeffrey did not go along on that trip. He stayed in his cell and read his scriptures.

On day two, the prosecution hauled Jeffrey's arsenal into court. Wooden boxes filled with ammunition, stacks of rifles, and numerous pistols were paraded before the jury. Photographs of the huge .50-caliber rifle that Jeffrey had bought appeared on the front page of the Cleveland *Plain Dealer* the next morning and were sent over the Associated Press wires. LaTourette was skillfully reconstructing the crime for the jury and the media.

LaPlante and Grieshammer didn't bother to question most of the prosecution's witnesses. They simply sat and listened to the testimony. Jeffrey spent the first two days of his trial reading passages from the Bible, Book of Mormon, and Doctrine and Covenants. Oftentimes, he didn't even bother looking at the parade of witnesses being called. Only once did he show any interest. When photographs of the Averys taken during the autopsies were introduced as evidence, Jeffrey pushed his scriptures aside and carefully examined each picture for several minutes after LaTourette handed them to LaPlante and Grieshammer to review. "When he studied those pictures I got really pissed," LaTourette said later. "I hated him more and more because it was clear that he was admiring his handiwork."

Judge Martin O. Parks's courtroom contained one large table which was used by both the prosecution and the defense. A podium in the center separated the two sides. LaTourette and LaPlante took the chairs closest to the lectern. Their assistants sat beside them and then, at the ends of the table, were the chairs that Chief Yarborough and Jeffrey used. Because of this arrangement, Yarborough and Jeffrey found themselves facing one another. Yarborough quickly made it his habit to stare directly at Jeffrey, hoping to make him nervous.

LaTourette's star witness, Richard Brand, testified on day three. Before he arrived, Yarborough and LaTourette took a roll of gray duct tape—the same kind used to bind and gag the Averys—and tore off four strips. They used the tape to make a rectangular outline on the courtroom floor. When it came time for Richard to describe the murders, LaTourette told him to step down from the witness stand and demonstrate for the jury exactly where he had put Dennis Avery when he and Danny had lowered him into the pit. Brand walked over to the taped outline, stepped inside, and dropped to his knees. He was only a few feet from Jeffrey. Holding the murder weapon in his hand, LaTourette left the podium and walked behind Richard. He dramatically raised the gun, pointing it directly at Richard's back.

Is this how Dennis Avery was murdered? he asked.

Yes, Richard had replied.

LaTourette wanted the jurors to visualize exactly what had happened. He had another reason for reenacting the scene. He wanted everyone in the courtroom, including Jeffrey, to see that the gun was pointed at Richard's back. Jeffrey had told his followers that he had looked Dennis in the eyes before shooting him. He had claimed that he had "pierced" Dennis Avery's heart. But LaTourette told the jury that Jeffrey had lied. "Dennis Avery was shot twice in the back," LaTourette proclaimed, "not in the chest, not in the heart." Richard told jurors that Jeffrey never showed any emotion when he executed the Averys. Even little Karen failed to bring any sign of remorse to his face.

Later, Jeffrey stared at Sharon and Debbie when they testified against him, but neither broke down. "Frequently, Jeffrey would tease in sexual overtones," Debbie said. "He would come up behind me and say things like he was going to run his tongue up and down my body." Once, she testified, Jeffrey joked about his scriptural teachings. "If this doesn't work out, I guess I'll become a pornographic writer," he was quoted as saying.

After four days of testimony, LaTourette rested his case. He felt confident that he had proved that Jeffrey was a con man who had simply set out to steal the group's money and had murdered the Averys to keep his other followers in line.

In keeping with LaPlante's let's-get-this-over-with strategy, the defense announced that it would not call any witnesses to defend Jeffrey. As expected, the jury quickly found him guilty of five aggravated murders and five counts of kidnapping.

On September 17 the "mitigation phase" of Jeffrey's trial began. "It is now our show, our turn," LaPlante nervously explained before the proceedings began.

"In Jeffrey's first trial, we told you he killed this family," Grieshammer explained to jurors during his opening remarks. "In this second trial, we will hopefully prove why."

In chronological fashion, LaPlante and Grieshammer began to tell the "Jeffrey Lundgren story" from birth to the murders. Along the way, they gently suggested that Jeffrey alone wasn't to blame for what had happened, that he too was a victim. They offered jurors two culprits: Jeffrey's parents and the RLDS Church. Don and Lois Lundgren had refused to come to their son's trial. Privately, they told friends that Jeffrey had "lost his mind." Although Jeffrey was thirty-nine when he killed the Avery family, the defense suggested that Don and Lois had "emotionally abused" their son by being overly strict and demanding. The defense's first witness, Jeffrey's uncle George Harvey Gadberry, described Don as a "stern" father but admitted during cross-examination that he'd never seen any evidence that Jeffrey had been physically abused as a child. Mary Bennett, Jeffrey's aunt, claimed that Don Lundgren "had such a hard look of sternness it would make anyone melt in their shoes." But the worst example of punishment that she could cite happened when Jeffrey was three years old and popped a handful of salted peanuts in his mouth. Jeffrey hadn't liked the taste and had started to spit them out when Don became angry at the waste of food. He forced Jeffrey to keep the peanuts in his mouth for more than thirty minutes, Bennett said. The jury did not seem too impressed by the tale.

Jeffrey's high school friend, Sarah Stotts, said Jeffrey had felt inferior as a teenager because he could never live up to his parents' expectations. But under cross-examination, Sarah admitted that she had no proof that Jeffrey had been mistreated at home.

When LaPlante and Grieshammer began calling witnesses to talk about Jeffrey's religious bent, LaTourette felt relieved. The prosecutor was certain that the defense had failed to convince anyone that Jeffrey had come from an abusive home.

Jeffrey's religious side was first described by Georgia Milliren, who fondly recalled how Jeffrey had taught Sunday school at Slover Park RLDS Church, but had eventually become disillusioned with the church. She was convinced that he was sincere. Much to the prosecution's irritation, Keith Johnson testified for the defense and claimed that Jeffrey was not a con man. "Jeffrey came to the point where he believed his own lies," said Keith. Even Kevin Currie, who had been terrified that Jeffrey was going to kill him, testified for the defense, saying that Jeffrey had built his life around his scriptures and was sincere in his teachings.

LaPlante called two expert witnesses to pull his case together. The first was William D. Russell, a professor of religion at Graceland College, who said that the Mormon religion was much more vulnerable to self-proclaimed prophets, such as Jeffrey, than other sects because of its belief in "continuing revelation" and acceptance of Joseph Smith, Jr., as a prophet. "I really don't have any doubt that Jeffrey thinks he is a prophet," said Russell, who added that he knew of at least twelve other self-proclaimed prophets who had broken from the RLDS just as Jeffrey had done. "He seems sincere," Russell said.

The defense's final expert witness, Dr. Nancy Schmidtgoessling, a Cincinnati psychologist, hammered home the point that Jeffrey was not a con man. She said that Jeffrey was drawn to religion because he felt inferior. Based on the eighteen hours that she had spent talking to Jeffrey and administering various psychological tests, Schmidtgoessling said that "Jeffrey was emotionally abused and did not feel accepted by his peers."

As a child, "he did not fit in. The only way for him to relate to people was through religion. He found a niche in religion. He found a way to relate to people and his religion shaped and focused him." The deeper Jeffrey delved into the scriptures, the more out of touch with reality he became.

In order to overcome his feelings of inadequacy, Jeffrey developed the opposite feelings. He developed a "grandiose" personality to the point that he came to believe that he was superior to everyone around him. Schmidtgoessling said that Jeffrey had an IQ of 124, which is 24 points higher than average, and had a much higher ability than most at memorizing material. Yet he couldn't hold a job or support his family. He blamed everyone but himself for his failures. He became extremely narcissistic and retreated further and further into a world of his own making. As was typical of narcissistic personalities, Jeffrey found it difficult to appreciate the suffering of others and was preoccupied with his own power.

The reason why he hated the Averys was because Dennis Avery reminded Jeffrey of his own secret weaknesses, Schmidtgoessling theorized. Cheryl's independence threatened Jeffrey's masculinity. "In a sense, Lundgren was killing part of himself," the psychologist testified. "In killing Dennis Avery, he was killing the parts of himself he detested. Jeffrey felt overrun by women. Dennis Avery had some of those same characteristics. He had a wife who pushed him around."

Finally, Schmidtgoessling said that Jeffrey had "no insight at all" about his own personality. He had cocooned himself inside a religious fantasy world and, in doing so, had convinced himself that "God had commanded him to kill. He really believes it was right to kill those folks."

When it was LaTourette's turn to question Schmidtgoessling, the prosecutor was blunt.

"Is Jeffrey insane?" he asked.

"No," Schmidtgoessling replied. Jeffrey knew that he was breaking the law when he killed the Averys.

That was all LaTourette wanted to know.

"What we had to present in mitigation was very subtle," LaPlante said later. "We knew from the start that Jeffrey was not beaten as a child. There was no evidence that he had been raped or abused. There wasn't really anything you could hang your hat on—where you could say, 'Ah-ha, this is why Jeffrey turned out this way,' but we felt there was enough there in his past and in his religion to make jurors see that there are degrees of illness and Jeffrey was way off the scale when it comes to mental disorders."

It was now time for LaPlante to play his last card: Jeffrey. In Ohio, a defendant facing the death penalty was allowed to make a final plea to jurors before he was sentenced. The law was designed to give a convicted murderer the opportunity to confess his sins, apologize, and beg for mercy. But Jeffrey had something else in mind. He wanted to teach a scripture class. LaTourette was furious when he learned what Jeffrey had planned, but he couldn't stop him. The prosecutor did, however, fuss over ground rules. "Lundgren wanted to use the lawyers' podium," LaTourette recalled. "I got mad. I was not going to dignify him by having him stand behind the podium. Paul [LaPlante] went nuts when I objected, but I didn't care.

This statement of his was nothing but a cheap way for him to get in a lot of crap."

LaTourette and LaPlante, the onetime close friends, argued bitterly in Judge Parks's chambers until Parks sided with LaTourette. Jeffrey could speak, but not behind the podium.

Spectators began gathering outside the courthouse before dawn on September 19, to hear Jeffrey. It would be the first time that he had spoken publicly since his capture. The courtroom held only sixty-five persons and the media took up many of those seats. Jeffrey was scheduled to begin his statement shortly after 10:00 A.M.

The local *News Herald* had described Jeffrey before his trial in a one-inch-high headline as a SILVER-TONGUED DEVIL. A radio station had arranged to broadcast his speech "live" from the courthouse. A television camera in the courtroom stood ready to relay Jeffrey's speech to five trucks parked in the town square, which would beam them to Cleveland and Kansas City television stations for news bulletins.

As the spectators waited, they talked among themselves and to reporters about Jeffrey. "I'd like to throw the switch that kills him," said one bearded man, standing next to another who wore a white T-shirt with the words FRY JEFFREY written on it in black block letters.

"Why waste the electricity on him?" a third spectator volunteered. "Should take that son of a bitch and shoot 'im in the head just like he shot 'em three little Avery girls."

Jeffrey had been awake all night in his cell scribbling his thoughts on a yellow legal pad. LaPlante and Grieshammer had urged him to keep his comments simple and concise, but he had ignored them. By the time he was brought to the courthouse, everyone was ready. Bailiff Glenn W. Kanaga, Sr., had held a lottery to determine which onlookers got seats. Sheriff's deputies had paraded reporters and spectators through a metal detector to check for weapons. A local radio announcer was on the air, giving his listeners background material—much like a sports commentator during a pre-game show. Judge Parks completed several routine courtroom chores and then told Jeffrey that he could begin. Jeffrey rose from his chair, glanced at his yellow legal pad one last time, cleared his throat, and faced the six men and six women who were to decide whether or not he should be put to death. He was wearing a light-brown jacket and brown polyester pants that Georgia Milliren had bought for him at a Salvation Army store. LaPlante's wife had washed and ironed Jeffrey's white shirt. His shoulder-length hair was pulled straight back and hung around his shoulders. In a calm, clear voice, Lundgren began.

"I am a prophet of God," he said. "I am even more than that—much, much more."

For five hours, Jeffrey spoke. He described his visions, quoted from the movie *The Highlander*, read numerous verses of scriptures, talked about chiasmus and the "pattern." He never apologized for killing the Averys. "Prophets have been asked by the Lord to go forth and kill since the beginning of time," he said. He ended his rambling discourse by quoting the Book of Mormon. "Repent ye, repent," he told the jurors. "For the Kingdom of God is close at hand. Prepare ye the way of the Lord."

The jury took less than two hours before recommending that Jeffrey be put to death. LaPlante and Grieshammer, both visibly upset, hurried from the courtroom without comment. LaTourette and Yarborough held a press conference.

Later that night, after Yarborough got home, he finally began to relax. Since the Averys' bodies were found, Yarborough had spent all of his time helping LaTourette prepare his case. The chief's dining-room table was covered with legal documents, newspaper clippings about religious cults, books about Mormonism.

"I feel good," he said, "because I think we were able to show that Jeffrey is not a prophet. He is a fat coward who is terrified unless he can hide behind his religious books. He is a baby killer."

Opening a box, Yarborough removed a well-worn, thick Bible. It had been Jeffrey's before it was confiscated, and Yarborough had spent hours studying it. Yarborough opened the book to chapter 6 of Revelation and the story of the Four Horsemen of the Apocalypse.

"Jeffrey made a mistake," the chief said, "when he read about the fourth rider." He read the verse aloud:

"And when he had opened the fourth seal, I heard the voice of the fourth beast say, Come and see. And I

*looked, and behold a pale horse; and his name that sat
on him was Death, and Hell followed with him . . ."*

Yarborough grinned.

"Jeffrey wasn't that rider," the chief explained. The justice
system, the state of Ohio, the prosecution was on that horse.
"We are death and we are going to see to it that Jeffrey goes
to hell for what he has done."

That night, for the first time in months, Chief Yarborough
got a good night's sleep.

Chapter 56

O N September 21, 1990, Judge Parks officially sentenced
Jeffrey to die in Ohio's electric chair. Parks chose April 17,
1991, as the execution date because it was on April 17 that
Jeffrey had murdered the Averys. The judge did not actually
expect Jeffrey to be electrocuted that soon. Death penalty
cases in Ohio are automatically appealed and it normally takes
seventy-seven months for a case to work its way through the
courts. LaTourette told reporters after the hearing that it would
take ten years for Jeffrey to exhaust his legal appeals. Even then,
there was a chance that his sentence might be commuted to life
without parole. Ohio had not executed anyone since 1963.

Jeffrey was unruffled when Parks sentenced him. Later that
afternoon, when LaPlante and Grieshammer went to speak with
Jeffrey in the Lake County jail, they found him relaxed. The
two attorneys weren't. Grieshammer liked Jeffrey and was
depressed. LaPlante felt irritated at the legal process. From
the start, he had argued that Jeffrey couldn't get a fair trial in
Lake County because of the extraordinary publicity the murders
had sparked. His suspicions were confirmed during voir dire,
the jury-selection process, when many of the potential jurors

admitted that they had already decided Jeffrey was guilty based on media accounts. Despite this, Judge Parks had refused to move the trial elsewhere. Instead, whenever prospective jurors said that they had already decided Jeffrey was guilty, Parks asked them if they could put aside their opinions and give Jeffrey a fair hearing. Nearly all had promised that they could. LaPlante wasn't certain they had.

Jeffrey ended up comforting his attorneys. "I told them that everything was okay."

What LaPlante and Grieshammer didn't realize, Jeffrey later explained, was that his death sentence was preordained. "This is all going according to God's game plan."

When Jeffrey was sentenced that morning, Judge Parks had made a point of saying that it was the "people of the state of Ohio" who had condemned Jeffrey to die. Parks was not personally doing it. Hadn't Pontius Pilate tried to wash his hands when he sentenced Jesus Christ to death? Jeffrey asked. "The scriptures say that a prophet must be rebuked by the people and that is what the judge said. 'The people of Ohio' have condemned me and now God is justified in destroying them.

"You see, God's tried all this before," Jeffrey explained. The inhabitants on earth had been destroyed eight times by God, he said. "The ground you walk on is made of bones." If people didn't "repent" after hearing Jeffrey's message, God would show Jeffrey how to continue opening the seven seals and the inhabitants of earth would be exterminated.

"God will simply start over."

Several events that happened during his trial were chronicled in the scriptures, he said. One of the biblical names that Jeffrey had given Richard Brand while the group was in West Virginia was "Bel" and in the Bible Bel was forced by God to bow down. During his testimony, Richard had been told by LaTourette to leave the witness chair and get down on his knees in the mock pit that had been outlined on the courtroom floor. At that point, "Bel was forced to bow before me, his lord and master," said Jeffrey.

Before Christ was crucified, he was mocked by his persecutors who lied about him. "LaTourette mocked and lied about me," Jeffrey said. "I am not a con man and I didn't shoot Dennis

Avery in the back. I looked him in the eyes and shot him in his chest."

Jeffrey insisted that LaTourette and the county coroners had intentionally identified the *exit* wounds in Dennis's back as the *entrance* wounds in order to make Jeffrey look like a coward. "I shot Mr. Avery in the chest. All you have to do is look at the wounds. The holes in the chest are smaller than the ones in his back, which proves I shot him in the chest."

But that was *not* what the wounds showed. The slugs that Jeffrey fired into Dennis were "hollow point" rounds designed to collapse and look like a "mushroom" on impact. Both had hit bones, which caused them to ricochet inside the body. During the autopsy, the bullets were recovered *inside* the corpse, according to Cuyahoga County Coroner Elizabeth K. Balraj and Lake County Coroner William C. Downing. There were no exit wounds. There were no bullet holes in Dennis Avery's chest. The only bullet holes were in his back. LaTourette hadn't lied. The proof was indisputable—to everyone but Jeffrey.

"They are lying. They will do anything to discredit me. I shot Dennis Avery in the chest."

Judge Parks had asked Jeffrey that morning during the sentencing hearing if he had anything that he wanted to say before the judge passed judgment. Jeffrey hadn't said anything. "But I thought about saying, 'Thank you, Judge, thank you, jury, and fuck you, Steve LaTourette.' "

Besides LaTourette, Jeffrey was irritated at Dr. Schmidt-goessling and her testimony that compared him to Dennis Avery. "I don't have any of the same characteristics as Dennis Avery. I would kill myself if I believed I did. . . . She said I have a profound hatred for women. That's stupid. I know more about womankind than most of the rest of the world because of what God has shown me. I have profound respect for women. . . ."

Now that the trial was over, God expected Jeffrey simply to wait, he said. "At some point, He will free me."

"I used to wonder," Jeffrey continued, "when this first began to happen—'Why me?' I think the simplest answer is that there was no one else to do it. It is what I was created for. I was created to put my life on the line. I was created to love the truth."

The convictions of Jeffrey and Alice left only one more major case. LaTourette had offered Damon Lundgren a plea bargain that would have required the nineteen-year-old to serve thirty years in prison, but Damon rejected the offer and instead insisted during his trial that he was innocent. Damon's lawyers claimed that Damon was dominated by his father and learned about the killings just hours before they were to occur. They said Damon did not participate directly in the shooting deaths. Prosecutors countered with testimony by Sharon, Debbie, Greg, and Richard. After deliberating for eight hours, a jury found Damon guilty of aggravated murder. During the mitigation stage, the defense called sixteen witnesses, including Bill Lord, Dale Luffman, and Donna Keehler. All three claimed Damon had been subjugated by his father. "He didn't have a chance," Bill Lord testified. "His father was over him all the time." In a fifteen-minute statement that caused many in the courtroom to weep, Damon begged the jury not to sentence him to death. "My whole life has been doing what my father told me to do. . . . I just want to tell you that I don't want to die. I have a whole lot of things I can contribute to society. . . . I'd like a chance to make up any way I can for some of the things my father did." The jury recommended that Damon be sentenced to life in prison.

Jeffrey's other followers, except for Ron Luff, agreed to plead guilty to reduced charges in order to avoid trials. Susan Luff pleaded guilty to five counts of conspiracy to murder, the same charges that Sharon and Debbie had accepted. Because Kathy Johnson was pregnant with Jeffrey's baby, her case was delayed during the summer. She was released on bond five months after her arrest. In June, Kathy gave birth to a daughter, whom she named Rasia, the Hebrew word for "rose." Kathy later pleaded guilty to obstructing justice. She had not been at the farm during the murders, but prosecutors said she was liable because she had not told anyone about the killings afterward. At her sentencing, Kathy was defiant. "I'm guilty of loving Jeff Lundgren," she said. "I'm not guilty of having assisted with anything he carried out." Kathy was sentenced to one year in prison.

Dennis and Tonya Patrick pleaded guilty to obstructing justice, the same charge as Kathy. But they were put on one-year probation and released. The difference between their sentences and Kathy's, Assistant Prosecutor Karen Kowall said, was that the Patricks "are very remorseful for what happened."

Danny Kraft, Jr., agreed to plead guilty to ten counts of aggravated murder and kidnapping after Jeffrey met with him privately in the Lake County jail and assured him that it was not necessary for him to stand trial. "Jeff is not a false prophet," Danny proclaimed during a two-hour speech that he delivered at his sentencing. "I understand how the killing of the Averys looks to people, but they are wrong. I cannot apologize for my assisting the prophet of God." Psychologist Paul R. Martin told Judge James W. Jackson that the twenty-six-year-old Kraft had been "brainwashed" by Jeffrey. In exchange for Danny's guilty plea, LaTourette recommended that Danny be sentenced to life in prison, rather than death. "He did fall under the spell of Jeffrey Lundgren," LaTourette said. "You're not going to get any argument from me that Jeffrey Lundgren is the most evil, vile, fat, smelly person ever to come into Lake County."

On December 5, Ron Luff's trial began in Toledo. Judge Parks had granted Luff a change of venue in October after Luff's attorney successfully argued that an unbiased jury could no longer be found in Lake County. Luff was found guilty of aggravated murder and kidnapping. However, the jury voted to spare his life and he was sentenced to 170 years in prison.

Before Alice and Jeffrey were sent to prison, they both asked Judge Parks to let them meet face-to-face in the Lake County jail one final time. Parks refused. Alice was sent to the Ohio Reformatory for Women in Marysville. Jeffrey was taken to death row at Ohio's maximum-security prison in Lucasville. Neither had regular access to a telephone, but they continued to correspond. Some days, Jeffrey would write as many as five letters to Alice. He was upset that she had described him as a "cold-blooded murderer" after her trial. She was irritated because he refused to "divorce" Kathy.

"Alice will not accept the fact that Kathy is my wife," he later explained. "She is angry. She is attacking me and rejecting the truth."

In order to placate Alice, Jeffrey told her in a letter that he was ending his relationship with "Mrs. Johnson." He was lying. He continued to correspond faithfully with Kathy. "If Alice repents, I will tell her the truth about Kathy, but if a lie is what will make her happy right now, then that's what I will give her. I will use delusion to tell her whatever she wants to hear. What is important is that she continues to believe. I love her and my job is to get her to the mountain [of the Lord] with Kathy and me."

Alice was skeptical when she got Jeffrey's letter. Not long afterward, she received a love letter from Jeffrey that contained vivid descriptions of various sexual acts that he wished they could engage in. In that letter, Jeffrey mistakenly referred to Alice at one point as Kathy. "He's writing that bitch the same love letters that he is sending me," Alice charged.

During Ron Luff's trial in December, Alice and Jeffrey were both called as potential witnesses and transferred from their respective prisons to the Lucas County jail in downtown Toledo. Both of them had access in the jail to telephones that were not routinely monitored by jail officials. They quickly arranged a conference call through an acquaintance outside the jail.

On the night before Jeffrey and Alice were scheduled to talk, Alice's opinion of her husband flipflopped by the minute. "Kathy is a bitch and Jeffrey is a liar," she said. "Everything he's ever told me is a lie. . . ."

Minutes later, she said, "You know, I'm still madly in love with that jerk. I always will be. There is nothing he could ever do to make me not love him."

Later, Alice was in tears. "Why doesn't Jeffrey ever tell me the truth? What am I, some kind of animal he keeps on a leash? I feel like a half-dead mouse that the cat keeps batting around. . . . I can't figure out why I still care. How can you continue to love a person who hurts you so much?"

On December 12, at 6:00 P.M., Alice and Jeffrey spoke for the first time since their arrest nearly one year earlier. They talked for nearly one hour, and afterward Alice felt triumphant. "I let him have it," she said gleefully. "I really grilled him about Kathy. I called him a liar."

Alice said that Jeffrey had assured her that he no longer cared about Kathy. In fact, he had agreed to write Kathy a "Dear John" letter and divorce her as his wife. Jeffrey had even offered to send the letter to Alice so that she could edit it and then mail it herself to Kathy.

"I really believe he is going to sever the tie this time," she said. The thought that Jeffrey might tip off Kathy beforehand about the letter apparently hadn't entered Alice's mind.

"Jeff told me that an angel had visited him in prison. It touched him and gave him a message from God," Alice explained. She had memorized what the angel had said: "Truly I say unto you, as a mongoose would rise against the cobra and consume it as its prey, so shall that which has come, rise against that which seems certain death. For I will turn your mornings into noonday . . . great shall be your joy . . . saith He that was and is and is to come. Lift up your voice in great joy for thou hast prayed mightily before my throne. Behold the measure is full, the hour of your deliverance by my hand draweth nigh."

On December 13, at 6:00 P.M., Alice and Jeffrey talked again, and during their conversation, Jeffrey assured Alice that he loved only her, not Kathy.

On December 16, Jeffrey and Alice talked once more. Afterward, Alice was ecstatic. Jeffrey had recited a love poem to her:

> *"Do you think I'm horny?*
> *I think you make me wild,*
> *And when the Lord does free you,*
> *I will make you big with child."*

God was going to release Jeffrey from prison within two years, Alice said. As soon as he was freed, he would come rescue her from Marysville and they would go see God together.

"He wants me to have another baby!" she gushed. "He is telling me the truth this time. I know it. I can feel it. He loves me. He loves me!"

On December 17, Alice and Jeffrey spoke for the final time. The next day, Alice was scheduled to be transferred back to Marysville prison. Jeffrey would leave shortly thereafter. They spoke for about an hour. All of the anger that Alice had felt earlier toward Jeffrey was gone. She apologized for calling him a "cold-blooded murderer." She had "gone to pieces," she explained, during her trial.

"I doubted you."

Alice told Jeffrey that she had gotten down on her knees in her cell after she had first arrived in Toledo and had prayed. "I was at the end of my rope. I told the Lord that I needed some proof, some evidence, that you were who you say you are. I said that I wanted to hear a voice." Alice was watching television later that same night in jail when she saw a news bulletin about Jeffrey. The reporter said that he was being brought to Toledo for Ron's trial. "I knew God was answering my prayer," she said. "Seeing something on television is just like having a visionary experience, isn't it?

"And now," Alice continued, "I have heard your voice on the telephone. You see, God answered my prayer. He gave me proof that you are who you say you are!

"I want you to know that I know you are right now, and I have never been so sure, and it feels so good."

"I understand," said Jeffrey.

The prophecy that the RLDS patriarch had made in 1969 about Alice had finally come true, she said.

You shall marry a companion whom I have prepared to bring forth my kingdom and he shall be great in the eyes of these people and shall do much good unto the children of men, for I have prepared him to bring forth a marvelous work and wonder.

"I am so ashamed of myself for doubting," Alice said.

Seconds later, she giggled. If she sent Jeffrey a pair of her panties would prison officials let him keep them? she asked.

No, Jeffrey replied, but he would have enjoyed receiving them. "Something like that would get me into a lot of shit."

"Well, we certainly both know what being in shit is like," Alice said.

They both laughed.

"Alice," he said. "I will come for you. I promise. You got to believe me. I am who I am. I am God's chosen one."

"I know you are," she said. "I do believe, Jeff. I really do."

"Hang in there, sweetheart," Jeffrey said.

"I will," Alice replied. "You don't have to worry about me anymore. . . . I'm not going to give up. I'm not going to quit. I'm not going to stop watching for you."

"Okay."

"And I'm not going to stop loving you."

"Thank you."

"I love you."

"Me too."

"I want you to know something."

"What?"

"I'd do it all again," Alice said. She was sobbing now.

"Thank you," he replied.

"Please take care of yourself."

"Hey, I can do it. You see, I'm unlike other people. I'm still just the same—big and strong. Okay? My faith never has wavered. . . ."

"I'm with you one hundred percent now," Alice said.

"Thank you."

"I'm very proud of you."

"Thank you," he said. "I'm very proud of you too."

"Oh, I'm so proud of you," she repeated. "I really am. . . . I love you."

"I love you too."

"I guess we should hang up now."

"Okay."

"Jeff," she said, her voice now a whisper. "I love you with all my heart."

She quickly got off the line.

"Alice?" Jeffrey replied. "Are you still there?"

He called her name once again.

"Alice?"

And then, after hearing no reply, Jeffrey began to cry and slowly hung up the phone.

Epilogue

JEFFREY D. *Lundgren*. Still on death row in Lucasville, Jeffrey continues to study his scriptures in search of a way to open the remaining seven seals in Revelation. Even though he is in prison, he continues to recruit new "disciples" by corresponding with people who have read about his case and expressed an interest in learning about the pattern. He has sent letters to some of his former followers warning them that when Christ returns to earth, He will free Jeffrey and encourage him to take revenge against those who have betrayed him. His case remains on appeal.

Alice Elizabeth Lundgren. When Alice returned to the women's prison in Marysville, she discovered that Jeffrey was still corresponding with Kathy Johnson. In March, Alice contacted the warden at Lucasville and had him add her name to a list of people whom Jeffrey is prohibited from contacting. She subsequently filed for a divorce. "I have a serious addiction problem," Alice said. "Jeffrey is as deadly to me as cocaine or heroin to some women. . . . I will never be completely free of what haunts me until I can stand over his grave—then it will be over, buried forever." Alice's case is currently under appeal. She continues to insist that she was powerless to stop Jeffrey because of years of emotional, sexual, physical abuse. Unless her conviction is overturned, she will not be eligible for parole until she serves 115 years.

Damon P. Lundgren. Currently serving a 120-year sentence, Damon will first be eligible for parole after 108 years. His tearful plea for mercy at his trial prompted an angry letter from Jeffrey, who told his son that he needed to worry more about what God thought of his actions than what jurors had to say.

Jason, Kristen, Caleb Lundgren. The minor children of the Lundgrens were placed under the care of Alice's parents, Ralph and Donna Keehler. Donna has forbidden her son-in-law to mention his religious beliefs in letters to his children.

Kathy Johnson. Kathy was scheduled for release from prison during the summer of 1991. For a short period, she was housed in the same women's prison as Alice in Marysville, but was later moved to a halfway house in Cleveland. The two women avoided each other while in prison. Kathy plans to move to Lucasville when she is freed so that she and Rasia can visit Jeffrey at the prison. She continues to insist that he is a prophet.

Keith Johnson. During Alice's trial, a BATF agent told the Lake County Prosecutor's Office that Keith was telling people that he was a prophet. The agent quoted Keith as saying, "If Jeff isn't the prophet, maybe I am." Keith later denied making such a claim. Keith lives with his parents and four sons in rural Missouri.

Richard Brand. As part of the deal that his attorney negotiated with prosecutors, Richard pleaded guilty to five counts of murder, but he was sentenced on only *one* of those counts. He received a prison term of fifteen years to life and will be eligible for parole after serving ten years.

Greg Winship. Greg also received a plea bargain, but it wasn't as good as Richard's even though Greg pleaded guilty to complicity to murder, a lesser charge. Richard's attorney had specified in his deal that his client could be sentenced on only one count. Greg's plea bargain did not contain any such limit. Because of this, Judge Mitrovich was free to sentence Greg to fifteen years to life in prison for *each* of the five counts levied against him. That came to a total of seventy-five years to life in prison. Greg will not be eligible for parole until he serves a minimum of twenty years.

Daniel D. Kraft, Jr. Currently serving a fifty-years-to-life prison term, Danny will not be eligible for parole until he serves thirty-seven years.

Debbie Olivarez, Sharon Bluntschly, Susie Luff. Because Debbie and Sharon cooperated fully with the prosecution and provided damaging testimony against Alice and Jeffrey, they expected to receive a lenient sentence from Judge Mitrovich. Instead, the judge sentenced them to the maximum prison term that he could: seven to twenty-five years in prison. Susie, who refused to cooperate with the prosecution, received the same sentence. All are housed in the same women's prison as Alice and will be eligible for parole in five years.

Ron Luff. Ron will not be eligible for parole until he serves 130 years.

Dennis and Tonya Patrick. The Patricks have returned to Independence, where they are trying to rebuild their lives.

Steven LaTourette. Although his willingness to grant plea bargains was criticized early on, LaTourette's handling of the Lundgren cases was widely praised. A political editor for a local newspaper predicted that LaTourette would be unbeatable in 1992 if he seeks reelection.

Dennis Yarborough and Ron Andolsek. Officer Andolsek prepared most of the evidence and testified at all three of the Lundgren trials. The stress of helping prosecute the cases caused him to suffer severe depression, he said, to the point that he felt suicidal. After the cases were resolved, Andolsek complained publicly about Judge Mitrovich's refusal to show leniency to Debbie Olivarez and Sharon Bluntschly. He also complained about the unequal treatment that Greg Winship received in comparison to Richard Brand. Andolsek has since returned to his regular duties on the Kirtland police force. In January, a local civic group honored Andolsek and Chief Yarborough with an award for distinguished public service. Yarborough remains Kirtland's police chief. He has declined offers from publishing houses and movie companies interested in telling his story. On May 3, 1991, he spent the night watching the Kirtland temple. He was afraid that pranksters or new followers of Jeffrey might attempt to deface it.

Reverend Dale Luffman. Shortly after Jeffrey's arrest, someone painted YOU'RE DEAD on the picture window of Luffman's home. Despite the threat, Luffman continues as RLDS stake president. When asked by a reporter from the Cleveland *Plain Dealer* if Jeffrey should be executed, Luffman said: "From a theological perspective our church believes life is sacred, but death is a part of life." In the case of Jeffrey, Luffman added, the death penalty was justified.

Donald and Lois Lundgren. Jeffrey's parents have refused to respond to letters that he has written them. Before Debbie Olivarez was arrested, she told Don and Lois that Jeffrey had considered killing his mother and recruiting his father into the group in order to get their money.

Shar Olson. Shar returned to Independence, where she remains friends with Dennis and Tonya Patrick. She continues to write regularly to Richard Brand, Greg Winship, and Debbie Olivarez.

Kevin Currie. "I understand the horror that took place," Kevin said at Jeffrey's trial, "but I still consider myself a friend of Jeffrey's." Even so, Kevin has an unlisted number and said that he still fears that Jeffrey might try to have him murdered. In the spring of 1991, Alice contacted Kevin and asked him to write her. "I'm still considering it," he said.

Dennis, Cheryl, Trina, Becky, and Karen Avery. The bodies of the Averys were returned to a suburb of Independence for burial. About 240 mourners attended the memorial service held at a "restoration" branch of the RLDS. The minister did not mention Jeffrey Lundgren, but in his eulogy, Elder Garth McCulloch warned mourners about following false prophets. "We must carefully lead," he said, "lest we are led astray."

Author's Note

THIS book is the story of Jeffrey Don and Alice Elizabeth Lundgren, and the murder of the Dennis Avery family. To date, I am the only author to interview the Lundgrens. I first met Jeffrey in April 1990 at the Lake County jail in Painesville, Ohio, four months after his arrest. I conducted sixteen separate interviews with him, most of which lasted five hours and took place after his trial and sentencing in September 1990. My interviews with Alice were done in the Lucas County jail in Toledo in November 1990. 1 spoke with her over a five-day period, usually five hours per session. Besides tape-recorded interviews, I also conducted numerous telephone interviews with both Lundgrens, and have received nearly fifty letters from Alice since she has been in prison. All of Alice's immediate relatives agreed to speak with me, including her parents, Donna and Ralph Keehler, her two sisters, Terri Buller and Susan Yates, and brother, Charles Keehler. I also met with the Lundgrens' three minor children, Jason, Kristen, and Caleb, and two of Jeffrey's relatives who asked not to be named. It is safe to say that I have spent close to two hundred hours talking to immediate family members and many more hours with the other persons interviewed for this book.

Although Jeffrey and Alice cooperated with me, I did not pay them or any other person for their cooperation. Nor did I permit Jeffrey, Alice, or anyone else mentioned in this manuscript any editorial control over its contents. All of my conversations with Jeffrey and Alice were on the record and I made no deals as to how either of them would be portrayed. None of the persons mentioned in this book was permitted to read any of the manuscript before it was published.

In addition to the personal interviews I conducted, this book also relies on numerous trial transcripts, confidential police and FBI records, and other information that previously has not been made public. Perhaps the most important of these confidential sources was seven hours of confessions that were videotaped by the Bureau of Alcohol, Tobacco and Firearms. While bits and pieces of these tapes were made public at the trials of Ron Luff and Alice Lundgren, the bulk of them have never been shown and their contents have remained secret. The tapes include statements by Ron Luff, Susie Luff, Richard Brand, Alice Lundgren, Dennis Patrick, and Tonya Patrick. Not only did I find these confessions useful in reconstructing the murders of the Avery family, but they also enabled me to observe the demeanor of the defendants shortly before or after their arrests. This proved particularly helpful months later when I interviewed Alice Lundgren and Dennis and Tonya Patrick in person, and observed Richard Brand and Ron and Susie Luff during their court appearances.

Besides Jeffrey, Alice, and their relatives, I also personally interviewed the following persons: Ron Andolsek, Tim Avery, Lisa Avery, Donna Bailey, Kevin Currie, William C. Downing, Charles R. Grieshammer, Marlene Jennings, Kathy Johnson, Keith Johnson, R. Paul LaPlante, Steven LaTourette, Bill Lord, Eleanor Lord, Dale Luffman, Judy Luffman, Georgia Milliren, Debbie Olivarez, Shar Olson, Dennis Patrick, Tonya Patrick, James Postlethwait, James H. Robbins, Laura Robbins, Hal Sappington, Ann Sherman, Muril Stone, Louise Stone, Hank Thompson, Bernie Wilson, Dennis Yarborough, Gail Yarborough. I held brief conversations with some twenty other persons who were involved in this affair in some way.

Readers should note that Sarah Stotts, Jacob Wilcox, Henry Thomas, Barbara Carter, Tom Miller, and Patti Miller are pseudonyms used to protect the privacy of real persons. All quotes attributed to them are actual statements. All other persons in this book are identified by their correct names. Statements by Jeffrey's aunt Mary Bennett and uncle George Gadberry were taken from their sworn testimony at Jeffrey's trial.

Fifteen other persons, including one of Jeffrey's followers, agreed to be interviewed, but asked that they not be identified. These included people who knew the Avery family in

Independence and in Kirtland, as well as former classmates of
Jeffrey's and church members who knew Alice as a teenager.

I attended all of Jeffrey's trial, and parts of the trials that
were held for Alice and Damon. I had access to transcripts of
those proceedings that I missed but felt were important.

During interviews, I found that people often recalled the
same events quite differently. I have noted major disparities
in the book, usually by giving more than one account, but in
minor cases, I have chosen the version that seemed most likely
to be true.

The most difficult information to verify dealt with the private
life of Alice and Jeffrey. Oftentimes, only the two of them were
present and they tell dissimilar accounts of what happened
during these private moments. I found Alice to be amazingly
forthcoming, particularly when describing her sexual practices
with Jeffrey. I was able to verify most of what she told me
by interviewing her relatives and longtime friends, such as
Louise Stone, whom Alice had confided in long before the
Avery family was murdered. In the few cases where I have
been unable to substantiate what Alice said, I have used the
words "Alice claimed" to warn the reader that her statements
cannot be corroborated. While I felt that Jeffrey was frank
during our talks, particularly when discussing his religious
beliefs and the murders, when it came to talking about his
sexual preferences and intimate relationships with Alice and
Kathy, I found his stories inconsistent and often blatantly
contrary to both women's versions. Once again, when I could
not corroborate Jeffrey's statements, I used the words "Jeffrey
claimed."

Whenever I described a character's feelings or thoughts in
the book, I have based that information on that person's recollection of their feelings and thoughts at that moment. I have
tried to verify this information when possible by questioning
eyewitnesses.

Information about the ships that Jeffrey served on during
his naval career was taken from each ship's log and sea
records stored at the Naval Historical Center in Washington,
D.C. I found these books and articles about the Mormon
religion helpful: "Before Mormonism: Joseph Smith's Use
of the Bible, 1820–1829," by Philip L. Barlow, *Journal of*

the American Academy of Religion; A Gathering of Saints: A True Story of Money, Murder and Deceit by Robert Lindsey; *The Mormons*, by Thomas F. O'Dea; *The Mormon Murders*, by Steven Naifeh and Gregory White Smith; *The Mormon Mirage*, by Latayne Colvett Scott; *Sidney Rigdon 1793–1876*, by F. Mark McKiernan; *Latter-Day Saint Beliefs: A Comparison Between the RLDS Church and the LDS Church*, by Steven L. Shields; *Defenders of the Faith: Varieties of RLDS Dissent*, by William Dean Russell; *An Illustrated History of the Kirtland Temple*, by Roger D. Launius; *No Man Knows My History: The Life of Joseph Smith*, by Fawn M. Brodie; *America's Saints: The Rise of Mormon Power*, by Robert Gottlieb and Peter Wiley; numerous pamphlets published by the Reorganized Church of Latter-Day Saints, and several articles published in *The Zarahemla Record*. Information about chiasmus was drawn from several sources including "Hebrew Poetry in the Book of Mormon," by Angela Crowell, *The Zarahemla Record; Kerygma*, by The Kerygma Study Program; "Chiasms in the Book of Mormon," by Raymond C. Treat, *The Zarahemla Record; Chiasmus in Antiquity*, by Wallace B. King. Information about Lake County was taken primarily from *Here Is Lake County, Ohio*, by the Lake County Historical Society.

These public officials provided me with help: Jamey Henderson, Department of Criminal Records, City Court, Independence, Missouri; Warden H. L. Morris, Ohio Reformatory for Women, Marysville, Ohio; Jack Bendolph, Southern Ohio Correctional Facility, Lucasville, Ohio; Sheriff James A. Telb, Richard D. Keller, and Sandi Guess, Lucas County jail; Jeffrey Farrone, Lake County jail. I also wish to thank Rob Whitehouse, staff writer, the *News Herald*; Maggi Martin, staff writer, and Curt Chandler, photographer, the Cleveland *Plain Dealer*; Bill McKay, reporter, and Belinda Prinz, producer, WJW TV-8, Cleveland.

As always, I am indebted to Patricia Hersch and Walter Harrington, two writers who gave me excellent editorial guidance, as well as, at William Morrow, my editor, Adrian Zackheim, and my copy editor, Joan Amico, and to Bob Mecoy at Avon Books. I am particularly grateful to my agent, Robert Gottlieb, and to Laura Shapiro and Irene Webb, all of the William Morris Agency. Special thanks to Yvonne M. Frament.

Others whose help I would like to acknowledge include the Reverend James C. Sprouse, the Reverend Richard G. Thayer, Toni Shaklee, Lynn and LouAnn Smith, Dr. C. T. Shades, Wayne and Donna Wolfersberger, and Carolyn Hunter. I wish to thank my parents, Elmer and Jean Earley, for reading this book in its earliest stages, and I am thankful for the support of my wife, Barbara, and children, Steve, Kev, and Kathy.

This book is dedicated to the memory of my sister, Alice Lee Earley, who died tragically at the age of sixteen, and my maternal grandmother, Belle Patterson, who inspired me with her poetry and artistic skills. I miss them both.